RESEARCH ON MOTIVATION IN EDUCATION

Volume 1

Student Motivation

RESEARCH ON MOTIVATION IN EDUCATION

Volume 1

Student Motivation

Edited by

RUSSELL AMES
University of Maryland Graduate School
  at The University College
College Park, Maryland

CAROLE AMES
Department of Human Development
University of Maryland at College Park
College Park, Maryland

ACADEMIC PRESS, INC.
Harcourt Brace Jovanovich, Publishers
San Diego   New York   Berkeley   Boston
London   Sydney   Tokyo   Toronto

ACADEMIC PRESS, INC.
1250 Sixth Avenue, San Diego, California 92101

United Kingdom Edition published by
ACADEMIC PRESS, INC. (LONDON) LTD.
24/28 Oval Road, London NW1 7DX

Library of Congress Cataloging in Publication Data

Main entry under title:

Research on motivation in education.

    Bibliography: p.
    Includes index.
    Contents: v. 1. Student motivation.
    1. Motivation in education--Addresses, essays,
lectures. I. Ames, Russell, Date   . II. Ames,
Carole.
LB1065.R47 1984   370.15'4   83-12315
ISBN 0-12-056701-6 (alk. paper)

PRINTED IN THE UNITED STATES OF AMERICA

88 89 90 91 92   10 9 8 7 6 5 4 3

Contents

PART I   THEORETICAL PERSPECTIVES

1. Principles for a Theory of Student Motivation and Their Application within an Attributional Framework
Bernard Weiner

2. Conceptions of Ability and Achievement Motivation
John G. Nicholls

PART II   THE STUDENT: INTERNAL MOTIVATIONAL FACTORS

3. The Motive for Self-worth
Martin V. Covington

4. Meaning and Motivation: Toward a Theory of Personal Investment
Martin L. Maehr

5. The Development of Achievement Motivation
Deborah J. Stipek

PART III   THE STUDENT'S ENVIRONMENT: CLASSROOM AND SITUATIONAL FACTORS

6. Competitive, Cooperative, and Individualistic Goal Structures: A Cognitive-Motivational Analysis
Carole Ames

7. Socioeconomic Status and Ethnic Group Differences in Achievement Motivation
Harris Cooper and David Y. H. Tom

Contributors

Numbers in parentheses indicate the pages on which the authors' contributions begin.

Carole Ames (1, 177), Department of Human Development, University of Maryland at College Park, College Park, Maryland 20742

Russell Ames (1), University of Maryland, Graduate School at The University College, College Park, Maryland 20742

Samuel Ball (313), Department of Education, University of Sydney, Sydney, N.S.W., 2006, Australia

Harris Cooper (209), Center for Research in Social Behavior, University of Missouri, Columbia, Missouri 65201

Martin V. Covington (77), Department of Psychology, University of California at Berkeley, Berkeley, California 94720

Richard deCharms (275), Graduate Institute of Education, Washington University, St. Louis, Missouri 63130

Kennedy T. Hill (245), Institute for Child Behavior and Development, University of Illinois at Urbana-Champaign, Champaign, Illinois 61820

Martin L. Maehr (115), Institute for Child Behavior and Development, University of Illinois at Urbana-Champaign, Champaign, Illinois 61820

John G. Nicholls (39), Educational Psychology, Purdue University, West Lafayette, Indiana 47907

Deborah J. Stipek (145), Graduate School of Education, University of California at Los Angeles, Los Angeles, California 90024

David Y. H. Tom (209), Center for Research in Social Behavior, University of Missouri, Columbia, Missouri 65201

Bernard Weiner (15), Department of Psychology, University of California, Los Angeles, Los Angeles, California 90024

Preface

It would be difficult to put a beginning date on the long and vigorous history of the study of motivation. The questions of why people pursue certain goals instead of others has been the subject of scholarly inquiry since the writings of Socrates, Plato, and Aristotle. Since the late nineteenth century, when philosophical psychology was replaced by experimental psychology, the systematic study of such motivationally related concepts as drives, needs, intentions, habits, and values has paralleled the history of psychology. Given such a long history of concern and interest, one might expect that motivation, as it relates to educational concerns and questions, would have been thoroughly studied. Only in the past 20 years, however, has the systematic study of motivational processes in education settings received significant and sustained attention by researchers in psychology and education.

This volume begins an attempt to review and integrate major recent contributions to the study of motivation in education. Broadly speaking, it is intended to provide a state-of-the-art summary of research on student motivation. The distinguished group of authors for this volume are all major contributors to theoretical and empirical literature and represent major programs of research. The theme of the volume is reflected by the chapter authors in their addressing such questions as: What is the "spring of action" in motivated behavior? How do cognitions and attributions function within the thought–action sequence and how do they develop? What are the roles of social context and sociocultural factors in cognitive-motivational processes? How can motivational processes be modified and optimized?

The volume has a decidedly cognitive focus, reflecting the zeitgeist of motivational research over the past decade. It is divided into four parts: (I) Theoretical Perspectives, (II) The Student: Internal Motivational Factors, (III) The Student's Environment: Classroom and Situational Factors, and (IV) Designs to Optimize Student Motivation. The first part focuses on the role of cognition and affect in motivation, and the subsequent chapters draw heavily on this framework. The second part focuses on person factors that meet specific criteria, namely, a traceable line of research, a specific application to the motivation of students, and an identifiable link with either or both of the theoretical paradigms in the first part. The third part focuses on factors in the student's environment, including specific social structure and broad societal and sociocultural factors. Chapters in the final part focus on interventions in the school environment that are aimed at optimizing student motivation and that have a substantial empirical base. A discussant chapter provides an integrative overview and critique of the work represented in the volume and points to areas for further research.

The impetus for this volume came from several symposia presentations sponsored by the Special Interest Group on Motivation in Education within the American Educational Research Association. In fact, the idea for this book can be traced back several years to an informal group of researchers who met on an ongoing basis to exchange research perspectives and findings. This group included, among others, Marty Maehr, Ken Hill, John Nicholls, Carol Dweck, Carole Ames, and Russell Ames. This dialogue has continued to benefit and enhance our thinking.

We have, in a sense, already acknowledged our indebtedness to the individual contributors to this volume, and we also wish to acknowledge our colleagues within the special interest group, whose commitment and enthusiasm promised to make this research area a fruitful one for ideas and inquiry. We are especially grateful to the staff of Academic Press for their enthusiastic response and commitment to this project and for their encouragement throughout the process of preparing the book. We hope that this volume serves well those scholars, researchers, students, and practitioners who desire to provide a knowledge base for the improvement of the quality of motivation in schools. We intend this volume to be the first of many on the topic of research on motivation. A second volume, now in progress, also holds these same high aspirations of providing a statement of the current research on motivation in education.

RESEARCH ON MOTIVATION IN EDUCATION

Volume 1

Student Motivation

Introduction

Russell Ames
Carole Ames

OVERVIEW OF MOTIVATION

This book is cast within the current zeitgeist of cognitive views of motivation. That is, motivation primarily is viewed to be a function of a person's thoughts rather than some instinct, need, drive, or state of arousal. The focus on thoughts can easily be traced to the assessment of needs via thought samples in Murray's work done in the late 1930s and subsequent work by McClelland and Atkinson in the early post–World War II period. In the early conceptions of motivation, a need or drive was viewed as the instigator or "spring of action," but in a cognitive approach, information encoded and transformed into a belief is the source of action. The intervening thought processes of perceptions and beliefs are the focus of study in a cognitive approach to motivation (see also Weiner, 1972, p. 2). It is this focus on thoughts, and specific thoughts related to action in particular, that we believe has led to the great increase in the knowledge base for motivation in education at both basic and applied levels. Current cognitive views focus on a variety of thoughts and determinants of action including, for example, attributions, information-seeking, metacognitive and cognitive strategies, emo-

1

tional states, and self-evaluations. While thoughts per se are viewed as a prime instigator of action, we see also a resurgence of interest in the study of emotion in the thought–action sequence and a continued re-analysis of the century-old question, initiated by Freud, of the nature of ego-defensive motives. The relative role of cognition versus emotion in motivation is still an unsolved puzzle, but we feel that some major advances in unraveling this apparent mystery have been made in the chapters contained in this volume.

Achievement theory, as represented in the works of McClelland and Atkinson, is the most immediate predecessor to the cognitive views of motivation in education presented in this volume. The roots of the achievement theory of McClelland (1955) and Atkinson (1954) can be seen throughout the book. Weiner and Kukla's (1970) work on attribution and motivation began with an attributional reinterpretation of the achievement motive and has demonstrated that causal attributions about success and failure are central components of the thought–action sequence. Further, these attributions have been shown to affect self-evaluations, instructional decisions, help-seeking, problem-solving strategies, emotions, and expectancies about future success, illustrating the variety of outcome variables. In addition to having direct linkages to attributional concepts of motivation, the chapters of Nicholls and Maehr cast ability attributions within the cultural context of the Protestant ethic, a framework fundamental to McClelland's view of achievement theory. Within achievement theory, competition with a standard-of-excellence is central, and chapters by Nicholls, Covington, Ames, and Stipek examine ability attributions as a function of the social comparative processes elicited by competition. Additional ties to achievement theory can be seen in the final three chapters of this volume. Specifically, Cooper and Tom examine as dependent variables those that represent the various classical measures of the motive to achieve, that is, the Thematic Apperception Test (TAT) and various derivatives. Hill's research is rooted in the Mandler and Sarason work on anxiety and achievement. Also, within achievement theory, achievement anxiety is related to a need to avoid failure. Finally, the origins of deCharms's work on training teachers in achievement motivation was based on McClelland's (see McClelland and Winter, 1969) work on training businessmen in the achievement motive. Thus, while the chapters in this volume have traceable historical roots to achievement theory, they are more directly associated with a cognitive–attributional approach to motivation. Certainly, Heider's (1958) volume is considered the seminal work on attribution theory, and others, namely, Jones and Davis (1965) and Kelley (1967), have been responsible for the further development and refinement of the theory. But the development and application of attribution theory to education has been carried forward predominantly by the work of Bernard Weiner.

The chapters in this volume represent a culmination of 10–15 years of work by a variety of researchers in the field of motivation in education. And, they truly represent what Weiner in 1972 (pp. 1–9) called second-level cognitive theory. That is, they deal with a variety of thoughts as related to actions. Nicholls, Covington, Stipek, and Ames each examine in great detail the specific attributions of ability and effort. Additionally, Covington and Ames in particular each elaborate on additional cognitions related to the environment (e.g., perceptions of past performance, reward structure, and other's performance). Maehr's chapter represents a true foray into the relatively unexplored area of a variety of cognitions associated with a general sense of "meaning." These cognitions include such things as beliefs about goals and values, as well as attributions and expectancies. Cooper and Tom's chapter uniquely represents a state-of-the-art empirical–analytical review, examining motivational research on social class and race. This research has been strongly grounded in achievement theory, and Cooper and Tom point to the need for further development and refinement of this important line of research through a more analytical analysis of specific cognitions, rather than the more global measures of the achievement motive. In summary, the value of the attributional approach to motivation has been in a microanalysis of the specific cognitions associated with the thought–action sequence; it is this precision that has allowed for the advance of prediction and control of motivation in educational settings over the last 15 years.

While we see the common cognitive–motivational orientation throughout the volume, the individual chapters do differ from each other in a variety of ways. In a broad sense, different foci have led to the basic organization of the book, beginning with theoretical views of Weiner and Nicholls, moving to a specific focus on factors within the student in the chapters of Covington, Maehr and Stipek, and then on to factors in the environment in the chapters of Ames and Cooper, and finally to the application of motivational principles to educational settings through the work of Hill and deCharms. These chapters also differ in how they address a number of themes that occur with some frequency throughout the volume. In the early paragraphs of this introduction, we have already alluded to many of these themes. The themes are captured in how the various authors address the following questions:

1. What is the basic spring of action in motivated behavior—a desire for information, an ego-related motive, some emotional state or valued goals?

2. How do attributions function within the thought–action sequence?
3. What role do culture and social class play in influencing cognitions in motivation?
4. How does the social structure of the classroom affect motivationally related thoughts and subsequent actions?
5. How can students' motivational tendencies be changed toward some desired motivational state?

SPRING OF ACTION: RATIONALITY VERSUS EMOTION AND EGO-DEFENSIVENESS

The contrasting views on this theme are best captured in the writing of Weiner, on the one hand, versus the work of Nicholls and Covington on the other. For Weiner, the basic spring of action is a rational search for understanding, and his work is concerned with how people answer *why* questions, for example, "Why did I fail?" This logical orientation clearly underlies his focus on the typical cause–effect linkages and perceived causal dimensions involved in answering these types of questions. For Covington, the basic impetus for action is the desire to protect one's sense of self-worth, particularly by maintaining a belief that one is able. Nicholls proposed that the desire to demonstrate high ability or to avoid demonstrating a low ability is a prime motivator, at least under certain conditions. Conceptual differences in these approaches derive from alternative conceptions of rationality.

For Weiner, rationality is a logical analysis of cause–effect relations; and thus hedonism, which implies illogic, is irrational. Nicholls and Covington, in contrast, have a broader view of rationality. Rationality is defined relatively in terms of the goals the student is pursuing; if students are attempting to avoid demonstrating low ability, they may make attributions which protect that sense of ability and subsequently engage in actions serving that purpose. Partly in response to this dilemma, C. Ames poses some very different motivational systems, each with a different spring of action, theorizing that under certain conditions, Weiner's logical analysis of causes framework holds, while under other circumstances, the Covington–Nicholls' framework for protecting the sense of ability holds. One condition, according to C. Ames, involves whether or not students perceive themselves as operating in a competitive or noncompetitive environment.

In fact, Nicholls, Covington, and Ames all propose that there is an alternative to the ego-defensive spring of action. Nicholls characterizes this state as one in which persons are focused externally on the task, as opposed to internally on themselves wondering whether or not they are able, and he calls this state "task involvement." Covington and Ames discuss individualized-mastery approaches in which students perceive an effort–outcome covariation. These three authors agree that in this state, students focus on effort and effort-related strategies, rather than on concerns about whether or not they are able. Despite the differences in the approaches offered by Weiner, Covington, and Nicholls with respect to the source of motivation, all of these chapters are similar in that they describe approaches heavily steeped in attribution theory.

ATTRIBUTIONS: THE ROLE OF ABILITY AND EFFORT

While Weiner's framework addresses the broad spectrum of attribution by classifying possible internal, external, stable, variable, controllable, and uncontrollable factors, much of the work in motivation in education has focused on the interactive role of ability and effort attributions. The chapters by Nicholls, Covington, Stipek, and Ames deal extensively with this issue. Nicholls and Stipek explore different meanings of ability and effort and their interaction from early childhood to adulthood. Of particular interest is the development of the belief in a compensatory trade-off between effort and ability; that is, less ability means you must apply more effort and high effort may imply low ability when success is not achieved. Stipek presents a developmental model of achievement cognitions showing how age-related conceptions of ability and effort are affected by the classroom environment and performance feedback. Nicholls and Covington show how the desire to protect one's self-concept of ability is culturally learned; and all four chapters examine the role of competition on the interplay of ability and effort attributions. These chapters clearly point out that a self-concept of ability can be protected by either exerting effort and succeeding, leading to an inference of high ability, or by withholding effort (e.g., procrastinating) and failing, but nevertheless avoiding an inference of low ability because no effort to succeed was made.

While attributions to ability may inhibit or enhance motivation, depending on the situational context, an attribution to effort is seen as the cognitive element leading to proactive, intentional action. The effort–outcome covariation belief is viewed as the thought segment most closely tied to the action in the thought–action sequence. Within classic expectancy-value theory (Lawler, 1973), the belief that if one tries one can, immediately presages a particular action. Furthermore, Weiner's attributional reinterpretation of the achievement motive suggests that those who take responsibility for outcomes are those who believe that their success is due to effort and their failure due to a lack of effort. Effort attributions in student motivation, at face value, would seem central to any discussion of student motivation, and each chapter focuses on these effort beliefs in some unique and interesting ways. Weiner classifies effort as an attributional factor of variable intensity and direction internal to and under the control of the student. Certainly, the views of the other authors are consistent with this basic definition. Covington, however, stresses the role of effort as a "double-edged sword" in its implications for student ability and self-worth. Nicholls and Ames stress the negative effects of competitive reward structure on effort beliefs; and, of course, deCharms's *origin* is a student who takes personal responsibility for actions and outcomes, believing strongly in his or her ability to bring about desired outcomes through exerting effort. We believe the study of ability and effort attributions is consistent with the overall theme of the book, which suggests that the study of the microanalysis of motivationally related cognitions is critical to understanding student motivation.

ROLE OF CULTURE AND SOCIOECONOMIC STATUS IN INFLUENCING COGNITIONS IN MOTIVATION

"Are the findings culturally bound?" is a question often raised about many areas of social psychological research. Two chapters address this topic directly: one theoretically and another empirically. Maehr has a long history of work on the topic of culture and motivation and he is now proposing a theory of personal investment in which the cultural meaning of an achievement event becomes the central concept within a theory of motivation. The theory as articulated by Maehr in his chapter suggests that we find different motivational characteristics of people as a function of the meaning they place on these achievement events. This meaning concept makes it easy, then, to explain cultural differences in achievement motivation because different cultures place different meanings on different kinds of goals, events, and actions. Thus, Maehr suggests (1) that persons bring a certain package of meaning to a situation, (2) that the features of the situation affect the meaning that arises in the situation, and (3) that meaning mediates personal investment. He also articulates how beliefs about the self, perceived goals of behavior in a situation, and perceived action possibilities determine the nature of the meaning of an event or situation. For example, the act of asserting oneself in an achievement situation may have different cultural meanings, positive and negative. These meanings may result in different approaches to achievement as a function of the values placed on this act such that in some cultures, achievement in the sense of doing better than someone else is highly valued, while in other cultures it receives quite a low value.

Cooper and Tom, in their chapter, attack the problem of culture and socioeconomic status (SES) from an empirical view by using recently developed statistical procedures for synthesizing research. They have done an extensive review of research on the effect of culture and SES on achievement motivation and have summarized this research using these metaanalytical procedures. Their chapter is a broad-based review covering current and historical literature on SES and race on motivation. A cornerstone piece in a historical trace of the literature, however, is represented by Katz's (1967) article on academic motivation in minority-group children. Whereas Katz looked at some variables very similar to the ones that Cooper and Tom examine in their chapter and concluded that not much research had been done up to that point, Cooper and Tom's review shows that a great deal of research has evolved since 1967. Cooper and Tom's empirical approach allows for a thorough review and update of the literature published on this subject, not only since 1967, but also incorporating much of the same literature that Katz examined. Their chapter clearly shows that SES is a more important determinant of achievement motivation than race or ethnicity. But, as they note, these variables are really pseudovariables or proxies for underlying variables associated with the meanings different socioeconomic statuses, races, and ethnic groups place on achievement strivings. These meanings probably are closely tied to different values and goals regarding striving for success and seem to result in different attributions for success and failure. While most of the literature reviewed by Cooper and Tom does not address motivation in this detail, they use their review and summary as the basis for a call for the microanalytic study of cognitions, which is so central to the research reported in this volume.

The cultural issue has both theoretical and practical significance for motivation in education. From a theoretical point of view, cross-cultural research allows us to test and validate theories and hypotheses in different cultural settings, so that we can then examine the generalizability of any particular theoretical paradigm. From a practical standpoint, the cultural issue is important because we are concerned in this country about how to improve educational opportunities for various minorities and special groups. Many of these groups differ in terms of SES and culture. The cornerstone variable in cross-cultural research relates to the underlying values in the culture, and differences in values become the significant motivational factor. A key aspect of Maehr's chapter is the theory of personal investment showing how different motivational meanings relate to underlying values that are held by the individual or by the culture. Even in the Cooper and Tom chapter, it seems clear that many of the cultural differences that have occurred in motivation have been explained in terms of some value-related concept. Thus, the values and goals of individuals serve as the basis for the different meanings placed on achievement in different cultures. The environment clearly has an impact on these different meanings—hence the view that SES is a good proxy for a broad base of contextual factors that affect motivationally related beliefs. We now turn to a discussion of the immediate and specific context factors of competition and its impact on motivationally related thoughts and actions.

COMPETITION AND MOTIVATION

Six of the nine chapters in this volume (Nicholls, Covington, Maehr, Stipek, Ames, and Hill) deal directly with the effects of competition on motivation and the underlying psychological process of social comparison. In contrast to the popular notion held by some that competition leads to enhanced motivation, all of these chapters uniformly indicate that competition leads to a number of debilitating motivational impacts. The varied research thrusts have identified some previously unknown problems that are associated with motivational impacts of competition that relate to specific self-referent attributions, emotions, and information utilization and attention.

Nicholls, Covington, and Ames's chapters suggest that competition is debilitating because it places the student in an ego-involved, threatening, self-focused state rather than a task-involved, effort- or strategy-focused state. They show that the debilitating effects of motivation are most clearly seen as negative self-worth and self-esteem and corresponding low-effort behaviors resulting in a general lack of effective performance. Stipek traces children's conceptions of ability as a function of development and shows how social comparison processes come to play an important role in this process. C. Ames's chapter provides clear evidence for the direct link between competitive versus noncompetitive environments and specific attributions to ability and effort. Hill's chapter looks at the emotional consequences associated with social comparison and competition—that is, anxiety; and Maehr's chapter examines how competition affects the kinds of goals that students pursue. In essence, competition seems to focus the student on a global and uncontrollable sense of ability, increasing student concern with demonstrating high ability and avoiding the demonstration of low ability. Several of these chapters also look at the motivational consequences of alternative social structures associated with competitive, individualized, or cooperative learning. Ames delineates the different meanings of success and effort-related actions within each of these structures, showing how motivation is *qualitatively* rather than *quantitatively* different within each structure. The ultimate value of such research on a controversial issue like competition in education and society is not in polemics, but in clearly identifying the motivational qualities of each structure so that a more rational choice can be made among the various alternatives educators have to motivate students.

MOTIVATIONAL CHANGE

The issue of whether or not motivation can be changed is most clearly addressed in the last section of the book. In this section, two chapters are presented in which the authors trace their own research, over time, showing that with a careful theoretical base, interventions can be designed to have an impact on students' motivation. And further, this impact can be empirically verified. It is clear, from the reading of these chapters, that programs for motivational change must evolve from an understanding of the thought–action sequence as characterized in an attributional approach. The chapters in this section differ in that one chapter focuses on environmental plans and techniques that help students deal with and reduce anxiety; the other focuses more on how students can change in their general internal psychological states relevant to motivation. Hill's work focuses on teaching students test-taking strategies to reduce anxiety and on changing the nature of the test situation itself so that less anxiety is elicited. DeCharms's chapter describes a long history of research on student motivation in school settings, showing that the achievement motivation of children and adolescents can be changed by training them in new thought–action patterns. The thoughts in these thought–action patterns clearly represent what

Weiner characterizes as second-level cognitions. The thoughts involve a variety of cognitions, including goals, attributions, conceptions of self, origin and pawn experiences, and expectancies. These programs are multifaceted in the sense that teachers, students, administrators, and the educational environment are all included in an overall plan to enhance and develop motivation in an educational setting.

The term that has been used to describe these two programs of research is *school–university collaborative research.* We believe that these two programs of school intervention, change, evaluation, and research are the forerunners of a great deal of work to be done in the 1980s on the design of instruction and training of teachers and students to enhance motivation. The time has come when there appears to be enough basic research to support a variety of approaches to motivational change programs.

THE VALUE OF MOTIVATION IN EDUCATION

As with advances in research and development in all fields, we now have alternative courses of action related to motivation that were hitherto unknown. The motivational research reported in this volume, for example, suggests that some commonly used educational practices (i.e., test-taking formats and reward structures) may have a debilitating effect on motivations. We also know from the work of Covington, Hill, and de-Charms that we can increase mastery orientation, motivation of students with high test anxiety, and achievement motivation of lower-SES school children, respectively. Further, as we come to understand the development of motivation as well as motivational differences among cultures, we find that students may be motivated to achieve quite a variety of different goals (e.g., friendship, recognition, as well as achievement). Thus, the research reported in this volume takes a giant step toward increasing our knowledge of how to systematically increase the motivation of students for both academic and nonacademic goals, through training or manipulating the environment. Additionally, the research reported here suggests that it is possible to increase the motivation of students who differ in level of anxiety, achievement motivation, SES, and race. With such knowledge comes the power and responsibility to change; but what changes are desirable or have highest priority?

We know it might be possible to increase the motivation of students for achievement as well as for affiliation, power, or other motives, but which motive is educationally valuable or desirable? Given our knowledge of individual differences in motivation, should we attempt to achieve what Nicholls has termed *motivation equality*. While such value questions are not directly addressed in the chapters in this volume, they are certainly embedded in many of the chapters and will be raised in the minds of many readers. As this research advances, it will be necessary for researchers and policymakers to address these value questions. Nevertheless, we believe that motivation should be given a central role in evaluating the quality of education, particularly when considering children of different cultural backgrounds, abilities, and attainment levels. Thus, advances in research on motivation, as represented by the chapters in this volume, may help educators and policymakers understand the dynamics of equality and quality in education, so that research-based choices are available as educational programs are planned and implemented.

REFERENCES

Atkinson, J. W. Explorations using imaginative thought to assess the strength of human motives. In M. R. Jones (Ed.), *Nebraska symposium on motivation* (Vol.2). Lincoln: University of Nebraska Press, 1954.

Heider, F. *The psychology of interpersonal relations*. New York: Wiley, 1958.

Jones, E. E., & Davis, K. E. From acts to dispositions: The attribution process in person perception. In L. Berkowitz (Ed.), *Advances in experimental social psychology* (Vol. 2). New York: Academic Press, 1965.

Katz, I. The socialization of academic motivation in minority group children. In D. Levine (Ed.), *Nebraska symposium on motivation* (Vol. 15). Lincoln: University of Nebraska Press, 1967.

Kelley, H H. Attribution theory in social psychology. In D. Levine (Ed.), *Nebraska symposium on motivation* (Vol 15). Lincoln: University of Nebraska Press, 1967.

Lawler, E. E. *Motivation in work organizations*. Monterey, CA: Brooks/Cole, 1973.

McClelland, D. C. Some social consequences of achievement motivation. In M. R. Jones (Ed.), *Nebraska symposium on motivation* (Vol. 3). Lincoln: University of Nebraska Press, 1955.

McClelland, D. C., & Winter, D. G. *Motivating economic achievement*. New York: Free Press, 1969.

Weiner, B. *Theories of motivation: From mechanism to cognition*. Chicago: McNally, 1972.

Weiner, B., & Kukla, A. An attributional analysis of achievement motivation. *Journal of Personality and Social Psychology*, 1970, *15*, 1–20.

PART I

Theoretical Perspectives

1

Principles for a Theory of Student Motivation and Their Application within an Attributional Framework*

Bernard Weiner

A THEORY OF STUDENT MOTIVATION

The construction of a theory of student motivation creates some special problems and requires departure from prior theories of motivation. It surely seems unlikely that much of classroom behavior is governed by the sexual and aggressive instincts stressed by Freud, so the psychoanalytic approach offers relatively little theoretical help. In a similar manner, Hullian theory, which focuses on the reduction of biological needs and the survival relevance of behavior, also is far removed from classroom concerns. Thus, the two most historically influential motivational theories, with their building blocks of internal equilibrium maintenance (homeostasis) and its hedonic consequences, do not provide the needed conceptual tools to explain classroom motivation.

*This chapter was written while the author was supported by grant MH38014 from the National Institute of Mental Health.

15

If homeostasis and hedonism do not provide the foundation for a theory of student motivation, then what other principles might guide theory construction? The answer to this question must be directed by observations in the classroom, as opposed to the introspections of clinical patients or the behavior of hungry rats. These observations force the theorist to confront the fact that behavior reeks of cognitions (Tolman, 1932), that a wide variety of emotions are experienced and expressed in school, and that behaviors are both logical (rational) and illogical (irrational). With these in mind, I suggest that the following three general canons must be incorporated into a theory of student motivation.

1. A Theory of Motivation Must Include the Full Range of Cognitive Processes.

Prior to the advent of behaviorism, it was accepted that thoughts and mental processes play a crucial role in determining human action. But behaviorism buried this belief, with its conception of humans as robots, or machines with input–output connections. However, behaviorism no longer plays a dominant role in psychology, clearly because we are not robots, machines, or hydraulic pumps. A broad array of mental processes, including information search and retrieval, attention, memory, categorization, judgment, and decision-making play essential roles in determining why students behave as they do. This is consistent with the variety of cognitive processes that also play an important role in student learning. Just as behavior often is functional, aiding in goal attainment, cognitions also often serve adaptive functions for reaching desired end states. Cognitive functionalism must play as central a part in a theory of motivation as behavioral functionalism.

The focus on cognitions includes the study of conscious experience. One can make the argument (or at least *I* can) that the time spent thinking about sex and aggression is much greater than the time actively engaged in these actions. Furthermore, the time spent in these thoughts and the feelings that accompany mental events and behavior are just as worthy of study as the time spent in the activity itself. A theory of motivation is responsible for examining the experiential state of the organism and the meaning of an action; hence, the theory must embrace phenomenology and accept that one acts on the perceived, rather than the real, world.

Associated with this position is my belief that many (but not all) of the significant thoughts and feelings are conscious and known by the actor. This is similar to the attitude of Gordon Allport, who stated that the best way to gain information about an individual is to directly ask that person. We may not be aware of psychological processes, such as how we

(Heider, 1958; Kelley, 1967; Weiner, 1980a). This presumption serves the same function for attribution theory as the maxim that individuals strive to reduce sexual and aggressive urges performs for psychoanalytic theory. Both point out the basic springs of action, and focus attention on particular phenomena.

A causal attribution answers a *why* question, such as "Why doesn't Johnny like me?" "Why did she get a poor mark on the spelling quiz?" "Why did I fail to get a hit in the baseball game?" "Why did our political party lose the election?" Causal search is not indiscriminately displayed in all situations, for this would place great cognitive strain on the organism. Rather, search is most evident when there has been an unexpected outcome (e.g., failure when success was anticipated), and when a desire has not been fulfilled (e.g., there is interpersonal rejection) (see Folkes, 1982; Lau & Russell, 1980; Wong & Weiner, 1981). The reader might note that the preceding *why* questions all involve nonattainment of desired outcomes. One typically does not ask, "Why *does* Johnny like me?" unless this is an unexpected occurrence.

There are a number of reasonable speculations that account for the instigation of causal search given unexpected and aversive outcomes. One function of causal search and explanation is to reduce surprise (Pettit, 1981). Thus, for example, one might be startled when rejected for a date by a fiancé. The response to a *why* query, such as "I must meet a friend" or "I have a terrible headache," produces the explanation needed to account for the rejection, thereby reducing surprise and uncertainty. Another, and manifestly more important, function of causal search is to aid in subsequent goal attainment. Knowing why one has failed might increase later chances for success because pertinent instrumental actions can now be undertaken. Attributional analyses therefore are functional, and attribution theory falls within the broader study of cognitive functionalism.

As intimated previously, causal search is not confined to any single motivational domain. Individuals desire to know, for example, why their team has been defeated (an achievement concern, Lau & Russell, 1980), why they have been refused for a date (an affiliative concern, Folkes, 1982); and why they have lost an election (a power concern, Kingdon, 1967). The number of these perceived causes is virtually infinite, and is greatly dependent on the particular activity that is under consideration. In achievement situations, there is a great deal of documentation that success and failure often are ascribed to ability (including both aptitude and learned skills), some aspect of motivation (such as short- or long-term effort expenditure, attention), others (friends, family), physiological factors (e.g., mood, maturity, health), the difficulty or ease of the task, and luck (see, for example, Cooper & Burger, 1980; Frieze & Snyder, 1980). But in noneducational achievement contexts other factors may play dominant causal roles. For example, outcomes at athletic events can be ascribed to the coach, the umpire, or the play of the opponent, while occupational success and failure might be attributed to any of a number of personality traits, such as perceived honesty, or to the state of the economy.

A different set of causes is elicited in explaining interpersonal success or failure. In an affiliative context, acceptance or rejection of a dating request may be ascribed to prior behaviors (e.g., making a good impression, being too assertive), physical appearance, and the desires or state of the potential date (e.g., wanting to go out; having a boyfriend or prior engagement; see Folkes, 1982). And given a political contest and power concerns, election or defeat tends to be attributed to party identification, the personality characteristics of the candidates, and their stances on issues (Kingdon, 1967).

Inasmuch as the potential list of causes is considerable within any motivational domain, and because the specific causes differ between domains, it is essential to create a classification scheme or a taxonomy of causes. That is, the organization of causal thinking must be ascertained. In so doing, the underlying properties of causes are identified and their similarities and differences can be determined. The discovery of these bases for comparison, which are referred to as causal dimensions, has proven to be the key step in the construction of this attributional theory of motivation and emotion. I consider the movement from description to classification a necessary first stage in theory construction.

CAUSAL DIMENSIONS

Two methods of arriving at new knowledge, dialectic and demonstrative (following Rychlak, 1968), have been used to determine the basic dimensions of causality. I will focus here on the dialectic or nonexperimental method, for that best conveys the logic and the meaning of the uncovered dimensions (for a review of the empirical work, see Weiner, 1982).

The dialectic approach has involved a logical grouping of causes, discovery of an apparent contradiction in reasoning, and the emergence of a new dimension of causality to resolve the uncovered inconsistency. This rational and introspective examination within the attributional domain began with a differentiation between causes located within the person, such as intelligence, physical beauty, and personality, and causes considered outside of the person (environmental factors), such as the objective difficulty of a task, the prior engagement of a dating partner, or the popularity of one's political opponent. The internal–external distinction is primarily associated with Rotter's (1966) construct of locus of control, but this causal dimension also is captured with various other labels, such as person–environment or disposition–situation, and is evident in contrasts between origin–pawn (deCharms, 1968), intrinsic– extrinsic motivation (Deci, 1975), and freedom–constraint (Brehm, 1966). Within the achievement domain, such causes as aptitude, effort, and health commonly are considered internal to the person, whereas task difficulty, help from others, and luck are perceived among the environmental determinants of an outcome.

A number of psychological approaches recognize only the internal–external distinction among causes. However, a shortcoming of this one-dimensional taxonomy became evident when it was discovered that disparate responses regarding expectancy and evaluation are displayed, given causes with an identical locus classification. For example, in achievement-related contexts, failure perceived as due to lack of ability (aptitude) results in lower expectancies of future success than failure believed to be caused by a lack of effort (see, for example, Weiner, Nierenberg, & Goldstein, 1976). This disparity shows that these two causes differ in one or more respects, although both are considered to be properties of the person. A second dimension of causality therefore was postulated; it was labeled causal stability (see Heider, 1958; Weiner, 1979, 1980a). The stability dimension differentiates causes on the basis of their temporal consistency. For example, math aptitude or physical beauty are perceived as relatively enduring, in contrast to luck and mood, which are temporary and can vary within short periods of time. Because ability is perceived as more constant than effort, prior outcomes ascribed to ability are more predictive of the future than are outcomes ascribed to effort. Causal stability, which is one aspect of the broader dimension that I will hereafter refer to as constancy, accounts for the expectancy shift differences produced by these two causal ascriptions.

It has also been pointed out by Abramson, Seligman, and Teasdale (1978) that causes differ in their cross-situational generality. For example, one can fail at math because of poor math aptitude (specific), or low intelligence (general). Abramson et al. (1978) labeled this causal dimension globality. Globality is considered here as another aspect of causal constancy. Stability relates to temporal consistency, while globality is concerned with cross-situational consistency. Both temporal and situational considerations are aspects of causal constancy (and traits).

A third dimension of causality was then proposed when it became evident that some causes identically classified on both the locus and constancy dimensions yielded dissimilar reactions (see Litman-Adizes,

1978; Rosenbaum, 1972; Weiner, 1979). For example, failure attributed to lack of effort begets greater punishment than failure ascribed to ill health, although both may be conceived as internal and unstable causes. Introspection suggested a third causal property, labeled controllability. The concept of control implies that the actor "could have done otherwise" (Hamilton, 1980). Effort is subject to volitional control; individuals are held to be responsible for how hard they try. On the other hand, one cannot typically control inherited characteristics such as aptitude or some temporary states such as illness. Within the achievement domain, effort is the most evident example of a controllable cause, although so-called traits such as patience or frustration tolerance are often perceived by others as controllable.

Very recently, still a fourth dimension of causality has been suggested by this dialectic method, although this discovery raises a number of difficult issues that I do not want to address in the present context. This dimension is labeled intentionality, and was alluded to in an earlier work (Weiner, 1979).[1] Again evaluation played a key role in the isolation of a new dimension. Lack of effort and poor work strategies (see Anderson & Jennings, 1980) are both considered internal, unstable, and controllable causes. Yet failure due to a lack of effort would result in greater punishment from others than failure because of a poor use of strategy. Hence, still a fourth differentiation between causes may be necessary. It appears that effort and strategy differ in their intentional or premeditational quality: Given low effort, but not poor strategy, the negative consequences are foreseeable and the behavior is considered "irresponsible."

In most instances, controllability and intentionality highly co-vary (see Anderson, 1983). However, in some circumstances (e.g., negligence) there can be high controllability with low intentionality, while in other instances (the psychopathic killer who does not consciously want to kill) there is low controllability over an intended act. However, because of the more general lack of independence of control from intent, these two causes will be classified under the common category of *responsibility*.

In sum, at present three dimensions of causality have been identified, representing five causal distinctions:

1. Locus
2. Constancy
   a. Temporal Stability
   b. Cross-situational generality (globality)

---

[1]Among the difficulties encountered with this formulation is that intention and my subsequent usage of the responsibility concept are characteristics of a person or an act, but do not characterize a cause.

3. Responsibility
   a. Controllability
   b. Intentionality

These distinctions have been brought to light by a conceptual analysis of the language of the layperson. This analysis allows us to better understand common sense, or shared beliefs about psychological concepts that are used in everyday life. The dimensions reveal the meaning of a cause and represent the manner in which the causal world is organized. I believe that these dimensions are quite prevalent, and perhaps pancultural as well as present throughout much of history.

The discussion thus far has not elucidated a theory of motivation and emotion. Rather, it has merely been suggested that individuals seek to know the causes of events, and that these causes share certain characteristics and can be described with a few basic concepts. Theoretical development requires that the antecedents of causal inference be determined and, more importantly, that there be a demonstration of the consequences of causal attributions. This provides a S–O–R framework, with S (stimulus) broadly representing the determinants of causal decisions, R (response) loosely indicating psychological consequences, and O the mental capacities of the organism. Because of space limitations and the fact that motivational psychology is particularly concerned with consequences, very little of this chapter is concerned with the determinants of causal inference (see a review in Weiner, 1980a). I briefly turn to this issue now.

CAUSAL ANTECEDENTS

What determines the answers to questions such as "Why doesn't Johnny like me?" "Why did she get a poor mark on the spelling quiz?" "Why did I fail to get a hit in the baseball game?" Investigators within the attributional field have referred to this as the study of the "attributional process" (Kelley & Michela, 1980).

A wide variety of specific informational cues, psychological structures, processes, and hedonic biases have been related to causal inferences. For example, information such as the performance of others at a task, as well as the person's past performance at the specific and similar tasks, in part determine causal ascriptions for a current success or failure (see Kelley, 1967; Weiner, 1980a). Thus, for example, if all others fail, while the individual has a history of success at the task in question, then a current success will be ascribed to an internal and stable factor such as high ability. There has been some controversy regarding whether people in fact use consensus information (the performance of others) in making attributional judgments (see Kassin, 1979). But it is evident that pupils immediately compare their grades with those of others and college students want to know about the class "curve." The pattern and randomness of performance, objective characteristics of the task, covariation of performance with incentive, and persistence of behavior are just some of the other specific informational cues that help one determine whether a success or a failure was due to causes such as ability, effort, task ease or difficulty, and luck (see Weiner, 1980a).

Concerning the role of psychological structures, what are known as causal schemata, or rules that relate causes to effects, also affect causal attributions (see Kelley, 1972). For example, given high ability and success at an easy task, there will be a strong tendency to discount effort expenditure as a causal factor because ability is a sufficient cause of success in this instance. Among the psychological processes that influence causal decision making are attentional factors. The well-studied actor–observer difference in attribution, which refers to the tendency of actors to make situation attributions and observers to make trait attributions, has been related to the actor's attention to the environment and the observer's focus on the actor. Finally, regarding hedonic biasing, it is now well-established that individuals are more prone to take credit for success than to blame themselves for failure.

Just a few of the determinants of causal attribution have been outlined. It is evident that a wide array of cognitive factors influence the attribution process. Principle 1, enumerated earlier, thus is highly evident within an attributional approach to motivation.

CAUSAL CONSEQUENCES

I now turn to the issue of greater concern to motivational psychologists—the consequences of causal ascriptions. The discussion focuses primarily on goal expectancies and emotional reactions.

Expectancy of Success

It is quite evident that motivational indicators, including which goals are selected and how long instrumental activity is undertaken to reach those goals, are in part determined by the subjective estimates of goal attainment. Tolman (1932) has perhaps most extensively examined this issue, although social learning theorists, applying the concepts of locus of control and generalized expectancy, also have addressed the expectancy question. However, relatively little is yet known about the factors that influence subjective expectancy.

The attributional conception being proposed offers a simple yet far-reaching principle that accounts for the magnitude and direction of *expectancy change*. It is contended that expectancy shifts after attainment or nonattainment of a goal are dependent on the perceived constancy or invariance of the cause of the prior outcome. Considering performance on the same task, over a span of time, ascription of an outcome to stable factors produces greater typical shifts in expectancy (increments in expectancy after success and decrements in expectancy after failure) than do ascriptions to unstable causes. Thus, for example, success at math ascribed to mathematical aptitude is likely to result in greater certainty about future success in math than would a positive outcome ascribed to lucky guessing, or to unexpected help from others. In a similar manner, rejection of a dating request is likely to produce increased certainty about the improbability of a subsequent date if that rejection is ascribed to stable factors such as physical appearance or religious restrictions than if the refusal is perceived as due to a prior engagement or temporary illness of the rejector. Stated somewhat differently, if success (or failure) has been attained and if the conditions or causes of that outcome are perceived as remaining unchanged, then success (or failure) will be anticipated again with a reasonable degree of certainty. But if the conditions or the causes are subject to change, then there is reasonable doubt of the repetition of the previous outcome.

There is a great deal of experimental support for these statements, although I believe that the hypotheses concerning expectancy shifts rest on the shared meaning of cause–effect relations and are not subject to empirical refutation.[2] The wide array of content domains to which this principle has been brought to bear, and the empirical findings, include the following:

1. Success at academic tests and tasks attributed to stable factors such as high ability result in higher future expectancies than does success ascribed to unstable factors such as luck. In a similar manner, failure attributed to stable factors such as low aptitude results in lower future expectancies than does failure ascribed to unstable factors such as low effort. These findings have been reported by more than a dozen experimenters (e.g., Fontaine, 1974; Inagi, 1977; Kovenklioglu & Greenhaus, 1978; McMahan, 1973; Weiner *et al.*, 1976).

[2]One might examine the development of cause–effect thinking, or the cross-cultural representation of this mode of thought. However, lack of experimental support in an investigation of American adults would not lead to the questioning of the foundation of logic that is embodied within cause–effect linkages.

2. Occupation or job-related success ascribed to stable factors such as personality or knowledge results in higher future expectancies, and failure due to those stable factors produces lower future expectancies, than outcomes ascribed to unstable factors such as a changing sales territory (e.g., Orpen, 1980; Valle & Frieze, 1976).

3. Acceptance of a dating request because of stable reasons such as physical appearance gives rise to higher future expectancies, and rejection because of those causes results in lower future expectancies, than outcomes due to unstable factors such as a prior engagement or temporary illness (Folkes, 1982).

4. Positive and negative outcomes at skill-related tasks (ability attributions) produce greater typical expectancy changes than outcomes at chance-related tasks (luck attributions) (e.g., Masterson, 1973; Rotter, Liverant, & Crowne, 1961).

5. Rape victims ascribing a prior attack to their personal characteristics perceive future rape as less avoidable than victims attributing the attack to an ill-advised action on their part (such as walking in an unsafe section of the city; Janoff-Bulman, 1979).

6. Rejection of a scientific paper for publication because of perceived stable causes (ability, training, soundness of the research design) is less likely to result in resubmission of the manuscript than rejection due to perceived unstable causes (e.g., choice of reviewers; Crittenden & Wiley, 1980).

7. A criminal is perceived as a greater risk to society and receives a longer sentence if his or her crime is attributed to stable characteristics (e.g., "a bad seed") rather than unstable factors (e.g., temporary economic conditions; Carroll & Payne, 1976, 1977).

The preceding listing includes just a small sample of studies relating causal stability to expectancy of success. The attributional formulation points out that academic failure because of perceived lack of ability, occupational failure because of a poor personality, social rejection because of physical unattractiveness, rape because of characterological faults, scientific rejection because of unsound research and a crime perceived as due to some genetic dysfunction all are similar in that the outcome is perceived as due to a stable factor, and thus is expected to recur. On the other hand, academic failure because of perceived bad luck or lack of effort, job failure because of a difficult but changing sales territory, social rejection because of temporary illness, rape because of mistaken behavior, scientific rejection because of choice of reviewers, and crime perceived as due to temporary economic plight share the possibility that the future will be different because the outcome is attributed to unstable causes. I suggest that the linkage between perceived causal stability and expectancy change be considered a fundamental law in psychology.

Expectancy of Success, Achievement Change Programs, and Motivational Models

The application of the stability–expectancy linkage has been especially influential in the development of achievement change programs, although other theoretical concepts such as learned helplessness also have guided these plans. An attributional approach to achievement change begins with the assumption that the perception of why an event has occurred in an important determinant of subsequent action. If this assumption is correct, then it logically follows that a modification of causal perceptions should produce a change in action. In attributional change programs, there is a focus on altering the perceived causes of failure with the goal of enhancing achievement strivings (e.g., Andrews & Debus, 1978; Dweck, 1975; Zoeller, Mahoney, & Weiner, 1983).

The programs generally presume that attribution of failure to lack of ability is especially debilitating because ability is a stable, uncontrollable factor. Hence, the experimental participants frequently are children who tend to attribute academic failure to low ability. On the other hand, it is reasoned that ascription of failure to lack of effort (Dweck, 1975) or to poor strategy (Anderson & Jennings, 1980) is adaptive inasmuch as these factors are unstable and subject to volitional control.

The achievement change research studies generally follow a similar paradigm in which there is induced failure and information from the experimenter that promotes attributions to lack of effort or to poor work strategy. The data clearly reveal that ascription to these unstable, controllable factors enhances persistence toward the goal and augments performance, relative to a control group.

Note that in the change program research one can begin to discern the outlines of a more complete motivational theory, with antecedent information (feedback from an experimenter) altering causal perceptions (from, say, lack of ability to lack of effort). The causal dimension of the failure ascription then also shifts (from stable and uncontrollable to unstable and controllable), which, in turn, results in a higher expectancy of future success following a failure. Expectancy of success then influences a variety of motivational indexes such as the direction of goal-directed activity or the intensity, quality, and persistence of behavior.

This analysis also can be applied to the previous discussions of resubmission of a scientific paper and criminal justice. Antecedent information (such as comments from the reviewer, past history of scientific rejections) produces a cause for the current rejection. The stability of the cause influences the expectancy of subsequent acceptance, which affects the decision to resubmit the manuscript. In a similar manner, the prior history of the criminal as well as a multiplicity of other facts result in the assignment of a cause for a crime. The perceived stability of the cause leads to an estimation of the risk of this criminal to society, which influences the sentencing and parole decision.

In sum, an attributional theory of motivation, as presented thus far, takes the following form:

Causal antecedents → Causal ascriptions → Causal dimension
(constancy) → Expectancy of success → Action

This conceptual analysis is, as already evidenced, not limited to any specific content domain. Hence, the conceptual tools are provided for the construction of a general theory.

One shortcoming of the theory and discussion thus far is that there are immediate determinants of action in addition to expectancy of success. Certainly one motivational factor that has been overlooked, and neglected by other motivational theories, is the emotional reactions of an actor.

ATTRIBUTIONS AND AFFECT

It often is difficult to give proper emphasis to emotions within a cognitive theory of human motivation. It is now possible, however, to outline the place of affect within this attributional conception. The approach to emotions associated with this attributional theory has been discussed in great detail in other publications (see Weiner, 1980b, 1982; Weiner & Graham, in press). In this context, I merely want to indicate that cognitions are considered sufficient determinants of feeling states.

AFFECT AS A REACTION TO A CAUSAL ASCRIPTION

A number of research investigations have rather definitively documented that, in achievement-related contexts, there are multiple sources of affect following success and failure. Two research paradigms, one simulational and reactive, and the other retrospective and operant, were first used to document this position (Weiner, Russell, & Lerman (1978, 1979). In the former paradigm, participants are asked to imagine that a student succeeded or failed at an exam for a particular reason, such as hard work or bad luck. The subjects then report the intensity of affective reactions that they think might be experienced in this situation. Intensity is indicated on rating scales for a number of pre-selected affects. In the second paradigm, participants are asked to recall a time in life when they succeeded or failed for a specified reason. They also recount the affects they experienced at that time.

These studies reveal that one determinant of affect is the outcome of an action—success at achievement–related activities gives rise to happiness, regardless of the cause of that outcome. For example, given athletic competition, one tends to be happy following a victory whether the win is due to extra training, the poor play of the competitor, or to luck. In a similar manner, failure gives rise to frustration and sadness regardless of the reason for that outcome (see Weiner *et al.*, 1978, 1979).

In addition, and more germane to this chapter, emotions are discriminably related to particular attributions. Among the specific attribution–emotion linkages for success are ability–competence, long-term effort–relaxation, help from others–gratitude, and luck–surprise. That is, if one succeeds because of help from others, then gratitude is experienced; success due to luck gives rise to surprise; and so on. Among the unions for failure are low ability–humiliation, lack of effort–guilt, hindrance from others–anger, and luck–surprise. At times, then, causal attributions yield opposing reactions to success and failure (gratitude vs. anger given an attribution to others); on other occasions the reactions to success and failure are unrelated given the same causal factor (e.g., high long-term effort gives rise to relaxation for success but low effort produces guilt for failure); and in still other circumstances the ascription-mediated reactions to success and failure are identical, as when there is a luck attribution. However, it must be remembered that, given an attribution to luck, the affective constellation is postulated to be surprise plus happiness given success and surprise plus frustration given failure.

Finally, causal dimensions also play an essential role in affective life. It conclusively appears that a number of affects, including pride and self-esteem, anger, gratitude, guilt, pity, and hopelessness are related to causal dimensions in the following manner:

1. *Pride* and positive self-esteem are experienced as a consequence of attributing a positive outcome to the self, while negative self-esteem is experienced when a negative outcome is ascribed to oneself (Weiner *et al.*, 1978, 1979). It also is evident that pride can be experienced when a relation, friend, or even one's country has "succeeded" for perceived internal reasons. In these instances, the affective experience is mediated by personal identification. To paraphrase Kant, everyone can enjoy a good meal, but only the cook can experience pride. Pride and personal esteem are therefore self-reflective emotions and implicate the locus dimension of causality.

2. *Anger* is experienced, given an attribution for a negative, self-related outcome or event to factors controllable by others (Weiner, 1980c, 1980d; Weiner *et al.*, 1978, 1979; Weiner, Graham & Chandler, 1982). Thus, for example, anger is aroused when one is prevented from studying by a noisy roommate. In addition, anger is elicited when a negative, other-related outcome or event is perceived as being under the personal control of that other. Hence, a pupil failing because of a lack of effort tends to elicit anger from the teacher, just as a person in need of aid because of excessive drinking often elicits anger.

3. *Gratitude* is experienced, given an attribution for a positive, self-related outcome or event to factors controllable by others (Weiner *et al.*, 1978, 1979). Hence, one feels grateful for a gift, but not if the giver was forced to present the gift. Of course, the intensity of gratitude, as well as anger, is influenced by many factors in addition to the controllability of the cause, such as the value of the goal (see Tesser, Gatewood, & Driver, 1968).

4. *Guilt* is experienced when one has brought about a negative consequence for a personally controllable cause. Thus, for example, failure because of insufficient effort or excessive eating by an obese person tends to elicit guilt within the actor (Weiner *et al.*, 1978, 1979; Weiner, Graham, & Chandler, 1982).

5. *Pity* is felt when others are in need of aid or in a negative state due to uncontrollable conditions (Weiner, 1980c, 1980d; Weiner, Graham, & Chandler, 1982). Another's loss of a loved one because of an accident or illness, or difficulties because of a physical handicap, are prototypical situations that elicit pity. Note, therefore, that the perceived controllability of a cause for a negative outcome in part determines whether anger or pity is directed toward another. We feel angry toward the lazy, but pity toward the unable. We use our knowledge of this linkage to alter the emotions of others. When explaining why we missed an appointment, or arrived late for it, uncontrollable causes often are given. Pity is exacerbated when the cause of a negative state is stable as well as uncontrollable (e.g., we pity a blind person more than one with a temporary eye problem).

6. *Hopelessness and resignation* are elicited, given an attribution for a negative outcome to stable factors (Weiner *et al.*, 1978, 1979). That is, if the future is expected to remain as bad as the past, then hopelessness is elicited.

A word of caution about the preceding list is needed. Given a causal ascription, the linked emotion does not necessarily follow. For example, one may not put forth effort, yet will be free from guilt. Or one may ascribe success to help from others, yet not experience gratitude. In addition, one may feel guilty when succeeding because of luck or even when failing because of a lack of ability. But the dimension–affect relations discussed above are quite prevalent in our culture. This position is similar to the argument that there is a linkage between frustration and aggression, although frustration elicits reactions other than aggression, and aggression has other antecedents in addition to frustration.

AFFECT AS A MOTIVATOR OF ACTION

Without question, then, attributions and their properties guide feelings. But do feelings, as was argued for expectancies, play a role in action? To aid in answering this question, assume a scenario in which one succeeds and the success is attributed to volitional help from others. On the basis of the prior discussion, this is expected to give rise to gratitude. One might think that gratitude, in turn, promotes actions instrumental to the maintenance of the relationship, such as the purchase of a gift. This scenario suggests that following the perception of an event there is an attribution–emotion–action sequence; we think the way we feel and act on the basis of these feelings.

In a series of investigations, evidence has been provided supporting this line of reasoning (Meyer, 1980; Weiner, 1980c, 1980d). In these studies, subjects read a scenario such as the following:

> At about 1:00 in the afternoon you are walking through campus and a student comes up to you. The student says that you do not know him, but that you are both enrolled in the same class. He asks if you would lend him the class notes from the meeting last week, saying that notes are needed because he skipped class to go to the beach. (Alternate form: Notes are needed because of eye problems). [Weiner, 1980d, p. 676].

Perception of the controllability of the cause of the need (in these instances, "beach" or "eyes"), ratings of pity and anger (which are known to be linked to perceived controllability), and the likelihood of helping are assessed.

The data in these investigations reveal positive relations between perceived controllability, anger, and lack of help, as well as between perceived uncontrollability, pity, and help-giving. Thus, for example, subjects tend to perceive the cause of the "eye-problem" student as uncontrollable, report feeling pity, and indicate they would help.

These correlational data also provide evidence concerning the temporal organization to behavior, including the linkage between affect and action. The logic of the analysis is that if affect mediates the relation between thought and action, then partialling affect from the cause (controllability)–lending correlation will greatly modulate the magnitude of that correlation. On the other hand, partialling thoughts from the affect-lending relation should not influence the magnitude of that correlation. And this is indeed the pattern of findings. The relations between pity and helping, and anger and lack of help, are not altered when perceptions of controllability are statistically taken from the relation. On the other hand, the relations between controllability and withdrawal, and uncontrollability and help, are greatly reduced when the reactions of anger and pity are held statistically constant. In sum, emotions, rather than causal perceptions, appear to be the immediate motivators of action. As was previously stated, thoughts give rise to feelings, and feelings guide behavior.

Affects also are indirect motivators of behavior because they are salient antecedents of causal thinking. For example, it has just been contended that pity is a consequence of attributing another's plight to an uncontrollable cause, particularly if that cause is perceived as stable (e.g., blindness, or low aptitude). It also has been demonstrated that the affect of pity communicated by an observer indicates to the actor that the cause of his or her problem is stable and uncontrollable. Hence, the recipient of this message is likely to infer that there is nothing to be done about the current plight. Pity, therefore, may be an inhibitor of action. On the other hand, anger communicates to the recipient of this message that something can be done about his or her behavior, because the cause of the current negative state is perceived as under volitional control. Anger therefore might be a motivator of behavior. In sum, affects are important cues that guide the attribution process and therefore have indirect motivational significance (see Graham, 1982; Weiner, Graham, Stern, & Lawson, 1982).[3]

THE COMPLETE THEORY

It is now appropriate to summarize the previous pages and to present this attributional theory as currently formulated. As I indicated in an earlier publication (Weiner, 1979), this theory is not fixed, and the advantages of publishing a self-contained and final package have not been realized. This theory, shown in Figure 1, indicates that a variety of

[3]In addition to pity, there are a number of other indirect cues that inadvertently communicate uncontrollable causes of negative states, particularly low ability. For example, praise for success at an easy task, lack of criticism for failure at an easy task, unsolicited help, and not allowing a child extended time when attempting to answer a question are all cues that communicate low-ability messages.

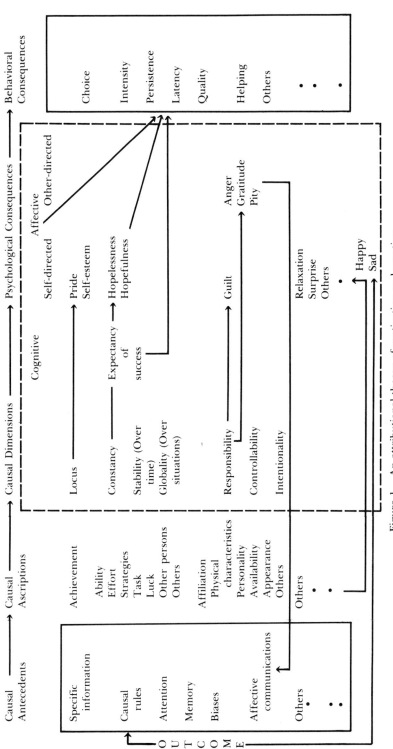

Figure 1. An attributional theory of motivation and emotion.

antecedents gives rise to specific causal ascriptions. The number of possible causal attributions is endless, but they can be characterized on the basis of three dimensions, comprising five distinctions. The constancy dimension is linked with expectancy changes and all the dimensions are uniquely related to particular affects, with controllability of special importance in interpersonal contexts. In addition, specific causes are associated with specific affects. Affect and expectancy, in turn, influence a variety of motivational indicators.

Consider, for example, the following scenario. A student tried hard but failed at a relatively easy task. This student has a history of failure, while all the other students were able to do well at this activity. On the basis of the specific past history and social norm data, as well as causal rules specifying that only little ability is needed for success at a relatively easy task if the person has tried, the inference made by the student is that he or she is "dumb." Low ability is a stable cause, producing low expectancy of future success. In addition, it generates feelings of humiliation and a lack of confidence. The teacher also notes the student's past history, the effort expended, and the performance of others, and concludes that this student is incompetent. This elicits pity and unsolicited help. These communications to the student serve as additional low-ability cues. The low expectancy of future success, accompanied by feelings of humiliation and expressions of pity and help, all contribute to lack of persistence in the face of future failure and performance decrements at achievement-related tasks.

Alternately, consider another possible scenario. A student did not study for a relatively difficult test and failed. This student has a history of success, and few of the other students did well at this test. On the basis of this information and use of causal rules, the inference is made by the student that he or she did not put forth sufficient effort. Lack of effort is an unstable cause, leading the student to anticipate the possibility of doing better on the next test. The lack of effort will produce guilt if the test is of some importance. The teacher also notes the student's past history and the performance of others, and concludes that the student was "wasting time." This elicits anger and perhaps withdrawal. These communications to the student serve as added low-effort cues. The maintenance of a high expectancy of success in the face of failure, accompanied by feelings of guilt and expressions of anger from the teacher, all contribute to increased intensity of performance given the anticipation of the next exam and produce increments in achievement-related behaviors.

These are, of course, merely two among many possible scenarios. In other instances the causal inferences may be less clear, the dimensional placement of the cause may be murky, the student reaction to failure because of lack of effort may not be guilt, there may be increased effort because one realizes he or she is incompetent, and so on. Thus, the hypothesized relations derived from the theory will not hold in all instances. However, many specific cases will fit within the conception, and the general analysis involving information search, causal decisions, expectancies, affects, and consequences is believed to be applicable in all cases.

A REEXAMINATION OF THE BASIC PRINCIPLES

It may be recalled that in the initial section of this chapter, three principles for the construction of a theory of student motivation were outlined. To what extent does the attributional theory that this been proposed adhere to these principles?

Principle 1 concerned cognitive processes, conscious experience, and the self. The key role of cognitive processes is especially evident in the antecedents of causal inference, which include specific information, causal rules, attention to and encoding of communications from others, memory, and other higher processes. Expectancy of success, which is virtually the only cognitive concept in expectancy-value theories, also is incorporated within the theory as a product of causal constancy. In addition, the theory is concerned with conscious experience: Awareness of causal attributions typically is assumed by investigators who make use of introspective reports to determine perceived causality. Finally, this theory is intimately tied to the self, inasmuch as (1) causal ascriptions often concern properties of the person, such as level of ability; (2) the emotional consequences of ascriptions include self-confidence and self-worth; and (3) the assumption of mastery strivings, which forms the heart of this attributional formulation, suggests growth and expansion of the self.

Principle 2 states that a theory should examine the full range of emotions. I know of no other motivational theory that incorporates the range of feelings that have been addressed here. Among the affects subsumed within the theory are pride and guilt, happiness and unhappiness, hopefulness and hopelessness, pity and anger, and so on. These are among the most prevalent affective reactions in the classroom.

Finally, regarding Principle 3, this attributional conception incorporates both rational decisions, as illustrated in the attribution process and the logic of cause–effect relations, as well as the irrational, such as hedonic biasing of attributions (attribution of success, but not failure, to the self).

A CONCLUDING NOTE

What, then, does the future hold? Many problems remain to be solved, including the number and the independence of the causal dimensions, methods for the measurement of affect and of causal thoughts, specification of the relationships of both expectancy and affect to action, and increasing the generality of the theory to additional domains. But the tools and building blocks for a theory of student motivation seem to be provided. We know, for example, that affects in the classroom include pity, guilt, feelings of incompetence, and the like. We realize that expectancies of future success, self-perceptions of ability, and positive evaluations for trying are part of life in the classroom. What is needed, then, is theoretical elaboration and refinement, and demonstration of theoretical value in the complex and overdetermined classroom setting.

REFERENCES

Abramson, L. Y., Seligman, M. E. P., & Teasdale, J. D. Learned helplessness in humans: Critique and reformulation. *Journal of Abnormal Psychology*, 1978, *87*, 49–74.

Anderson, C. A. The causal structure of situations: The generation of plausible causal attributions as a function of type of event situation. *Journal of Experimental Social Psychology*, 1983, *19*, 185–203.

Anderson, C. A., & Jennings, D. L. When experiences of failure promote expectations of success: The impact of attributing failure to ineffective strategies. *Journal of Personality*, 1980, *48*, 393–407.

Andrews, G. R., & Debus, R. L. Persistence and causal perceptions of failure: Modifying cognitive attributions. *Journal of Educational Psychology*, 1978, *70*, 154–166.

Atkinson, J. W. *An introduction to motivation*. Princeton, N.J.: Van Nostrand, 1964.

Brehm, J. W. (Ed.) *A theory of psychological reactance*. New York: Academic Press, 1966.

Carroll, J. S., & Payne, J. W. The psychology of the parole decision process: A joint application of attribution theory and information processing psychology. In J. S. Carroll & J. W. Payne (Eds.), *Cognition and social behavior*. Hillsdale, N.J.: Erlbaum, 1976.

Carroll, J. S., & Payne, J. W. Judgments about crime and the criminal: A model and method for investigating parole decisions. In B. D. Sales (Ed.), *Prospectives in law and psychology:* (Vol. 1) *The criminal justice system*. New York: Plenum, 1977.

Cooper, H. M., & Burger, J. M. How teachers explain students' academic performance. *American Educational Research Journal*, 1980, *17*, 95–109.

Crittenden, K. S., & Wiley, M. G. Causal attribution and behavioral response to failure. *Social Psychology Quarterly*, 1980, *43*, 353–358.

deCharms, R. *Personal causation.* New York: Academic Press, 1968.

Deci, E. L. *Intrinsic motivation.* New York: Plenum, 1975.

Dweck, C. S. The role of expectations and attributions in the alleviation of learned help-lessness. *Journal of Personality and Social Psychology,* 1975, *31,* 674–685.

Folkes, V. S. Communicating the reasons for social rejection. *Journal of Experimental Social Psychology,* 1982, *18,* 235–252.

Fontaine, G. Social comparison and some determinants of expected personal control and expected performance in a novel situation. *Journal of Personality and Social Psychology,* 1974, *29,* 487–496.

Frieze, I. H., & Snyder, H. N. Children's beliefs about the causes of success and failure in school settings. *Journal of Educational Psychology,* 1980, *72,* 186–196.

Graham, S. *Communicated sympathy and anger as determinants of self-perception and performance among black and white children.* Unpublished doctoral dissertation, University of California, Los Angeles, 1982.

Hamilton, V. L. Intuitive psychologist or intuitive lawyer? Alternative models of the attribution process. *Journal of Personality and Social Psychology,* 1980, *39,* 767–772.

Heider, F. *The psychology of interpersonal relations.* New York: Wiley, 1958.

Inagi, T. Causal ascription and expectancy of success. *Japanese Psychological Research,* 1977, *19,* 22–30.

Janoff-Bulman, R. Characterological versus behavioral self-blame: Inquiries into depression and rape. *Journal of Personality and Social Psychology,* 1979, *37,* 1798–1809.

Kassin, S. M. Consensus information, prediction, and causal attribution: A review of the literature and issues. *Journal of Personality and Social Psychology,* 1979, *37,* 1966–1981.

Kelley, H. H. Attribution theory in social psychology. In D. Levine (Ed.), *Nebraska symposium on motivation.* Lincoln, NB: University of Nebraska Press, 1967.

Kelley, H. H. Causal schemata and the attribution process. In E. E. Jones, D. E. Kanouse, H. H. Kelley, R. E. Nisbett, S. Valins, & B. Weiner (Eds.), *Attribution: Perceiving the causes of behavior.* Morristown, N.J.: General Learning Press, 1972.

Kelley, H. H., & Michela, J. L. Attribution theory and research. *Annual Review of Psychology,* 1980, *31,* 457–501.

Kingdon, J. W. Politicians' beliefs about voters. *American Political Science Review,* 1967, *61,* 137–145.

Kovenklioglu, G., & Greenhaus, J. H. Causal attributions, expectations, and task performance. *Journal of Applied Psychology,* 1978, *6,* 698–705.

Lau, R. R., & Russell, D. Attributions in the sports pages: A field test of some current hypotheses in attribution research. *Journal of Personality and Social Psychology,* 1980, *39,* 29–38.

Litman-Adizes, T. *An attributional model of depression.* Unpublished doctoral dissertation, University of California, Los Angeles, 1978.

McMahan, I. D. Relationships between causal attributions and expectancy of success. *Journal of Personality and Social Psychology,* 1973, *28,* 108–115.

Masterson, J. H. Expectancy changes with skill-determined and chance-determined outcomes. *Journal of Personality and Social Psychology,* 1973, *27,* 396–404.

Meyer, J. P. Causal attributions for success and failure: A multivariate investigation of dimensionality, formation, and consequences. *Journal of Personality and Social Psychology,* 1980, *38,* 704–718.

Orpen, C. The relationship between expected job performance and causal attributions of past success and failure. *Journal of Social Psychology,* 1980, *112,* 151–152.

Pettit, P. On actions and explanations. In C. Antaki (Ed.), *The psychology of ordinary explanations.* London: Academic Press, 1981.

Rosenbaum, R. M. *A dimensional analysis of the perceived causes of success and failure.* Unpublished doctoral dissertation, University of California, Los Angeles, 1972.

Rotter, J. B. Generalized expectancies for internal versus external control of reinforcement. *Psychological Monographs,* 1966, *80*(1, Whole No. 609).

Rotter, J. B., Liverant, S., & Crowne, D. P. The growth and extinction of expectancies in chance controlled and skilled tasks. *Journal of Psychology,* 1961, *52,* 161–177.

Rychlak, J. F. *A philosophy of science for personality theory.* New York: Houghton Mifflin, 1968.

Tesser, A., Gatewood, R., & Driver, M. Some determinants of gratitude. *Journal of Personality and Social Psychology,* 1968, *3,* 233–236.

Tolman, E. C. *Purposive behavior in animals and men.* New York: Appleton-Century-Crofts, 1932.

Valle, V. A., & Frieze, I. H. Stability of causal attributions as a mediator in changing expectations for success. *Journal of Personality and Social Psychology,* 1976, *33,* 579–587.

Weiner, B. A theory of motivation for some classroom experiences. *Journal of Educational Psychology,* 1979, *71,* 3–25.

Weiner, B. *Human motivation.* New York: Holt, Reinhart & Winston, 1980.(a).

Weiner, B. The role of affect in rational (attributional) approaches to human motivation. *Educational Researcher,* 1980, July–August, 4–11. (b)

Weiner, B. A cognitive (attribution)–emotion–action model of motivated behavior: An analysis of judgments of help-giving. *Journal of Personality and Social Psychology,* 1980, *39,* 186–200. (c)

Weiner, B. May I borrow your class notes? An attributional analysis of judgments of help-giving in an achievement-related context. *Journal of Educational Psychology,* 1980, *72,* 676–681. (d)

Weiner, B. The emotional consequences of causal ascriptions. In M. S. Clark & S. T. Fiske (Eds.), *Affect and cognition: The 17th Annual Carnegie symposium on cognition.* Hillsdale, N.J.: Erlbaum, 1982.

Weiner, B., & Graham, S. An attributional approach to emotional development. In C. Izard, J. Kagen, & R. Zajonc (Eds.), *Emotion, cognition, and action.* Cambridge, MA: Harvard University Press, in press.

Weiner, B., Graham, S., & Chandler, C. Causal antecedents of pity, anger, and guilt. *Personality and Social Psychology Bulletin,* 1982, *8,* 226–232.

Weiner, B., Graham, S., Stern, P., & Lawson, M. E. Using affective cues to infer causal thoughts. *Developmental Psychology,* 1982, *18,* 278–286.

Weiner, B., Nierenberg, R., & Goldstein, M. Social learning (locus of control) versus attribution (unusual stability) interpretations of expectancy of success. *Journal of Personality,* 1976, *44,* 52–68.

Weiner, B., Russell, D., & Lerman, D. Affective consequences of causal ascriptions. In J. H. Harvey, W. J. Ickes, & R. F. Kidd (Eds.), *New directions in attribution research* (Vol. 2). Hillsdale, N.J.: Erlbaum, 1978.

Weiner, B., Russell, D., & Lerman, D. The cognition–emotion process in achievement-related contexts. *Journal of Personality and Social Psychology,* 1979, *37,* 1211–1220.

Wong, P. T. P., & Weiner, B. When people ask "why" questions and the heuristics of attributional search. *Journal of Personality and Social Psychology,* 1981, *40,* 650–663.

Zoeller, C. *An attribution training program with mentally retarded adults in a workshop setting.* Unpublished doctoral dissertation, University of California, Los Angeles, California, 1979.

Zoeller, C., Mahoney, G., & Weiner, B. Effects of attribution training on the assembly task performance of mentally retarded adults. *American Journal of Mental Deficiency.* 1983, *88,* 109–112.

2

Conceptions of Ability and Achievement Motivation*

John G. Nicholls

THE INTENTIONAL APPROACH

Some young mathematicians had inveigled the great mathematician Johnny von Neumann, who invented game theory with his elegant "minmax" theorem, into playing poker with them.
(According to the theorem, there exists a technique called "optimal strategy" that simultaneously seeks to reduce to a minimum your opponent's chips while maximizing your own.)
That night, von Neumann raised every bet an opponent made. He seemed to bet without looking at his cards. Within 30 minutes, he had lost all his chips, paid the winners, and excused himself, muttering about some problems on his mind. At first, the remaining players were stunned, then they occupied themselves with an analytic recapitulation of his strategy. Finally, one player worked out the solution: "Hell, he wasn't trying to maximize his money, he was minimizing his time."

Ankeny, 1982

*Preparation of this chapter was supported in part by NSF Grant 7914252, University of Illinois and Harvard University subcontracts. Comments by Carolyn Jagacinski, Susan Nolen, and Michael Pataschnick are acknowledged with gratitude.

39

At first glance, von Neumann's behavior could appear irrational. When considered in terms of his goals, however, the behavior appears rational and, if the observers had known his goals in advance, they might have predicted his behavior. The approach to understanding behavior in terms of an individual's goals is the one that naive observers adopt when they empathize with others (Hoffman, Mischel, & Mazze, 1981). There are those who perceive this empathic stance as unscientific, but it may have value even for those who seek to predict the behavior of rats. Empathizing with rats has not been a generally approved strategy for predicting their behavior. Yet Garcia (1981) owns that "I always use anthropomorphism and teleology to predict animal behavior because this works better than most learning theories. I could rationalize this heresy by pointing to our common neurosensory systems or to convergent evolutionary forces. But, in truth, I merely put myself in the animal's place" (p. 151). This can be termed an intentional conception of behavior (Dennett, 1978). In this approach, behavior is predicted by assuming that individuals are goal-directed and that their behavior is a rational or economic attempt to gain their goals. If an action would not improve or would reduce an individual's chance of attaining her or his goals, we would not predict that action.

This does not imply that individuals are always conscious of their goals or that they could describe them in the terms used in an intentional analysis (Dennett, 1978). The intentional stance is the most effective one to adopt when facing a chess-playing computer. We are more likely to beat the computer if we act as if it is trying to play by the rules with the purpose of winning than if we study its wiring. Yet, we do not normally attribute to the computer consciousness of the rules or a desire to win.

Successful use of this approach to prediction of behavior depends on our ability to predict an individual's goals and to describe these goals clearly. If we cannot specify an individual's goals, we cannot judge what behavior will maximize the chances of achieving these goals and minimize the chances of avoiding undesirable outcomes. Achievement behavior is that in which the competence of one's behavior is at issue—where the goal is to be, or to appear to be, competent rather than incompetent. To apply the intentional approach to achievement behavior we must be able to predict when individuals will seek to be competent rather than incompetent and how they will judge their competence.

There is evidence that our reasoning concerning ability changes with age (e.g., Heckhausen, 1982; Nicholls, 1978; Ruble, Parsons, & Ross, 1976; Weiner & Kun, 1976). In the process of trying to integrate this developmental literature and relate it to theories of adult achievement motivation (Atkinson & Raynor, 1974; Kukla, 1972, 1978; Weiner,

1972) it struck me that different theories of adult motivation embody different conceptions of ability. Some (Atkinson & Raynor, 1974; Kukla, 1972) incorporate conceptions of ability that are akin to those that young children employ, whereas others (Weiner, 1972) embody the conception of ability found in adults and older children. If, in different situations, adults and older children use different conceptions of ability to evaluate their achievement behavior, theories based on only one conception of ability will not encompass this behavior. I argue that we do use different conceptions of ability in different situations. Because I see the conceptions of ability as the key to the understanding of achievement motivation, I describe them first. The next steps are to use the intentional framework to predict when each conception of ability will be used to evaluate performance and to derive predictions of subjective experience and overt behavior.

CONCEPTIONS OF ABILITY

We see the development of the concept of ability as a process of differentiation (Nicholls & Miller, in press), and have distinguished three levels of differentiation of ability and difficulty and four levels of differentiation of ability and effort. For the present purpose, it is sufficient to contrast the relatively undifferentiated conception of ability found in most 5-year-olds with the more differentiated conception found in most 12- and 13-year-olds.

The more differentiated conception of most adolescents is embodied in standard ability-testing procedures (Nicholls, 1978). Ability is defined with reference to the performance of others. A raw ability-test score must be compared with the performance of a suitable reference group if one is to make an adequate inference of ability. A valid ability-inference also requires evidence of optimum effort: the limit of one's ability will not be revealed if effort is low. Conversely, it is assumed that effort will increase performance, only up to the limit of one's present capacity. That is, ability is conceived as capacity—an underlying trait that is not observed directly but is inferred from both effort and performance, in a context of social comparison. When mature individuals believe their ability is low, they believe they lack capacity. This is not the case for young children (Nicholls & Miller, in press).

For young children, high ability is implied by learning or by success at tasks they are uncertain of being able to complete. They do not judge ability with reference to performance norms or social comparisons. They can be induced to adopt another's performance as a standard, but normally they make self-referenced rather than social-norm-referenced judgments of ability: high ability means improved performance or success on tasks in which there is some doubt concerning their success. Ability does not, in this case, imply an inferred trait. For young children, when more effort is needed for success, this implies more learning, which is more ability. Effort can have quite different implications for adults and older children. They realize that, though more effort produces more learning, higher effort can imply lower ability if others require less effort for the same performance. Effort is a two-edged sword (Covington & Omelich, 1979) only for adolescents and adults.

The perspective of younger children could be termed subjective. For them, the subjective experience of gaining insight or mastery through effort is the experience of competence or ability. For adults, a gain in mastery can lead to feelings of competence. But, it can lead to feelings of incompetence if, on adopting the more objective viewpoint that the young child lacks, they observe that their peers master more with equivalent effort or achieve the same with less effort.

I recall my first day on skis. I soon gained a pleasant sense of accomplishment from improving to the point at which I was able to negotiate reliably a gentle slope and make snowplow turns. I had applied effort and had improved; I felt competent in the less differentiated sense. The subsequent appearance of two highly skilled small children produced a momentary shock to this sense of competence. However, because I had spent less time and effort than these children had, my poor showing compared with theirs did not indicate a lack of capacity. By employing more fully the conception of ability as capacity I saved something of the initial sense of accomplishment that was based on the less differentiated conception. When the less differentiated conception of ability is the goal of behavior, it is as if we ask "How do I master this task?" and feel competent if we gain in mastery. When the conception of ability as capacity is the goal, our concern is better expressed by the question "What do I have to do to show superior capacity?" or "Can I show I am intelligent?"

If we were forced to choose but one prototypical conception of ability, it would probably be the more differentiated conception (Heckhausen, 1982; Jagacinski & Nicholls, 1982; Maehr & Nicholls, 1980). Behavior directed at developing or demonstrating ability in the less differentiated sense encompasses what White (1959) has termed *competence motivation*. Consideration of such behavior as achievement behavior is justified because of the continuity between the developmentally earlier and the later, more complex, conception of ability (Heckhausen, 1982; Nicholls & Miller, in press). In addition, the first form of achievement motivation is an important ingredient of outstanding creative achievement (Nicholls, 1972; 1979). A theory of achievement motivation that lacks the potential to deal with such outstanding achievements would be incomplete.

SUBJECTIVE EXPERIENCE AND CONDITIONS THAT ENGAGE EACH CONCEPTION OF ABILITY

If we apply the differentiated conception to ourselves we attempt to evaluate our capacity: an enduring trait that distinguishes us from others and affects our future chances of performing well compared with them. For such judgments, we must compare our own and others' effort and attainment. A less external perspective is needed to judge ability in the less differentiated sense. In this case we need not consider the effort or attainment of others or distinguish ourselves from them. The concern is whether we have mastered a task or improved our mastery. Thus, I use the term *task-involvement* to refer to states where our concern is to develop or demonstrate (primarily to oneself) high ability in the less differentiated sense. *Ego-involvement* refers to states where our concern is with developing or demonstrating (to self or others) high rather than low capacity. In the latter case we must compare the effort and performance of self and others and thus be more publicly self-aware (Carver & Scheier, 1981).

Activation of the different conceptions of ability also involves different perceptions of the purposes of our effort or learning. If we are task-involved, we seek to improve our mastery or to master things we are uncertain we can do. To learn is to demonstrate ability in the less differentiated sense. In other words, learning or mastery will be an end in itself. In ego-involved states, our concern is whether, by learning or mastering, we will demonstrate superior capacity. We must calculate whether learning or mastering will serve our end of demonstrating high rather than low capacity. Learning will, therefore, be more likely to be experienced as a means to an end when we are ego-involved. It follows that when we are task-involved, we will attempt to learn if we see an opportunity to do so and, when doing so, will feel we are doing what we want to do. Our learning will be endogenously attributed (Kruglanski, 1975). We will feel we are learning freely. When ego-involved, on the other hand, we will feel more constrained. Our learning will be more exogenously attributed and we will not attempt to learn if this appears unlikely to enable us to demonstrate high capacity.

The intentional framework can also be used to predict when we will employ the more, rather than the less, differentiated conception. Let us start with Robert White's (1959) observation that individuals presented with skill tasks offering a moderate challenge will attempt to improve their mastery of these tasks. Provided there is no physiological or psychological stress and task-extrinsic incentives are not salient, such tasks will elicit attempts to demonstrate or develop ability in the less differentiated sense. Improvement of performance through effort will produce feelings of competence. The question is, what situational factors will transform this goal to the goal of demonstration of high versus low capacity?

The general answer is that, when we are working on skill tasks, factors that increase concerns about evaluation of our ability will increase use of the differentiated conception. This is because the more differentiated conception enables a more adequate or more complete evaluation of ability. If our concern is to evaluate our ability, knowledge that we have learned through effort is inadequate. Was the improvement simply due to the ease of the task? Was it effort rather than ability that led to improvement? As when we use an intelligence test to assess a child's ability, we have to employ the conception of ability as capacity to adequately evaluate our competence.

Perhaps the most common practice, in experiments and in classrooms, that would induce a concern about evaluation of one's ability is the announcement that "this is a test," implying "we are evaluating an important ability." If the importance of the test is emphasized or if it is presented as a test of abilities that are already highly valued, this should heighten concerns about one's ability. Interpersonal competition on valued skill tasks also emphasizes the importance of personal competence. By emphasizing comparison with others, competition also highlights the relevance of the differentiated conception. Thus, when the skills in question might be thought important, and when evaluative, test-like, or competitive conditions prevail, the use of the conception of ability as capacity should increase: Ego-involvement should increase. Further, manipulations that increase encoding of self-relevant information, especially those that increase encoding of information relevant to public views of the self should increase ego-involvement. This is because the conception of ability as capacity involves a more public perspective on the self. Manipulations such as use of an audience or the making of videotapes of individuals (Carver & Scheier, 1981) increase public self-awareness. Thus, when we are performing skill tasks, such conditions should increase ego-involvement—the tendency to use the conception of ability as capacity to evaluate oneself.

EVIDENCE

I started with evidence that the concept of ability changes with age. I postulated that adults can use either the more- or the less-differentiated conception of ability. Then, using the intentional approach, I derived predictions of (1) the nature of subjective experience when we want to demonstrate ability in the more- or less-differentiated sense and (2) the conditions that will make us concerned about our ability in the more- rather than the less-differentiated sense. The predictions were derived by asking what inferences we must make when we have a given concern: to learn versus to evaluate our capacity. It is time to see how these commonsensical (but, I believe, logical) derivations look in the light of empirical research.

Jagacinski and Nicholls (1983) had students estimate their feelings of competence on passing a class assignment after high versus low effort. Students expected higher effort to lead to greater gains in competence. However, in a competitive condition, when performance was equal, perception of higher effort was associated with perception of lower ability. Thus, students employed the conception of ability as capacity wherein effort is seen to improve competence but, when other things are equal, higher effort implies lower ability. No such effect was found in a more task-involving learning-for-learning's-sake condition. In this study and in several replications (Jagacinski, Nicholls, & Burton, 1983), higher effort was expected to produce equal or greater perceived ability in task-involvement.

Carole Ames and her associates have studied attributions and affect in competitive and in more task-involving conditions. Competition produces more satisfaction with performance when high ability is attributed to the self (Ames, Ames, & Felker, 1977). In noncompetitive situations, higher perceived effort is associated with higher satisfaction (Ames *et al.* 1977) and effort attributions are higher (Ames & Ames, 1981). These findings indicate that the less differentiated conception—in which what is accomplished through effort is the basis of perceived competence— was used more in noncompetitive conditions. A complementary picture emerged in a study in which students were able to report either attributions or self-instructions (Ames & McKelvie, 1983). Competition produced more ability and difficulty attributions. More effort attributions and strategies for task-completion (self-instructions) indicate that the less-differentiated conception was used more in the noncompetitive condition.

A study by Diener and Srull (1979) and two by Scheier and Carver (in press) found that self-awareness, especially public self-awareness, increased interest in the performance of others and increased self-reinforcement on the basis of comparison with others' performance. These findings support the hypothesis that public self-awareness will increase use of the differentiated conception wherein ability is judged relative to that of others.

Several studies also support the hypothesis that ego-involving conditions—practices that engage the differentiated conception—produce more exogenous attributions and reduce intrinsic interest in tasks. Ryan (1982) found more interest in tasks after performance in a neutral condition than after an "intelligence test" condition. Similarly Deci, Betley, Kahle, Abrams, and Porac (1981) found interest in puzzles was higher after individual performance than after success in competition with another person. Deci, Schwartz, Sheinman, and Ryan (1981) found teacher reports of use of social comparison to control student behavior were highly correlated with use of coercive (exogenous) control techniques and not strongly associated with use of non-coercive methods. Children of teachers who favored use of social comparison and coercion reported less intrinsic interest in schoolwork. These findings support the linking of use of social comparison with exogenous attribution.

The preceding studies (and others reviewed in Nicholls, 1980) support the initial predictions. Most generally, situational factors affect use of more- versus less-differentiated conceptions of ability. More specifically, testlike and competitive conditions and public self-awareness tend to engage the conception of ability as capacity. That is, these conditions induce ego-involvement. Secondly, ego-involving conditions increase exogenous attribution and reduce task-intrinsic interest.

TASK DIFFICULTY PREFERENCE AND PERFORMANCE

Given that the less differentiated conception of ability is employed in more or less neutral achievement situations and that the conception of ability as capacity is employed in more evaluative conditions, the way is clear for derivation of predictions of behavior in these different conditions. The general theoretical assumption is that behavior will be economically directed at the goal of demonstrating high rather than low ability. The first step is to establish how our expectations of demonstrating high versus low ability in each sense vary with task difficulty and performance feedback. It will then be clear what behavior will most economically lead to demonstration of high rather than low ability. The less-differentiated conception of ability is simpler so the derivations for task-involvement are simpler.

TASK-INVOLVEMENT

When we employ the less-differentiated conception of ability, we see more effort as leading to more learning, which amounts to more ability. Within this framework, perceptions of task difficulty are directly related to our expectancies of success. If a task is seen to require high effort or if our chances of success or failure on it appear uncertain, it will appear moderately difficult and success will imply high ability. If a task appears likely to yield to slight effort, it will appear easy and offer little chance of learning or of demonstrating high ability. Finally, if no amount of effort appears likely to produce success, the task will appear highly difficult and will offer no chance of demonstrating ability. In short, tasks that appear to demand moderate to high effort will offer the best chances for demonstrating ability in the less-differentiated sense. It follows that when we are task-involved, we will not choose tasks or set goals that make either success for failure appear certain. We will prefer challenging tasks—those in which we have moderate subjective probabilities of success.

If, when task-involved, we have no choice of tasks, effort should be strongest on tasks where effort appears necessary for demonstration of high ability: tasks that appear moderately challenging. As long as we expect effort to lead to improvements in mastery we should, when task-involved, apply effort and thereby gain in mastery.

From an educational perspective, task-involvement appears an ideal state. Learning is an end in itself, our feelings of competence are a function of perception of learning, and we act to maximize our chances of learning and minimize behavior that will not produce gains in mastery. This is not the case when we are ego-involved.

EGO-INVOLVEMENT

When we are ego-involved, our own expectancies of success and the amount of effort we expect to need for success are insufficient basis for estimating task difficulty or our chances of demonstrating ability. When we employ the conception of ability as capacity, task difficulty is defined with reference to the performance of our peers. If many others can do a task, this shows it is easy and success does not indicate high ability, whereas failure indicates low ability. If many others cannot do a task, it is difficult and success indicates high ability, whereas failure does not indicate low ability. Thus, our expectancies of demonstrating ability depend on perceived normative difficulty (how well others do or how well we expect them to do) as well as on our own expectancies of success. To be "smart" we must be above average.

If we have low perceived ability (in the differentiated sense) we will only expect to succeed on normatively easy tasks—tasks where many succeed and where success will merely enable us to avoid demonstrating low ability. Thus, if we have low perceived capacity, we will see little opportunity of demonstrating high ability. A feeling of lack of capacity indicates that we believe our best is probably not good enough. We will, therefore, have little reason to choose tasks close to the limit of our perceived ability. But, we can avoid demonstrating low ability and even keep our options partially open. If we retain some commitment to demonstrating high rather than low ability, normatively difficult tasks offer the best option. Failure will not imply incompetence and such choices are consistent with the remote but perhaps not impossible goal of demonstrating high ability. If, however, repeated failure or social input has lowered our perceived ability to a point at which we are certain we cannot demonstrate high ability, it would be irrational to remain committed to this goal (see Klinger, 1975). If we cannot simply opt right out of the situation, very easy tasks will enable us to avoid demonstrating low ability with the minimum amount of subjectively fruitless effort. In short, our commitment to demonstrating high rather than low ability will decline as we become more certain we lack ability and our preference will change from tasks in which we feel almost certain to fail to tasks in which we are almost certain to succeed. From the perspective of someone who is task-involved, either preference would appear unrealistic or irrational. Neither offers a chance to improve our mastery. Yet, given our goal of avoiding demonstration of low capacity, these choices are rational.

When we are unable to choose our own tasks, extreme levels of normative difficulty will prove less threatening. Moderate difficulty levels will be more threatening because we expect to fail where failure indicates low ability. Because we think of ability as capacity, the expectation of failure at these tasks will be likely to induce self-derogatory feelings or anxiety. We will feel in danger of revealing a basic personal inadequacy that we can do little to alter. This will impair our performance, especially on complex tasks (Arkin, Kolditz, & Kolditz, in press; Sarason, 1975; Wine, 1971). We may see some advantage in lowering our effort to minimize the extent to which failure will indicate lack of capacity (Frankel & Snyder, 1978). This would also reduce attainment. Or, if we are certain our ability is low, we will not attempt to demonstrate ability. We will see no point in expending any more effort than necessary to keep teachers or experimenters off our backs. We would not become ego-involved and would even avoid success. Again, performance would be impaired.

If we retain some commitment to demonstrating high rather than low ability, anxiety and effort reduction are less likely on normatively easy or very difficult tasks than on intermediate tasks. Failure on a very difficult task cannot reveal our incompetence and, who knows, we may strike it lucky. If the task is normatively easy we will expect that high effort will produce success, which will save us from looking stupid. Thus, our performance will not be impaired at levels of extreme difficulty. In summary, when we are ego-involved and believe our capacity is low, we will avoid moderate normative-difficulty levels or "realistic" challenges and will perform our worst if obliged to work on such tasks.

If, on the other hand, we believe we have high capacity, ego-involving situations will present relatively little threat to our sense of competence. We will expect to succeed and, thereby, to demonstrate high ability at moderate normative-difficulty levels. Like all people when they are task-involved, we will see our best chance for demonstrating high rather than low ability on tasks where we have moderate expectancies of success. We will choose such tasks rather than those that appear so normatively easy or difficult as to establish neither high nor low ability. We will expect effort to produce success and, thereby, expect to appear competent at moderate normative difficulty levels. We will, therefore, perform effectively when we are assigned such tasks. We will not expect to look stupid at high difficulty levels and will also perform effectively on these tasks (except if they appear impossibly difficult). We may relax on tasks we think are normatively easy and thus perform worse than if we thought they were difficult and even worse than ego-involved individuals who doubt their competence.

In short, if we perceive our capacity as high, our levels of aspiration will look realistic or rational to task-involved individuals and our performance will not be impaired by anxiety, self-protective effort-reduction, or a sense of hopelessness. Because learning is a means to the end of demonstrating high capacity, our learning might suffer on complex tasks that demand sustained involvement and problem finding (Condry & Chambers, 1978). But on shorter tasks, our performance will be similar in task- and ego-involving situations.

EVIDENCE

Many of the studies, reviewed here subsequently, employed measures of resultant achievement motivation, test anxiety, or self-esteem rather than measures of perceived ability. Much confusion has resulted from the uncritical assumption that resultant achievement motivation measures, test anxiety measures, and the like measure what their names denote (Nicholls, 1976b). There is a reasonable case for treating most measures of resultant achievement motivation, test anxiety, self-esteem, and self-concept as measures of perceived ability in the differentiated sense (Kukla, 1972, 1978; Nicholls, 1980). Klinger and McNelly's (1969) evidence that achievement motivation scores reflect perceived status is consistent with this view. Confirmation of present predictions with these different scales also supports their construct validity as measures of perceived ability.

Let us first consider general contrasts between task- and ego-involvement and then the more detailed predictions for ego-involvement. First, difficulty preferences, then performance or attainment. In task-involvement, task difficulty preferences for all individuals were expected to be realistic. That is, all individuals should prefer tasks in which they have moderate probabilities of success. In ego-involvement, those with high perceived ability should show similar preferences but as perceived ability declines, preference for more extreme (high or low) probabilities of success should increase.

A direct comparison of task- and ego-involving conditions is provided by Raynor and Smith's (1966) study of task choice with puzzles in what they termed achievement-oriented and relaxed conditions. In the *achievement-oriented* condition, puzzles were presented as valid intellectual ability measures that subjects should find challenging and it was emphasized that this was an important part of the experimental session. In the *relaxed* condition, the experimenter adopted a casual manner, the importance of the puzzles was played down and nothing specific was said about them beyond explaining procedures. Subjects experienced these conditions as less different than Raynor and Smith had intended. Nevertheless, the predicted differences between conditions was obtained. There was a strong tendency for low- more than high-resultant motive (perceived ability) students to take extreme risks in the achievement-oriented condition and an appreciably weaker tendency in the same direction in the relaxed condition.

In several risk-taking studies with a motor task, under relaxed conditions, Schneider (1973, Chapter 4) found no differences between individuals who were high and those who were low in resultant achievement motivation. However, in one study (Schneider, 1973, Chapter 5), low motive (low perceived ability) subjects took more extreme risks. This study differed from the earlier ones in that the experimenter was not neutral, but a teacher in the students' school. It was, therefore, hypothesized that this difference between the motive types occurred only when self-esteem was threatened. A subsequent experiment, comparing a nonevaluative, matter-of-fact task-presentation with one in which the task was presented as a valid measure of ability, supported this hypothesis and the present predictions. More extreme risks on the part of low- as compared with high-resultant motive students occurred only in the ego-involving condition (Jopt, 1974, p. 196). Most other risk-taking studies have employed tasks and/or conditions that would induce ego-involvement. In these studies, more extreme risks were found in low- than in high-resultant motive individuals (Nicholls, 1980). When clearly nonevaluative conditions are created (Buckert, Meyer, & Schmalt, 1979; Trope, 1979), the predicted preference for moderate probability of success levels in both high- and low-perceived-ability individuals is found. Thus, difficulty preferences in task- and ego-involvement contrast in the predicted manner.

It was also predicted that, in ego-involvement, preference for very low probabilities of success would be most common among individuals who perceive their ability as low, but not so low that they have given up commitment to demonstrating high rather than low ability. Preference for very high probabilities of success should be most common in those who are more certain they lack ability and who, consequently, lack commitment to demonstrating high rather than low ability. Two studies using ego-involving conditions support these predictions. Sears (1940) found that children who set very high goals showed a stronger wish for high achievement in diverse activities and made more negative evaluations of their performance in these activities than did others. They acted "as if they never felt they were doing well enough" (Sears, 1940, p. 523). These findings support the prediction that perception of inadequate ability and commitment to demonstrating high ability leads to preference for low probabilities of success. Those selecting unrealistically low goals were distinguished from others by greater responsiveness to nonachievement incentives. This indicates lack of commitment to demonstrating high ability. They were also prone to lower their goals still further after manipulated success. This also implies the rejction of the goal of demonstrating high ability (Sears, 1940, 1941) predicted in those who prefer high probabilities of success. Moulton (1965) found that students with lowest and with intermediate levels of resultant achievement motivation chose more extremely high or low probability levels than did students with higher resultant motivation. Further, as predicted, the lowest motive group (lowest perceived ability) selected high probabilities of success more than the intermediate group, whose bias was toward low probabilities of success.

Thus, there is support for all the predictions of task difficulty preference in task- and ego-involvement. From an educational point of view, the salient fact is that task-involvement favors, for all students, the type of choice that should be most conducive to learning: preference for moderate risk or realistic challenge. Ego-involvement, however, produces selection of tasks that would not facilitate learning in students with low perceived ability.

When we present students with tasks of a given difficulty level, rather than allow students to choose difficulty levels, their attainment or performance is also predicted to depend on whether they are task- or ego-involved. In school, it is common for students to be presented tasks that are normatively moderately difficult or tasks in which the range of possible scores will indicate whether their ability relative to that of others is high or low. If the situation induces ego-involvement, low-perceived-ability students should expect to perform worse than others and, thereby, to demonstrate lack of capacity. Students with high perceived ability will expect effort to lead to demonstration of high capacity. Accordingly, performance of low- but not high-perceived-ability students will be impaired. If task-involvement is induced, however, all will expect to gain in mastery through effort and will perform effectively. A variety of studies comparing test-like and more neutral conditions (e.g., Entin & Raynor, 1973; Gjesme, 1974; Paul & Eriksen, 1964; Sarason, 1959) confirm these predictions. Ego-involving conditions lowered the performance of students with low- but not those with high-perceived ability. Students with low perceived ability performed better when they were task-involved than when they were ego-involved. They performed worse than high-perceived ability students in ego-involving conditions. Similar results were obtained in comparisons of performance when self-awareness was heightened (Brockner, 1979; Brockner & Hulton, 1978) versus when task-focus was induced. Comparisons of neutral conditions and conditions where evaluative observers were present produced the same results (Ganzer, 1968; Shrauger, 1972). (See also Carver, Blaney, & Scheier, 1979; Carver & Scheier, 1981; Kuhl, 1981.) Brockner and Hulton (1978) also found the predicted lower anxiety among low-perceived-ability students in task-involvement. In review, there is a considerable amount of support for the predicted effects of task- versus ego-involving conditions on performance on normatively moderate-difficulty tasks where individuals are likely to expect that success indicates high capacity and failure indicates low capacity.

Ego-involving conditions were further predicted to produce diminished performance in high-perceived-ability individuals when they believe tasks are normatively easy or when they feel sure they are outperforming others. When they believe tasks are moderately difficult or that they are falling behind others, they will expect effort to lead to demonstration of high ability. They would, therefore, perform effectively in the latter cases. Low-perceived-ability students are expected to perform their worst at moderate difficulty levels or when told their performance is below average. Unlike high-perceived-ability students, they would not relax when they perceive that tasks are normatively easy or when informed that they are demonstrating high ability.

The predicted effects of social comparison feedback were obtained by Weiner (1966) and by Weiner and Schneider (1971) who told students they were doing either much better or much worse than others. Perez (1973) and Schalon (1968) also found the predicted effects of feedback indicating that students were performing below average. The major, predicted, normative-task-difficulty effects were obtained by Karabenick and Youssef (1968), (for easy and moderately difficult tasks) by Kukla (1974), by Sarason, Mandler, and Craighill (1952), and (for moderate- and high-difficulty conditions) by Sarason (1958, 1961). (The results of the last study were not entirely as predicted, but this may have been due to variations in the extent to which ego-involvement was induced [Nicholls, 1980].)

Finally, it was predicted that when low-perceived-ability individuals are certain they lack ability they should also lack commitment to demonstrating ability and avoid successes that might indicate high ability. This phenomenon was demonstrated by Marecek and Mettee (1972). When told they had displayed above-average ability, only students who were both low in self-esteem (perceived ability) and certain of this low self-evaluation did not improve on a retest. All other students improved on the retest. (The situation was not test-like until the retest.) The individuals who were certain of their low self-evaluations improved their performance when the task was presented as a luck task: where success would not indicate high ability. This finding confirms the view that, in the skill situation, they were avoiding demonstration of high ability.

All in all, the predictions of task choice and performance are fairly consistently supported by relevant experimental data. However, the thesis that performance impairment in ego-involvement occurs when we expect to demonstrate low ability, specifically in the differentiated sense, is not directly established by the preceding evidence. Miller (1982) obtained support for this claim by comparing sixth graders who had attained the conception of ability as capacity with those who had not, in an ego-involving situation. After a manipulated series of failures designed to induce doubts about their ability, these students were presented tasks said to be of moderate normative difficulty, where failure would imply low ability. Only those with the conception of ability as capacity showed lower performance than those in a control group that initially suc-

ceeded. The more and the less mature students did not differ in perception of ability. Thus, the difference in performance must have reflected
their conceptions of ability, not just the level of ability they believed they
had. There was no impaired performance in mature or immature students who were told the (second) task was highly normatively difficult. If
impaired performance resulted merely from expectancy of failure or
noncontingency (helplessness), the "difficult" task should have produced greater impairment—failure would appear most likely and effort
most fruitless in this condition. Yet it was the moderate difficulty condition, in which failure would indicate incompetence, that produced impairment. Thus, Miller's findings support the proposed role of perceptions of capacity as opposed to mere expectancies of failure or perceived
noncontingency.

There appears to be no experimental evidence concerning the effects
of task- versus ego-involvement on performance of more-complex learning tasks that require sustainment of involvement over days rather than
minutes and in which significant cognitive restructuring is required.
Task-involvement, where learning is an end in itself, should sustain
more effective functioning in these cases. Support for this prediction is
provided by evidence that significant adult achievement is favored by a
personal disposition toward task-involvement rather than ego-involvement (Nicholls, 1979, 1983).

AN ILLUSTRATION

Virginia Valian (1977) describes the motivational problems she experienced in graduate school and the way she overcame these. Hers is a
story of a change from ego- to task-involvement.

> I wrote my papers only at the last minute, and I never . . . worked an intellectual
> problem through to its conclusion. I did enough to get by [p. 164]. In addition to
> feeling competitive, I felt resentful: work was an onerous obligation [p. 171].
> . . . for much of the time I was preoccupied with questions about my ability
> . . . How smart was I compared to so-and-so? How creative was I? . . . There was
> no end to these questions. They plagued me. They interfered with my work. I
> worried about whether I was smart enough to solve such-and-such a problem
> instead of getting on with trying to solve it . . . the only escape . . . is to put the
> question of ability in its proper place, which is, I think, no place at all. Ability is not
> important. The important thing is how much you can come to understand . . . [p.
> 172]. [The result is new rewards from working.] One is the continual discovery
> within myself of new ideas; the other is deeper understanding of a problem [p.
> 174]. [When evaluation of one's capacity is not an issue, gains in understanding
> can be intrinsically satisfying and occasion feelings of competence.]

OTHER THEORIES OF TASK CHOICE AND
PERFORMANCE

PREDICTIONS

Comparison of the predictions of the present theory with those of others is complicated by the fact that others often do not distinguish normative difficulty from subjective probability of success. Atkinson, for example, holds that "degree of difficulty can be inferred from the subjective probability of success" (1957, p. 362). For young children, subjective probabilities of success are equivalent to perceived task difficulty (Nicholls & Miller, 1983). They are, according to the present position, also equivalent in task-involvement. This is not so in ego-involvement or when individuals make explicit judgments of task difficulty rather than the implicit judgments made in task-involvement. Atkinson (1957, 1969) cites evidence that higher-resultant-motive individuals have higher expectancies of success at given difficulty levels. This indicates that difficulty and subjective probability of success should not always be equated and this contradicts a basic assumption of Atkinson's theory.

When theories fail to distinguish between normative difficulty and subjective probability of success, it is difficult to interpret their predictions precisely. When Atkinson predicts preference for extreme probabilities of success, does he mean this or does he mean extreme levels of normative difficulty? Because most level-of-aspiration studies employ only indexes of probability of success, I will assume subjective probability of success was intended. Atkinson's theory (1957, 1965) predicts choice of tasks in which subjective probabilities of success are intermediate in those with high resultant motivation (perceived ability) and more extreme preferences in those with low resultant motivation. However, Atkinson's predictions do not distinguish factors favoring unrealistically high rather than low risks, whereas the present position does. Kukla's (1978) theory predicts preference for intermediate subjective risks in all subjects and stronger preference, at this level, on the part of high- versus low-perceived-ability individuals. Meyer, Folkes, and Weiner (1976) also predict intermediate probability preferences in all subjects.

If Atkinson were wholly correct, both Meyer et al. (1976) and Kukla (1979) would have to be wrong. According to the present position both Meyer et al. and Kukla are right in task-involving circumstances, whereas Atkinson is right when ego-involvement is induced. The evidence supports this position. It also supports the additional predictions of the present theory that distinguish preference for extremely high versus low probabilities of success in ego-involvement. The other positions do not discriminate between these extreme probability preferences. Thus, the present theory is more comprehensive and more specific.

The theories that make the most explicit predictions of performance as a function of task difficulty or normative feedback are those of Kukla (1972) and Atkinson (1965). The fact that these theories do not distinguish normative difficulty from subjective probability of success means, as noted previously, that their predictions lack precision. At one point, for example, Kukla (1972) presents as consistent with his theory, evidence that low-resultant-motive individuals perform better when half their peers are predicted to fail than when the odds of success are clearly higher or lower (Atkinson, 1958). At another point he holds that evidence that low-resultant-motive individuals perform better on a normatively easy task than on an intermediate-difficulty task (Kukla, 1974) supports his theory. This inconsistency would not be possible if predictions had been framed in terms of normative difficulty cues. Kukla's predictions of performance are, however, similar to the present predictions for task-involvement in that all individuals are expected to perform most effectively when they believe high effort is necessary for and likely to produce task-mastery. There is no place in his formulation for the various demonstrated effects that the present position predicts for ego-involvement. For example, effects of anxiety in low-perceived-ability individuals at moderate normative-difficulty levels are not mentioned. Nor does Kukla predict the avoidance-of-success phenomenon (Marecek & Mettee, 1972).

Atkinson's predictions, as modified by Revelle and Michaels (1976), are framed in terms of subjective probability of success, which is held to be equivalent to difficulty. Relevant studies employ normative feedback or normative difficulty cues. So, the predictions must be considered in these terms. When this is done, Revelle and Michaels' predictions are seen to be reasonably compatible with the present predictions for ego-involvement. In both positions, low perceived ability (or low-resultant-achievement motive) individuals are predicted to perform worst at moderate normative difficulty levels and high-perceived-ability individuals are expected to perform worst at easy and at extremely difficult tasks.

Revelle and Michaels' position differs from Kukla's and the present one, in that they do not predict that low-resultant-motive subjects will outperform high-motive subjects when told they have outperformed others (Weiner, 1966; Weiner & Schneider, 1971). Kukla (1972) argues that this effect is mediated by perception of low task-difficulty consequent on this "success" feedback. It seems more plausible to assume, as in the present position, that low-perceived-ability subjects accept such normative feedback as reasonably accurate and take it as evidence that their ability may be higher than expected. In any event, Atkinson's theory does not predict this phenomenon. Nor does Atkinson predict effective performance in task-involving situations or the fact that task-involvement fosters significant real-world achievement.

The concept of learned helplessness has been used to explain impaired performance. In a revision of the helplessness hypothesis (Abramson, Seligman, & Teasdale, 1978) employing the attributional concepts of Weiner, Frieze, Kukla, Reed, Rest, and Rosenbaum (1971), personal and universal helplessness are distinguished. Bandura (1977) distinguishes lack of a sense of efficacy from belief in an unresponsive environment. These distinctions are equivalent to the present distinction between perception of low ability and perception of a normatively very difficult task. Thus, it might appear that these positions employ the differentiated conception of ability. In fact, the two conceptions are confounded in both positions. When Bandura (1977, p. 195) implies that self-efficacy will be enhanced by improved behavioral functioning, the less-differentiated conception is implied. Abramson *et al.* (1978) see performance impairment as primarily a consequence of perception of noncontingency between one's own behavior and the outcomes. This also implies the less-differentiated conception because noncontingency can result from low capacity or high normative task-difficulty. In ego-involvement, the behaviorial consequences of perception of noncontingency depend on the perceived reasons for noncontingency. Perception that "difficulty" in achieving success reflects a lack of capacity should be more debilitating than perception of a normatively difficult task, though both involve perception of noncontingency. I cited evidence that it is not noncontingency per se that impairs performance. (See also Frankel & Snyder, 1978.) However, noncontingency will impair performance in young children (Ramey & Finkelstein, 1978). For them, difficulty and ability are imperfectly differentiated. High difficulty implies low ability and both are indicated by noncontingency (Nicholls & Miller, 1983).

Bandura (1977) and Abramson *et al.* (1978) are concerned with many issues (such as generalization of performance impairment and alleviation of phobias) that I have not considered. But the distinction between task- and ego-involvement, which they do not make, has important implications for attempts at remediation. As the preceding studies show, task-involvement minimizes performance impairment whereas ego-involvement increases it. In a similar vein, Carver and his associates (Carver, 1979; Carver, Blaney, & Scheier, 1979; Carver & Scheier, 1981) have shown that expectancies of success and self-awareness both affect behavior. An expectation of failure impairs persistence most when public self-awareness is high. When self-awareness is reduced, an expectation of failure impairs performance less. (See also Kuhl, 1981). In this respect, Carver's position and the present one are similar.

Covington and Beery (1976) do not make predictions of performance that are sufficiently explicit to enable clear comparisons of theories. However, they also hold that task choice and effort will be less conducive to learning when individuals (especially those with low-perceived capacity) judge their ability in relation to that of others. Heckhausen and Krugg (1982) and Rheinberg (in press) present a similar thesis. Maehr (1983) also makes similar and additional distinctions.

INTERNAL CONSISTENCY OF THEORIES

Theories can be compared in terms of their intrinsic qualities—internal consistency, or method of construction—as well as their efficiency in predicting phenomena. A theory is more than a set of predictions. A set of predictions about the way high- and low-perceived-ability individuals feel and behave does not constitute a theory. Standing behind the predictions of the present theory are two premises: (1) Cognitions and overt actions reflect rational or economical attempts to attain goals; and (2) The different conceptions of ability can define the goals of action. Predictions were derived in a logical fashion from these premises. Thus the predictions have a direct and logical link to a more general conception of action and the theory can be examined for logical consistency.

Kukla's position is similar in assumptions and derivation to the present theory. The major difference is that the present theory holds that ability is not always construed in the same way, whereas Kukla employs the less differentiated conception of ability. It is, therefore, encouraging that his predictions resemble the present predictions for task-involvement.[1]

Atkinson's is an intentional theory in that behavior is assumed to be a function both of expectations of success and failure and of the value of these outcomes. However, the intentional approach is not used to derive

[1]In fact, Kukla's (1972) theory of performance embodies a less differentiated conception of difficulty and ability (Nicholls & Miller, 1983b) than his theory of task choice (Kukla, 1978). The result is that his predictions of performance are closer to the present predictions for task involvement than are his predictions for task choice. The latter predictions fall partway between the present predictions for task- and ego-involvement. There is no reason to hold that we always experience pure states of task- and ego-involvement. There will surely be situations in which we employ partially differentiated conceptions of ability, for example, where we judge ability on the basis of performance relative to others and do not take effort into account. I have avoided discussing these possibilities, not because they are unimportant, but because it seemed clearer and simpler to focus on the extremes of the continuum.

predictions. For Atkinson (1957), "The strength of motivation to perform some act is assumed to be a multiplicative function of the strength of the motive, the expectancy (subjective probability) that the act will have as a consequence the attainment of an incentive and the value of the incentive" (p. 360–361). These are premises as well as predictions. These statements are not derived from a more general conception of action or from higher-order assumptions. Thus, one cannot submit Atkinson's statements to a test of internal logical consistency. However, it is interesting that Atkinson's predictions resemble those made here for ego-involvement, whereas the conception of ability he uses is that which is employed in task-involvement. (When Atkinson holds that probability of success can be inferred from task difficulty he employs the undifferentiated conception [Nicholls & Miller, 1983].) Yet, his predictions are more like those derived when it is assumed that individuals seek to demonstrate high rather than low ability in the differentiated sense. This indicates that if Atkinson's position could be examined for internal consistency, inconsistency would be found.

For Carver and Scheier (1981), success rather than demonstration of ability is the goal of achievement behavior (1981, Chapter 10). Yet, they subsequently qualify this position with Atkinson's assumption that success is more valued on more difficult tasks (p. 260). This assumption does not derive from their position, but follows naturally from the present assumption that demonstration of ability is the goal of achievement behavior. Further, when they discuss task choice (1981, Chapter 13), they adopt the suggestion of Meyer *et al.* (1976), Trope (1979), and Weiner and Kukla (1970) that task choice reflects the fact that moderately difficult tasks are most diagnostic of one's ability. Thus, they do not sustain their initial position. In other respects, Carver and Scheier's position and the present position are rather similar.

I have not done justice to the richness of any of the other positions. My position has derived something from each of them. But, it seems that the assumptions that achievement behavior is a rational attempt to develop or demonstrate ability and that ability can be construed in different ways enable logical derivation of a relatively internally consistent theory that predicts task choice and performance as well or better than the alternative theories.

ATTRIBUTION THEORY

Weiner's (1972, 1979; Weiner *et al.*, 1971) attribution theory approach to achievement motivation is based on an analysis of commonsense reasoning about the causes of success and failure on skill tasks. Weiner has not adopted the commonsense, intentional approach to prediction of behavior on the basis of individuals' goals and of the behavior necessary to attain these goals. However, Weiner's approach has been applied to many other domains. Of these I will consider only the relations between attributions and affect and the relations between effort and ability attributions.

There are several categorizations of the causal factors we employ to explain success and failure (Weiner, 1979). All embody the assumption that we employ the differentiated conception of ability, in that ability, effort, and task difficulty are treated as distinct factors with clearly different properties. However, when we employ the less differentiated conception, ability, effort, and difficulty are less perfectly differentiated than when we employ the differentiated conception. Until now, most attribution theory research, including my own (e.g., Nicholls, 1975, 1976a), has not allowed for this possibility that casts new light on some aspects of attribution theory.[2]

ABILITY AND EFFORT ATTRIBUTIONS

There has been considerable interest in the nature of the relationship between perceived effort and ability. Kepka and Brickman (1971) found that, when performance was equal, students perceived hypothetical individuals with higher perceived ability as having applied less effort. It appears that Kepka and Brickman's subjects employed the differentiated conception of ability, wherein individuals with higher capacity are presumed to need less effort to achieve a given outcome. Felson and Bohrnstedt (1980), however, found teachers' judgments of the effort and ability of their students to be positively related. They imply that their result raises doubts about the ecological validity of Kepka and Brickman's study. This does not follow. Nor does it follow that, as one might suspect, Felson and Bohrnstedt's subjects employed the less differentiated conception. Use of the differentiated conception of ability does not always mean that effort and ability will be seen as negatively related. Children who demonstrate attainment of the differentiated conception of ability (by explaining that the harder working of two others who gain the same score is less able) also recognize that more able students usually try harder and get higher grades (Nicholls & Miller, in press). Kepka and Brickman also found that people generally expect

---

[2]Note, however, that Weiner (in press) points out that the meaning of causal factors can vary. For example, effort can be seen as a stable personal trait or as something that varies across time and tasks.

more able students to try harder even though they expect more able students to have tried less when they score the same as less able students. Ability, motivation, and attainment are indeed generally positively correlated. One can recognize this even though one believes that able students do not need to try as hard as less able students to achieve as well as they do. Felson and Bohrnstedt appear to have assessed general beliefs about the way ability and effort are related in the real world and to have confused this with the ways we infer ability or effort. The finding that judgments of effort and ability are positively related is not a sufficient basis for inferring that individuals are employing the less differentiated conception of ability. On the other hand, there may be times when positive associations do indicate use of the less differentiated conception. In evaluative situations, judgments of their own ability and effort are positively related in children who have not attained the concept of ability as capacity, but these judgments are negatively related in older children (Nicholls & Miller, in press; Rholes, Blackwell, Jordan, & Walters, 1980). For adults, positive relations are found in task-involving situations and negative relations in ego-involving situations (Jagacinski *et al.*, 1983). That is, in task-involving situations, adults can feel they have learned more and feel more competent if they have tried hard.

This may help explain the finding that students with high-resultant-achievement motivation judge their ability more highly when they apply more effort whereas students with low resultant motivation infer higher ability when they apply less effort (Touhey & Villemez, 1980). The high-resultant-motive students' judgments are consistent with the description of task-involved individuals for whom higher effort implies greater competence. The low-resultant-motive students' judgments correspond to the picture of ego-involvement. There is evidence that individuals with high perceived ability or high resultant motivation are more disposed to be task-involved (Harter & Connell, in press). Given an absence of doubts about their capacity, they may rarely ask the question, "Am I smart enough?" Instead they may focus on strategies for task mastery (Diener & Dweck, 1978). Individuals with low-perceived ability may, however, be disposed to see almost any skill task as a test of their ability—to become ego-involved. Touhey and Villemez's (1980) findings are paradoxical from the point of view of attribution theory in which it is implicitly assumed that the concepts of effort and ability are fixed in meaning. However, they appear explicable within the present framework.

From an educational point of view, the advantages of task-involvement, where higher effort implies higher ability are again evident. The findings of Touhey and Villemez (1980) and Harter and Connell (in press) indicate that students with high-perceived ability may not only have feelings of greater competence. They may also have the added advantage of being more able to forget about their capacity and become intrinsically involved in learning.

ATTRIBUTIONS AND EMOTION

A question of early interest to attribution theorists was whether effort or ability attributions were more important as predictors of achievement affect. If this question is considered from the point of view of the differentiated conception (which is implicit in attribution theory) it is difficult not to come to the conclusion that ability attributions are the important determinants of affect. Conversely, effort attributions should only be important to the extent that, when performance is constant, higher effort implies lower ability. High ability indicates that future success is likely (Weiner, Nierenberg, & Goldstein, 1976). If success occasions pleasure, attribution of high ability to oneself should maximize expectancies of continued success and feelings of pleasure or pride. If the differentiated conception is employed, a belief that success reflected high effort should imply lower ability and less chance of continued success. This would produce less satisfaction. If ability and effort attributions both mediate affect, how could high-perceived ability and high-perceived effort both occasion pleasure? Surely ability attributions are the main mediators of achievement affect? But, suppose this conclusion was not supported and that positive affect was maximized when success was attributed to high effort and that negative affect was maximized when failure was attributed to low effort. This would mean that we would always maximize our gains and minimize our losses by trying as hard as possible. As Kukla (1978) notes, it is clear that we often do not do this. But if we did, causal attributions could serve no purpose. To maximize our gains and minimize our losses we would only need to assure ourselves that we had tried hard. We would have no reason to consider the role of factors such as ability, difficulty, or luck because effort can be perceived directly. We must control for effort and difficulty to infer our capacity but we do not have to control anything to judge our effort. We do not need to make causal attributions to judge our effort. Thus, if effort attributions were the prime mediators of achievement affect, causal attribution theory would be irrelevant to achievement motivation.[3]

---

[3]Spontaneous causal attributions should be infrequent when individuals are task-involved. More precisely, attributions to the full range of causal factors will be unlikely. In task-involvement, the concern is with mastering tasks rather than with distinguishing the contributions of ability, effort, and difficulty to outcomes. When they are ego-involved, individuals are concerned with distinguishing the contributions of effort and ability (capacity) to performance. Spontaneous causal attributions are, therefore, more likely in this

I could not persuade myself that I never make causal attributions or that I always try hard. Therefore, for as long as I also persisted in thinking in terms of the differentiated conception of ability, I had to conclude that ability attributions must be the critical mediators of achievement affect. Evidence consistent with this thesis was found in an ego-involving situation where success and failure were manipulated (Nicholls, 1975) and with students' attributions for their recalled academic successes and failures (Nicholls, 1976b). Thus, feelings about success and failure appeared to reflect the extent to which they are attributed to ability (see McFarland & Ross, 1982). However, others (e.g., Weiner & Kukla, 1970) found effort to be more important. This paradox appeared to be resolved by the suggestion that, although we prefer to have high ability, we recognize that effort is virtuous (Covington & Omelich, 1979; Nicholls, 1976a; Sohn, 1977). We recognize that effort is socially approved and, when placed in a teaching role, we reward effort more than ability (Lanzetta & Hannah, 1969; Weiner, 1979).

This, however, does not seem to be the whole truth. If we are task-involved, higher effort can indicate greater learning and greater competence—thus, perception that success resulted from high effort could occasion feelings of competence and positive affect. Evidence in support of this prediction is presented by Ames et al. (1977). They found more positive affect associated with higher-perceived effort in an individual goal situation, but not in an ego-involving context. (See also Ames, this volume.)

The picture became more complex when it was shown that different attributions were associated, not merely with different amounts of emotion, but with different emotions (Weiner, 1979; Weiner, Russell, & Lerman, 1979). But, if the meanings of ability and effort can change, the associations between given attributions and specific affects might also change. Brown and Weiner (1982), for example, found embarassment diminished and guilt increased when effort was low. These results make sense in ego-involvement where (if performance is fixed) low effort would enhance perceived ability and thus minimize the embarrassment that would follow demonstration of low ability. At the same time, low effort would produce guilt: We feel bad if we do not do our best. Effort would be a two-edged sword (Covington & Omelich, 1979) in ego-involvement. In task-involvement, however, higher effort can indicate greater competence. In this case, therefore, higher effort should minimize both guilt and embarrassment. These predictions were confirmed with task-involving and ego-involving scenarios by Jagacinski et al (1982).

state. In most studies, however, causal attributions are elicited by explicit questions about the causes of outcomes.

When students are ego-involved, they are faced with the choice of trying hard and experiencing greater embarrassment (if they fail) or applying less effort and experiencing more guilt. In task-involvement, effort minimizes both guilt and embarassment. Again, from the perspective of education, task-involvement appears the more desirable psychological state.

In retrospect, the attempt to establish the relative importance of different attributions as mediators of achievement affect and of linkages between specific attributions and specific emotions appears absolutist. The meanings of ability and effort are not fixed. They differ in task- and ego-involvement. Correspondingly, the relations among perceptions of effort, and ability, and emotions also vary.

VALUES, DEVELOPMENT, AND EDUCATION

THE AIMS OF EDUCATION

Throughout this chapter, I have argued that task-involvement will produce the most desirable educational outcomes. This view does not derive purely from psychological theory and research. It also derives from a value position on what the outcomes of education should be. This position is that each student should develop his or her intellectual potential to the fullest possible extent. If teachers maintain optimum motivation for intellectual development in all their students, they will achieve a legitimate form of educational equality. This would not mean equal attainment. It would mean that all students would develop their intellectual potential equally: to the fullest possible extent (Nicholls, 1979).

Ego-involving classrooms appear bound to maximize inequality of motivation and, therefore, unequal development of intellectual potential. Within classrooms, perceived ability and attainment are generally positively correlated (Bloom, 1976; Schwarzer, 1981). Ego-involvement selectively impairs the learning of those with low perceived ability. This will confirm their perception of low ability and further diminish their attainment. From them who lack ability will be taken away the will to improve even that which they have. On the other hand, classrooms that sustain task-involvement are more likely to maintain equal and optimum motivation for intellectual development; particularly the development of logical thought (Nicholls, 1983). Equal and optimum development of intellectual potential is, however, but one possible aim of education. One could see the purpose of schooling is to select and prepare students for work in a meritocratic economic system where personal worth and income depend on status in the system. In this view, ego-involving, competitive, classrooms would be a model for a meritocratic economic system in which rewards are dependent on capacity and effort rather than on need or ascribed status. Acceptance of the justice of this sort of schooling would prepare students for acceptance of the wider social and economic order and their status in it. In this view, test anxiety and unrealistically high goal setting could be seen as an unfortunate but necessary phase in the process whereby those who doubt their ability come to terms with their status. Low performance-expectations, low effort, and adoption of low goals could be seen as evidence of acceptance of this status. The consequent reluctance to work for anything but task-extrinsic incentives could, in turn be seen as justifying a scarcity of rewards and subservient roles. Though alienated, students with low perceived ability would feel little justification for complaint so long as their problems appear to reflect their own lack of ability or effort. My argument is that, in ego-involvement, a greater readiness to learn is a consequence of perception of high ability. However, it could be seen as a legitimate basis for more reward, freedom, responsibility, and leadership roles.

A proponent of a meritocratic, capitalist position would not, however, want a significant proportion of the population to give up learning before it had acquired competence in the basic skills needed even in the lowest status occupations. Extreme levels of ego-involvement could, thereby, cause the system to collapse. In fact, age-related changes in the concept of ability and in teaching practices appear designed to ensure attainment of minimum levels of competence in most of the population before ego-involvement is given full rein.

AGE-RELATED CHANGES

Developmental changes in the conception of ability appear calculated to make growing children progressively more susceptible to concerns about their ability and more likely to have their learning and emotional well-being disrupted in ego-involving conditions. Preschool children's optimism is evident in their performance expectations (Stipek, in press) and in their occupational aspirations (Gottfredson, 1981). This optimism and readiness to try despite failure gradually diminishes with age. This appears, in part at least, a consequence of the development of the conception of ability as capacity.

When learning indicates ability, all children have the possibility of feeling competent. This possibility fades in the early school years as children come to understand that being able means being more able than others (Nicholls, 1978; Nicholls & Miller, 1983). At the same time, they realize that success is more impressive when few succeed and become correspondingly more concerned about performing well compared to others (Nicholls & Miller, 1983; Ruble & Frey, 1982). In other words, they become more inclined to become ego-involved. These developments may make it increasingly difficult for teachers to approve of one child's performance without thereby implying another's incompetence (Miller, Brickman, & Bolen, 1975).

Motivational problems in students with low attainment and low perceived ability can become more extreme in early adolescence when the conception of ability as capacity is established. For a young child, an expectation of demonstrating low ability does not involve much more than an expectation that one cannot do a task. For adolescents, it has the additional and more serious implication that one will be revealed as lacking a fundamental personal trait, capacity, which cannot be easily modified. This can constitute a more serious threat to self-esteem. Further, in ego-involving situations, younger children's perceptions of effort and ability are positively correlated: higher effort implies higher ability. But when ability is conceived as capacity, higher effort can imply lower capacity. Thus, when they are ego-involved, adolescents can face the prospect that high effort will show that they lack the stable personal trait, capacity. For these reasons, the expectation that one might "look stupid" produces more severe performance impairment in adolescents than in younger children (Miller, 1982; Nicholls & Miller, in press). The concept of ability as capacity also makes it more difficult for teachers to praise adolescents for effort and improvement without thereby implying low ability (Meyer, Bachmann, Biermann, Hempelmann, Ploger, & Spiller, 1979). Adolescents' tendency to value ability is also likely to conflict with the tendency of teachers to reward effort. In short, as children mature, increasing numbers of them are likely to infer that they lack ability and, in ego-involving situations, the consequences of low perceived ability for learning and emotional well-being become increasingly negative (Nicholls & Miller, in press).

The problems associated with the development of the concept of ability can hardly be solved by slowing or reversing the process of intellectual development. These problems can be minimized by classroom methods that maintain task-involvement. However, the general trend across the grades is for an increase in practices that foster ego-involvement and diminsih task-involvement (Eccles, Midgley, & Adler, 1983). As Eccles *et al.* observe, it is likely that these grade-related changes in teaching practice contribute to the age-related declines in diverse indexes of achievement motivation that they document. Ego-involvement also leads to most performance impairment and maladaptive goal-setting in students with low-perceived ability. Thus, these age-related changes appear calculated to produce increasing inequality of academic motivation.

VALUES AGAIN

Could the parallels between age-changes in the concept of ability and school practices be the outcome of random occurrences? Might not this conjunction of individual and social patterns be evidence of a divine purpose, namely, the promotion of capitalism and the defeat of the "secular humanism" espoused by John Dewey and like thinkers? For Dewey (1938/1963), education should be democratic.

> [It should] engage the learner in the formation of the purposes which direct his activities in the learning process [p. 67]. [Learning should also be an end in itself.] What avail is it to win prescribed amounts of information about geography and history, to win ability to read and write, if in the process the individual loses his own soul: loses his appreciation of things worthwhile, of the values to which things are relative; if he loses desire to apply what he has learned and, above all, loses the ability to extract meaning from his future experiences as they occur [p. 49]. [When preparation for occupations is made the controlling end,] the potentialities of the present are sacrificed to a suppositious future . . . . The ideal of using the present simply to get ready for the future . . . shuts out the very conditions by which a person can be prepared for his future . . . . Only by extracting at each present time the full meaning of each present experience are we prepared for doing the same thing in the future [p. 49].

Dewey hoped that education could promote more fulfilling work by promoting personal and intellectual development. The progress of society and individual development would, he hoped, both be promoted by education. Instead, Bowles and Gintis (1976) argue, the economic system ensured that progressive education would not prevail in the schools, let alone influence the world of work. In the domains of politics and individual rights, our society is at least formally democratic and egalitarian. But, according to Bowles and Gintis, Dewey overlooked the fact that

> the hierarchial division of labor in the capitalist enterprise is politically autocratic. Moreover, his central thesis as to the economic value of an educational system devoted to fostering personal growth is untrue in capitalist society. Dewey's view requires that work be a natural extension of intrinsically motivated activity. The alienated work of corporate life is inimical to intrinsic motivation [p. 46].

Educational researchers have developed and validated a variety of teaching methods that diminish ego-involvement and promote task-involvement (see Covington & Beery, 1976; Maehr, 1976; 1983; Nicholls, 1983). Some teachers spontaneously employ or adopt such practices

(Nicholls, 1983). These practices are, however, far from widespread. This is explicable if, in fact, many parents and teachers have not been stimulated to question seriously the view that the existing socioeconomic status ranking is valid and that the purpose of schooling is to select and prepare students for their place in it. If this is true, we may see no fundamental changes in schooling until our conceptions of society and of the role of education are transformed.

REFERENCES

Abramson, L. Y., Seligman, M. E. P., & Teasdale, J. D. Learned helplessness in humans: Critique and reformulation. *Journal of Abnormal Psychology*, 1978, 87, 49–74.

Ames, C., & Ames, R. Competitive versus individualistic goal structures: The salience of past performance information for causal attributions and affect. *Journal of Educational Psychology*, 1981, 73, 411–418.

Ames, C., Ames, R., & Felker, D. Effects of competitive reward structure and valence of outcome on children's achievement attributions. *Journal of Educational Psychology*, 1977, 69, 1–8.

Ames, C., & McKelvie, S. *Achievement attributions and self-instructions under competitive and individualistic goal structures.* Paper presented at American Educational Research Association meeting, Montreal, April 1983.

Ankeny, N. C. Using game theory, via poker to examine Regan's fiscal '83 budget. *New York Times*, February 14, 1982.

Arkin, R. M., Kolditz, T. A., & Kolditz, K. K. Attributions of the test anxious student: Self-assessments in the classroom. *Personality and Social Psychology Bulletin*, in press.

Atkinson, J. W. Motivational determinants of risk-taking behavior. *Psychological Review*, 1957, 64, 359–372.

Atkinson, J. W. Towards an experimental analysis of human motives in terms of motives, expectancies, and incentives. In J. W. Atkinson (Ed.), *Motives in fantasy actions and society*. New York: Van Nostrand, 1958.

Atkinson, J. W. The mainsprings of achievement-oriented activity. In J. D. Krumboltz (Ed.), *Learning and the educational process*. Chicago: McNally, 1965.

Atkinson, J. W. Comments on papers by Crandall and Veroff. In C. P. Smith (Ed.), *Achievement-related motives in children*. New York: Sage, 1969.

Atkinson, J. W., & Raynor, J. O. *Motivation and achievement*. Washington, D.C.: Winston, 1974.

Bandura, A. Self-efficacy: Toward a unifying theory of behavioral change. *Psychological Review*, 1977, 84, 191–215.

Bloom, B. S. *Human characteristics and school learning*. New York: McGraw-Hill, 1976.

Bowles, S., & Gintis, H. *Schooling in capitalist America*. New York: Basic Books, 1976.

Brockner, J. Self-esteem, self-consciousness, and task performance: Replications, extensions, and possible explanations. *Journal of Personality and Social Psychology*, 1979, 37, 447–461.

Brockner, J., & Hulton, A. J. B. How to reverse the vicious cycle of low self-esteem: The importance of attentional focus. *Journal of Experimental Social Psychology*, 1978, 14, 564–578.

Brown, J., & Weiner, B. *Affective consequences of ability versus effort ascriptions: Empirical controversies, resolutions, and quandaries.* Unpublished manuscript, University of California, Los Angeles, 1982.

Buckert, U., Meyer, W. U., & Schmalt, H. D. Effects of difficulty and diagnosticity on choice among tasks in relation to achievement motivation and perceived ability. *Journal of Personality and Social Psychology*, 1979, 37, 1172–1178.

Carver, C. S. A cybernetic model of self-attentional processes. *Journal of Personality and Social Psychology*, 1979, 37, 1251–1281.

Carver, C. S., Blaney, P. H., & Scheier, M. F. Reassertion and giving up: The interactive role of self-directed attention and outcome expectancy. *Journal of Personality and Social Psychology*, 1979, 37, 1859–1870.

Carver, C. S., & Scheier, M. F. *Attention and self-regulation: A control-theory approach to human behavior.* New York: Springer-Verlag, 1981.

Condry, J. D. & Chambers, J. Intrinsic motivation and the process of learning. In M. R. Lepper & D. Greene (Eds.), *The hidden costs of reward: New perspectives on the psychology of human motivation.* Hillsdale, N.J.: Erlbaum, 1978.

Covington, M. V., & Beery, R. *Self-worth and school learning.* New York: Holt, Rinehart, & Winston, 1976.

Covington, M. V., & Omelich, C. L. Effort: The double-edged sword in school achievement. *Journal of Educational Psychology*, 1979, 71, 169–182.

Deci, E. L, Betley, G., Kahle, J., Abrams, L., & Porac, J. When trying to win: Competition and intrinsic motivation. *Personality and Social Psychology Bulletin*, 1981, 7, 79–83.

Deci, E. L., Schwartz, A. J., Sheinman, L., & Ryan, R. M. An instrument to assess adults' orientations toward control versus autonomy with children: Reflections on intrinsic motivation and perceived competence. *Journal of Educational Psychology*, 1981, 73, 642–650.

Dennett, D. C. *Branstorms: Philosophical essays on mind and psychology.* Montgomery, VT: Bradford, 1978.

Dewey, J. *Experience and education.* New York: Collier Books Edition, 1963. (Originally published, Kappa Delta Pi, 1938.)

Diener, C. I., & Dweck, C. S. An analysis of learned helplessness: Continuous changes in performance, strategy, and achievement cognitions following failure. *Journal of Personality and Social Psychology*, 1978, 36, 451–462.

Diener, E., & Srull, T. K. Self-awareness, psychological perspective, and self-reinforcement in relation to personal and social standards. *Journal of Personality and Social Psychology*, 1979, 37, 413–423.

Eccles (Parsons), J., Midgley, C., & Adler, T. Age-related environmental changes and their impact on achievement behavior. In J. G. Nicholls (Ed.), *The development of achievement motivation.* Greenwich, CN: JAI Press, 1983.

Entin, E. E., & Raynor, J. O. Effects of contingent future orientation and achievement motivation on performance in two kinds of tasks. *Journal of Experimental Research in Personality*, 1973, 6, 314–320.

Felson, R. B., & Bohrnstedt, G. W. Attributions of ability and motivation in a natural setting. *Journal of Personality and Social Psychology*, 1980, 39, 799–805.

Frankel, A., & Snyder, M. L. Poor performance following unsolvable problems: Learned helplessness or egotism? *Journal of Personality and Social Psychology*, 1978, 36, 1415–1423.

Ganzer, V. J. Effects of audience presence and test anxiety on learning and retention in a serial learning situation. *Journal of Personality and Social Psychology*, 1968, 8, 194–199.

Garcia, J. Tilting at the paper mills of academe. *American Psychologist*, 1981, 36, 149–158.

Gjesme, T. Goal distance in time and its effects on the relations between achievement motives and performance. *Journal of Research in Personality*, 1974, *8*, 161–171.

Gottfredson, L. S. Circumscription and compromise: A developmental theory of occupational aspirations. *Journal of Counseling Psychology Monograph*, 1981, *28*, 545–579.

Harter, S., & Connell, J. P. A model of the relationships among children's academic achievement orientation. In J. G. Nicholls (Ed.), *The development of achievement motivation*. Greenwich, CN: JAI Press, in press.

Heckhausen, H. The development of achievement motivation. In W. W. Hartup (Ed.), *Review of child development research* (Vol. 6). Chicago: University of Chicago Press, 1982.

Heckhausen, H., & Krugg, S. Motive modification. In A. Stewart (Ed.), *Motivation and society: Essays in honor of David C. McClelland*. San Francisco: Jossey Bass, 1982.

Hoffman, C., Mischel, W., & Mazze, K. The role of purpose in the organization of information about behavior: Trait-based versus goal-based categories in person cognition. *Journal of Personality and Social Psychology*, 1981, *40*, 211–225.

Jagacinski, C. M., & Nicholls, J. G. *Concepts of ability*. Paper presented at American Educational Research Association meeting, New York, March 1982.

Jagacinski, C. M., Nicholls, J. G., & Burton, J. T. *Conceptions of ability and effort and related affects*. Paper presented at American Educational Research Association meeting, Montreal, April 1983.

Jopt, J. U. *Extrinsiche motivation und liestungsverhalten*. Unpublished dissertation, Ruhr University Bochum, West Germany, 1974.

Karabenick, S. A., & Youssef, Z. I. Performance as a function of achievement motive level and perceived difficulty. *Journal of Personality and Social Psychology*, 1968, *10*, 414–419.

Kepka, E. J., & Brickman, P. Consistency versus discrepancy as cues in the attribution of intelligence and motivation. *Journal of Personality and Social Psychology*, 1971, *20*, 223–229.

Klinger, E. Consequences of commitment to and disengagement from incentives. *Psychological Review*, 1975, *82*, 1–25.

Klinger, E., & McNelly, F. W. Fantasy need achievement and performance: A role analysis. *Psychological Review*, 1969, *76*, 574–591.

Kruglanski, A. W. The endogenous–exogenous partition in attribution theory. *Psychological Review*, 1975, *82*, 387–406.

Kuhl, J. Motivational and functional helplessness: The moderating effect of state versus action orientation. *Journal of Personality and Social Psychology*, 1981, *40*, 155–170.

Kukla, A. Foundations of an attributional theory of performance. *Psychological Review*, 1972, *79*, 454–470.

Kukla, A. Performance as a function of resultant achievement motivation (perceived ability) and perceived difficulty. *Journal of Research in Personality*, 1974, *7*, 374–383.

Kukla, A. An attributional theory of choice. In L. Berkowitz (Ed.), *Advances in Experimental Social Psychology* (Vol. 11). New York: Academic Press, 1978.

Lanzetta, J. T., & Hannah, T. E. Reinforcing behavior of "naive" trainers. *Journal of Personality and Social Psychology*, 1969, *11*, 245–252.

Maehr, M. L. Continuing motivation: An analysis of a seldom considered educational outcome. *Review of Educational Research*, 1976, *46*, 443–462.

Maehr, M. L. On doing well in science: Why Johnny no longer excels; why Sarah never did. In S. G. Paris, G. M. Olson, & H. W. Stevenson (Eds.), *Learning and motivation in the classroom*. Hillsdale, N.J.: Erlbaum, 1983.

Maehr, M. L. & Nicholls, J. G. Culture and achievement motivation: A second look. In N. Warren (Ed.), *Studies in cross-cultural psychology* (Vol. 2). New York: Academic Press, 1980.

Marecek, J., & Mettee, D. R. Avoidance of continued success as a function of self-esteem, level of self-esteem certainty, and responsibility for success. *Journal of Personality and Social Psychology*, 1972, *22*, 98–107.

McFarland, C., & Ross, M. Impact of causal attributions on affective reactions to success and failure. *Journal of Personality and Social Psychology*, 1982, *43*, 937–946.

Meyer, W-U., Bachmann, M., Biermann, U., Hempelmann, M., Ploger, F-O., & Spiller, H. The informational value of evaluative behavior: Influences of praise and blame on perceptions of ability. *Journal of Educational Psychology*, 1979, *71*, 259–268.

Meyer, W-U., Folkes, V., & Weiner, B. The perceived informational value and affective consequence of choice behavior and intermediate difficulty task selection. *Journal of Research in Personality*, 1976, *10*, 410–423.

Miller, A. T. *Self-recognitory schemes and achievement behavior: A developmental study.* Unpublished doctoral dissertation, Purdue University, 1982.

Miller, R. L., Brickman, P., & Bolen, D. Attribution versus persuasion as a means for modifying behavior. *Journal of Personality and Social Psychology*, 1975, *31*, 430–441

Moulton, R. W. Effects of success and failure on level of aspiration as related to achievement motives. *Journal of Personality and Social Psychology*, 1965, *1*, 399–406.

Nicholls, J. G. Creativity in the person who will never produce anything original and useful: The concept of creativity as a normally distributed trait. *American Psychologist*, 1972, *27*, 717–727.

Nicholls, J. G. Causal attributions and other achievement-rleated cognitions: Effects of task-outcomes attainment value and sex. *Journal of Personality and Social Psychology*, 1975, *31*, 379–389.

Nicholls, J. G. Effort is virtuous, but it's better to have ability: Evaluative responses to perceptions of effort and ability. *Journal of Research in Personality*, 1976, *10*, 306–315. (a)

Nicholls, J. G. When a scale measures more than its name denotes: The case of the Test Anxiety Scale for Children. *Journal of Consulting and Clinical Psychology*, 1976, *44*, 976–985. (b)

Nicholls, J. G. The development of the concepts of effort and ability, perception of own attainment, and the understanding that difficult tasks require more ability. *Child Development*, 1978, *49*, 800–814.

Nicholls, J. G. Quality and equality in intellectual development: The role of motivation in education. *American Psychologist*, 1979, *34*, 1071–1084.

Nicholls, J. G. An intentional theory of achievement motivation. In W-U. Meyer & B. Weiner (Chairpersons), *Attributional approaches to human motivation.* Symposium presented at the Center for Interdisciplinary Studies, University of Bielefeld, West Germany, August, 1980.

Nicholls, J. G. Conceptions of ability and achievement motivation: A theory and its implications for education. In S. G. Paris, G. M. Olson, & H. W. Stevenson (Eds.), *Learning and motivation in the classroom.* Hillsdale, N.J.: Erlbaum, 1983.

Nicholls, J. G., & Miller, A. T. Development and its discontents: The differentiation of the concept of ability. In J. G. Nicholls (Ed.), *The development of achievement motivation.* Greenwich, CN: JAI Press, in press.

Nicholls, J. G., & Miller, A. T. The differentiation of the concepts of difficulty and ability. *Child Development*, 1983, *54*, 951–959.

Paul, G. L. , & Eriksen, C. W. Effects of test anxiety on "real-life" examinations. *Journal of Personality*, 1964, *32*, 480–494.

Perez, R. C. The effect of experimentally induced failure, self-esteem, and sex on cognitive differentiation. *Journal of Abnormal Psychology*, 1973, *81*, 74–79.

Ramey, C. T., & Finkelstein, N. W. Contingent stimulation and infant competence. *Journal of Pediatric Psychology*, 1978, *3*, 89–96.

Raynor, J. O., & Smith, C. P. Achievement-related motives and risk-taking in games of skill and chance. *Journal of Personality*, 1966, *34*, 176–198.

Revelle, W., & Michaels, E. J. The theory of achievement motivation revisited: The implication of inertial tendencies. *Psychological Review*, 1976, *83*, 394–404.

Rheinberg, F. Achievement evaluation: A fundamental difference and its motivational consequences. *Studies in Educational Evaluation*, in press.

Rholes, W. S., Blackwell, J., Jordan, C., & Walters, C. A developmental study of learned helplessness. *Developmental Psychology*, 1980, *16*, 616–624.

Rotter, J. B. *Social learning and clinical psychology*. Englewood Cliffs, N.J.: Prentice-Hall, 1954.

Ruble, D. N., & Frey, K. S. Self-evaluation and social comparison in the classroom: A naturalistic study of peer interaction. In S. Nelson-LeGall (Chair) *Social Comparison: Implications for education*. Symposium presented at American Educational Research Association meeting, New York, March 1982.

Ruble, D. N., Parsons, J. E., & Ross, J. Self-evaluative responses of children in an achievement setting. *Child Development*, 1976, *47*, 990–997.

Ryan, R. M. Control and information in the intrapersonal sphere: An extension of cognitive evaluation theory. *Journal of Personality and Social Psychology*, 1982, *43*, 450–461.

Sarason, I. G. The effects of anxiety, reassurance, and meaningfulness of material to be learned in verbal learning. *Journal of Experimental Psychology*, 1958, *56*, 472–477.

Sarason, I. G. Relationships of measures of anxiety and experimental instructions to word association test performance. *Journal of Abnormal and Social Psychology*, 1959, *59*, 37–42.

Sarason, I. G. The effects of anxiety and threat on solution of a difficult task. *Journal of Abnormal and Social Psychology*, 1961, *62*, 165–168.

Sarason, I. G. Anxiety and self-preoccupation. In I. G. Sarason & C. D. Spielberger (Eds.), *Stress and anxiety* (Vol. 2). Washington, D.C.: Wiley–Hemisphere, 1975.

Sarason, S. B., Mandler, G., & Craighill, P. G. The effect of differential instructions on anxiety and learning. *Journal of Abnormal and Social Psychology*, 1952, *47*, 561–565.

Schalon, C. L. Effect of self-esteem upon performance following failure stress. *Journal of Consulting and Clinical Psychology*, 1968, *32*, 497.

Scheier, M. F., & Carver, C. S. Self-directed attention and the comparison of self with standards. *Journal of Experimental Social Psychology*, in press.

Schneider, K. *Motivation unter Erfolgsrisiko*. Gottingen: Hogrefe, 1973.

Schwarzer, R. *The development of academic self-concept with respect to reference groups in school*. Paper presented at International Society for the Study of Behavioral Development meeting, Toronto, August 1981.

Sears, P. S. Levels of aspiration in academically successful and unsuccessful children. *Journal of Abnormal and Social Psychology*, 1940, *35*, 498–536.

Sears, P. S. Levels of aspiration in relation to some variables of personality: Clinical studies. *Journal of Social Psychology*, 1941, *14*, 311–336.

Shrauger, J. S. Self-esteem and reactions to being observed by others. *Journal of Personality and Social Psychology*, 1972, *23*, 192–200.

Sohn, D. Affect-generating powers of effort and ability self-attributions of academic success and failure. *Journal of Educational Psychology*, 1977, *69*, 500–505.

Stipek, D. J. Young children's performance expectations: Logical analysis or wishful thinking? In J. G. Nicholls (Ed.), *The development of achievement motivation*. Greenwich, CN: JAI Press, in press.

Touhey, J. C., & Villemez, W. J. Ability attribution as a result of variable effort and achievement motivation. *Journal of Personality and Social Psychology*, 1980, *38*, 211–216.

Trope, Y. Uncertainty-reducing properties of achievement tasks. *Journal of Personality and Social Psychology*, 1979, *37*, 1505–1518.

Valian, V. Learning to work. In S. Ruddick & P. Daniels (Eds.), *Working it out*. New York: Pantheon, 1977.

Weiner, B. The role of success and failure in the learning of easy and complex tasks. *Journal of Personality and Social Psychology*, 1966, *3*, 339–343.

Weiner, B. *Theories of motivation: From mechanism to cognition*. Chicago: Markham, 1972.

Weiner, B. A theory of motivation for some classroom experiences. *Journal of Educational Psychology*, 1979, *71*, 3–25.

Weiner, B. Some methodological pitfalls in attributional research. *Journal of Educational Psychology*, in press.

Weiner, B., Frieze, I. H., Kukla, A., Reed, L., Rest, S., & Rosenbaum, R. M. *Perceiving the causes of success and failure*. Morristown, NJ: General Learning Press, 1971.

Weiner, B., & Kukla, A. An attributional analysis of achievement motivation. *Journal of Personality and Social Psychology*, 1970, *15*, 1–20.

Weiner, B., & Kun, A. *The development of causal attributions and the growth of achievement and social motivation*. Unpublished manuscript, University of California, Los Angeles, 1976.

Weiner, B., Nierenberg, R., & Goldstein, M. Social learning (locus of control) versus attributional (causal stability) interpretations of expectancy of success. *Journal of Personality*, 1976, *44*, 52–68.

Weiner, B., Russell, D., & Lerman, D. The cognition–emotion process in achievement-related contexts. *Journal of Personality and Social Psychology*, 1979, *37*, 1211–1220.

Weiner, B., & Schneider, K. Drive versus cognitive theory: A reply to Boor and Harman. *Journal of Personality and Social Psychology*, 1971, *18*, 285–262.

White, R. W. Motivation reconsidered: The concept of competence. *Psychological Review*, 1959, *66*, 297–333.

Wine, J. Test anxiety and direction of attention. *Psychological Bulletin*, 1971, *76*, 92–104.

PART II

The Student:
Internal Motivational Factors

3

The Motive for Self-worth

Martin V. Covington

L. Frank Baum's charming fantasy, *The Wizard of Oz,* presents a penetrating allegory of mankind's quest for self-acceptance. The cowardly lion, the most beloved member of that intrepid band of adventurers, sought acceptance by reason of brave deeds. The scarecrow, sensing the inadequacy of straw and cloth, sought to fill the void with brains and in so doing to become worthy by reason of brilliance. Finally, the tin woodsman quested for a heart and the approval of others through acts of kindness.

Latterday wizards in the form of social and behavioral scientists seek to understand the processes by which the basic human need for personal and social acceptance develops, how it is nourished, and how it is often frustrated. The purpose of this chapter is to explore current research on the motive for self-worth, especially as it pertains to school achievement. In the first section I review recent social psychological research on self-serving bias in achievement dynamics. This sets the stage for the more particular exploration of classroom motivation that follows in successive sections of the chapter. Finally, in conclusion, I return to the Emerald City of Oz. The evocative genius of Baum's story lies primarily in the Wizard's handling of the adventurers' requests that they be granted self-acceptance as a gift, and by magical means. The Wizard's tour de force is a lesson for parents, teachers, and educational researchers alike.

Copyright © 1984 by Academic Press, Inc.

SELF-SERVING BIAS IN ACHIEVEMENT

One of the major organizing principles of psychology is the assumption that individuals act in ways that promote a positive self-identity in order to gain the approval of others and to disassociate oneself from actions or events that might attract negative social sanctions. I refer to this general tendency for the establishing and maintenance of a positive self-image as the *self-worth motive*. In contemporary terms, the laboratory study of the dynamics of self-interest in the achievement context is focused largely on the tendency of individuals to take personal responsibility for their successes and to attribute their failures or shortcomings to external causes that do not reflect on their worth as a person. This dual tendency has been referred to variously as self-serving bias (Miller & Ross, 1975), egocentric perception (Heider, 1958), and attributional egotism (Snyder, Stephan, & Rosenfield, 1976). It is generally presumed that such biases or distortions are manifestations of a more basic motive for self-acceptance. This presumption of motivated cognitions is called here the *egotism hypothesis*.

As is often true of research, much of the intense current interest in this topic is generated from controversy. Beginning in the 1970s, observers have increasingly criticized the egotism hypothesis. It has been said, for example, that this construct has been used far too loosely, without sufficient definition, and often without proper empirical justification. By far the most influential critics have been Miller and Ross (1975). Basically, these investigators raised the intriguing possibility that much of what had passed for egocentric bias may be explained equally well, and more simply, in nonmotivational terms. For instance, as already noted, the one finding on which the egotistic position mainly rests is that individuals tend to accept less personal responsibility for their failures than for their successes. Miller and Ross reasoned that because people are more likely to expect success than failure, and because individuals tend to take more responsibility for expected outcomes (Feather, 1969), then simple cognitive, information-processing biases can also account for the positive relationship found between success and internal attributions to one's ability.

The reaction to the Miller and Ross challenge was swift and on the whole constructive. One reaction took the form of a counterchallenge to the validity of various information-processing explanations of previous egotism studies. For instance, in the example just presented, it has subsequently been demonstrated that individuals do not always expect success, thereby calling into question the presumed logical basis on which individuals make internal attributions for success (Zuckerman, 1979). At the same time, other researchers in the egotism tradition produced a second generation of experiments designed to demonstrate the presence of self-serving biases that could not be readily interpreted in nonmotivational terms and for which various methodological objections raised by Miller and Ross could not reasonably apply (e.g., Covington & Omelich, 1978; Zuckerman, 1979).

As a result of these activities a more convincing case has been established for self-serving, motivationally driven biases than was previously available. But by far the most important outcome of this controversy has been a deeper, more systematic understanding of the processes by which egotism tendencies operate, and how logical, rational considerations limit and mediate egotistical dynamics. The basis for this potential rapprochement of cognitive and affective processes was a recognition of the need to differentiate between distortions in one's privately held beliefs about self (or self-image) and the biasing of one's public image. As Miller (1978) explained it, this first type of bias presumes an unwitting, unconscious distortion of object causality, whereas the latter type of distortion likely involves a conscious manipulation or management of the impression that one makes on others. Miller reasonably argued that while the majority of earlier egotism studies were concerned with establishing the presence of unconscious bias in the service of one's private image, public-presentational elements were also undoubtedly operating, especially in the concern of the subject for how the experimenter viewed him or her. Thus, the possibility exists for a confounding of two related yet distinctive motivational processes, one dealing with perceptual bias and the other with descriptive distortion (Frankel & Synder, 1978; Ross, 1977).

This private–public distinction provides the basis for an understanding of the dynamic interaction between rational considerations and self-aggrandizing motives. Although the role of the "constraints of reason", as Heider called them (1958), are not yet well understood in the creation of private image-making, there is little doubt that deliberate, logical calculations enter into the construction of public images in order to balance egotistic tendencies against the need to maintain credibility in the eyes of others (Frey, 1978; Schlenker, 1975). Specifically, individuals constantly shift their public images depending on circumstances. For example, the degree to which the individual presents a positively skewed social-image depends on (1) how much information others have about the individual (Hendricks & Brickman, 1974); (2) whether or not the information on which the person bases his or her self-portrayal remains anonymous (Schneider, 1969); and (3) whether or not the individual will

be expected to perform in the future in ways consistent with the prof-
fered image. To the extent that individuals are likely to be held responsible for their self-evaluations or their credibility challenged, positive
biases are reduced and public portraits are painted in a more modest
fashion.

On the basis of these and related findings (e.g., Arkin, Appelman, &
Burger, 1980), it has been concluded that a multistep process is probably
at work when individuals make achievement attributions for success and
failure (Riess, Rosenfeld, Melburg & Tedeschi, 1981). First, persons
arrive at a private assessment of causes that may be biased unconsciously
both by the need to maintain a sense of competency and by information-
processing factors. Second, these private perceptions may then undergo
further distortion as a result of public-presentational concerns, which in
turn are balanced to accommodate the social realities of the moment.
Seen in this way, such apparently nonselfish behaviors as modesty and
self-deprecation are not necessarily counterproductive to underlying
hedonistic goals, but actually may further them. This reasoning has been
extended to those confounding reversals where the individual actually
takes more responsibility for failure than for success. Weary (1979) has
coined the phrase *counter-defensive attributions* to cover this case. Presumably, on some occasions, accepting rather than denying one's responsibility for failure casts the individual in a better light. Miller (1978) has
worried that such a proposal runs the risk of overinclusiveness, that is, it
may allow *any* differential pattern of attributions for success and failure
to be interpreted as self-serving. While this concern must be taken seriously, considerable evidence for the counterdefensive hypothesis has
nonetheless been generated (Arkin *et al.*, 1980; Covington and Omelich,
1978). One intriguing aspect of this counterdefensive process that serves
to underscore the intensity of the need for self-aggrandizement even in
failure is reported by Baumeister and Jones (1978). When subjects were
forced by circumstances to accept an unfavorable description of themselves, they appeared to compensate by enhancing their self-descriptions
on traits of which observers had no knowledge.

The research reviewed in this first section leads to a far more sophisticated view of the parameters within which a self-worth motive operates
than was prevalent in the early 1970s. The evidence suggests that individuals strive to maintain both private and public images that are not
only internally consistent with one another, but also credible in the eyes
of others. According to this view, behaviors that at times may appear
counterintuitive to such self-serving goals are in reality carefully calculated moves to maximize one's sense of value in the long run. This broad
perspective provides a sound footing for the following examination of

the self-worth motive as expressed in the context of school learning. While educators scarcely need be told that school achievement is motivated, the laboratory-based research reviewed thus far gives ample empirical validation for their suspicions, and in the process provides several important insights into educational theory and practice. First, the distinction between private and public image-making, a concept not yet widely appreciated in educational circles, holds a number of implications for school learning. Second, a conceptual basis for the dynamic interplay between motivational and information-processing factors in achievement behavior has been established. Third, the research also provides a unifying theoretical and empirical basis for understanding a bewildering array of self-handicapping behaviors encountered in the classroom, ranging from procrastination, to cheating, to setting impossibly high goals for oneself. All of these actions can be seen as strategies in the struggle to protect a sense of personal worth.

For their part, applied educational psychologists bring to the study of achievement motivation a keen interest in the social context in which these dynamics are played out, a theme barely alluded to in the available laboratory research. Also, much is known about the developmental features of the struggle for an acceptable self-image and how classroom learning structures and grading systems affect the outcome of this drama. Moreover, there is considerable evidence on the accumulating negative effects of self-handicapping strategies on the individual's ability to cope. Finally, an important literature is just beginning to emerge concerning the implications of self-worth motivation for instructional design. It is to these various topics that I now turn.

THE DYNAMICS OF FAILURE-AVOIDING BEHAVIOR

In the classroom achievement context, self-perceptions of *competency* become the dominant manifestation of the self-worth motive. Given our society's tendency to equate the ability to achieve and human value, it is not surprising to find that many students come to believe that they are only as good as their accomplishments, and that to fail makes them unworthy of the approval of others. Because ability is perceived to be a central ingredient to academic success, it is understandable that efforts to protect a sense of ability is a major preoccupation among students. Pupils of all ages, from kindergartan to college, value ability (Harari & Covington, 1981; Nicholls, 1975, 1976; Sohn, 1977), and, particularly among older students, prefer to be seen by others as achieving by means of ability rather than by dint of personal effort (Covington & Omelich, 1979b; 1979c; Nicholls, 1976). Teachers also value ability. For example, outside the limited instructional context of rewarding effort as a means to promote learning, a teacher's selection of students regarding their suitability for prestigious jobs depends largely on perceived ability (Kaplan & Swant, 1973).

However, linking one's sense of worth to ability is a considerable gamble because perceptions of intellectual adequacy are easily threatened by failure, and schools as institutions are often failure-prone. This is because schools provide insufficient successes for students at all ability levels due to their competitive nature. Sociological observations of typical classrooms (Alshuler, 1973) suggest that students are forced to compete among themselves for a fixed number of rewards (e.g., grades) that are unequally distributed within the classroom. This inequity is perpetuated by the practice of grading "on the curve," which forces a few students to succeed at the expense of the many. In this competitive context, grades become valued for their scarcity and hence as evidence of ability. For example, an individual's reputation as a bright student would be enhanced if he were the only child singled out for special praise. If the performances of a number of other classmates were also acknowledged as outstanding, the task would likely to perceived as a relatively easy one, certainly not requiring extraordinary ability. Moreover, not only are successes fewer in competitive environments but the very fact of competition alters the perceived causes of these successes (and failures as well) by exaggerating the importance of the role of ability in achievement (Ames & Ames, 1981; Ames, Ames, & Felker, 1976). Such a perceived ability–outcome linkage culminates in a state of demoralization for many students. Finally, in competitively oriented classes there is a greater consensus among peers and teachers as to each student's ability level (Rosenholtz & Wilson, 1980), a condition of certainty that helps pave the way for the negative dynamics described next.

STRATEGIES TO AVOID FAILURE

A combination of a scarcity of rewards and an undue emphasis on ability forces many students to struggle simply to avoid failure rather than to strive for success. A wide assortment of defensive strategies are available for avoiding failure or at least for avoiding the implications of failure, should it occur. Because this arsenal of self-serving tactics has been catalogued in detail elsewhere (Beery, 1975; Birney, Burdick, & Teevan, 1969; Covington & Beery, 1976), the primary focus here is on the nature of the basic mechanisms involved through the use of selected examples.

Obviously, the most direct way to avoid school failure is simply not to participate. This time-honored strategy with its many variations is well-known to teachers: appearing eager to answer a question, gambling that the teacher will call on someone else who appears less certain; busily taking notes, hopefully too busy for the teacher to interrupt; or slouching down in one's seat to avoid notice. Other manifestations of this strategy are an unwillingness to do work that is not absolutely required or doing as little as possible on required assignments, and in its most extreme forms, absenteeism and chronic inattention. Naturally, noninvolvement is not without risk, because teachers expect students to try and teachers reward and punish students accordingly. For this reason, nonparticipation tactics are often combined with other ploys, such as false effort. Students may act interested and involved in their school assignments without any real commitment and in ways that avoid entirely the risk of failure. For example, the individual may feign attention during a classroom discussion, may ask a question for which the answer is already known or may give the outward appearance of thinking by adopting a quizzical, pensive expression. These deceptions are a standard feature of classroom life, and when used sparingly can act as buffers against the everyday stresses of learning.

Far more harmful, however, are those failure-avoiding strategies required to meet the situation in which the student is obliged to participate, yet expects to fail. Here, the student might not be able to avoid failure, but might at least attempt to side-step the implications of failure. As a group these strategies seek to shift the personal causes of failure away from the internal attribution of ability toward external factors beyond the individual's control or responsibility. In short, the individual blames poor performance on other things and argues that failure is not indicative of academic potential, and is therefore not a real measure of worth.

One manifestation of this strategy is to set unattainable personal performance goals. Although success becomes impossible under such circumstances, at least failing an excessively difficult task reveals little about one's capabilities because few others could succeed against such odds. Another example is procrastination. By handicapping themselves through the tactic of studying only at the last minute, procrastinators can hardly be blamed for failure, and if they succeed these persons will appear highly able because they achieved with so little effort (Beery, 1975). A final example of this general strategy is the *underachiever*, who by not trying provides no information about actual ability and consequently experiences little shame when failure occurs. Indeed, underachievers often make a virtue out of inaction by downgrading the importance of the work they refuse to do. They may even come to take a perverse pride in failure as a mark of nonconformity (Bricklin & Bricklin, 1967).

Another set of failure-avoiding strategies takes a somewhat different tact: the ensuring of success. Failure-avoiding students tend to prefer either highly difficult tasks—for reasons already given—or very easy assignments that permit the setting of aspirations well below one's ability level (Altkinson & Raynor, 1977; Birney *et al.*, 1969). This latter strategy guarantees success of a sort, as in the case of the individual who publicly announces before each examination that he or she will be satisfied with just a passing grade. There are social payoffs to be gained as well by forming an impression of personal modesty. Unfortunately, however, when aspirations are set so low that there is little or no risk of failure, success becomes entirely predictable and loses its reward value. In short, because there is no real challenge, there can be no genuine pride in accomplishment.

Even this brief analysis of the nature and expression of failure-avoiding strategies makes clear that these tactics typically lead to the very failures that students are attempting to avoid. Despite the fact that these tactics may temporarily reduce the immediate anxiety and distress of failure, in the long run they are self-defeating. It is for this reason that we refer to students who repeatedly use these tactics as *failure prone*. The root problem here is not so much one of low ability, but of anchoring one's sense of worth in achievement coupled with persistent self-demands for academic perfection. Many failure-avoiding individuals suffer from excessively high standards so that success becomes an even more remote possibility (see Birney *et al.*, 1969). Although the available evidence suggests that the excessive use of failure-avoiding tactics and the presence of unforgiving personal standards are predisposed through early negative child-rearing experiences (Coopersmith, 1967; Davids & Hainsworth, 1967), it is equally clear that students also acquire unrealistic, self-defeating aspirations in competitive school environments (Ames, 1978, 1981).

Efforts to maintain a belief in one's ability to achieve in competitive settings is a far more complex and dynamic process than can be captured in the laboratory. As Beery and I have written elsewhere (Covington & Beery, 1976):

> In the minute-by-minute reality of classroom life, each student is constantly changing his achievement strategies depending on events. One moment we may find a student trying all out on an assignment—in effect, seizing at success with both hands—because the odds are favorable to him; yet in the next instant his paramount concern is to play it safe, perhaps by waiting for others to answer the

teacher's question before committing himself. Such a nonstop performance is worthy of a virtuoso. It is played out largely at an unconscious level with virtually automatic moves and countermoves that depend on the student's intuitive estimates of success and the stakes involved. . . . Yet for all the complexity involved, this drama has but one central purpose—the protection of the individual's sense of worth and dignity (pp. 61–62).

The preceding analysis of failure-avoidance strategies supposes that the dynamics of ability maintenance generally involve two fundamental elements: the manipulation of effort level by students and the availability of discounting excuses. In this section I review the research evidence for the causal role of effort and excuses both in protecting a sense of competency in the event of failure and in aggrandizing ability in the case of success.

Failure Dynamics

In the event of failure, effort expenditure represents a potential threat to one's sense of worth because a combination of high effort and failure implies low ability (Heider, 1958; Kun & Weiner, 1973). Conversely, as has been seen, not trying is likely to be an effective strategy for minimizing information about one's abilities. This line of reasoning assumes that under the threat of failure, inaction is likely to be a motivated behavior. Alternatively, of course, lack of effort could simply be interpreted as a rational decision to husband one's resources in situations where the likelihood of success is low. Which interpretation is most consistent with the evidence? Two kinds of evidence are pertinent. First, if threat is a key mediator of effort level, as assumed by the egotism view, then self-estimates of effort expenditure should be minimized following failure. This expectation has been confirmed (Covington & Beery, 1976; Miller, 1976). Second, because a defensive interpretation supposes that effort is threatening, then the reduction of threat should correspondingly enhance effort expenditure and perhaps even increase performance as well. One way to eliminate threat, as was seen, is to work on a task of such difficulty that failure can now be attributed to characteristics of the environment rather than to the individual. In contrast, given rational considerations alone, effort is unlikely to increase if one is confronted with a task believed to be more difficult than those previously failed. The accumulated evidence suggests that describing a task as highly difficult improves the performance of those who chronically worry about failure (Feather, 1961, 1963; Karabenick & Youssef, 1968; Sarason, 1961).

While these studies point to the likely presence of self-serving elements in effort expenditure, there is no indication here of the compelling nature of such maneuvering or of the interpsychic conflict that results from the use of such strategies as inaction and procrastination. In this connection, it has been shown (Covington, Spratt, & Omelich, 1980) that while a low-effort profile in failure predictably forestalled ability diminution, not trying also triggered negative self-referent labels such as "unmotivated" and "lazy." The willingness of some students to endure such social and personal stigma, especially in light of the need to manage favorable public impressions, suggests something of the degree to which they are driven to avoid the implications of failure (Bricklin & Bricklin, 1967).

To summarize, several points have been made thus far: (1) failure to maintain a sense of ability causes negative affect and a loss of self-respect; (2) student manipulation of effort expenditure plays a key role in avoiding the threat of failure; and (3) excuses can deflect the implication that one lacks ability. Each of these points has been demonstrated in a single experiment (Covington & Omelich, 1979c). College students were asked to estimate their academic ability and to introspect their affective reactions to each of four different kinds of test failure: little effort (study) (e^-); little effort but with an excuse (e^-/x); high effort only (e^+); and high effort with an excuse (e^+/x). The excuse accompanying high effort was that the instructor's test emphasized different portions of the material than those studied by the student; little effort in failure was justified by reason of illness. The results of the study are presented in Figure 1. For the moment consider only the shame and self-perceptions of ability variables.

It can be seen that students experienced the greatest shame under conditions of high effort (e^+) and the least under low effort (e^-). Additionally, shame was reduced when excuses were available to explain inaction or why effort did not pay off. Affective (shame) ratings were regressed on ability estimates. Results supported the causal assumption that shame follows from decreased perceptions of ability. Thus shame resulted from perceiving oneself as incompetent, and evidence of incompetency in turn depended on the condition of failure, primarily amount of effort expended and the presence or absence of an excuse (For review, see Covington & Omelich, in press).

In order to round out our understanding of these failure-avoiding dynamics, briefly consider the role of the plausibility of externalizing

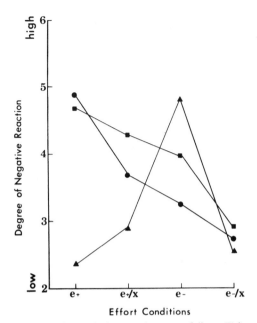

Figure 1. Teacher and student reactions to classroom failure. Triangles indicate teacher's punishment of student; squares indicate student shame; circles indicate self-perceptions of ability.

excuses. If, as concluded earlier, perceived ability maintenance can succeed only to the extend that self-serving explanations remain credible in the eyes of others, then egotism would be expressed only when multiple explanations for failure are possible. Couching this hypothesis in terms of our previously described effort–excuse paradigm, students would likely attribute higher levels of ability to self than to others in those situations where information about ability remains ambiguous (e^-; e^-/x; e^+/x). Conversely, in that single situation where low ability represents an unambiguous explanation for failure (e^+), egotism tendencies should be temporarily suspended and a more modest view of one's gifts prevail. These predictions were confirmed (Covington & Omelich 1978). Moreover, when plausible, nonability explanations for one's failure were available, not only did our subjects attribute greater ability to themselves, but also they believed that others accepted these inflated self-images. This latter tendency, referred to as *egocentricity* by Jones and Nisbett (1971) underscores the fact that success in maintaining a flattering view of self depends on the expectation that others will also agree. Without such assurance, doubts about one's credibility will likely arise and force a readjustment in egotistic tendencies. Thus in terms of the present research, when egotism occurred, egocentricity also prevailed, making self-deception complete.

Success Dynamics

What are the self-worth dynamics in the event of *successful* performance? To what extent do effort and ability attributions moderate pride, and what is the evidence regarding the aggrandizement of ability in success? To answer these questions, Omelich and I conducted a companion study on success using an identical paradigm to the one just described for failure (Covington & Omelich, 1979b). As before, college students were asked to judge their ability and to introspect their reactions to success (pride) under comparable hypothetical conditions of high and low effort expenditure. It was anticipated that pride would increase as a positive function of effort expenditure, despite the fact that trying harder causes lowered ability estimates, even in success (Kelley, 1971, 1973). We reasoned that such self-perceived-ability-diminution mechanisms would play little part in mediating pride for two reasons. First, ability estimates should remain high, irrespective of degree of effort expenditure, because success at a difficult task is preemptive evidence of ability (Fontaine, 1974; Harvey & Kelley, 1974; Kun & Weiner, 1973). Second, any negative affect triggered by ability diminution, slight as it might be, should be further offset by the fact that effort expenditure is itself a source of pride in success (Weiner, 1972, 1974; Weiner, Heckhausen, Meyer, & Cook, 1972; Weiner & Kukla, 1970).

These assumptions were supported. Effort enhanced pride in success, while offsetting the countervailing negative impact of lower ability estimates. Because successful performance aggrandizes ability, on balance, there appears little need here for the distorted, self-serving reports of reduced effort expenditure that often accompany failure (Covington & Beery, 1976; Miller, 1976). For most students, public acknowledgment of effort appears not to be too high a price to pay for success. Nonetheless, some students have discovered the self-serving value of minimizing the role of effort even in success. The most extreme example is the student who bemoans a lack of preparation for an upcoming test but in reality has secretly studied very hard. Doing this not only makes such a "closet" achiever appear unusually capable if successful, but also protects a reputation for brilliance if unsuccessful. Generally, however, defensive maneuvering seems less likely in successful circumstances than in those of failure, and success may even be the occasion for claims of personal modesty regarding one's intellectual gifts.

TEACHER REWARDS AND PUNISHMENT

The plausibility of self-serving excuses and the need to maintain an aura of public credibility simply reiterate a universal constraint on the task of coping with achievement stress that confronts us all, adults and children alike. However, for students there is a special complication arising out of the nature of the teaching–learning process. Youngsters must also balance the use of failure-avoiding strategies against the realities of teacher rewards and punishment. A number of studies clearly indicate that although the major determinant of positive teacher evaluation is high achievement, teachers also reward effort (Blumenfeld, Hamilton, Bossert, Wessels, & Meece, 1977; Eswara, 1972; Rest, Nierenberg, Weiner, & Heckhausen, 1973). Students who are seen as having expended effort are rewarded more in success and punished less in failure than those who do not try.

Thus, in effect, many students must thread their way between the threatening extremes of high effort—with its implications for low ability, should they fail—and no effort at all. It is for this reason that effort has been characterized as a *double-edged sword* (Covington & Omelich, 1979c). Excuses appear to be a basic ally in achieving this precarious balance. This point is illustrated by the failure data presented in Figure 1. In addition to gathering information on student estimates of their academic ability and their accompanying affective reactions, Omelich and I also asked our subjects to adopt the role of teachers and to punish hypothetical students under the same four conditions of failure. The results are entirely consistent with the research on teacher punishment just cited. From Figure 1 it can be seen that teachers punish diligent students less than those who do not try. Effort is critical for students, too, but in a different way. This incompatibility is best demonstrated by comparing the data for teacher punishment with that for students' self-estimates of ability and affective reactions to failure. The incompatibility of student and teacher reactions was most striking under conditions of failure with high effort (e^+). While teachers punished students least under these conditions, students felt most incompetent and experienced the greatest degree of personal dissatisfaction and shame. In contrast, while low effort (e^-) substantially reduced student discomfort, it did so at the cost of a considerable increase in teacher punishment. As has been remarked, the data suggest that excuses operate to maintain a psychological balance between trying and not trying. For example, teachers made allowance for low effort if the student had a plausible explanation for why he or she did not study (e^-/x). Without an excuse the same low effort (e^-) was severely punished. At the same time, excuses acted to reduce student shame and feelings of worthlessness regardless of effort level.

In the case of student success, we found a far more positive situation (Covington and Omelich, 1979b). There was little evidence for the teacher–student incompatibility of values seen in failure outcomes. Teacher rewards were maximized under those conditions for which student pride and satisfaction were highest (e^+) and, conversely, teachers rewarded least those kinds of accomplishments for which students took the least pride (e^-). In short, success allowed students to share the best of two possible worlds—they could appear *virtuous* by reason of effort and *able,* too. This is not to suggest that there is no potential for student–teacher disharmony in success. Additional data gathered on achievement perferences indicated that students preferred to be perceived as both able and hardworking in the event of success. However, when students were forced to choose between these two positive characteristics, they picked ability. Thus while these two sources of pride need not be incompatible, it is the self-enhancement of ability and feelings of competency that command the student's highest priority.

DEVELOPMENTAL TRENDS

The child's conception of the relationship between effort, ability, and outcome has an important developmental history. For preschool and kindergarten children, ability and effort are basically indistinguishable (Harari & Covington, 1981; Nicholls, 1978; Stipek, 1981). These youngsters believe that individuals who try hard are smart and that because of their efforts they become even smarter. In effect, effort is both an indicator of ability and synonymous with it. Indeed, young children hold an inherently incremental view of ability (Blumenfeld, Pintrich, Meece, & Wessels, 1981; Dweck, 1983). They believe that ability is a repertoire of skills that increases with experience and effort, or as one first-grade student put it, "If you study it helps the brain and you get smarter" (Harari & Covington,1981, p. 25). Only as children approach the middle-elementary school years do they begin to distinguish between ability and effort as independent dimensions, but even so, effort is still considered the overwhelming causal factor in achievement. In time, however, this perceived dependency of outcome and ability on effort is replaced by a view of intelligence as a stable, immutable entity, unaffected by industry or zeal (Blumenfeld *et al.,* 1981). As a result, for many junior-high-school pupils, and for virtually all high-school students, effort is no longer seen as either a precondition or a guarantor of success, and ability alone becomes a sufficient condition for high accomplishment (Harari & Covington, 1981). By this stage of development, the inverse, compensatory relationship between effort and ability is sufficiently in place so that, as we have seen, high effort comes to imply low ability, especially in failure. Also, the self-serving advantages of effort-level distortion become apparent. Among most young adults, low effort in success is believed to be indicative of brilliance, while low effort expenditure in failure deflects causes away from the stable, internal attribution of ability. In sum, young children experience no conflict of teacher–student values of the kind documented among older students. By trying harder, young children capitalize on the rewards of good conduct and are perceived as being smart both by themselves and by their peers. The available evidence suggests that the shift from an incremental to an entity theory of ability, although likely an inevitable developmental process (Ruble, Boggiano, Feldman, & Loebl, 1980; Veroff, 1969), is accelerated by peer-group competition.

Several points of theoretical and practical importance to the curriculum and instruction enterprise have been made in this section. To recap, insufficiency of available rewards is a key factor in the initiation and maintenance of failure-avoiding behaviors, a situation that in turn is caused primarily by a competitive classroom atmosphere. It is also clear that the strong causal link between variations in self-perceptions of ability and pride in success and of shame in failure add momentum to a preoccupation with the aggrandizement and protection of one's ability in the classroom. One unfortunate result of this is a potential teacher–student conflict of values regarding ability and effort.

THE CONSEQUENCES OF FAILURE AVOIDANCE

A primary consequence of the prolonged or excessive use of failure-avoiding strategies, in general, is a progressive deterioration of the individual's will to learn. Psychologically speaking, this involves a transformation in the person from being success-oriented to becoming failure-prone and then, ultimately, failure-accepting. It has been argued that such a process is initiated and sustained in large part by the competitive nature of school achievement. Not only does defensive maneuvering tend to set up the failures that students are trying to avoid, but by adopting such self-defeating techniques, students progressively cut themselves off from an already scarce supply of classroom rewards. This

process of deterioration can take months or even years, but its onset can
be quite rapid as demonstrated by the research of Flowers (1974). This
investigator found that by simply instructing previously successful students to criticize themselves when they were unsure of a test answer, he
could precipitate an immediate deterioration of achievement scores. Obviously, worry and doubt interfere with performance, but the ease with
which a failure dynamic can be established, especially among students
who were reasonably confident to begin with, is of concern.

COPING AND EGOTISM

A major premise of the self-worth position is that the need for self-
protection is universal, and that it is the strategic quality of self-de-
fense—its frequency, timeliness, and sense of proportion—rather than
the mere presence or absence of egotism—that differentiates successful
from unsuccessful students. One implication of this position is that for
some seemingly successful students, defensiveness provides the motive
power for outstanding achievement. A case in point is the overstriver
(Beery, 1975; Covington & Beery, 1976). These academically successful
individuals have adopted a strategy of avoiding failure by succeeding!
Overstrivers achieve through a combination of high ability, overprepared-
ness, and slavish attention to detail. But what may be seen as a virtue to
the teacher—high achievement via effort—is what makes the overstriver
especially conflicted. By relying heavily on effort, this student becomes
successively more vulnerable to the implications of failure should it occur. Thus, failure-avoidance can take on many guises, even the appearance of success.

Little is known about the role of egotism as a potentially positive force
in sustaining the will to learn (see Lazarus, 1983). Nor is it clear when
the need for self-justification overturns the requirements of credibility
and social approval with a result that the individual lapses into dysfunctional behaviors such as underachievement or overstriving. Nonetheless,
we can profitably speculate on these matters in anticipation of complete
evidence. The private–public-image distinction introduced earlier
should prove helpful here. Some individuals are known to harbor private self-doubts yet struggle to maintain a praiseworthy public image of
competency. To the extent that there is uncertainty about the accuracy
of one's negative self-appraisal due to the successful maintenance of a
positive public image, individuals are probably more likely to seek out
success. Such striving may represent an effort to reduce uncertainty in a
positive direction and to prove one's worth both to self and to others
(Coopersmith, 1967; Swann, 1982). Low self-concept males in particular

have been shown to exhibit such a private–public discrepancy (Covington & Omelich, 1979c; Covington & Omelich, 1978), which likely reflects
the general tendency toward defensiveness among males in matters of
ability (Synder *et al.*, 1976; Stephan, Rosenfield, & Stephen, 1976;
Streufert & Streufert, 1969; Wolosin, Sherman, & Till, 1973). In contrast, students who are so convinced of their incompetency that they
have given up the struggle for both self-approval and the approval of
others are unlikely to attempt success. This self-deprecatory pattern is
frequently found among females (Covington & Omelich, 1978). In this
connection, Marecek and Mettee (1972) found that females who were
certain of their inability performed well only if they believed the outcomes depended on chance, presumably because "lucky" successes
would not oblige them to do well on future occasions.

In summary, then, the will to learn likely depends as much on the
certainty with which the individual holds a given self-concept of ability
and on the degree of *discrepancy* between publicly and privately held
images, as it does on the *level* of self-perceived competency per se. As
long as students are somewhat uncertain about the causes of their
failures, even when such uncertainty is the product of defensive man-
uevering, they may respond well to praise and success.

ATTRIBUTIONS TO SUCCESS AND FAILURE

The struggle to maintain a positive image and the progression from
successful coping to defending and eventually to despair can be concep-
tualized most simply in terms of the kinds of causes individuals attribute
to their successes and failures. Over the past decade investigators have
identified a remarkably consistent set of attributional and behavioral
patterns (Ames, 1978; Weiner, 1972; Weiner & Kukla, 1970). Success-
oriented students tend to attribute their successes to a combination of
skill and effort, and their failures to a lack of proper effort. In contrast,
failure-accepting students attribute their successes, infrequent as they
are, to external factors such as luck, task ease or to the generosity of a
teacher, while failure is ascribed to a lack of skill and ability. Because
these students perceive success as beyond their control, they tend to
withhold self-praise as being unjustified and also actively avoid success
because it implies an obligation to succeed again, something they believe
themselves incapable of (Marecek & Mettee, 1972; Mettee, 1971). Con-
comitantly, because these students see failure as due to personal inadequacies, they are predisposed to severe self-criticism (Ames & Felker,
1979).

For simplicity sake, consider these two extreme attributional positions—the one success oriented, the other failure accepting—as anchor points on a continuum of coping, with the former locus representing an effective struggle for adaptation and the latter a failure or actual abandonment of defenses. Clearly, the attributional pattern of success-oriented individuals is positive and uplifting. In effect, success inspires further confidence because it is taken as evidence of one's ability to do well whereas failure signals the need to try harder. Such an interpretation, even if defensively driven, robs failure of much of its threat.

For failure-accepting students, by contrast, it is difficult to imagine a more devastating pattern of attributions: blaming oneself for failure, yet taking little credit for success. Feeling that one is at the mercy of capricious forces beyond one's control is demoralizing, especially when failure threatens self-worth. In its extreme manifestations, we can characterize such individuals as having experienced a massive failure of defenses, and as a result they become completely convinced of their incompetency. It is this group of individuals that has often been associated with the phenomenon of learned helplessness (Heckhausen, 1980; Schwarzer, 1981; Wortman & Brehm, 1975). Learned helplessness has been described as a state of inaction and depression arising from a realization that the individual's efforts are ineffectual in obtaining reinforcement (Abramson, Seligman, & Teasdale, 1978). As implied by this definition, earlier explanations of learned helplessness attributed indifference primarily to a condition of effort noncontingency (e.g., "Why try when it does not help?"). However, more recently researchers in the self-worth tradition have stressed the importance of intervening ability attributions in this self-defeating dynamic (e.g., "Trying does not work because I lack ability."). For example, Synder and his colleagues (Frankel & Synder, 1978; Snyder, Smoller, Strenta, & Frankel, 1981) reasoned that if inaction is solely the result of reaching the logical conclusion that effort does not pay off, then the introduction of even more difficult tasks would simply increase helplessness. However, as noted earlier, a defensive explanation would predict increasing effort since failing a difficult task reduces the threat to self, thereby freeing the individual to do his or her best. The results of this series of experiments by Snyder favored a self-worth, ability-linked interpretation of learned helplessness.

FAILURE ACCEPTANCE

There is little systematic evidence on the psychological mechanisms by which repeated failure is translated into progressive demoralization. All we know with reasonable certainty is that self-perceived-ability diminution, effort level, and the availability of excuses are central elements in this process. The key causal role of these three interrelated factors is demonstrated in a study by Covington & Omelich (1981) that was conducted in the naturally occurring context of repeated test-taking failures in the classroom. College students enrolled in a large mastery-based psychology course were allowed to take several parallel forms of the same test, with additional study interspersed, in order to achieve their highest grade-goal aspirations. In this process many students never attained even their minimally acceptable goals, and as a consequence experienced repeated feelings of failure. These students were asked to attribute causes to each failure as it occurred, to indicate the degree of shame they experienced, and to rate their chances for future success. Regression analyses of these data indicated that the decreased future expectancies and negative affect that followed a *first* failure depended largely on lowered self-estimates of ability, thereby corroborating our previously described findings with single, isolated failures using a role-playing methodology (Covington & Omelich, 1979c; Covington *et al.*, 1980). As failures accumulated, self-perceived ability diminution was accelerated largely because low ability progressively became a sufficient reason for failure due to the increasing implausibility of alternative, self-serving explanations such as insufficient opportunity to study. Correlatively, the more that students studied over the course of the test–retest cycle, the more salient effort expenditure became as a cue for inability. In short, repeated failure not only caused decreases in self-perceived *levels* of ability, but because of its increasing saliency as an explanation for failure, ability perceptions also became a more important causal *source* of distress and hopelessness. These data also suggested that for those students initially low in self-concept of ability, repeated failure simply accelerated these negative dynamics, a conclusion that can also be reached on the basis of several laboratory investigations (Feather, 1969; Feather and Simon, 1971a, 1971b; Markus, 1977). Moreover, it appeared that the greater resistance of highly self-confident individuals to this debilitating process occurred because of their tendency to attribute failure to causes other than inability. This research also complements the aforementioned learned helplessness work of Snyder and his colleagues by underscoring the centrality of self-perceptions of ability in the process of progressive demoralization. It also suggests that one of the keys to personal resiliency in the face of failure is the continuing plausibility of attempts to externalize responsibility.

As failures mount, however, plausible self-serving explanations become more difficult to maintain and as a consequence one's public image is more likely to become congruent with already prevailing self-doubts.

According to a consistency theory position (Festinger, 1957; Secord & Backman, 1961, 1965) the pressures for psychological congruence should further act to reduce inconsistencies between one's own self-perceptions, one's behavior, and the reactions of others to these behaviors. From this reasoning it follows that in order to maintain self-consistency, habitually failing students ought to seek out and prefer unfavorable, negative evaluations from others (Deutsch & Solomon, 1959), act in ways that present an image of incompetency, and even go so far as to handicap their efforts at success (Aronson & Carlsmith, 1962; Berglas & Jones, 1978; Taylor & Huesmann, 1974). Each of these predictions has found support in the literature, suggesting that in some circumstances self-consistancy may be more valued than self-validation. However, each of these results has also been challenged by contrary research evidence. Generally, these objections arise out of the fact that laboratory subjects are anything but consistent in their behavior. As has been seen, individuals are highly sensitive to the circumstances of self-disclosure and readily alter their public presentational images to fit the demands of credibility (e.g., Arkin *et al.*, 1980). The seemingly contradictory nature of the consistency and egotism literature may be largely resolved if we assume that both self-presentational and self-consistency needs operate simultaneously but that the ascendancy of one tendency over the other, and its form of expression, depends on where on the continuum, from effective coping to dysfunctioning, individuals find themselves. For example, considerable benefits may accrue from accepting, even embracing, an image of low ability as one begins losing the struggle for ability maintenance. In this connection, Weiner and Kukla (1970) have emphasized the survival value of perceived low ability in releasing the individual from responsibility. In contrast, as long as an individual is coping successfully with periodic failure, the maintenance of a self-image and a public-image of competency provides the necessary resiliency to continue to achieve.

INSTRUCTIONAL GUIDELINES:
A MOTIVATIONAL APPROACH

Now consider the instructional implications of the diverse array of research findings reviewed thus far. Any fully comprehensive set of guidelines for curriculum and instructional development must take into account the ubiquitous motive for self-worth, the complex dynamics of self-serving ability maintenance, and the fundamental requirement that the threat of failure be offset not only by reducing the frequency of failure but also by altering its psychological meaning. Obviously, this is no small task. Realistically, resentment and frustration are inevitable outcomes of any evaluative process where so much is at stake, and schooling is no exception, with its clear implications for future occupational placement. Thus the threat to the learner can only be moderated, not banished, but hopefully before it destroys the will to learn. In this spirit of cautious optimism we can now turn to several guidelines for enhancing and sustaining success-oriented motivation in schools.

ESTABLISHING A SUFFICIENCY OF REWARDS

The research reviewed here underscores the paramount need to increase the number of classroom rewards available so that students are no longer forced simply to avoid failure for the lack of opportunity to pursue success. Providing sufficient rewards requires a basic alteration of competitively oriented achievement structures. A number of researchers are investigating novel learning systems designed to provide sufficient rewards either through competition with absolute standards of excellence, through self-competition, or by means of cooperative peer learning. This diverse group of experimental learning structures can be loosely termed *equity* paradigms given their focus on the importance of sufficient rewards for all students, irrespective of ability level. Comprehensive reviews of these systems are found in Covington and Beery (1976), Kulik, Kulik and Cohen (1979), and Thomas (1980). For our present purposes, a few brief examples suffice. One type of equity structure features the use of absolute teacher-based performance standards such that any number of students can achieve a given grade so long as their accomplishments exceed the teacher's preannounced criteria. In such a *mastery*-learning context (Block, 1977), students set a series of intermediate grade goals of their own choosing on their way toward the more distant final achievement objective. Other equity approaches involve *contract* learning in which individual students establish work agreements with teachers. Such contracts specify what is to be done by the student, the quality of work required, and the kind of payoffs that are contingent on completing the job. Contracts often involve an analysis of potential task difficulties and the creation of plans to overcome learning obstacles. A third quite different approach involves *cooperative* learning in which peers set group-achievement goals, divide the work into manageable subtasks that are often self-assigned on the basis of individual interest or experience, and allocate rewards in a mutually acceptable fashion (Martin, 1976).

Overall, equity structures have the effect of redefining success in terms of exceeding one's own goals or standards rather than surpassing the accomplishments of others. With an adequate supply of self-rewards thereby possible, students can, in principle, act in a more success-oriented manner. Naturally, however, plentiful rewards by themselves are not sufficient to promote a will to learn. Students must also accept their newly won successes as caused by their own skillful effort. This process of gaining a sense of personal control over events involves the strengthening of a positive effort–outcome attributional linkage, and the simultaneous offsetting of a belief in ability as the dominant cause of achievement.

STRENGTHENING AN EFFORT–OUTCOME COVARIATION

As has been shown, competition serves to increase the saliency of ability as the major perceived cause of success and failure; and, when failure is attributed to a lack of ability, task involvement wanes. Learned helplessness is but one example of this. As will be recalled, in the case of helplessness, the perceived ability–outcome linkage, and its increasing causal importance as failures mount, accounted for the progressive sense of demoralization. In contrast, it has been demonstrated that a strong self-perceived effort–outcome linkage—as typically found among younger students and among success-oriented persons—serves to encourage the individual's will to learn even when failure is the temporary result of trying. Effort-linked performance outcomes also enhance a compatibility of teacher–student values, especially as illustrated in the event of achievement success.

As a group, equity structures seem well suited to the task of shifting emphasis from ability to effort as the dominant cause of successful performance. For example, learning how to divide a complex classroom assignment into more manageable subparts—in effect, making a difficult task easier—has the advantage of increasing the likelihood of success without necessarily lowering aspirations. Also, students should have less reason to avoid trying for fear that it will reflect poorly on ability should they fail. Other interpretations of failure are now possible. Failure may occur because of improper task analysis, unrealistically high aspirations, or because of inappropriate effort, factors within the student's power to correct. Moreover, mastering small units of material, one at a time, appears to be an effective means for learning to accept credit for one's successes, especially among ability-uncertain individuals (Marecek & Mettee, 1972; Mettee, 1971).

ENHANCING A POSITIVE EFFORT—AFFECT LINKAGE

If, as has been shown, degree of pride in success and degree of shame in failure depend largely on self-perceptions of ability, then task involvement is likely to continue only as long as the individual succeeds in aggrandizing ability. When all goes well, resulting feelings of pride act as a potent source of self-reinforcement—but pride in ability, not necessarily pride in accomplishment. Once failure threatens one's self-perception of ability, and shame results, individuals are likely to remove themselves from the task, especially those who already doubt their ability. Thus, from an instructional viewpoint a shift is needed from an ability—affect dependency to an effort-based valuation so that self-praise in success comes to depend to a greater degree on effort expenditure, and self-criticism in failure becomes linked to attributions of insufficient or improper effort.

Such a transformation is difficult to achieve at any time, but especially in competitive environments, which tend to accentuate prideful reactions to success and shameful reactions to failure (Ames & Felker, 1979; Crockenberg, Bryant, & Wilce, 1976). In effect, this means that competitive settings breed an atmosphere of exaggeration in which success and failure become psychologically remote from one other. There is little middle ground for the more subtle qualifications of the kind suggested by John Holt (1964) when he urged that schools need to establish a semantic distinction between failure and nonsuccess. In the present situation, one can take little solace in failing despite having tried hard, nor can one appreciate the benefits of success other than for its self-aggrandizing value. Again, equity learning approaches, with their emphasis on achievement via effort and their discouragement of improper or low effort, would appear at least in theory to strengthen a positive effort—affect linkage.

As has already been remarked, there is ample reason for caution in accepting these or any guidelines. A finely balanced appreciation must always be maintained between the presumed benefits of a recommendation, on the one hand, and its potentially offsetting costs, on the other. A case in point is the reinforcement value of grades. In a competitive context, good grades are valued as evidence of ability, primarily because of their scarcity. So, will noteworthy accomplishments still retain their incentive value when they become more commonplace and when it is clear to students that effort has replaced ability at least temporarily as the critical factor in achievement? Questions of this kind can only be resolved empirically. Yet to my knowledge no research has addressed this particular issue. Nor has any attempt been made to evaluate the extent to which particular instructional systems enhance the kinds of effort-oriented linkages stressed in the guidelines, and whether or not by their strengthening, these attributions cause achievement gains and a corresponding reduction in failure-driven, defensive tactics (see Scheirer & Kraut, 1979). For this reason, I submit that a comprehensive motivational analysis of actual classroom learning structures is a next and urgently needed step in ongoing research on achievement behavior.

INSTRUCTIONAL RESEARCH IN ACHIEVEMENT MOTIVATION

As part of the Berkeley Teaching/Learning Project, my colleagues and I (Covington, 1983, 1984; Covington & Jacoby, 1972; Covington & Omelich, 1979a) have undertaken a motivational analysis of the mastery learning paradigm, one of the *equity* structures described earlier. Because of the prototypical nature of this research, and its relevance to all aspects of the proposed instructional guidelines, it deserves a detailed treatment here. It is important to note at the outset, however, that our focus on a mastery paradigm was basically a matter of convenience. Any of the other equity structures mentioned earlier are equally appropriate candidates for such analyses.

To reiterate, a mastery paradigm involves a criterion-referenced grading arrangement in which absolute performance standards must be met by each student in order to achieve different grade levels; for example, so many points for an A, so many points for a B, and so on. Any number of students can receive a given grade as long as they exceed the performance criterion. Additionally, students have several test–retest opportunities to attain the criterion. Thus, a mastery paradigm should satisfy our guidelines for promoting success-oriented motivation. Presumably, absolute standards permit sufficient opportunities for individual successes, irrespective of the grade-goal aspirations of all other students, a circumstance that should reduce a sense of peer-group competition and moderate negative affect such as test anxiety. Moreover, when standards of performance are well defined, as in this case, failure to achieve the standard should motivate students to try harder (Kennedy & Willcutt, 1964). At the same time, multiple testing opportunities should also strengthen the perceived linkage between effort and performance and should lead to higher achievement.

In order to test the many causal hypotheses implied here, it was necessary to compare the impact of the basic structural elements of the mastery paradigm with those of more traditional instructional approaches

(Covington & Omelich, 1980). Accordingly, some 500 students in a large introductory psychology course at the University of California, Berkeley, were randomly assigned either to a criterion-referenced or to a norm-referenced grading condition (i.e., "grading on the curve"). Students within each grading condition were then assigned to either a one-try or a two-try examination sequence. Students in the two-try group had the option of taking a second parallel form of each midterm test at no penalty after additional study.

After students were assigned to either the criterion-referenced or norm-referenced condition, and the advantages and disadvantages of each system explained, both groups were found to be equated for grade aspirations, confidence that these goals would be obtained and were equal in the value they placed on doing well in the course. Moreover, the fact that these groups were subjected to a variety of unique procedures, including extensive self-report assessments, minimized the likelihood of a Hawthorne-type effect favoring the nontraditional system. Finally, unknown to all students, the two grading systems were yoked so that the average grade for the norm-referenced group was pegged at the average for the criterion-referenced group. Thus while actual performance levels could vary between groups, students in the two conditions shared equivalent grading distributions, a necessary control because course evaluations have been shown to depend on the grades students receive (Vasta & Sarmiento, 1979).

Across these experimental manipulations, we gathered data throughout the semester on several key motivation dimensions, including (1) *system fairness:* the degree to which each student experienced a reduced sense of peer competition and grading ambiguity; (2) *system internality–control:* the extent of subjective correspondence between effort expended and grade attained; (3) *grade aspirations:* each student's minimally acceptable grade and highest aspired grade; and (4) *confidence:* the degree of assurance that one's minimal goals would be achieved. Before the course began, data were also gathered on several learner characteristics, including student self-perceptions of academic ability.

The overall analysis of this complex data set is best understood in three steps. First, by contrasting the reactions of the prototypic mastery group (a combination of absolute standards–multiple-tests) with the responses of students under a conventional paradigm (relative standards–single test), we established that the mastery system was, indeed, superior both in terms of test performance and on all the preceding motivational dimensions. As a second step, the sources of this superiority were established. For example, we found that performance superiority depended entirely on the presence of multiple-test opportunities. Absolute standards contributed nothing to this performance advantage, suggesting that quality of performance may depend more on the level of standards demanded for a given grade than on whether or not these objectives are couched in absolute or in relative terms. Higher grade-goal *aspirations* and increased *confidence* also depended exclusively on the presence of multiple testing. However, important motivational benefits did arise from the presence of absolute standards. For instance, increased student perceptions of *system fairness* depended entirely on absolute standards. Moreover, enhanced perceptions of personal control via effort depended on a combination of absolute standards and multiple-test options.

The third level of analysis is most germane to our present interests. If a mastery system enhances achievement and promotes relevant attributional linkages, as it appears to do, then what are the causal relationships among these factors? For example, while the presence of absolute standards may promote a reduction in a sense of peer competition, does this condition lead in turn to enhanced performance or to greater task involvement and confidence as presupposed by our guidelines? In order to evaluate the causal relationships involved in such hypotheses, we cast the entire data set in the temporally ordered array shown in Figure 2. Two midterm test sequences, 1 and 2, each containing a test-retest cycle, have been broken out separately. Student motivational reactions follow

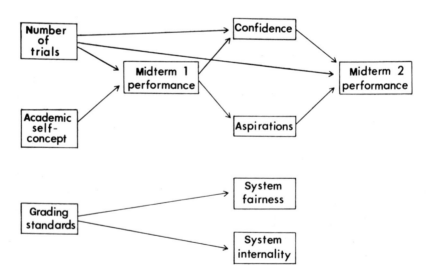

Figure 2.   Path diagram of the influence of number of test trials and self-concept level on classroom motivation and performance.

rather than precede Midterm 1 test performance on the grounds that such reactions crystallized for students only after some experience with the test-taking systems. The primary method for analyzing this system of variables is path analysis (Anderson & Evans, 1974; Duncan, 1966; Werts & Linn, 1970). To simplify the presentation here, only selected pathways significant at the .01 level are shown in the form of unidirectional arrows. These path coefficients are derived by regressing each dependent variable of interest in turn on each antecedent variable, and can be interpreted causally according to the assumptions of path analysis.

A key consideration in the instructional guidelines was the need to reduce the dependency of performance on self-perceptions of ability. Aided by Figure 2, we see that academic self-concept as an antecedent factor exerted a significant influence on Midterm 1 performance (accounting for some 42% of the explained test variance!). However, the forward impact of self-estimates of ability on Midterm 2 performance was negligible. Under the mastery paradigm, variations in subsequent performance no longer appeared to depend on academic self-concept (now accounting for only 7% of the variance). Yet these same self-perceptions continued to exert a substantial impact on performance under the traditional paradigm. Why should this be? In the case of mastery learning the otherwise influential role of ability perceptions was largely offset by enhanced performance. These performance gains were the result of a complex network of factors. Specifically, we note with reference to the top portion of Figure 2, moving from left to right, that increases in Midterm 1 performance were triggered by the presence of the multiple-test option, and it was these performance gains that led in turn to increased aspirations and confidence. Finally, these enhanced motivational factors contributed directly to the increased test performance on Midterm 2. In short, the multiple-testing option set up a recursive upward cycle of motivation-driven successful performances that temporarily suppressed otherwise important ability self-perceptions.

At the same time, regarding other aspects of our guidelines, there was a strengthening of the critical effort–outcome covariation from several sources. First, the opportunity for retesting increased the absolute amount of effort (study) expended by mastery students. Second, mastery students experienced a greater sense of correspondence between this increased commitment to effort and subsequent test gains (*system internality*), a relationship nurtured entirely by the presence of absolute standards, as indicated in the lower portion of Figure 2.

Evidence on the strengthening of a positive effort–affect– performance covariation comes from the phenomenon of belated success. Despite many initial failures, most mastery students eventually succeeded in reaching their personal grade goals for each midterm through persistent study and a second test-taking. Indeed, approximately 60% of all initial mastery failures were followed by successful second-test performances. Is belated success more self-reinforcing (pride-evoking) than an initial success, and if so, to what extent is such pride mediated by self-perceptions of effort rather than ability? Our evidence (Covington & Omelich, 1981) suggests that belated success evokes more personal satisfaction than first-time success. Moreover, only after an initial failure does effort level begin to mediate pride in later success with a corresponding reduction in ability attributions as mediators. Corroborative evidence from the laboratory indicates that pride is maximized when individuals achieve up to capacity through hard work (Brickman & Hendricks, 1975; Weaver & Brickman, 1974). Thus a multiple-test option not only promotes achievement gains but encourages outcomes that are more prideful by reason of increased effort expenditure.

One concern expressed in the guidelines was the possible negative consequences of providing a condition of plentiful rewards. Because a scarcity economy no longer prevails under mastery conditions, would not a disproportionate number of high scores rob achievement of its incentive value, especially because noteworthy performances are no longer a mark of ability? Actually, competition exists in a mastery system, if not also among most other equity paradigms. It is only the type and focus of competition that shifts, in the present case from peer-group competition to competing with the standards of the instructor. Hopefully, the basis for self-evaluation also shifts from invidious social comparisons to one of task persistence and to the satisfaction that derives from self-improvement, irrespective of the achievement of others. Our evidence suggests that the value of noteworthy performances did not decrease even though they were more frequent. This undoubtedly occurred in part because of the aforementioned positive psychological mechanisms associated with belated success.

Finally, it is important to consider the impact of individual success and failure experiences. Because more testing opportunities inevitably invite a greater absolute number of failure experiences, ironically enough, the mastery system may be ill suited for students suffering from self-doubts of ability. In this connection, previously described research (Covington & Omelich, 1981) indicated that as failures accumulate, low-ability explanations increase due to the progressive implausibility of alternative self-serving hypotheses. It will also be recalled that this progressive demoralization was most pronounced among those students already doubtful of their ability to achieve. It is true, of course, that low self-concept mastery students performed better than did their counterparts in the traditional instructional system. It is also true that the disruptive effects of a negative self-concept on performance were largely offset by the positive features of mastery learning. Nevertheless, it is still possible that doubtful students may have suffered self-perceived ability decrements due to repeated test failures. Although such doubts may be no particular handicap under mastery learning, might they not impede performance in other situations that place a high premium on ability?

To explore the possibility of self-perceived ability diminution we examined the various patterns and frequencies of success and failure experiences among students under the two systems (Covington & Omelich, 1982). Basically, we found that mastery students resisted self-perceived ability diminution to a significantly greater degree than did students under the traditional system. This was also true for low-self-concept-of-ability students. This outcome can be explained in part by the psychological benefits of belated success. However, even among those mastery students who were disappointed with *all* their test performances, self-perceived ability diminution was also lessened. Is this outcome the product of defensive maneuvering of the kinds documented earlier? To answer this question we considered two self-serving strategies designed to protect ability: attributing failure to task difficulty, thereby externalizing blame, and devaluating the importance of the achievement task. As to the first of these possibilities, all students, both mastery and traditional, perceived the tests as more difficult following an initial failure. However, this tendency was no more pronounced among mastery students. As to the second tactic of devaluating task importance, the data suggested a slight tendency toward devaluation as the course progressed, but again no differential trends emerged as a function of the instructional system. What then was operating in the mastery paradigm to promote confidence and to maintain self-perceptions of ability despite the negative attributional consequences of repeated failure? Further path-analytic treatment of the data pointed to increasing performance gains as the responsible factor. It can be concluded that as long as students show progressive gains in test performance, then individual failure experiences along the way—although perhaps temporarily demoralizing—have little influence on overall motivational reactions. A traditional testing system may allow for more self-serving excuses in the event of failure, such as bad luck, ambiguous grading practices, or test unfamiliarity, and thereby protect a sense of self-worth for a time. But mastery learning provides a far more potent source for maintaining a sense of self-worth: an increasing sense of competency.

Again, it is important to note that this analysis is not intended as a brief for mastery learning as much as an exercise in the assessment of a motivationally based model for curriculum development and evaluation. Despite its demonstrated effectiveness, the mastery paradigm, like any other single approach to instruction can not incorporate all the various factors known to stimulate achievement and student motivation. For example, largely absent here is an opportunity for students to participate in decisions about what to learn and a sense of freedom for how to proceed (Hammock & Brehm, 1966). A programmatic analysis of the many different components of an effective classroom climate, taken singly and in hybrid combination, will undoubtedly reveal a whole family of instructional options, some of which are more effective for one purpose than for others, and more effective with some kinds of students than with others. For example, in this latter connection Covington & Jacoby (1972) have shown that personal course-satisfaction depends in part on whether or not there is a match between student work-style, such as a preference to achieve independently, and the kind of course structure.

CONCLUSIONS

This chapter has focused on the implications for school learning of the individual's need to establish and maintain a personal sense of worth, and specifically on the understandable tendency among students to avoid the implications of failure. We have explored the delicate balance between constructing a favorable self, and public impression that promotes a resiliency to failure, on the one hand, and the need to accommodate to social realities, on the other, so that egotistic tendencies do not ultimately prove dysfunctional. Seen in this light, the educator's task in designing curriculum experiences should be to promote the twin interests of self-validation *and* self-accuracy. In this enterprise, we must never dismiss or belittle ability as a major ingredient in achievement. Indeed, even in the example of a mastery learning paradigm, the impact of ability was not negated as much as simply suspended temporarily for the immediate purposes of acquiring a particular subject-matter competency. The culprit in the story is not the fact that achievement depends heavily on ability, but rather that personal worth may become associated with ability. It is this fateful linkage, equating ability and performance with personal value, that must be recognized and dealt with. For one thing this means that educators must actively promote among students theories of intelligence that are conducive to the productive use of the mind and to a life-long involvement in learning. As already noted, youngsters who believe that ability is a repertoire of skills that can be endlessly expanded through instruction and experience are more likely to focus on the task at hand, to display greater intrinsic involvement, and are less preoccupied with learning as a test of their worth. In contrast, children who hold a view of intelligence as a stable, immutable trait worry far more about personal inadequacies and seek to reassure themselves through comparison with others. The former view of ability is quite reminiscent of the beliefs held by very young children in which, it will be recalled, ability was seen as an incremental process that depended on hard work (Harari & Covington, 1981). Research indicates that not only do achievement structures patterned along the lines of equity paradigms promote an incremental view of intelligence (Dweck, 1983), but that instructional curricula expressly designed to teach for problem-solving skills, such as the *Productive Thinking Program* (Covington, Crutchfield, Davies, & Olton, 1974), also promote the idea that ability is an evolving, ever-expanding process.

Thus, I paraphrase an old adage: It is not how much you have that counts, but what you use of what you *think* you have! The Wizard of Oz understood this message profoundly, and how it applied to individuals. Consider the scarecrow who sought after a brain or, as we have termed it, ability. The issue was not that the scarecrow lacked brains. After all, he had saved Dorothy and her friends from one disaster after another by his quick thinking. The scarecrow was smart enough, but what he needed was confidence. But not the false confidence that arises out of a gift magically bestowed. Rather the scarecrow needed a self-assurance born out of a recognition that, no matter what his IQ rating, he was *acting* intelligently. How do you convey this message to a scarecrow, or for that matter to a child? The Wizard confided to the scarecrow that he already had brains, but what he did not have was the external trappings of wisdom, something possessed by all other learned persons: A diploma. Once a diploma was bestowed, and the issue settled, the scarecrow immediately began searching for a way to get Dorothy back home rather than continuing his search for self-acceptance. One would like to think that the Wizard also understood that through the process of searching for brains, the scarecrow had learned to make the best use of his abilities by overcoming repeated challenges, and in the end enhanced what he thought he never had. This kind of insight would have qualified the Wizard as an early, if not the first, advocate of an incremental theory of intelligence.

REFERENCES

Abramson, L. Y., Seligman, M. E. P., & Teasdale, J. D. Learned helplessness in humans: Critique and reformulation. *Journal of Abnormal Psychology*, 1978, *87*, 49–74.

Alshuler, A. S. *Developing achievement motivation in adolescents.* New Jersey: Educational Technology Publications, 1973.

Ames, C. Children's achievement attributions and self-reinforcement: Effects of self-concept and competitive reward structure. *Journal of Education Psychology*, 1978, *70*, 345–355.

Ames, C. Competitive versus cooperative reward structures: The influence of individual and group performance factors on achievement attributions and affect. *American Educational Research Journal*, 1981, *18*, 273–288.

Ames, C., & Ames, R. Competitive versus individualistic goal structures: The salience of past performance information for causal attributions and effect. *Journal of Educational Psychology*, 1981, *73*, 411–418.

Ames, D., Ames, R., & Felker, D. Informational and dispositiohal determinants of children's achievement attributions. *Journal of Educational Psychology*, 1976, *68*, 63–69.

Ames, C., & Felker, D. W. Effects of self-concept on children's causal attributions and self-reinforcement. *Journal of Educational Psychology*, 1979, *71*, 613–619.

Anderson, J. G., & Evans, F. B. Causal models in educational research: Recursive models. *American Educational Research Journal*, 1974, *11*, 29–39.

Arkin, R. M., Appelman, A. J., & Burger, J. M. Social anxiety, self-presentation, and the self-serving bias in causal attribution. *Journal of Personality and Social Psychology*, 1980, *38*, 23–35.

Aronson, E., & Carlsmith, J. M. Performance expectancy as a determinant of actual performance. *Journal of Abnormal and Social Psychology*, 1962, *65*, 178–182.

Atkinson, J. W., & Raynor, J. D. *Personality, motivation and achievement.* New York: Hemisphere, 1977.

Baumeister, R. F., & Jones, E. E. When self-presentation is constrained by the target's knowledge: Consistency and compensation. *Journal of Personality and Social Psychology*, 1978, *36*, 608–618.

Beery, R. G. Fear of failure in the student experience. *Personnel and Guidance Journal*, 1975, *54*, 190–203.

Berglas, S., & Jones, E. Drug choice as a self handicapping strategy in response to noncontingent success. *Journal of Personality and Social Psychology*, 1978, *36*, 405–417.

Birney, R. C., Burdick, H., & Teevan, R. C. *Fear of failure.* New York: Van Nostrand, 1969.

Block, J. H. Motivation, evaluation, and mastery learning. *UCLA Educator*, 1977, *12*, 31–37.

Blumenfeld, P., Hamilton, V. L., Bossert, S., Wessels, K., & Meece, J. Teacher talk and student thought: Socialization into the student role. In J. Levine & M. Wang (Eds.), *Teacher and student perceptions: Implications for learning.* Hillsdale, NJ: Erlbaum, 1977.

Blumenfeld, P. C., Pintrich, P. R., Meece, J., & Wessels, K. *The influence of instructional practices on children's criteria for judging ability, effort and conduct.* Paper presented at the Annual American Educational Research Association meeting, Los Angeles, April 1981.

Bricklin, B., & Bricklin, P. M. *Bright child—poor grades.* New York: Dell, 1967.

Brickman, P., & Hendricks, M. Expectancy for gradual or sudden improvement and reaction to success and failure. *Journal of Personality and Social Psychology*, 1975, *32*, 893–900.

Coopersmith, S. *The antecedents of self-esteem.* San Francisco, Ca & London, England: Freeman, 1967.

Covington, M. V. Motivated cognitions. In S. G. Paris, G. M. Olson, & H. W. Stevenson (Eds.), *Learning and motivation in the classroom.* New York: Erlbaum, 1983.

Covington, M. V. Strategic thinking and the fear of failure. In J. Segal, S. Chipman, & R. Gloser (Eds.), *Thinking and learning skills: Relating instruction to basic research.* Hillsdale, NJ: Erlbaum, 1984.

Covington, M. V., & Beery, R. *Self-worth and school learning.* New York: Holt, Rienhart, & Winston, 1976.

Covington, M. V., Crutchfield, R. S., Davies, L. B., & Olton, R. M. *The productive thinking program: A course in learning to think.* Columbus, OH: Merrill, 1974.

Covington, M. V., & Jacoby, K. E. *Thinking psychology: Student projects* (Sets 1 and 2). Berkeley: Institute of Personality Assessment and Research, University of California, 1972.

Covington, M. V., & Omelich, C. L. *Sex differences in self-serving perceptions of ability.* Unpublished manuscript, Department of Psychology, University of California, Berkeley, 1978.

Covington, M. V., & Omelich, C. L. Are causal attributions causal? A path analysis of the cognitive model of achievement motivation. *Journal of Personality and Social Psychology,* 1979, *37,* 1487–1504. (a)

Covington, M. V., & Omelich, C. L. It's best to be able and virtuous too: Student and teacher evaluative responses to successful effort. *Journal of Educational Psychology,* 1979, *71,* 688–700. (b)

Covington, M. V., & Omelich, C. L. Effort: The double-edged sword in school achievement. *Journal of Educational Psychology,* 1979, *71,* 169–182. (c)

Covington, M. V., & Omelich, C. L. *A psychological and behavioral cost/benefits analysis of mastery learning.* Paper presented at the Annual Western Psychological Association meeting, Los Angeles, April 1980.

Covington, M. V., & Omelich, C. L. As failures mount: Affective and cognitive consequences of ability demotion in the classroom. *Journal of Educational Psychology,* 1981, *73,* 796–808.

Covington, M. V., & Omelich, C. L. Achievement anxiety, performance and behavioral instruction: A cost/benefits analysis. In R. Schwarzer, H. Van der Ploeg, & C. Speilberger (Eds.), *Test Anxiety Research* (Vol. 1). Amsterdam: Swets & Zeitlinger, 1982.

Covington, M. V., & Omelich, C. L. Controversies or consistencies? A reply to Brown and Weiner. *Journal of Educational Psychology,* in press.

Covington, M. V., Spratt, M. F., & Omelich, C. L. Is effort enough or does diligence count too? Student and teacher reactions to effort stability in failure. *Journal of Educational Psychology,* 1980, *72,* 717–729.

Crockenberg, S., Bryant, B., & Wilce, L. The effects of cooperatively and competitively structured learning environments on inter- and intrapersonal behavior. *Child Development,* 1976, *47,* 386–396.

Davids, A., & Hainsworth, P. K. Maternal attitudes about family life and child rearing as avowed by mothers and perceived by their underachieving and high-achieving sons. *Journal of Consulting Psychology,* 1967, *31,* 29–37.

Deutsch, M., & Solomon, L. Reactions to evaluations by others as influenced by self-evaluation. *Sociometry,* 1959, *22,* 93–113.

Duncan, O. D. Path analysis: Sociological examples. *American Journal of Sociology,* 1966, *72,* 1–16.

Dweck, C. S. Theories of intelligence and achievement motivation. In S. Paris, G. Olson, &

H. Stevenson (Eds.), *Learning and motivation in the classroom.* Hillsdale, NJ: Erlbaum, 1983.

Eswara, H. S. Administration of reward and punishment in relation to ability, effort, and performance. *Journal of Social Psychology,* 1972, *87,* 137–140.

Feather, N. T. The relationship of persistence at a task to expectation of success and achievement-related motives. *Journal of Abnormal and Social Psychology,* 1961, *63,* 552–561.

Feather, N. T. Persistence at a difficult task with an alternative task of intermediate difficulty. *Journal of Abnormal and Social Psychology,* 1963, *66,* 604–609.

Feather, N. T. Attribution of responsibility and valence of success and failure in relation to initial confidence and task performance. *Journal of Personality and Social Psychology,* 1969, *13,* 129–144.

Feather, N. T., & Simon, J. G. Attribution of responsibility and valence of outcome in relation to initial confidence and success and failure of self and other. *Journal of Personality and Social Psychology,* 1971, *18,* 173–188. (a)

Feather, N. T., & Simon, J. G. Causal attributions for success and failure in relation to expectations of success based upon selective or manipulative control. *Journal of Personality,* 1971, *39,* 528–541. (b)

Festinger, L. *A theory of cognitive dissonance.* Stanford, CA: Stanford University Press, 1957.

Flowers, J. V. The effect of self-reinforcement and self-punishment on test performance in elementary school children. Paper presented at the Western Psychological Association meeting, San Francisco, 1974.

Fontaine, G. Social comparison and some determinants of expected personal control and expected performance in a novel task situation. *Journal of Personality and Social Psychology,* 1974, *29,* 487–496.

Frankel, A., & Synder, M. L. Poor performance following unsolvable problems: Learned helplessness or egotism? *Journal of Personality and Social Psychology,* 1978, *36,* 1415–1423.

Frey, D. Reactions to success and failure in public and in private conditions. *Journal of Experimental Social Psychology,* 1978, *14,* 172–179.

Hammock, T., & Brehm, J. W. The attractiveness of choice alternatives when freedom to choose is eliminated by a social agent. *Journal of Personality,* 1966, *34,* 546–554.

Harari, O., & Covington, M. V. Reactions to achievement behavior from a teacher and student perspective: A developmental analysis. *American Educational Research Journal,* 1981, *18,* 15–28.

Harvey, J. H., & Kelley, H. H. Sense of own judgmental competence as a function of temporal patterns of stability–instability in judgment. *Journal of Personality and Social Psychology,* 1974, *29,* 526–538.

Heckhausen, H. *Motivation and Handeln.* Berlin: Springer, 1980.

Heider, F. *The psychology of interpersonal relations.* New York: Wiley, 1958.

Hendricks, M., & Brickman, P. Effects of status and knowledgeability of audience on self presentation. *Sociometry.* 1974, *37,* 440–449.

Holt, J. *How children fail.* New York: Dell, 1964.

Jones, E. E., & Nisbett, R. E. The actor and the observer: Divergent perceptions of the causes of behavior. In E. E. Jones, D. E. Kanouse, H. H. Kelley, R. E. Nisbett, S. Valins & Bernard Weiner, (Eds.), *Attribution: Perceiving the causes of behavior.* Morristown, NJ: General Learning Press, 1971.

Kaplan, R. M., & Swant, S. G. Reward characteristics in appraisal of achievement behavior. *Representative Research in Social Psychology,* 1973, *4,* 11–17.

Karabenick, S. A., & Youssef, Z. I. Performance as a function of achievement motive level and perceived difficulty. *Journal of Personality and Social Psychology*, 1968, *10*, 414–419.

Kelley, H. H. Causal schemata and the attribution process. In E. E. Jones, D. E. Kanouse, H. H. Kelley, R. E. Nisbett, S. Valins & Bernard Weiner, (Eds.), *Attribution: Perceiving the causes of behavior*. Morristown, NJ: General Learning Press, 1971.

Kelley, H. H. The processes of causal attribution. *American Psychologist*, 1973, *28*, 107–128.

Kennedy, W. A., & Willcutt, H. C. Praise and blame as incentives. *Psychological Bulletin*, 1964, *62*, 323–332.

Kulik, J. A., Kulik, C. C., & Cohen, P. A. A meta-analysis of outcome studies of Keller's personalized system of instruction. *American Psychologist*, 1979, *34*, 307–318.

Kun, A., & Weiner, B. Necessary versus sufficient causal schemata for success and failure. *Journal of Research in Personality*, 1973, *7*, 197–207.

Lazarus, R. A. The costs and benefits of denial. In S. Breznitz (Ed.), *Denial of stress*. New York: International Universities Press, 1983.

Marecek, J., & Mettee, D. R. Avoidance of continued success as a function of self-esteem, level of esteem certainty, and responsibility for success. *Journal of Personality and Social Psychology*, 1972, *22*, 98–107.

Markus, H. Self-schemata and processing information about the self. *Journal of Personality and Social Psychology*, 1977, *35*, 63–78.

Martin, J. F. *An observational study of cooperative learning among junior high school children*. Unpublished doctoral dissertation, Harvard University, 1976.

Mettee, D. R. Rejection of unexpected success as a function of the negative consequences of accepting success. *Journal of Personality and Social Psychology*, 1971, *17*, 332–341.

Miller, D. T. What constitutes a self-serving attributional bias? A reply to Bradley. *Journal of Personality and Social Psychology*, 1978, *36*, 1221–1223.

Miller, D. T., & Ross, M. Self-serving biases in the attribution of causality: Fact or fiction? *Psychological Bulletin*, 1975, *82*, 213–225.

Miller, D. T. Ego involvement and attribution for success and failure. *Journal of Personality and Social Psychology*, 1976, *34*, 901–906.

Nicholls, J. G. Causal attributions and other achievement-related cognitions; effects of task outcome, attainment value, and sex. *Journal of Personality and Social Psychology*, 1975, *31*, 379–389.

Nicholls, J. G. Effort is virtuous, but it's better to have ability: Evaluative responses to perceptions of effort and ability. *Journal of Research in Personality*, 1976, *10*, 306–315.

Nicholls, J. G. The development of the concepts of effort and ability, perception of academic attainment, and the understanding that difficult tasks require more ability. *Child Development*, 1978, *49*, 800–814.

Rest, S., Nierenberg, R., Weiner, B., & Heckhausen, H. Further evidence concerning the effects of perceptions of effort and ability on achievement evaluation. *Journal of Personality and Social Psychology*, 1973, *28*, 187–191.

Riess, M., Rosenfeld, P., Melburg, V., & Tedeschi, J. T. Self-serving attribution: Biased private perceptions and distorted public descriptions. *Journal of Personality and Social Psychology*, 1981, *41*, 224–231.

Rosenholtz, S. J., & Wilson, B. The effect of classroom structure on shared perceptions of ability. *American Educational Research Journal*, 1980, *17*, 75–82.

Ross, L. The intuitive psychologist and his shortcomings: Distortions in the attribution process. In L. Berkowitz (Ed.), *Advances in experimental social psychology* (Vol. 10). New York: Academic Press, 1977.

Ruble, D. N., Boggiano, A. K., Feldman, N. S., & Loebl, J. H. Developmental analysis of the role of social comparison in self-evaluation. *Developmental Psychology*, 1980, *16*, 105–115.

Sarason, I. G. The effects of anxiety and threat on the solution of a difficult task. *Journal of Abnormal and Social Psychology*, 1961, *62*, 165–168.

Scheirer, M. A., & Kraut, R. E. Increasing educational achievement via self-concept change. *Review of Educational Research*, 1979, *49*, 131–150.

Schlenker, B. Self-presentation: Managing the impression of consistency when reality interferes with self-enhancement. *Journal of Personality and Social Psychology*, 1975, *32*, 1030–1037.

Schneider, D. J. Tactical self-presentation after success and failure. *Journal of Personality and Social Psychology*, 1969, *13*, 262–268.

Schwarzer, R. *Stress, Angst und Hilflosigkeit*. Stuttgart, Germany: Kohlhammer, 1981.

Secord, P. F., & Backman, C. W. Personality theory and the problem of stability and change in individual behavior: An interpersonal approach. *Psychological Review*, 1961, *68*, 21–32.

Secord, P. F., & Backman, C. W. An interpersonal approach to personality. In B. A. Maher (Ed.), *Progress in experimental personality research* (Vol. 1). New York: Academic Press, 1965.

Synder, M. L., Smoller, B., Strenta, A., & Frankel, A. A comparison of egotism, negativity, and learned helplessness as explanations for poor performance after unsolvable problems. *Journal of Personality and Social Psychology*, 1981, *40*, 24–30.

Snyder, M. L., Stephan, W. G., & Rosenfeld, D. Egotism and attribution. *Journal of Personality and Social Psychology*, 1976, *33*, 435–441.

Sohn, D. Affect-generating powers of effort and ability self attributions of academic success and failure. *Journal of Educational Psychology*, 1977, *69*, 500–505.

Stephen, W. G., Rosenfield, D., & Stephen, C. Egotism in males and females. *Journal of Personality and Social Psychology*, 1976, *34*, 1161–1167.

Stipek, D. Children's perceptions of their own and their classmates' ability. *Journal of Educational Psychology*, 1981, *73*, 404–410.

Streufert, S., & Streufert, S. C. Effects of conceptual structure, failure, and success on attribution of causality and interpersonal attitudes. *Journal of Personality and Social Psychology*, 1969, *11*, 138–147.

Swann, W. B. Self-verification: Bringing social reality into harmony with the self. In J. Suls & A. G. Greenwald (Eds.), *Psychological perspectives on the self*. Hillsdale, NJ: Erlbaum, 1982.

Taylor, S. E., & Huesmann, L. R. Expectancy confirmed again: A computer investigation of expectancy theory. *Journal of Experimental Social Psychology*, 1974, *10*, 497–501.

Thomas, J. W. Agency and achievement: Self-management and self-regard. *Review of Educational Research*, 1980, *50*, 213–240.

Vasta, R., & Sarmiento, R. F. Liberal grading improves evaluations but not performance. *Journal of Educational Psychology*, 1979, *71*, 207–211.

Veroff, J. Social comparison and the development of achievement motivation. In Smith, C. P. (Ed.), *Achievement-related motives in children*. New York: Sage, 1969.

Weary, G. Self-serving attributional biases: Perceptual or response distortions? *Journal of Personality and Social Psychology*, 1979, *37*, 1418–1420.

Weaver, D., & Brickman, P. Expectancy, feedback and disconfirmation as independent factors in outcome satisfaction. *Journal of Personality and Social Psychology*, 1974, *30*, 420–428.

Weiner, B. *Theories of motivation: From mechanism to cognition*. Chicago: Markham, 1972.

Weiner, B. (Ed.) *Achievement motivation and attribution theory.* Morristown, NJ: General Learning Press, 1974.

Weiner, B., Heckhausen, H., Meyer, W., & Cook, R. Causal ascriptions and achievement behavior: A conceptual analysis of effort and reanalysis of locus of control. *Journal of Personality and Social Psychology,* 1972, *21,* 239–248.

Weiner, B., & Kukla, A. An attributional analysis of achievement motivation. *Journal of personality and Social Psychology,* 1970, *15,* 1–20.

Werts, C. E., & Linn, R. D. Path analysis: Psychological examples. *Psychological Bulletin,* 1970, *74,* 193–213.

Wolosin, R. J., Sherman, S. J., & Till, A. Effects of cooperation and competition on responsibility attribution after success and failure. *Journal of Experimental Social Psychology,* 1973, *9,* 220–235.

Wortman, C. B., & Brehm, J. W. Responses to uncontrollable outcomes: An integration of reactance theory and the learned helplessness model. In L. E. Berkowitz (Ed.), *Advances in experimental social psychology.* New York: Academic Press, 1975.

Zuckerman, M. Attribution of success and failure revisited, or: The motivational bias is alive and well in attribution theory. *Journal of Personality,* 1979, *47,* 245–287.

4

Meaning and Motivation: Toward a Theory of Personal Investment

Martin L. Maehr

INTRODUCTION

TOWARD A THEORY OF HUMAN MOTIVATION

The topic of motivation stands as singularly interesting—and important—in the realm of human affairs. Artists and musicians worry about the loss of creative verve and the will to keep on performing (see Henahan, 1982). The business establishment worries about the loss of productivity and quickly assigns an important role to motivation (see Ouchi, 1981). This volume stands as one of many pieces of evidence that motivation is likewise important in the enterprise known broadly as education. Perhaps it was Freud (see Boring, 1950) that made motivation a significant part of scientific psychology. Freud, however, was not needed to create an awareness of the importance of motivation in education on the part of teachers, parents, and even students themselves. As a teacher, father of three, and still a student, I can personally attest to the relevance of systematic study of the force or forces that drive, direct and excite us.

Recently, the study of motivation in school settings has been profoundly influenced by theories of achievement motivation (e.g., Atkinson & Raynor, 1974; Hill, 1980; Maehr, 1974a; Nicholls, 1983; Weiner, 1979). This, of course, is not surprising as schools are manifestly concerned with achievement. That is, they are concerned with acquiring and demonstrating competence, with doing things that require skill and which enhance ability. Achievement motivation theory is clearly concerned with such issues. But it is equally clear that not all those associated with or in schools are concerned with achievement. All may at some time or at some place be concerned with acquiring and demonstrating competence but not necessarily in a particular school setting at a particular time. Other goals, other intentions, other attractions, continually intrude. Even achievement in the classroom occurs in response to non-achievement concerns: Children have been known to do their homework not to acquire competence, but to keep their allowance intact. Minority group students may not exhibit any evidence of achievement motivation in a classroom but may show it elsewhere (Maehr, 1974b; Maehr & Nicholls, 1980).

Certainly, those who apply achievement theory have always recognized this to one degree or another. In a significant sense, achievement theory grew out of a theory of human motivation, but within the realm of educational research the broader framework has not always been as evident as has been the focus on a particular motive or motivational pattern. While the increasing focus on achievement motivation has probably served scholarly purposes reasonably well, it may not be sufficient for the practitioner. It is my assumption in writing this chapter that classroom motivation must be viewed in the broader context of motivation theory. Therewith, I outline a theory of human motivation that grows out of current research on achievement as well as other social motives. In the course of outlining such a theory, it is hoped that a viable perspective for educational research as well as practice will be evident. The realization of that hope will not be left entirely to chance: throughout, the classroom is the assumed arena for the antecedent–consequent relationships envisioned by the theory.

TOWARD A THEORY OF PERSONAL INVESTMENT

The theory presented in this chapter is neither new nor novel. Its intellectual forbears are readily evident, its overlap with other theories all too obvious. In several ways it is more a perspective than a formal theory as such. It attempts to integrate propositions and models from several sources into a more comprehensive scheme and thereby sacrifice specificity in avoiding intellectual provincialism. The goal is to construct a framework reasonably acceptable to scholars but hopefully also useful to the practitioner. Most immediately, the theory grows out of past and current work on the role of social and cultural context in determining motivational patterns in performing achievement tasks (e.g., Maehr, 1974b, 1976, 1978, 1983; Maehr & Nicholls, 1980; Maehr & Kleiber, 1981). Increasingly, I am choosing to call it a Theory of Personal Investment because that term seems to reflect both the phenomenological nature of the constructs employed as well as the emphasis on choices, values, and intentions in the broad arena of life. In a preliminary way, the character of the theory is reflected in three primary working propositions:

1. The study of motivation begins and ends with the study of behavior.
2. The meaning of a situation to the behaver determines behavior.
3. The meaning of a situation to the behaver can be assessed and its origins determined.

MOTIVATION AND BEHAVIOR

It may seem strange indeed to stress at the outset that the study of motivation begins and ends with the study of behavior. Historically, the study of motivation has been associated with internal processes: needs, drives, expectancies, goals, intentions, et cetera. The recent emphases on attributions (Weiner, 1979), self-determination (Deci, 1980), personal causation (deCharms, 1968), sense of competence (Harter, 1980, 1982; Harter & Connell, in press), and other cognitive variables have not varied greatly from this tradition. Moreover, it is already evident that the argument presented here ultimately places considerable weight on the subjective side: the meaning that a person associates with the situation. Yet, talk about motivation has often gone astray by not retaining an awareness that it is what is observed that prompts motivational inferences (see Maehr, 1974b). One does not ask about the motivation of a child to read or do arithmetic because one sees a need, motive, or desire. The initiating factor in prompting discussions about motivation obviously relates to something that is seen, to behavior. The question, of course, is—What is it that the child or person does that prompts motivational questions? This issue deserves attention at the outset, because it is basic to the understanding of motivational processes.

Whenever theorists and practitioners talk about motivation, they seem to refer to a wide variety of activities. On closer examination, however, the behavior on which they base motivational inferences is in fact more limited. Tentatively, it may be suggested that most motivational talk in educational circles arises out of five identifiable types of behavior patterns. When one or more of these patterns is observed, it is then that motivational inferences are made. In an important sense these behaviors are the beginning and end of motivational research and theory. The study of motivation begins with observations of the existence and variations in these patterns; the goal of motivation research is to understand, predict and explain such variation and existence.

DIRECTION

The apparent choice among a set of action possibilities is a first indicator of motivation. When an individual attends to one thing and not another, it is then that we are likely to infer that he is motivated in one way, but not in another. The choices that individuals make between behavioral alternatives suggest motivational inferences. When a student selects one course and rejects another or chooses to shoot baskets rather than do his homework, it is at this point that we make motivational inferences. Similarly, when a child attends to a learning task while a peer persists in "cutting up," it is then that we use the term motivation. Thus, in the case of school, work, or play, it is the observation of a choice that has been made between certain possibilities that determines the inference that motivation of some kind is involved. Strictly speaking, of course, choice is not a simple behavioral observation. It is in reality an inference that is made when it is observed that a person does one thing when it is assumed that other possibilities were open to him. It is the designation or attribution of choice among alternatives that prompts motivational inferences.

PERSISTENCE

Persistence is the second behavioral pattern that forms the basis for motivational inferences. When an individual concentrates attention on the same task or event, for a greater or lesser period of time, it is then that observers are likely to infer the existence of a greater or lesser degree of motivation. In the classroom, a student's tendency to stick to a task without being distracted is often the cue that leads one to infer that the child is "highly motivated." It is the extended period spent in the laboratory that is taken as an index of a scientist's motivation. And one can multiply such examples across almost any area of human activity. Clearly, observations concerning persistence can sum up to a critical indicator of motivation. However, it is worth noting that persistence may, in fact, be viewed as an instance in which the same direction in behavior is retained. In other words, the person repeatedly chooses the same (or closely similar) behavioral alternatives while simultaneously rejecting other alternatives. In an important sense, then, the behavioral pattern of persistence is really just another example of a choice that is made or a behavioral direction that is taken.

CONTINUING MOTIVATION

The behavioral pattern that is strikingly suggestive of powerful motivational forces is the return to a previously encountered task or task area on one's own, without apparent external constraint to do so. It is the child who proceeds to use a free moment to do additional problems, or check out an extra book to find out a bit more about insects, or try out a physics experiment in his father's workshop who is thought to be really motivated. Maehr (1976; see also Fyans, Kremer, Salili, & Maehr, 1981; Maehr & Stallings, 1972; Salili, Maehr, Sorensen, & Fyans, 1976; Sorensen & Maehr, 1976) has referred to this pattern as "continuing motivation (CM)" and explicated its nature and origins in a preliminary way, relating it particularly to work on intrinsic motivation (Deci, 1975). In passing, it may be noted that while from the standpoint of motivation theory this may be viewed as just another index of motivation, CM takes on special significance for teachers, particularly in the early grades. As discussed by Maehr (1976) elsewhere, CM is a crucial educational outcome for many educators, the thing they are really trying to produce. That does not make it especially easy to identify or measure, or help us in our theorizing, but it does underscore the necessity of including it as a behavioral pattern indicative of motivation and necessary to be explained by motivation theory. Moreover, it should be added that we can distinguish this pattern from persistence. Whereas in the case of persistence, the person keeps on working on a task, in the case of CM, there is an interruption and a spontaneous return.

ACTIVITY

Activity level is a fourth behavioral index of motivation. Some persons seem to be more active than others; they do more things. While this basic observation has merit, several qualifying factors should be noted. In some ways, activity level is a more complex and less reliable indicator than choice, persistence and continuing motivation. First, physiological factors are likely to be implicated in many instances, much more so than in the case of the three previous patterns. Moreover, it may be noted that in the case of some classroom situations, the motivation pattern is not one of activity, but direction. Whether or not activity level is a predominant indicator of motivation in the majority of classrooms, it is most certainly a pattern to be taken into account in the wider scheme of things.

PERFORMANCE

The final example of a behavioral pattern that characteristically prompts motivational inferences is variation in performance. If variation in performance cannot be readily explained in terms of variation in competence, skill, or physiological factors, then a motivational inference is frequently made. Teachers can readily cite "curious" instances where "A students" slump and do "C work" as well as examples of "C students" who "get serious" and increase their grade-point averages. Sometimes, these slumps and jumps can be related to the acquisition of a necessary skill. Sometimes, physiological factors, such as illness are involved. However, when such explanations are, for one reason or another, found wanting, a motivational explanation is likely to be invoked.

It might be noted that performance level is in no sense a pure measure of motivation. Performance level is a product of a variety of factors, including a combination of the motivational patterns already reviewed. That is, choice, persistence, CM, and activity level are all likely to be reflected in performance level. One might even argue that it is, at best, a very crude measure of motivation. Yet, it is a behavioral pattern that is typically taken seriously in the discussion of motivation, perhaps because performance level is often the "bottom line" in the rationale for studying motivation. In any event, because variation in level of performance often leads to motivational inferences, this particular pattern of behavior finds a rightful place in the present taxonomy.

These clearly overlapping behavioral patterns may or may not be all-inclusive. Most certainly, they need further elaboration as specific instances and issues arise. They need specification as measurement and research procedures are constructed. Moreover, it may be fairly argued that they do not in each instance represent "pure observations" but rather judgments about behavior. But for the moment, they suffice to suggest what it is that we are talking about when we say that a person is or is not motivated. To put it more bluntly, motivation is, in the first instance, behavioral patterns such as outlined above. When, for example, the teacher asks how to motivate students, she or he is probably asking how to direct students to do one thing (e.g., reading) and avoid other things (e.g., socializing, fighting, or daydreaming). Further, the teacher is concerned with some degree of persistence at these activities, and, most especially, hopes that they occur, not only when demanded, but also in the free moments in school, home, or elsewhere. Moreover, she expects—and rightly so—that persistence and continuing motivation to attend to the "right" activities will eventuate in increased levels of performance. In other words, it can readily be argued that the previously defined behavioral patterns are, in fact, what practitioners are talking about when they talk about motivation. Identifying motivation with certain behavioral patterns not only has theoretical value, it also accords with practical demands placed on motivation theory. It is these patterns that must be explained.

THE CONCEPT OF PERSONAL INVESTMENT

MOTIVATION BEHAVIOR PATTERNS AND PERSONAL INVESTMENT

While there is obvious value in stressing the primary data base for motivational inferences, there is also value in considering whether there might be certain unifying principles which underlie these somewhat disparate behavioral patterns. What type of conceptual scheme might bind these patterns together? Ultimately, that is the burden of a comprehensive theory. On the way to the development of such a theory a lesser thought or two may suffice. In this regard, the metaphor of personal investment (PI) may prove helpful. Kelly (1982) and others (e.g., Kuhlen, 1964) have used this term in discussing a wide array of tasks that individuals pursue, the weight they place on these, and the general direction of their lives. The metaphor implicit in the term *personal investment* possibly does capture the underlying meaning of these somewhat disparate patterns that I have associated with motivation. That is, when behavioral direction, persistence, performance, CM, and variation in activity level are observed, one might suggest that a person is in effect investing his or her personal resources in a certain way. Personal resources in this case refer largely to time, talent, and energy. Note that the image here is primarily one of *distributing* resources. The stress is not on the *availability* of the resource. The implicit motivation model, then, is one that stresses motivational differences rather than deprivation (see Maehr, 1974b, 1978; Maehr & Nicholls, 1980) without denying the possibility that differential levels of motivation may characterize different persons. Clearly, just as individuals may distribute their resources differently so they may also have more or less to distribute. It has been argued that the assumption of motivational differences rather than deprivation is desirable in the study of motivation in persons of varying cultural background (see Maehr, 1974b, 1978; Maehr & Nicholls, 1980). It may also be argued (see Maehr & Kleiber, 1980; 1981) that this must be the initial assumption in making cross-age comparisons, but clearly one cannot rule out the existence of differential levels of motivation. The aged often seem to give up, lose the will to live; psychological depression at all age levels may be associated with passivity—and the reader can add his or her own example. The point is that personal investment is a felicitous term for expressing the dual possibilities that persons exhibit both qualitative and quantitative differences in motivation.

SOURCES OF PERSONAL INVESTMENT:
THE ROLE OF MEANING

Granted that a certain set of behavioral patterns summed up by the term *personal investment* represents a stimulus for our research, it is necessary to move to the second step. What are the antecedents of these patterns? What brings them into existence? What modifies or enhances them? What are the sources of personal investment?

There are a variety of answers that one can give to these questions. The central answer that I propose to give is that the meaning of the situation to the person is of primary significance. One can readily identify an assortment of stimuli, events and processes that would seemingly affect personal investment. The effects of such external factors, however, are filtered through the perceptions of the person and are mediated by the meanings imposed on them by the individual involved. An illustration or two may underscore that rather simple but basic point. There is perhaps no more generally accepted motivational principle than that which psychologists are wont to call the "law of effect." Presumably in accord with this principle, it is often assumed that success at a task should increase motivation and failure decrease it. And so, we have regularly heard that "nothing succeeds like success" and "nothing fails so miserably as failure." But the fact of the matter is that success does not succeed in enhancing motivation and failure does not, in many obvious cases, serve to reduce it. That point should now be firmly embedded in psychological theory and should be just as firmly established in educational practice as well. Apparent success or failure at a task does not necessarily mean that the person feels that he or she succeeded or failed. As several decades of research from an expectancy X value framework (e.g., Feather, 1982) should have made clear, it is the subjective definition of success and failure that counts (see also, Frieze, 1980; Frieze, Shomo, & Francis, 1979). How well one does on a task is a most subjective judgment.

Quite apparently, persons not only perceive success and failure differently because they have different standards for their performance, but also because they make different judgments about the worth of the task. Cross-cultural studies are one source for illustrating this point. Most practicing educators are aware that students place different values on school tasks quite apart from their ability to perform. That this may be the critical feature in explaining cross-cultural variation in achievement patterns has been recently illustrated in a series of cross-cultural studies (Duda, 1980, 1981; Fyans, Salili, Maehr, & Desai, 1983; Willig, Harnisch, Hill, & Maehr, 1983). Generally, it seems that individuals project different pictures of what they would like to be or become. They derive these pictures from personal experiences within their own culture so that Navajo (Duda, 1980, 1981), Black, White, and Hispanic (Willig *et al.*, 1983) and persons around the world (Fyans *et al.*, 1983) all have their own pictures of the nature of successful achievement. But the critical point is that, as events are interpreted as conforming to these pictures of achievement, they are associated with success. Simply, a performance outcome, or any information that is perceived as indicating that we are becoming what we want to become, is readily defined as success (see Ames, 1984; Maehr & Nicholls, 1980). Of course, events, outcomes and information to the contrary eventuate in perceptions of failure.

Such a brief sketch of the role of meaning in mediating personal investment leaves much be be desired. Yet, it should underline the essential character of my argument. Meaning is the critical determinant of motivation. Whether or not persons will invest themselves in a particular activity depends on what the activity means to them. Persons, it may be assumed, characteristically bring a certain package of meanings with them into a situation, which determines their behavior in the particular situation at hand. There are also features of any given situation that affect the meanings that may arise there for the person. It is these meanings that determine personal investment.

ON THE MEANING OF MEANING

Having asserted the importance of meaning, it is necessary to define it. What is meant by meaning? Of what is it composed? How does it mediate personal investment?

The nature and structure of meaning can be defined and explored in a variety of ways. Focusing particularly on the meaning of achievement to the achiever, my colleagues and I have explored a number of different possibilities. Briefly, this search has necessarily employed a variety of procedures and yielded an interesting array of definitions of achievement and its causes. Amidst this variation, however, there are also points of convergence. With some risk, it is possible to designate these and to suggest a meaning structure that may prove useful in pursuing the origins of personal investment.

Three basic facets of meaning may be designated as critical in determining personal investment in a specific situation: (1) beliefs about self, (2) perceived goals of behavior in a situation, and (3) perceived alternatives for pursuing these goals or the action possibilities. First, it may be noted that some version of these three constructs is regularly employed in discussions of human motivation. In particular, this conception draws heavily on earlier work in choice and decision-making (see Messick & Brayfield, 1964). The three components, self, goals and action possibilities, are, under one guise or another, the essential features of most such theories. However, the special way I define these components is important and deserves fuller elaboration. Moreover, in defining them it is well to keep firmly in mind that they always operate collectively. They are interrelated and overlapping in nature and function, as should be quite evident.

ACTION POSSIBILITIES

The term "action possibilities" refers to the behavioral alternatives or options that a person perceives to be available to him or her in any given situation. One will act in terms of what is perceived as possible. It is not very likely that an aboriginal living in the Northern Territory of Australia will take up the cello, especially if he has not seen a cello. But besides what is perceived to be available in one's world, there is a parallel perception of what is appropriate to do in terms of sociocultural norms that exist for the individual. Playing the violin is not truly a realistic option for many students in the United States—even though they have seen one and even though they know a bit about its properties. Playing the violin simply is not the thing to do. That is, it is not behavior that is encouraged and rewarded by one's reference groups. It is something done by others, in other groups and contexts and is, therefore, alien to one's identity. In order to entice such a person into becoming a violinist, one would have to provide more than simple instruction in the existence of stringed instruments. In spite of extensive information about the violin, violin playing, careers in music, and so on, the child may still develop no interest—particularly if violin playing is not really an inherent part of his cultural world. This all may be fairly obvious, yet it is well to recognize that it is an absolutely critical facet of the motivational process. When wondering why a person does or does not do something, one has to consider first whether that something is in fact a part of his or her world. Opportunity is the sine qua non. In some ways, this is most clearly evident in the case of those who become elite performers. In this regard, the research of Bloom (1982a; 1982b) provides a very interesting example. Bloom and his colleagues have been studying world class performers in five areas: (1) athletics (tennis players, swimmers), (2) musicians (pianists), (3) mathematicians, (4) artists (sculptors), and (5) neuroscientists. There are many facets to this most fascinating study. One of them fits in most appropriately with the points being made here. These performers, in an important sense, were born into the "right families." The families valued the particular activity involved. They promoted and rewarded it. They also knew how to facilitate it. Not that this alone was sufficient, because not all children in a particular family would eventually develop their talent to the same degree as the one who actually became the elite performer; yet, the opportunity had to be there.

All in all, then, whether or not one wishes to define action possibilities as a motivational component, it is clear that one dare not ignore the component. Thus, one cannot really say much that is definitive about choice and direction in behavior unless one knows something about the possibilities from which such choices are made or the directional alternatives that are real to the person. Choosing to go to college may be a real choice among alternatives—and this represents motivation for one. For another, it may represent no choice at all and be of questionable value as an indicator of motivation.

SENSE OF SELF

There are a variety of ways to define selfhood and a wide array of components is viewed as more or less integral to this concept. Here the term *sense of self* is rather generally defined as the more- or less-organized collection of perceptions, beliefs, and feelings related to who one is. Sorting through the literature, it is possible to designate a number of different components of selfhood that figure prominently in motivation (e.g., Maehr, 1978; Maehr & Braskamp, 1983). Among these, one must certainly include judgments about one's competence (see Harter, 1980, 1982, Harter & Connell, in press). Few facets of selfhood have been as thoroughly and systematically researched as this one. Moreover, the research has underscored the importance of subjective judgments about one's competence in understanding school performance. But in any event, forced to concentrate my attention, this facet of selfhood certainly represents as good a choice to consider as any.

By sense of competence, I refer more specifically to a subjective judgment a person might make about his or her ability to perform effectively. It is, simply put, the judgment that one can do something or that one cannot. This judgment varies in degree and extent. Thus, it may be limited to one particular area or generalized broadly across a variety of performance domains. Some will view themselves as more competent in their abilities, some as less competent. In any case, I am referring to a subjective judgment that a person makes about his or her ability to succeed at a task if he or she tries.

The importance of judgments about one's competence has long been a critical feature of my thinking about behavior (see Haas & Maehr, 1965; Maehr, Mensing & Nafzger, 1962). Our early research indicated quite simply that individuals tend to do what they feel competent to do (see Ludwig & Maehr, 1967). That conclusion is not invalidated by subsequent research but *is* shown to be simplistic. In particular, it may be noted that recent research on motivation and achievement has indicated that one's sense of competence will likely guide preferences and choices that have a major impact on the continuing development of talent and ability (see Kukla, 1978; Maehr, 1983; Maehr & Willig, 1982; Nicholls, 1983). Those who have a high sense of competence in a performance area are not only more than likely to continue performing in that area, they are also more than likely to initiate and maintain activities which enhance their ability. They will challenge their ability, test it and, thereby, enhance it. Those who are less sure of their competence need special encouragement from others if they are to confront the kind of challenge that is likely to be self-enhancing. It seems, then, that at an early stage of experience with an area of activity, persons develop a sense of competence which serves as an inner guide toward the performance and practice of self-enhancing tasks. In one study (Fyans & Maehr, 1979), this problem was already powerfully evident in the fourth grade. I suspect that it may be a reality before that time in many areas of activity.

So, sense of competence is by itself a powerful determiner of whether or not individuals will invest themselves in a given area of activity. But as is noted here later, sense of competence is also important as it interacts with other facets of meaning, particularly with goals that are salient for the individual in a particular situation.

GOALS

The term *goal*, as employed here, refers to the motivational focus of the activity: What does the person expect to get out of performing? What is the value of the activity? More concretely, how does a person define *success* and *failure* in the situation?

The Nature of Goals

In a general way, the use of the term as a critical construct implies certain working assumptions about human nature. The term suggests an intentional psychology (see Klinger, 1977) in which the organism makes plans (see Miller, Galanter, & Pribram, 1960) and lives the present in terms of the future as much as in light of the past (see Allport, 1955). It is not necessary to assume that individuals spend considerable amounts of time identifying these goals and planning how to attain them. As a matter of fact, in most cases, persons seem quite nongoal oriented. That is, they seem to live from moment to moment, situation to situation— without thought about ends. Contextual constraints and demands, aside from whatever purposes they might have, seem primary. By employing the term *goal*, I have no intentions of ignoring the apparent fact that individuals spend very little time thinking about goals and purposes in what they are doing at any given moment. My suggestion, however, is that individuals do operate in terms of what a given situation yields for them. They have latent knowledge of what they hope and expect from specific situations and, if properly cued, can state this. Moreover, these beliefs about the situation should and will affect their behavior in predictable ways. In short, it is possible simply to ask people what they hope to accomplish in a given situation with a realistic hope that they can provide accurate answers.

Parenthetically, it may be noted that in practice we have been inclined to use what we have rather flamboyantly termed a "retrospective critical incident technique" in assessing goals. That is, we have asked persons to reflect on a past experience in which they experienced success–failure

TABLE 1

Example of Item Employed In Assessing Goals[a]

For this item indicate on a five point scale, ranging from "Definitely Does Not" (1) to "Definitely Does" (5), how each experience described in the item relates to this question. THINK ABOUT TIMES WHEN YOU TRULY FELT GREAT, SATISFIED, OR POSITIVE ABOUT YOURSELF AND THE WORLD. Was it because you:

	Definitely does not				Definitely does
Accomplished something others could not do	1	2	3	4	5
Pleased someone important to you	1	2	3	4	5
Showed you were competent	1	2	3	4	5
Experienced adventure–novelty	1	2	3	4	5
Understood something for the first time	1	2	3	4	5
Received an unexpected financial bonus for a job well done	1	2	3	4	5
Were totally involved in what you were doing	1	2	3	4	5
Realized you had more money than you thought you did	1	2	3	4	5
Received recognition–prestige	1	2	3	4	5
Won	1	2	3	4	5
Demonstrated your religious commitment	1	2	3	4	5
Showed how intelligent you were	1	2	3	4	5
Were totally responsible for the outcome	1	2	3	4	5
Enhanced your status	1	2	3	4	5
Showed acts of charity toward others	1	2	3	4	5
Fought for a cause	1	2	3	4	5
Sacrificed personal gain to help another	1	2	3	4	5

[a]Adapted from Braskamp and Maehr, 1983. Reprinted by permission of the authors.

or positive–negative emotion of some type and then asked them to provide an analysis of this situation. An example of one format in which such a query has been presented is found in Table 1. By no means, however, has such inquiry been confined to such a structured approach (see later). But in all instances, the design involves eliciting from persons examples of cases in which they could convey the important incentives in their lives. In any event, perhaps these few words and Table 1 will make the concept of goals, as used here, a bit more concrete.

Variety of Goals

Anyone reasonably acquainted with the vagaries of human behavior must be aware of the likelihood that a number of goals may be operative in guiding how persons invest time, talent and energy. So-called "need theories" of human motivation suggest a broad range of goal possibilities. The work of Henry Murray (1938), for example, outlines a number of so-called "needs," which in the present context, could be thought of as goals. Certainly, the particular needs selected from this list for special attention by McClelland and his colleagues (1953; Atkinson, 1958) would suggest possible goals of what is here termed *personal investment*. Thus, *n*Ach, *n*Aff, and *n*Power, in particular, might be considered as examples of goal possibilities. Without citing further examples it is possible to suggest that there are indeed a number of goals that one can logically identify. Or perhaps one can more properly say that there are various goal taxonomies available. These various goal possibilities quite properly remain of interest as the study of human motivation is pursued. Mindful of these alternatives, I intend to focus on four goal possibilities which grew out of my own research. This work suggests that four broad "goal categories" may be designated in considering achievement patterns in the schools. These categories may be labeled as follows: task, ego, social solidarity, and extrinsic rewards. A brief word about each of these is in order.

The task goal category may be viewed as embracing two somewhat different purposes in performance. First, there is the performance situation described by Csikszentmihalyi (1975; 1978), in which the individual is totally absorbed in a task and where social comparisons of performance are remote or are virtually nonexistent. Second, there is the competence motivation situation initially described by White (1959, 1960, pp. 97–140) and currently the object of considerable research (e.g., Harter, 1980, 1982; Harter & Connell, in press).

Ego goals refer to intentions that relate to doing better than some socially defined standard, especially a standard inherent in the performance of others. Whereas, task-oriented goals are at most self-competitive, ego goals are explicitly socially competitive (see Maehr & Sjogren, 1971). Achieving the goal inevitably involves beating someone, doing better than another, winning, being the best.

Social solidarity goals are not always thought of, strictly speaking, as achievement goals. Yet, any serious consideration of achievement in the classroom can hardly ignore the fact that pleasing significant others is apparently a critical factor in many instances. Thus, in interaction with a teacher, the student may wish to demonstrate that he or she has good intentions, means well, tries hard, and in this sense is a good boy or girl. To those with social solidarity goals, faithfulness is more important than demonstrating competence, excelling others or simply having fun in doing something. Clearly, demonstrating good intentions is an acceptable means of gaining social approval, not only in various stations in life, but most specifically in the classroom. It is that means of gaining social approval that is especially designated by the category, social solidarity.

Extrinsic rewards refer to a class of goals that are often designated or associated with earning money, a prize, or some other desideratum, not, strictly speaking, inherent in the performance of the task itself. Presumably, such rewards are, in fact, alien to the task in an important sense. More importantly, they are alien to the individual's personal reasons for performing the task. One might suggest that it is more appropriate to view these goals not as ends in themselves, but rather as means to other ends. They are subgoals, if you will, the attaining of which facilitates reaching other personal and more intrinsic goals. In any event, recent work on the social psychology of extrinsic–intrinsic motivation (Deci, 1975, 1980; Harter, 1980; Lepper & Greene, 1978) has made it quite clear that any comprehensive understanding of achievement must consider the role that external rewards play in controlling achievement, not only in the world of work, but also in school.

Goals and Behavior

The ultimate point about goals, however, is that they affect behavior. How variations in goals might be followed by variation in behavior is at least implied in the definition and description of goal possibilities. Overall, it should be evident that behavior is differentially oriented toward externally-administered and controlled evaluation and reward under the various goals. Extrinsic rewards are necessary to sustain behavior when extrinsic goals are held. When the behavior is defined as leading to extrinsic ends, then extrinsic rewards must be regularly administered to sustain the behavior. In a phrase, when a task is defined as *work*, it is only done when *pay* is forthcoming. To create the kind of spontaneous learning pattern suggested by the concept of "continuing motivation" (Maehr, 1976), a task–goal orientation must be fostered. Only as one is oriented toward doing a task, apart from the evaluation placed on it by others, will one continue doing it when there are no others evaluating it. Thus, viewing a task as interesting in its own right or as an opportunity to enhance one's competence will likely eventuate in continuing motivation. Doing a task to please others or to earn a grade is not likely to foster a love of learning for its own sake.

Additional examples along this line could be given, but to broaden the range of possibilities a somewhat different type of example might be presented. This example relates to the interaction of two meaning systems: sense of self and goals. A common goal condition in many class-rooms is the ego-condition. Under this condition, success is associated with doing better than others. Fine and well if one not only has ability but also confidence in this ability. Of course, there is a long line of research regarding the differential performance of individuals in com-petitive situations. Beginning with the work of Atkinson and his col-leagues (see for example, Atkinson & Feather, 1966; Atkinson & Ray-nor, 1974) and continuing with work in areas as diverse as the classroom (Hill, 1980) and sports arena (Roberts, 1982, in press). The evidence has converged on one central point: persons differ drastically in their re-sponse to what is here labeled an ego–goal condition. Building on the work of Kukla (1978), Nicholls (1979, 1983), and Roberts (1982, 1983), I attribute such variations in response to variations in the individual's sense of competence (Maehr, 1983). Those who lack a sense of compe-tence, not surprisingly, demonstrate avoidance patterns in a situation in which competence is externally evaluated and compared. Those who feel competent approach the situation with optimism. Not only do they feel that they have nothing to fear, they have something to gain: another chance to demonstrate how able they are. But my purpose is not to describe a particular case but to make two general points. First, the example illustrates how goals affect an important class of behaviors. Second, the example suggests how meaning systems can interact in de-termining behavior.

For a final illustration of how goals might influence behavior, I turn to a situation of enduring interest to researchers interested in achievement behavior: confrontation of challenge. Teachers as well as researchers are interested in the conditions under which a person is likely to attempt a challenging task, continue performing when things are difficult or re-turn to solve the difficult, unsolved problem. While not every facet of this concern can be pursued here, it may prove of interest to review a set of hypotheses that have evolved out of our work in this regard. This set of hypotheses suggests rather specifically how goals modify challenge-seeking behavior. One way of summing up the essential predictions comprised under each goal category is to construct four graphs which describe the level of motivation in relationship to subjective probability of success. Four graphs along this line are presented in Figure 1. Fur-ther, they imply hypotheses for which there are, at this point, varying degrees of empirical support. However, they help to express the func-tion of goals in a very concrete, specific, and testable fashion.

Considering the graphs, it can be seen that the prediction in the case of the task goal condition (Figure 1 [a]) is that all will exhibit the choice–performance patterns which Atkinson (1957) limits to persons

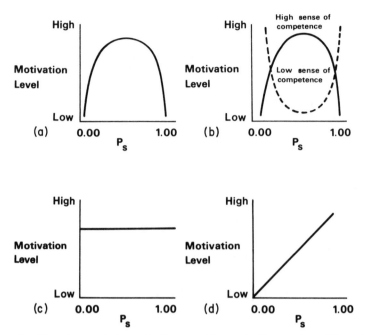

Figure 1.   Hypotheses relative to challenge seeking under four goal-conditions: (a) task goal condition; (b) ego goal condition; (c) social solidarity condition; (d) extrinsic rewards condition.

with high achievement motivation. In the ego condition (Figure 1 [b]), however, perceived competence mediates challenge-seeking. Those who perceive themselves as competent are attracted to challenge; the reverse is true for those who are lacking in a sense of competence. The overall patterns portrayed are roughly those proposed by Atkinson (1957; see also Atkinson & Feather, 1966; Atkinson & Raynor, 1974), except that perceived competence rather than resultant achievement motivation (RAM) is the moderating variable (see Kukla, 1978; Nicholls, 1979; Maehr, 1983). Figure 1 (c) suggests that social solidarity is a condition in which motivation is not low. More important, however, is the suggestion that motivation does not vary with subjective probability of success (P_s). There is no preference for or against challenge-seeking in this condition. Level of challenge is irrelevant. Figure 1 (d) articulates a well-known proposition of choice and decision theory (e.g., Messick & Brayfield, 1964) to the effect that individuals tend to maximize rewards. In the choice between an assured path to obtaining an extrinsic reward and a less certain one, the prediction is that the person will choose the more certain one. There is no value in uncertainty or in confronting a challenge when the reward is overwhelmingly extrinsic in nature.

Such a brief sketch of the behavioral possibilities inherent in various goal conditions has definite limitations. At best, it illustrates how that facet of meaning, goals, serves to modify the nature and occurrence of personal investment. Possibly also, it serves as a kind of heuristic device, stimulating further study, specification and definition. In any event, the loose threads must be left dangling in order to provide that bigger picture of meaning, motivation, and personal investment.

ANTECEDENTS OF MEANING

The thrust of the discussion thus far can be summarized in two propositions:

1. Persons invest themselves in certain activities depending on the meaning that these activities have for them.
2. Meaning is composed of three interrelated cognitions: goals, self-concepts, and action possibilities.

But what determines meaning?

Certainly, no one could expect a full and complete answer to this question in one short chapter, if at all (see Maehr & Braskamp, 1983). It is, however, possible to suggest certain factors that are likely to be important in this regard. In broad outline, one may think of meaning and personal investment as having their source in the dual factors of situation and person and in a complex of person X situation interactions. While such designation is sufficient for certain purposes, the outline of factors presented in Figure 2 may have greater utility. Figure 2 outlines four antecedent categories: task design, personal experience, information, and sociocultural context. Additionally, it may be suggested that underlying the effects of all other factors, are developmental–maturational factors. In particular, it seems evident that cognitive development would play a major role in modifying the function of these factors. Suggested more directly by the figure is the proposition that different external factors are likely to affect the various components of meaning differentially. Thus, one may surmise that previous learning and personal experience are likely to have a major impact on one's sense of self, whereas the broader sociocultural milieu in which the student participates would be especially important in defining action possibilities.

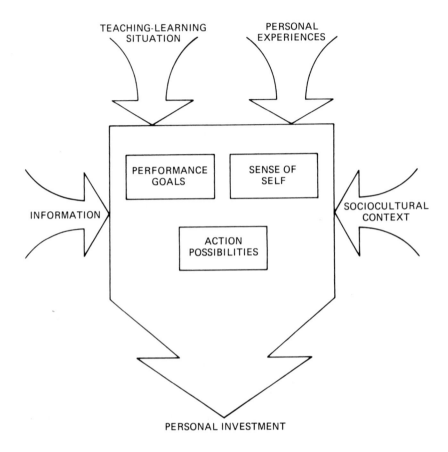

Figure 2.   Antecedents of meaning and of personal investment.

Each of these types of antecedents is important and each has been the subject of at least some research. Recognizing that the antecedents of meaning are many and diverse, I focus on the four causal categories portrayed in Figure 2. With no pretense of exhausting the discussion on the point, the goal is to illustrate rather than catalogue or fully specify.

PERSONAL EXPERIENCE AND MEANING

First, it should be noted that each individual comes to any situation with a "package of meanings" derived from past experiences. That is, an individual is likely to hold a particular set of goals characterized by certain views of self and to be especially aware of a particular set of behavioral options. Thus, one can readily think of individuals who approach each task as if it were a competitive game in which some win and others lose. Similarly, a student is likely to hold a general sense that he or she can or cannot do math problems. In other words, individuals typically bring a complex of meanings derived from the past to each new situation. If you will, *meaning* as here defined may be viewed as a feature of one's personality, an enduring characteristic acquired through previous learning and experience that tends to exhibit itself in the present.

In reviewing the research on personality and motivation, there are several conclusions that can be reached which have special relevance in the present case. First, it is difficult to ignore a continuing effect of previous experiences on the way one approaches achievement situations. This point was made early on in the study of achievement motivation, perhaps most notably by McClelland and his colleagues (e.g., McClelland, 1961). While more recent work has tended to concentrate less on enduring personal traits than on cognitions that arise in achievement situations (e.g., Maehr & Nicholls, 1980), it is difficult to ignore the baggage of beliefs, thoughts, and meanings that the achiever is likely to bring to any given situation. Beliefs about self, goal preferences, awareness and acceptance of behavioral options that a person may hold in any situation undoubtedly have their precedents; they have a developmental history. While we know all too little about such history, we do know that certain social experiences are critical in the determination of these enduring meanings. Thus, for example, sense of competence in a given area is significantly affected by the appraisal of past performances (Maehr, Mensing, & Nafzger, 1962; Haas & Maehr, 1965; Ludwig & Maehr, 1967). These motivational orientations, of course, are often formed outside the school setting and are not always amenable to change by teachers.

THE TEACHING–LEARNING SITUATION

Under the first category of causes, personal experiences, emphasis is placed on the experiential background of individuals, what they bring to any given achievement situation as the result of where they have been, psychologically. Because each person brings a slightly different assortment of meanings to any given situation, one can expect individual differences in motivational patterns. However, past experience alone does not determine present meaning. The present situation counts! There are at least two aspects of the teaching–learning situation that affect the meanings held by the persons involved: *social expectations* and *task design*.

Social Expectations

In a classroom, as in any social group, social organization of some kind tends to emerge. Norms and roles come into being and social status is assigned. This social organization occurs somewhat apart from the formal curriculum. It is frequently peer initiated and peer controlled. Such organization is accompanied by sets of expectations for the participants, collectively and individually. The social group may, in an informal and nonexplicit fashion, develop its own performance norms, punishing the "rate buster" and rejecting the laggard. Moreover, along with expectations applicable to all participants there are also expectations pertinent to specific individuals. Thus, the role that an individual plays in a group is accompanied by different expectations for achievement and such expectations in turn are reportedly followed by varying levels of performance. For example, persons who are assigned a leadership role or who are accorded higher status are likely also to exhibit higher performance levels (Maehr, 1974a, b, 1978). Expectations are also associated with race and gender as well as with certain personal characteristics (e.g., Maehr, 1978).

Of course, this is all fairly basic group process theory. This theory, however, has a special relevance in the present instance. The suggestion that I wish to make is that such expectations affect achievement-related behavior as they affect the meanings that individuals hold in the situation. Thus, the expectations of the group orient individuals to strive for certain goals. The love of learning for its own sake is not in high evidence among many learning groups and woe be it unto the lone student who does view learning as "fun." She or he certainly cannot admit to it publicly. Moreover, the definition of individuals within the group is likely to define not only who they are but also what they can do. People have been known to show more achievement motivation when they are assigned a leadership role than when they are merely followers (Zander & Forward, 1968). The argument of this chapter is that this occurs because the assignment has in effect changed their view of themselves, what they can do, and the purposes of such doing. The change in meaning that has accompanied the shift in roles affects the personal investment exhibited.

Other examples and illustrations could be given, but the point should by now be self-evident: any consideration of why a student does or does not invest his or her time, talent and energy in a particular situation must involve the social expectations extant. The expectations affect the person's perception and definition of goals, action possibilities and sense of self. Change the situation, the peers, or both, and meaning and personal investment will also change.

Task Design

An important feature of any teaching–learning situation, of course, is the task itself. In this regard, it may be noted that several features of this task may affect the meaning that the task will have for the student.

First, the task may in and of itself elicit personal investment. Some tasks are in their very nature simply more attractive, interesting and inherently motivating than others. Why this is true is not altogether clear, but research on intrinsic motivation (e.g., Deci, 1975) seems to suggest that a task that possesses a certain optimum level of uncertainty and unpredictability tends to be generally attractive. While social experiences can reduce the search for novelty, new information and challenge, it appears that human beings are innately attracted to those features in tasks.

In reviewing task-related factors that determine motivation, it is natural to move quickly from physical and structural features to the social–psychological conditions which surround task performance. In this regard, performance appraisal looms as a potentially critical factor. Going beyond the mere communication of success and failure it appears that the *way* that performance appraisal is carried out may have far reaching, and often unintended consequences. Thus, for example, a growing number of studies (Fyans, *et al.,* 1981; Hill, 1980; Maehr, 1976; Maehr & Stallings, 1972; Salili *et al.,* 1976) has indicated that placing stress on tests and the teacher's evaluation of performance can have an essentially negative effect. While an emphasis on such external evaluation may momentarily enhance the performance of some students, it also has negative effects on continuing motivation (Maehr, 1976). That is, when stress is placed on external evaluation, students are less likely to continue working on the task on their own, seeking new challenges and new opportunities in this regard. They may perform for the evaluator, or when the implied reward–punishment of the evaluation is present. Remove this, however, and their motivation decidely wanes.

Interpreting these results in terms of personal investment theory, the suggestion is that evaluation conditions tend to affect the individual's definition of the goals implicit in the task (see Maehr, 1983). Specifically, external evaluation tends to rule out the establishment of more intrinsic task-related goals. Therewith, students are likely to be responsive only when extrinsic rewards are a prominent feature of the situation. Assuming that a major intent of instruction is to foster a continuing and independent interest in the subject matter, it is self-evidently desirable to foster a task–goal orientation. Reducing the emphasis on external evaluation tends to serve this purpose. Moreover, an emphasis on external evaluation may also foster a kind of competitive atmosphere. That is, in the present terms, it may serve to create an ego–goal orientation.

Similar to, and perhaps implicit in the issue of evaluation or performance appraisal, are matters of degree of freedom or choice that can be allowed in the performance of an instructional task. A number of recent studies have taken up this issue and the results are instructive. Generally, it has been found that choice and freedom are particularly significant in determining "continuing motivation." Interpreting the results in terms of personal investment theory, one might propose that variation in the degree of freedom of choice offered affects the meaning of the situation to the persons. More specifically, allowing a high degree of freedom likely fosters task goals; exercising control likely fosters extrinsic goals.

In any event, it should be quite clear that task design will affect meaning and personal investment. Certainly the preceding review of this basic assertion is more illustrative than exhaustive, but it should serve to underline the essentials of my proposal. The complementary factors of social expectations and task design account for a considerable share of the variance in motivation and achievement across classrooms. Personal investment theory suggests that they do so by changing the meaning of the task for the persons involved.

INFORMATION

A fourth factor of significance in determining meaning and personal investment is termed very simply: information. While one may imagine that information has a role to play in all facets of meaning that lead to personal investment, its role is perhaps most self-evident in regard to behavioral options. An example should make the point. Vocational information (or misinformation) likely plays an important role in determining choices that are made in taking a path to achievement. Seemingly simple matters such as setting forth the relationship between skills needed to proceed along one or another career path may change frustration to positive action. Individuals choose on the basis of perceived options. These options are in part determined by the information available to them. Of course, such information can be made available in a variety of ways: through formal or informal instruction, through literature or through the visible examples of models. But clearly the conveying of information influences the options perceived by the person.

THE SOCIAL–CULTURAL CONTEXT

Fifth, and finally, social–cultural factors likely play a major role in determining meaning of the task and therewith in creating personal investment. Most obviously, social–cultural factors play their roles in making certain behavioral options more salient and acceptable than others. To a significant extent, it is one's social–cultural group that determines that a given area is an acceptable area in which to perform. Thus, a given social–cultural group may define a task as desirable, repulsive or irrelevant. In this regard, Barkow (1975) points out that a prestige ranking of a task within a particular social–cultural group may by itself best explain the motivation exhibited by members of that group. Recently, the possible effects of social–cultural factors on the meaning of achievement has been rather directly studied. One's culture appears to affect achievement not only by defining what success and failure means (Maehr & Nicholls, 1980) but also by delineating how success and failure should be pursued (Fyans *et al.*, 1983).

For various reasons, I have been forced to present the antecedents of meaning with broad strokes and many details have been left unstated. The sources of meaning are multiple, diverse, and exceedingly complex. Yet, within the statements made above there are reasonably clear guidelines about lines of research that may be followed in pursuing the antecedents of meaning. Indeed, our own research, as well as that of others, has already provided concrete examples of how one might increasingly tie down the specific causes of meaning systems which affect personal investment.

TOWARD THE ASSESSMENT OF PERSONAL INVESTMENT

The discussion thus far has been highly theoretical; at points, speculative. Before concluding, then, it may be well to call attention to the fact that the preceding perspectives can be and currently are being operationalized.

It should be self-evident that a theory of personal investment or, for
that matter, any reliable understanding of motivation, cannot be attained without the development of measurement techniques; and, it can
also be fairly argued that it is impossible to develop valid assessment
procedures without theory. It is theory that tells one *what* and, to some
extent, *how* to measure; it is measurement that makes theory specific,
concrete—and useable. The development of assessment procedures is
really the first test of validity of a theory and so our research at this early
stage has paid attention to how one might measure the constructs that
have been proposed. While the development of a theory of personal
investment as alluded to here involves the specification of a number of
different measurement and assessment procedures, the one that has
claimed our primary attention so far revolves around the assessment of
meaning. More specifically, our attention has been primarily claimed by
the meanings that an individual might characteristically bring to any
given situation as a result of previous personal experiences or, more
specific still, our focus has been on relatively enduring goals and judgments about self that might influence how one invests his or her energy,
talent, and time.

Following the basic guidelines of the theory, it was assumed that individuals, if properly cued, could specify the goals that were important to
them and could and would provide reliable and valid information about
their feelings toward self. The theory is a cognitive theory and the assumption is that certain conscious thoughts that one has are critical in
determining behavior. How one might assist persons to specify relevant
goals and elicit judgments about themselves remains of interest. Suffice
it to say that a range of procedures has been employed, including structured (Duda, 1980, 1981) and unstructured (Braskamp, Fowler, & Ory,
1982) interviews, semantic differential procedures (Fyans *et al.*, 1983),
questionnaires of varying format (Ewing, 1981; Farmer, Maehr, &
Rooney, 1980) and even survey instruments designed for administration
over the phone (Duda, Maehr, & Kleiber, 1983). It is of special interest
that such work has apparently yielded a psychometrically sound instrument for studying meanings critical to determining personal investment
and motivation. Predictably, we have termed the instrument in question,
the *Inventory of Personal Investment* and have endeavored to exhibit a bit
of creativity in assigning it a nickname: $_IP_I$. Further, experimentation
with the instrument has yielded information interesting in its own right
about the differences in meanings that guide different persons. And
already, a variety of uses for the instrument are evident (see Maehr &
Braskamp, 1983).

While space and specific intent of this chapter permits only passing reference to such measurement efforts, it should be clear that such efforts were and are being made. Moreover, the character of these efforts may shine through to clarify further the assumptions underlying the theory that is emerging. Above all, the point is that evidence is being gathered that meanings which are associated with personal investment can be reliably assessed.

CONCLUSION

As a graduate student in the 1950s, I was alternatively fascinated by and disparaging of the wave of subjectivism that was beginning to flood the beachhead made by scientific psychology. Standing on the shoulders of Thorndike, Skinner's dicta made us all aware that it was what could be *seen* that counted. The students of Hull were willing to make inferences but within a distinctively constrained framework. Piaget had not yet experienced a rebirth and Tolman was just a chapter in Hilgard's (1956) *Theories of Learning,* which we all read and occasionally memorized. To be good scientific psychologists, we thought we had to be hard-headed behaviorists. That also meant forgetting about such "soft" constructs as self-concept and self-actualization. It also made us wary of thinking about the role of goals and purpose in determining human behavior because this smacked of teleology.

Faced with conducting my dissertation research, I had a sinful desire to study self-actualization. I had read Carl Rogers and Abraham Maslow and was enthralled. I had read Gordon Allport and was sure that he provided the appropriate integration of all the thoughts that had been popping around in my head, but I was dissuaded from indulging myself in the study of the subjective. In retrospect, I can truly say that it was good advice that I received. The time was not then right for studying selfhood, purpose, or values, particularly if one was a student hoping to complete a doctorate in a reasonably short period of time. Basic work on cognition and motivation had to be done first. Basic methodologies had to be developed and procedures constructed before one could hope to attain a level of success in the study of the subjective. It is my belief that that work has now been done and I suggest a return to the kind of interests that were indeed expressed several decades ago by the likes of Rogers, Maslow, and Allport. Hopefully, this chapter has provided not only an example of how such a study might be pursued but suggests also the implications that pursuing such study might hold in developing a psychology of motivation for the practitioner.

REFERENCES

Allport, G. W. *Becoming: Basic considerations for a psychology of personality.* New Haven: Yale University Press, 1955.

Ames, R. Help-seeking and achievement orientation: Perspectives from attribution theory. In B. DePaulo, A. Nadler, & J. Fisher (Eds.), *New directions in helping.* New York: Academic Press, 1984.

Atkinson, J. W. Motivational determinants of risk-taking behavior. *Psychological Review,* 1957, *64,* 359–372.

Atkinson, J. W. (Ed.). *Motives in fantasy, action, an society.* New York: Van Nostrand, 1958.

Atkinson, J. W., & Feather, N. T. (Eds.). *A theory of achievement motivation.* New York: Wiley, 1966.

Atkinson, J. W., & Raynor, J. O. (Eds.). *Motivation and achievement.* New York: Wiley, 1974.

Barkow, J. W. Attention structure and the evolution of human psychological characteristics. In M. R. A. Chance & R. R. Larsen (Eds.), *The social structure of attention.* London: Wiley, 1975.

Bloom, B. S. The role of gifts and markers in the development of talent. *Exceptional Children,* 1982, *48,* 510–522. (a)

Bloom, B. S. The master teachers. *Phi Delta Kappan,* 1982, *63,* 664–668, 715. (b)

Boring, E. G. *A history of experimental psychology* (2nd ed.). New York: Appleton-Century-Crofts, 1950.

Braskamp, L. A., & Maehr, M. L. *Inventory of personal investment.* Measurement instrument available from authors, University of Illinois, Urbana-Champaign, 1983.

Braskamp, L. A., Fowler, D. A., & Ory, J. C. *Faculty development and achievement: A faculty's view.* Manuscript submitted for publication, 1982.

Csikszentmihalyi, M. *Beyond boredom and anxiety.* San Francisco: Jossey-Bass, 1975.

Csikszentmihalyi, M. Intrinsic rewards and emergent motivation. In M. R. Lepper & D. Greene (Eds.), *The hidden costs of reward.* Hillsdale, NJ: Erlbaum, 1978.

deCharms, R. *Personal behavior.* New York: Academic Press, 1968.

Deci, E. L. *Intrinsic motivation.* New York: Plenum, 1975.

Deci, E. L. *The psychology of self-determination.* Lexington, MA: Heath, 1980.

Duda, J. Achievement motivation among Navajo students: A conceptual analysis with preliminary data. *Ethos,* 1980, *8-4,* 316–337.

Duda, J. *A cross-cultural analysis of achievement motivation in sport and the classroom.* Unpublished doctoral dissertation, University of Illinois at Urbana-Champaign, 1981.

Duda, J., Maehr, M. L., & Kleiber, D. A. Motivational orientations in the later years. Research in progress.

Ewing, M. E. *Achievement orientations and sport behavior of males and females.* Unpublished doctoral dissertation, University of Illinois at Urbana-Champaign, 1981.

Farmer, H., Maehr, M. L., & Rooney, G. *Attribution and values for personal success, failures, and future goals.* Unpublished manuscript, 1980. (Measurement instrument available from Department of Educational Psychology, University of Illinois at Urbana-Champaign).

Feather, N. T. (Ed.). *Expectations and actions: Expectancy-value models in psychology.* Hillsdale, NJ: Erlbaum, 1982.

Frieze, I. H. Beliefs about success and failure in the classroom. In J. H. McMillen (Ed.), *The social psychology of school learning.* New York: Academic Press, 1980.

Frieze, I. H., Shomo, K. H., & Francis, W. D. Determinants of subjective feelings of success. In *Teacher and student perceptions of success and failure: Implications for learning.* Unpublished paper presented at the LRDC Conference, Pittsburg, PA, October 25–26, 1979.

Fyans, L. J., Jr., Kremer, B., Salili, F., & Maehr, M. L. The effects of evaluation conditions on continuing motivation: A study of the cultural, personological, and situational antecedents of a motivational pattern. *International Journal of Intercultural Relations,* 1981, *5,* 1–22.

Fyans, L. J., Jr., & Maehr, M. L. Attributional style, task selection and achievement. *Journal of Educational Psychology,* 1979, *71,* 499–507.

Fyans, L. J., Jr., Salili, F., Maehr, M. L., & Desai, K. A. A cross-cultural exploration into the meaning of achievement. *Journal of Personality and Social Psychology,* 1983, *44,* 1000–1013.

Haas, H. I., & Maehr, M. L. Two experiments on the concept of self and the reactions of others. *Journal of Personality and Social Psychology,* 1965, *1,* 100–105.

Harter, S. A model of intrinsic mastery motivation in children: Individual differences and developmental change. In W. A. Collins (Ed.), *Minnesota symposium in child psychology* (Vol. 14). Hillsdale, NJ: Erlbaum, 1980.

Harter, S. Developmental perspectives in the self-system. In M. Hetherington (Ed.), *Carmichael's manual of child psychology.* New York: Wiley, 1982.

Harter, S., & Connell, J. P. A structural model of the relationships among children's academic achievement and their self-perceptions of competence, control, and motivational orientation in the cognitive domain. In J. Nicholls (Ed.), *The development of achievement motivation.* Greenwich, CT: JAI Press, in press.

Henahan, D. The mystery of the dropout composer. *New York Times* (Section 2—Music Review), Sunday, March 14, 1982, pp. 1; 23.

Hilgard, E. *Theories of learning* (2nd ed.). New York: Appleton-Century-Crofts, 1956.

Hill, K. T. Motivation, evaluation, and testing policy. In L. J. Fyans, Jr. (Ed.), *Achievement motivation: Recent trends in theory, and research.* New York: Plenum, 1980.

Kelly, J. R. Leisure in later life: Roles and identities. In N. Osgood (Ed.), *Life after retirement.* New York: Praeger, 1982.

Klinger, E. *Meaning and void: Inner experience and the incentives in people's lives.* Minneapolis: University of Minnesota Press, 1977.

Kuhlen, R. G. Developmental changes in motivation during adult years. In J. E. Birren (Ed.), *Relations of development and aging.* Springfield, IL: Thomas, 1964.

Kukla, A. An attributional theory of choice. In L. Berkowitz (Ed.), *Advances in experimental social psychology* (Vol. 11). New York: Academic Press, 1978.

Lepper, M. R., & Greene, D. (Eds.). *The hidden costs of reward: New perspectives on the psychology of human motivation.* Hillsdale, NJ: Erlbaum, 1978.

Ludwig, D. J., & Maehr, M. L. Changes in self concept and stated behavioral preferences. *Child Development,* 1967, *38,* 453–467.

McClelland, D. C. *The achieving society.* New York: Free Press, 1961.

McClelland, D. C., Atkinson, J. W., Clark, R. A., & Cowell, E. L. *The achievement motive.* New York: Appleton-Century-Crofts, 1953.

Maehr, M. L. *Sociocultural origins of achievement.* Monterey: Brooks/Cole, 1974. (a)

Maehr, M. L. Culture and achievement motivation. *American Psychologist,* 1974, *29,* 887–896. (b)

Maehr, M. L. Continuing motivation: An analysis of a seldom considered educational outcome. *Review of Educational Research,* 1976, *46,* 443–462.

Maehr, M. L. Sociocultural origins of achievement. In D. Bar-Tal & L. Saxe (Eds.), *Social psychology of education: Theory and research.* New York: Wiley, 1978.

Maehr, M. L. On doing well in science: Why Johnny no longer excels; why Sarah never did. In S. Paris, G. Olson, & N. Stephenson (Eds.), *Learning and motivation in the classroom.* Hillsdale, NJ: Erlbaum, in press.

Maehr, M. L., & Braskamp, L. A. *Personal investment: Motivation, achievement, and life satisfaction.* Book in preparation.

Maehr, M. L., & Kleiber, D. The graying of America: Implications for achievement motivation theory and research. In L. J. Fyans, Jr. (Ed.), *Achievement motivation.* New York: Plenum, 1980.

Maehr, M. L., & Kleiber, D. A. The graying of achievement motivation. *American Psychologist,* 1981, *36,* 787–793.

Maehr, M. L., Mensing, J., & Nafzger, S. Concept of self and the reaction of others. *Sociometry,* 1962, *25,* 353–357.

Maehr, M. L., & Nicholls, J. G. Culture and achievement motivation: A second look. In N. Warren (Ed.), *Studies in cross-cultural psychology* (Vol. 3). New York: Academic Press, 1980.

Maehr, M. L., & Sjogren, D. Atkinson's theory of achievement motivation: First step toward a theory of academic motivation? *Review of Educational Research,* 1971, *41,* 143–161.

Maehr, M. L., & Stallings, W. M. Freedom from external evaluation. *Child Development,* 1972, *43,* 177–185.

Maehr, M. L., & Willig, A. C. Expecting too much or too little: Student freedom and responsibility in the classroom. In H. Walberg & R. Luckie (Eds.), *Improving educational productivity: The research basis of school standards.* Chicago: NSSE Series in Contemporary Issues in Education, 1982.

Messick, S., & Brayfield, A. H. (Eds.). *Decision and choice.* New York: McGraw-Hill, 1964.

Miller, G. A., Galanter, E., & Pribram, K. H. *Plans and the structure of behavior.* New York: Holt, Rinehart & Winston, 1960.

Murray, H. A. *Explorations in personality.* New York: Oxford University Press, 1938.

Nicholls, J. G. Quality and inequality in intellectual development: The role of motivation in education. *American Psychologist,* 1979, *34,* 1071–1084.

Nicholls, J. G. Conceptions of ability and achievement motivation: A theory and its implications for education. In S. G. Paris, G. M. Olson, & H. W. Stevenson (Eds.), *Learning and motivation in the classroom.* Hillsdale, NJ: Erlbaum, in press.

Ouchi, W. *Theory Z corporations: How American business can meet the Japanese challenge.* Reading, MA: Addison-Wesley, 1981.

Roberts, G. C. Achievement motivation and sport behavior. In R. Terjung (Ed.), *Exercise sport science review.* Philadelphia, PA: Franklin Institute Press, 1982.

Roberts, G. C. Achievement motivation in children's sport. In J. G. Nicholls (Ed.), *The development of achievement motivation.* Greenwich, CT: JAI Press, in press.

Salili, F., Maehr, M. L., Sorensen, R. L., & Fyans, L. J., Jr. A further consideration of the effects of evaluation on motivation. *American Educational Research Journal,* 1976, *13,* 85–102.

Sorensen, R. L., & Maehr, M. L. Toward the experimental analysis of "continuing motivation." *Journal of Educational Research,* 1976, *69,* 319–322.

Weiner, B. A theory of motivation for some classroom experiences. *Journal of Educational Psychology,* 1979, *71,* 3–25.

White, R. W. Motivation reconsidered: The concept of competence. *Psychological Review,* 1959, *66,* 297–333.

White, R. W. Competence and the psychosexual stages of development. In M. R. Jones (Ed.), *Nebraska symposium on motivation.* Lincoln: University of Nebraska Press, 1960.

Willig, A. C., Harnisch, D. L., Hill, K. T., & Maehr, M. L. Sociocultural and educational correlates of success–failure attributions and evaluation anxiety in the school setting for Black, Hispanic, and Anglo children. *American Educational Research Journal,* 1983, *20,* 385–410.

Zander, A., & Forward, J. Position in group, achievement motivation, and group aspirations. *Journal of Personality and Social Psychology,* 1968, *8,* 282–288.

5

The Development of Achievement Motivation

Deborah J. Stipek

A CONCEPTUAL FRAMEWORK

Developmental issues are relevant to all theoretical approaches to achievement motivation. Developmental processes must be considered whether, for example, independence training, reinforcement contingencies, or cognitions are assumed to explain behavior in achievement settings. To train independence, performance demands made on children must be continually modified as children develop new competencies. What constitutes an effective reinforcer also changes as a function of experience and age. And achievement-related cognitions naturally change as a result of children's developing information-processing skills.

Achievement-motivation theorists have, to varying degrees, acknowledged the relevance of developmental factors. But as the popularity of theories rise and fall, so also do particular developmental concerns in the achievement-motivation literature. For many years, consistent with Mc-Clelland's and Atkinson's model of achievement motivation, developmental researchers examined primarily the effect of early socialization experiences on presumably stable individual differences in achievement striving. Thus, researchers studied explicit independence training (Rosen & D'Andrade, 1959; Winterbottom, 1958), or other child-rearing practices believed to affect achievement motivation and achievement behavior (Crandall, 1967).

145

Reinforcement models are usually given brief review in theoretical discussions of achievement motivation because strict learning theorists have not paid particular attention to achievement behaviors per se. Rather, they have assumed that behavior in achievement settings follows the same principles that apply to all behavior. Ironically, simple behavioral models have probably influenced the practice of teaching (at least of teacher training) more than any theoretical model exclusively concerned with achievement behavior (see Anderson & Faust, 1973; Ausubel, Novak, & Hanesian, 1978). Although some recent educational psychology texts (see Biehler & Snowman, 1982; Clifford, 1981) discuss more cognitive theories of motivation, developmental change has not been a major concern in behavioral research, except inasmuch as the effectiveness of reinforcers change as a function of a child's age and experience.

To be sure, from a practical standpoint, developmental change in achievement behavior is our primary concern. However, in recent years the view that cognitions determine behavior has gained adherents among social psychologists and personality theorists. In developmental psychology, given the prominence of Piaget's view that cognitive development involves qualitative change, it is not surprising that many researchers have begun to investigate the relevance of cognitive developmental change for achievement motivation (see review chapters by Ruble, 1980; Stipek, in press).

Consistent with current interest in cognitive constructs believed to underlie achievement behavior, this chapter focuses on recent developments in our understanding of developmental change in achievement-related cognitions—performance expectancies, self-perceptions of competence, and perceptions of the cause of achievement outcomes—and in the cognitive processes (e.g., information processing) assumed to mediate change in these cognitive constructs. Children's processing of performance feedback is emphasized because interpretation of evaluative feedback is assumed to be the most important factor in the development of these achievement-related cognitions.

Briefer consideration is given to development regarding several affect-related motivational constructs that are believed to influence achievement behavior, including the value children place on achievement outcomes, their affect regarding school in general, and their emotional response to specific achievement outcomes.[1] Developmental change in

---

[1]*Values* here refer to the positive or negative valence, in Lewinian terms, of the attitude object, which in this case is performance outcomes. *Affect* is used rather than *attitude* to emphasize the affective, as opposed to the cognitive, components of attitudes. Here *affect* refers to both the child's evaluation of school (e.g., its positive or negative valence) and the emotional responses associated with being in or thinking about school. Emotional re-

children's goals in engaging in academic tasks, that is, their perception of the reason for engaging in a task, is also mentioned.

The chapter is based on the view that the development of achievement motivation can only be understood in terms of an ongoing interaction between children and their educational environments. This perspective is different from that taken in early developmental research related to achievement motivation that assumed a unidirectional socialization model in which children were "molded" by their parents and other socializing agents. It is also a departure from more recent developmental research (including my own) that focuses on the effect that changes in cognitive capacities have on achievement-related cognitions and behavior, with only passing acknowledgment of the impact of the child's environment on the development of achievement-related cognitions. Although the home environment is acknowledged to influence achievement motivation, this chapter focuses on the school environment.

An interactive approach is taken because changes in the classroom environment, such as, performance demands, direct encouragement for achievement striving, incentives, reinforcement, and so forth, accompany changes in children's achievement-related cognitions. These changes in the environment presumably occur largely in response to changes in the child. But they also may reinforce, extend, or delay those changes. A comprehensive model of achievement motivation therefore needs to consider changes taking place within the child, in the environment, and perhaps most importantly, the interaction between these two sets of variables. We begin with a review of observed changes in achievement behavior and in the achievement-related constructs that are believed to mediate achievement behavior.

DEVELOPMENTAL CHANGE IN ACHIEVEMENT MOTIVATION CHARACTERISTICS

ACHIEVEMENT BEHAVIOR

In the absence of comparative observational data, some of the claims made here about age changes in achievement behavior are based on my

---

sponses to specific performance outcomes refer to the child's emotional state as a consequence of succeeding or failing in an academic task. These distinctions follow from conventional views of attitudes as consisting of cognitive, affective, and behavioral components (see Freedman, Sears, & Carlsmith, 1981).

own informal observations, which need to be validated in systematic observational research. Note also that there is huge variation in children's behavior in achievement settings at any age. Whereas some of the cognitive developmental variables discussed in this chapter appear to be relatively uniform, behavioral changes are far from universal. Nevertheless, there are apparently developmental trends in behavior which need to be explained. These trends are particularly important to understand because children manifest negative or self-defeating behaviors in achievement settings with increasing frequency as they get older and advance in grade in school.

Picture for a moment a prototypical preschool. Most children, if not all, are actively engaged in some self-initiated activity. Learning situations are approached eagerly and with apparent confidence. Failure occasionally occurs (e.g., the tower of blocks falls over when the final block is added; the puzzle does not get put together). But, my own observations suggest that failure rarely causes serious emotional anguish—mild frustration perhaps, but no obvious shame or embarrassment. Frequently, the goal or the rules of the game are changed (e.g., a game of building a tower is changed to a game of knocking down the tower; puzzle pieces that would not fit properly into the frame are piled up or spread out over the table). Children's attention seems to be focused on the process more than on the outcome of their efforts and there is little apparent anxiety about external evaluation of their products.

When children enter first grade they encounter a more structured educational environment, in which they are required to complete specific learning tasks designated by the teacher. Nevertheless, I have observed relatively few signs of performance anxiety or fearfulness about academic tasks among first graders. Rather, many teachers have informed me that their first-grade students' primary motivational problem concern working independently in a structured academic environment. For example, young students often fail to listen to instructions given to the whole class, and then one by one they approach the teacher to find out what they are supposed to do on an assignment. Or they ask for help, whether they need it or not, presumably because they enjoy the personal contact with the teacher. However, they typically approach their work enthusiastically and confidently.

Unfortunately, later on in elementary school, many children approach learning tasks less confidently. Maladaptive failure–avoidance and learned helpless behaviors observed in elementary classrooms have been poignantly described by Covington and Beery (1976) and other astute classroom observers (e.g., Holt, 1964; Jackson, 1968). Anxiety about failure and external evaluation can be seen in the child who never volunteers an answer, exerts little effort on assignments, or selects the easiest or the impossibly difficult tasks. The "helpless" child may seek help unnecessarily or give up without ever trying. Not all children in the upper elementary grades manifest these self-defeating behaviors, but typically the higher the grade in school, the more likely these behaviors will be observed.

There is some research evidence to support these proposed graderelated changes in achievement behavior. Rholes, Blackwell, Jordan, and Walters (1980) found that preschool-age children were less susceptible to the behavioral effects (i.e., learned helplessness) of experimentally induced failure than were older children. Miller (1982) similarly found impaired performance for sixth graders, but not for second graders who had experienced a series of failures. Weisz (1979) provides further evidence for retarded children, who presumably experience a significant amount of failure in achievement settings. In his study, retarded children did not manifest relatively more maladaptive achievement behavior in an experimental setting than normal children until the later grades of elementary school.

What accounts for these changes in children's achievement behavior? Consistent with the view that achievement behavior is influenced by children's cognitions, we review concomitant changes observed by researchers on several cognitive dimensions. Developmental change in the value children place on achievement outcomes, their affect toward school in general, their emotional response to specific achievement outcomes, and their perceptions of the reasons for engaging in achievement tasks are also discussed. Then we consider explanations for developmental change in these motivational constructs, with specific attention to the evaluative feedback children receive, attend to, and process.

COGNITIONS

Three interrelated cognitions are considered particularly relevant to achievement behavior: performance expectancies, self-perceptions of competence, and perceptions of the cause of achievement outcomes (Weiner, 1979). With regard to performance expectancies, studies find consistently that children's expectations for success at academic performance remain high, often unrealistically high, until about the second or third grade, and continue to decrease, on the average, throughout the elementary grades. For example, in a nonexperimental, longitudinal study Entwisle and Hayduk (1978) asked children entering first and second grade to predict the grades they would receive in math and reading. Nearly all first-grade children maintained high expectations despite teachers' and parents' low expectations for some children and despite grades indicating, on the average, lower performance than the children had predicted. Not until the end of the second grade did children's expected grades correlate fairly well with their actual performance.

Experimental studies have produced further evidence suggesting that young children typically overestimate their future performance and that performance predictions decrease with age (Clifford, 1975, 1978; Goss, 1968; Parsons, Moses, & Yulish-Muszynski, 1977; Parsons & Ruble, 1972, 1977; Phillips, 1963; Stipek & Hoffman, 1980; see Stipek, in press for a review). In all of these studies, until the age of about 6 or 7 years, children maintained high expectations for success despite poor performance on past trials. Results of my own studies on young children's expectations for success on experimental tasks are typical of other researchers' findings. In one study (Stipek & Hoffman, 1980), we gave children a balance task that allowed us to experimentally control performance outcomes. The goal of the task was to raise a platform to the top of a tower without a metal ball falling off. Preschool-age children's predictions for their own future performance were unaffected by their past performance histories on this task. They almost invariably expected to get the platform to the top, even though they barely got the platform off the base without the ball falling off on four previous trials. The predictions of second and third graders, and to some degree, of kindergarten and first graders, declined as a function of the cumulative failure experience.

This same tendency to be optimistic about the probability of success, despite past objective evidence that would suggest future failure to most adults, has been found in studies of young children's accuracy in predicting their memory (Flavell, Friedrichs, & Hoyt, 1970; Yussen & Berman, 1981; Yussen & Levy, 1975). These researchers have found that preschoolers grossly overestimate the amount of information they will remember, despite poor performance on previous identical memory tasks. Over the first few years of school, children's performance predictions on experimental tasks and in studies of metamemory increasingly reflect objective past performance feedback (that is, lower predictions are associated with poorer past performance).

Children's self-perceptions of competence have also been found to decline, on the average, over the elementary school years. Studies have found, for example, that young children's ability ratings are not as affected by objective success or failure feedback as are older children's (Ruble, Parsons, & Ross, 1976; Shaklee, 1976; Shaklee & Tucker, 1979). Younger children are not just inaccurate, they typically overestimate their ability or performance level. Generally children are found to have uniformly positive perceptions of their competence until about the second grade; their self-evaluations increasingly correlate with teachers' evaluations of objective performance criteria as they advance through the elementary grades (Eshel & Klein, 1981; Nicholls, 1978, 1979). Further evidence suggests a relatively steep decline in self-evaluations soon after children enter junior high (Rosenberg, 1979; Simmons, Blyth, Van Cleave, & Bush, 1979; Simmons, Rosenberg, & Rosenberg, 1973; see Parsons, Midgley, & Adler, in press, for a review).

Perceptions of the cause of achievement outcomes also change with development. Children in the early elementary grades seem to emphasize effort as a cause, whereas older children attribute performance outcomes to ability and other factors, in addition to effort (Parsons, 1974). This shift, which is discussed in more detail later, probably occurs primarily because younger children do not differentiate effort and ability. In adolescence, individuals rate ability as a more important cause of performance outcomes than effort, whereas younger children tend to rate effort as the more important cause (Nicholls & Miller, in press).

VALUES

Although values formally figure into the original expectancy × value theories of achievement motivation (e.g., Atkinson, 1964), values have been given considerably less attention by achievement motivation theorists and researchers than have expectancies. Yet, clearly a child who cares little about academic achievement is not likely to exert much effort in achievement contexts, regardless of his or her expectation for success or any other achievement-related cognition. To be sure, values vary among children in any age group. However, there may be systematic developmental shifts that need to be considered in a developmental theory of achievement motivation.

My own research on children in kindergarten and first grade suggests that "academic achievement" per se is of little concern to these young children (Stipek, 1981; Stipek & Tannatt, in press). Indeed, as will be seen later, academic achievement is not fully differentiated from conduct. Over the first few years of school, children learn to differentiate between academic achievement and good behavior and they learn that academic achievement is valued in our society.

There is some evidence to suggest that young children treat the classroom more as a social environment than as an academic environment. Brophy and Evertson (1981) report a decline, over the elementary school grades, in personal, nonacademic, and approval-seeking child-initiated contacts with teachers, and an increase in child-initiated academic contacts. These data suggest that social needs decline and academic concerns increase over the elementary school years.

As children enter adolescence, peer approval increases in importance, as does demonstrating physical prowess. Consequently, for some students, school achievement may decline in value. Adolescents who have experienced considerable academic failure in school may be especially likely to devalue school achievement in order to maintain a favorable self image. For other adolescents who have begun to consider long term educational and occupational aspirations, academic achievement may increase in importance.

These hypothesized shifts in values surely have important implications for achievement behavior. Very young children, for example, may concentrate on being "good" more than on performing well. Some adolescents may actually exert effort to *avoid* high academic performance to maintain good peer relations. Other adolescents may begin, for the first time, to take school work seriously. Regrettably, because so little attention has been given to the effect of achievement values on achievement behavior, we can only speculate about what this relationship might be.

AFFECTS

Research on affect toward school in general typically reports increasingly negative evaluations as children advance in grade school (Neale & Proshek, 1967; Parsons, Adler, Futterman, Goff, Kaczala, Meece, & Midgley, in press; Yamamoto, Thomas, & Karns, 1969). A particularly sharp decline in positive affects has been observed among young adolescents in junior high (Haladyna & Thomas, 1979).

There is little evidence on developmental change in the emotional lives of children in achievement contexts, or on emotional responses to particular achievement outcomes. Weiner, Anderson, and Prawat (1982) provide evidence that fourth and fifth graders use many more negative than positive affective labels to describe their emotional lives in the classroom, but no comparable data is available at other age levels.

GOALS

There is some evidence suggesting a developmental change in children's perceived goals in engaging in achievement behavior. Studies find that, compared to older children, younger children are more likely to claim that they engage in achievement-related behaviors to satisfy their own needs for mastery (i.e., they are *intrinsically* motivated); older children are more likely than younger children to report extrinsic reinforcement (e.g., grades) as a reason for engaging in achievement-related activities (i.e., they are more *extrinsically* motivated; Blumenfeld & Pintrich, 1982; DeCharms, 1980; Gottfried, 1981; Harter, 1981a). This shift from perceived intrinsic or extrinsic motivation is especially marked at the beginning of junior high (Parsons, Midgley, & Adler, in press). Harter (1981a) reports a marked decrease in reported preference for challenging as opposed to easy assignments occurring also at the beginning of junior high.

SUMMARY

In summary, it has been proposed that, on the average, children value academic achievement more as they progress through school, but their expectations for success and self-perceptions of competence decline, and their affect toward school becomes more negative. Children also become increasingly concerned about achievement outcomes and the reinforcement (e.g., high grades) associated with positive outcomes and less concerned about intrinsic satisfaction in achieving greater competence.

Developmental change on all of these achievement-motivational dimensions is likely to influence children's behavior in achievement settings. Indeed, it may explain, in part, the proposed increase in maladaptive failure-avoidance and learned helpless behavior. It is therefore important to explore possible explanations for the cognitive and affective changes. Performance evaluation is undoubtedly an important factor in the development of these achievement-motivational constructs. What teachers' emphasize in evaluation (e.g., conduct, effort, or outcome) informs children what is valued and thus presumably influences their own values. Performance feedback also serves as a basis for both children's achievement-related cognitions (e.g., expectations, perceived competence, and performance attributions) and emotions (e.g., happiness, disappointment, fear, pride, shame). Over time, performance feedback can influence attitudes toward school in general or toward specific subject matter, and it serves as an incentive (goal) for future achievement-related behaviors.

The nature of the performance feedback children receive in school changes with grade. Also changing, as a result of socialization and the development of information-processing abilities, are children's attention to, and processing of, evaluative feedback. These changes in the school environment and in the child are presumed to mediate the changes in the preceding achievement-motivational constructs. Accordingly, next we examine developmental change in the evaluative feedback children receive, attend to, and process.

PERFORMANCE FEEDBACK

Feedback takes many forms in the classroom, including social evaluation ("The teacher said I was a good speller."), symbolic evaluation ("The teacher usually puts a star on my paper, or an 'A' "), objective past performance, ("I usually get 100% on my spelling test."), or normative feedback ("I usually get the highest score in the class."). The following sections review developmental change regarding how children process these different kinds of performance feedback, the kind of feedback they attend to, and the kind of feedback that is most prominent in their classroom.

SOCIAL EVALUATIVE FEEDBACK

Young children may attend more to social reinforcement—praise or criticism—than to objective, symbolic or normative feedback directly related to their performance. Thus, a nice, socially reinforcing, or encouraging teacher is probably a more important factor in young children's achievement-related cognitions than is their actual performance on tasks. The evidence on this proposition is scarce, but generally supportive.

Spear and Armstrong (1978) found that, compared to older elementary school children, kindergarten and first-grade children's performance on motor and learning tasks was relatively more affected by social reinforcement statements made by adults than by peer comparisons. There is additional evidence suggesting that young children attend to and respond more to social reinforcement than to "objective" feedback (Lewis, Wall, & Aronfreed, 1963; Meid, 1971).

Lewis et al. (1963), for example, gave first and fifth graders a binary probability choice task. Reinforcement for pushing the left and right levers was given with a ratio of .70:.30. Half of the children in each grade were given verbal praise and the other half were given correctness feedback (a green light) for each "correct" choice. Only the first graders who received social reinforcement pulled the left lever with increasing frequency, consequently maximizing the amount of praise they received. These results indicate that the first graders, but not the fifth graders, were more responsive to the social reinforcement than to the objective correctness feedback.

In a dissertation by Meid (1971, described in Harter, 1978), 6- and 10-year-olds were given objective information regarding their past performance (high, medium, and low) and adult verbal reinforcement or feedback (praise, no comment, and mildly negative comments). The younger children's expectations for performance on a subsequent task were based entirely on the social feedback, even when the social feedback conflicted with the objective feedback. The older children took both objective feedback and social feedback into account in their expectancy statements.

Young children's focus on social reinforcement and their relative inattention to other indices of performance outcomes may be related to their relative inexperience with adults who are not in a parenting or caretaking role. Young children may regard their teachers as they regard their parents, rather than as adults who have a more narrowly defined role. Children's attention to objective performance feedback may increase, in part, because they become aware that teachers' regard for children is to some degree conditional upon academic performance.

Adult evaluation may also carry greater weight with younger than with older children because until children reach concrete operations, they apparently attribute full evaluative and moral authority to adults. Furthermore, guided by what Kohlberg (1969) refers to as the "good boy" or "good girl" principle of moral behavior, they are especially concerned about pleasing adults. Accordingly, young children are concerned about teacher approval and they may internalize the teachers' verbal feedback at face value without questioning its legitimacy, whether or not the feedback is at all linked to good performance.

What aspects of the educational environment in the early-elementary grades might contribute to young children's primary attention to social evaluation? In the kindergarten and first-grade classrooms that I have observed social reinforcement seems to be the predominant form of evaluative feedback. Symbolic evaluative feedback (e.g., happy faces and stars) is also common, but this is often given in conjunction with verbal comments. Teachers of young children may use social reinforcement naturally because the children respond to it. However, children who experience the rare kindergarten teacher who emphasizes objective outcomes or grades might attend to these more "mature" forms of evaluation earlier than children who experience the more typical teacher who relies primarily on social reinforcement.

Given this emphasis on social reinforcement, it is perhaps not surprising that young children have a positive view of their competency and high expectations for success. The social reinforcement young children receive directly regarding the products of their achievement activities is typically positive. My own observations suggest that the products of preschool-age children's achievement efforts, for example, are usually not criticized unless some rule of conduct is broken (e.g., the drawing is made on the wall rather than on a piece of paper). Even then, the criticism is most likely directed to the forbidden act, not the quality of the product. Who would dare reply to a 5-year-old exhibiting his or her uninterpretable drawing, "What an ugly picture, you sure can't draw very well."

Brophy (1981) also points out that praise in early elementary school classrooms is not always contingent on good performance. Anderson, Evertson, and Brophy (1979) found that first-grade children in reading groups were just as likely to be praised following reading turns with mistakes as they were following errorless reading turns. Brophy (1981) describes many reasons for which praise is given, aside from providing evaluative performance information. Thus, the teacher may say "good" to a child at the end of a reading turn to "balance out" the many error corrections made while the child was reading. Young children presumably accept this praise at face value, interpreting it as a positive judgment of their reading competence, in contrast to children after the age of about 12 years, who have been found to interpret praise of relatively low performance as an indication of *low* ability (Meyer, Bachmann, Biermann, Hempelmann, Ploger, & Spiller, 1979).

The amount of positive feedback children receive in the classroom may also decrease during the elementary school grades. Blumenfeld, Wessels, Pintrich and Meece (1981) found that positive academic feedback constituted a higher proportion of teacher comments to second graders than to sixth graders. They suggest that the grade difference in positive reinforcement resulted from different instructional organizations typical of second and sixth grade classrooms. Second graders are more likely to receive instruction in small groups than are sixth graders. Consequently, the younger children have more opportunity to receive positive social feedback directed toward them individually.

Social evaluation may be salient for young children, then, in part because they are particularly attentive to and accept at face value the positive social evaluation they receive, and they receive a considerable amount of positive social evaluation, some of which is not contingent upon good performance.

SYMBOLIC FEEDBACK

Children receive symbolic feedback regarding their performance in a variety of forms. Grades, of course, are the prevailing form of symbolic performance feedback, but smiling faces, gold stars, and other more idiosyncratic forms are common, especially in the early elementary school grades. For children to base their performance-related cognitions on symbolic feedback they must understand the representational quality of the symbol and they must process and interpret this feedback much in the same way that they would use objective feedback.

Some symbols (e.g., happy faces) given in the early grades are explicitly related to social approval and because they are probably not fully differentiated from social reinforcement, they may affect achievement-related cognition and affects earlier than grades. Teachers in kindergarten and first grade undoubtedly reinforce the link between social approval and symbolic feedback by giving social and symbolic feedback simultaneously (e.g., "You did a very good job on this assignment; I am putting a star, or an 'A,' at the top of your paper"), thereby inculcating the value of such symbols of achievement. Grades, however, would not affect achievement-related cognitions or emotions until children learn their value and meaning (i.e., that they reflect teacher or parent approval). The age at which good grades are perceived as desirable is probably largely dependent on the degree to which early elementary school teachers and parents emphasize grades and the degree to which significant adults give approval contingent upon high grades.

There is some variation in findings regarding the age at which children's own perceptions of their competence reflect accurately the grades they have received. Entwisle and Hayduk (1978) found in the study described earlier that children's expected grades did not correlate significantly with their actual performance until the end of second grade. Nicholls (1978, 1979) has found that children's self-ratings of ability were not significantly related to grades or ratings given by the teacher until third or fourth grade. Eshel and Klein (1981) report a steady increase in the correlations between middle-SES children's expected and actual grades in math and reading from first through fourth grade, with the largest increment occurring between the second and third grade. This pattern was less regular for lower-SES children.

Gradually, grades and other kinds of symbolic performance feedback take on their own value. However, the performance information derived from grades may change during middle childhood. Most children probably learn that a good grade is more desirable than a bad grade soon after they enter school. But evidence to be discussed later suggests that the normative information contained in grades is not as relevant to younger children as it is to older children. A first grader may be just as proud receiving an A when every child in the class receives an A as he or she would be if only a few A's were given. For older children, the same symbolic feedback may be valued primarily because of the normative information it provides.

"Objective feedback" is used here to denote correctness, with no additional evaluative or normative information. Children are given objective feedback on their academic work as early as kindergarten, and definitely in first grade. Yet, as noted previously, considerable evidence suggests that objective feedback does not have the same meaning, and consequently does not mediate achievement-related cognitions in the same way for younger and older children. Recall, for example, that experimental studies indicate that despite compelling past objective performance evidence to the contrary, preoperational children typically predict successful future performance and maintain positive perceptions of their competence.

Performance feedback increasingly influences children's achievement related cognitions over the early elementary school grades. Research on children's interpretation of feedback and other developmental changes in children's thinking suggest several explanations for these observed changes in their use of objective performance feedback. The two explanations discussed subsequently—cognitive processing and wishful thinking—are not mutually exclusive. Rather, they may both contribute to developmental change in children's performance-related cognitions.

Cognitive Processing

Evidence that young children expect success and maintain high perceptions of ability even after a series of objective failure experiences suggests that they are unable to process and integrate a sequence of past failures. This interpretation is consistent with Inhelder and Piaget's (1964) observations that preoperational children have difficulty integrating temporally separate events.

Even if young children attend to and process objective past performance information, that information may not always have the same implications for future performance that it has for older children. Note that past performance is relevant to future performance only if some stability in performance is assumed. Older children and adults presumably believe that past performance reflects ability level, and since ability is somewhat stable, future performance should partly reflect past performance.

There is some evidence suggesting that young children do not have a concept of ability as a stable trait that has implications for future performance. Dweck (in press) proposes that young children have an "incremental" view of ability; they assume that ability is unstable and, to some degree, influenced by practice and effort. Consistent with Dweck's conceptualization is research suggesting that, for young children, ability and effort are undifferentiated (Karabenick & Heller, 1976; Kun, 1977; Nicholls, 1978).

Interviews of young children provide further evidence of an "incremental" view of competence. In one study, I asked children to explain their assessments of their own and their peers' ability in school. Of the kindergarten and first graders, 28% discussed their work habits, including effort (Stipek, 1981). A few of the children who referred to competence or ability in their explanations of a peer's poor performance (e.g., "He's not very smart in reading") hastened to add, "If he practices he'll be smarter." In a second interview study on children's concept of ability (Stipek & Tannatt, in press), "work habits" (references to effort, following directions or finishing work) were commonly used by children through the second and third grade to explain "smartness" ratings they gave to themselves and their peers. Indeed, 44% of the kindergarteners and first graders and 49% of the second and third graders explained ratings of their classmates' "smartness" in terms of their work habits. Approximately a third in each grade group (preschool through third grade) explained their own "smartness" rating in terms of work habits. Harter and Chao (reported in Harter, 1981b) similarly found that 4- and 5-year-olds typically believed that an unsuccessful child merely needed to practice a skill to improve performance. One second grader in a study by Harari and Covington (1981) succinctly explained the relationship between ability and effort: "If you study, it helps the brain and you get smarter" (p. 25).

Nicholls (1978) has studied children's reasoning about effort and ability by showing them films of children doing math problems with varying levels of effort and success. His results suggest that until the age of about 10 or 11, children do not understand the compensatory relationship between effort and ability (i.e., that given equal outcomes, higher effort implies lower ability), or that ability implies limits in the extent to which effort can increase performance. The youngest children in his study (aged 5 and 6 years) did not distinguish between effort, ability, and outcome; children from about the age of 7 to 10 distinguished effort and outcome as a cause and effect, but ability, "in the sense of capacity which can increase or limit the effectiveness of effort," was not understood (p. 812). Kun, Parsons, and Ruble (1974) similarly report that not until children were 10 years old did they understand that effort is more facilitative for high- than for low-ability individuals.

It is not surprising that children of elementary school age do not differentiate between effort, ability, and outcome. Teachers themselves do not always differentiate these dimensions in their feedback. According to Apple and King (1978), praise is usually given more for social behavior or school-appropriate behavior than on the basis of the quality of children's products. A teacher's "good" may refer to the child's good conduct (e.g., working alone quietly), effort, or the quality of his or her work, or all of these simultaneously. Many verbal comments do not clearly indicate on which of these dimensions the teacher is commenting. Throughout the elementary grades the basis for verbal or other evaluative feedback is often ambiguous. Blumenfeld, Pintrich, Meece, and Wessels (1982) comment that grades on compositions, for example, "may be based on numerous standards which are ambiguous to the child. Spelling, grammar, length, and penmanship may be considered, along with the nature and accuracy of the information mentioned or the originality of the ideas expressed" (p. 408). Children's interpretation of the feedback may therefore be no less undifferentiated than it is given.

It is noteworthy that the concept of effort itself may be more global for younger than for older children. Blumenfeld et al. (1982) argue that children in the first few grades in school do not explicitly consider the quality or nature of effort (e.g., persisting, applying alternative strategies, or seeking help). According to these researchers, trying is synonymous with good conduct for young children. In their study, the second graders', but not the sixth graders' ability perceptions were negatively related to the proportion of criticism about conduct they received. Sixth graders apparently discounted academically irrelevant information about conduct when assessing ability, whereas the second graders' perceptions of their ability declined as a function of the amount of behavioral criticism they received.

Together these studies indicate that young children are not likely to attribute objective failure to a stable factor which limits the potential effectiveness of effort. So when consistent failure performance feedback is received, even if it is "processed" it need not dampen future expectations, as it would logically for an adult in most situations.

Recent evidence, however, indicates that preschool-age children's failure to take objective past performance feedback into account in formulating expectancy and competency judgments cannot be entirely explained by either cognitive deficiencies in integrating a sequence of feedback, or their perceptions of the implications of past performance for future performance. We found, for example, that the same preschoolers who failed to use their own past failure in formulating future expectancy judgments used this information in an adult-like logical fashion when making judgments about another child's performance (Stipek & Hoffman, 1980). Young children's expectancies for success on the balance task after four failure experiences were just as high as their expectations after four success experiences. However, the same children expected another child who had failed the task four times to do much more poorly than the other child who had succeeded four times. Judgments about the other child indicated that these 3- and 4-year-old children were quite capable of processing the past performance information and of applying that information in their judgments about future performance. But for some reason they did not apply negative past performance information in judgments about their own performance.

In another study, kindergarten through third graders were asked to rate their own and their classmates' competence on a scale of one to five. The youngest children's ratings of their classmates', but not their own, competence were significantly associated with teachers' ratings, suggesting that these kindergartners and first graders considered poor past performance information in their judgments of classmates' competence, but they did not use this information in judgments about their own competence (Stipek, 1981). Results of this second study suggest that the tendency to apply negative performance feedback in achievement-related judgments about other children prior to applying negative feedback in judgments about their own competencies extends beyond the preschool years.

A follow-up study using the expectancy paradigm described previously provides evidence that preoperational children are, under certain conditions, capable of using past objective performance information in expectancy judgments, but that whether the children make a judgment regarding their own or another child's performance is not the only relevant variable (Stipek, Roberts, & Sanborn, 1983).

We used the aforementioned balance task (Stipek & Hoffman, 1980). Sixty 4-year-olds were randomly assigned to six different conditions: Half of the children in each age group made predictions for their own performance ("self") and half made predictions about another child's performance ("other"). Within the self and other conditions, 10 of the children received a marble specifically for every color-coded interval the cart passed on the tower before the ball fell off; 10 children were promised a bag of marbles if the cart reached the top; and 10 children were offered no reward. To render the "other" conditions realistic, we used a videotape of a real child the same age and gender. In all conditions the sequencing of outcomes was the same: 1, 3, 1, 2, 1 out of a possible of six intervals. Before any feedback and before the fourth, fifth, and sixth trials, children were asked to make performance predictions.

Compared to children who received no reward for their own performance, children who received a marble for every color the cart passed on the tower, without the metal ball falling off, made much more realistic predictions (i.e., predictions declined as a function of cumulative failure). We replicated this effect twice. We hypothesize that children made more realistic predictions when a reward was made contingent on the specific level of performance because this reward made outcomes more salient. This effect deomonstrates again children's competence to use negative objective feedback regarding their own performance under certain circumstances.

Apparently, even preoperational children are capable of integrating objective feedback and perceiving the significance of that information for future performance, because their predictions indicate that they process performance information in this adult-like logical fashion under some circumstances. Factors other than cognitive deficiencies in processing the information must therefore explain their frequent failure to apply past objective failure information. One possible factor is discussed next.

Wishful Thinking

According to Piaget (1925, 1930), preschoolage children often do not differentiate between their wishes and their expectations. He claims that both infants' and preoperational children's perceptions of causality are based on contiguity. But an understanding of the nature, or the "how" of many causal relationships comes later. Thus, "whenever the contiguous events are in harmony with the child's desire, this desire is perceived as the total or partial cause (Piaget, 1925, p. 64, my translation). Thus, Piaget (1930) reports that some preoperational children believe that they are responsible for the movement of the moon, the stars, and the clouds.

Extending this analysis to achievement outcomes, we might expect that young children lack a full understanding of the behaviors instrumental to success and are seduced, by their observations of continguity between desiring and achieving success, into believing that success was brought about by personal desires. Perhaps, when making judgments about their own future performance, children sometimes confuse their desires with their "objective" judgment (i.e., they believe that their desire for success is sufficient to bring it about); when another child's performance is judged, there is no personal desire to interfere with processing objective performance evidence.

Piaget's analysis suggests that children might have higher expectations for their own performance than for the performance of another child in part because they have a stronger desire for their own success. If this analysis is correct, then we should be able to raise children's expectations for another child by making the other child's success desirable to them. Our manipulation of the reward value of the subject's own and another child's performance outcomes in the study mentioned above was done to examine the effect of desires on performance expectations. Our assumption was that children would desire another child's success more if they received a reward contingent on it. Accordingly, we compared the expectations of 4-year-old children who were told that they would receive a bag of marbles contingent on the performing child's outcome to the expectations of children who received no reward.

Children making predictions about their own performance, with no reward, had significantly higher expectations for future performance on Trials 4, 5, and 6 than children who received no reward for the other child's performance. This is essentially a replication of our previous finding that preschoolage children had higher expectations for their own performance after failure than for the performance of another child (Stipek & Hoffman, 1980). However, when a reward was dependent on achieving the highest level of success possible, children's expectations for another child were raised to about the same level as their expectations for their own unrewarded performance. That is, as hypothesized, this reward condition enhanced judgments about the other child's future performance. The young child's predictions were also significantly correlated to the performance level that they claimed they "wanted" to achieve.

There is some empirical support, then, for the proposition that "wishful thinking" causes young children to ignore past performance feedback inconsistent with their desire for a successful outcome. If desired future outcomes are caused by wishing them, past performance is irrelevant!

Summary

Given the preceding characteristics of the youngest elementary school-age children's thought, it is not surprising that they maintain relatively high expectations and positive perceptions of their competencies, despite objective feedback to the contrary. Even if they process objective failure on a task, the failure probably does not have the same implications for competence and future performance that it would have for an older child or an adult. The young child is likely to attribute the failure to an unstable cause and all that is needed is a little practice, a little more effort, or even a strong desire for success. Note that this "immature" view of performance is probably consistent with most young children's experience. They develop competencies at such a rapid pace that, in fact, what they cannot do today, they often can do tomorrow.

Even middle-elementary-school-age children apparently make achievement-related judgments somewhat differently from older children and adults. According to Nicholls (1978), children's concepts of effort and ability are not fully differentiated until about the age of 11 years. Consequently, it is likely that until the later elementary grades, children maintain a relatively high level of optimism for future performance regardless of objective past performance information.

An important qualifier in this depiction of the youngest children's thinking is important. There is some evidence suggesting that children's performance judgments do not reflect an inability to process objective information and, although preoperational children may lack a concept of stable ability, they do understand that past performance is predictive of future performance. Our research has shown that minor experimental manipulations will result in preschoolage children making judgments similar to those an adult would make. Taken together, research evidence suggests that children are cognitively able, but disinclined to process and apply negative objective performance feedback as an adult would, at least in most situations.

NORMATIVE FEEDBACK

Older children and adults often interpret an outcome as success or failure in terms of how their performance compares to others. While even preschool-age children seem to be able to make social comparisons (Mosatche & Bragonier, 1981; Ruble, Feldman, & Boggiano, 1976), children tend not to compare their performance with other children until at least the second grade (Boggiano & Ruble, 1979; Ruble, Boggiano, Feldman, & Loebl, 1980; Veroff, 1969). Moreover, their self-evaluations are relatively unaffected by comparative information regarding their performance (Ruble, Parsons, & Ross, 1976; Ruble *et al.*, 1980).

Further evidence suggesting that young children do not consider normative information in their competency evaluations comes from the study we did in which children in preschool through third grade were asked to explain their competency ratings for themselves and their classmates (Stipek & Tannatt, in press). Whether the rating was for a specific competency or "smartness" in general, the older the child, the more likely he or she was to refer to performance relative to others or to the difficulty level of a task the child being rated could perform.

All children can surpass their own past performance level, but not all children can surpass the performance level of peers. By failing to compare their performance to other children, young children are spared one potential source of information indicating low competence. Their relative lack of interest in comparing performance and in normative information may explain, in part, why they are able to maintain high expectations and a positive view of their competencies. An important question for developmentalists is whether children tend not to compare their performance to other children because they are cognitively unable to process comparative information, or because they simply are not motivated to obtain comparative information.

Whatever children's "natural" inclinations toward social comparison are, environmental changes undoubtedly reinforce a shift toward increasing concern and attention to normative information. Most children are not exposed to an age-stratified educational context, in which the same demands and expectations are made on all of the children in the group, until they begin school. Classroom practices which provide normative information, such as ability grouping, sometimes occur as early as kindergarten. However, the amount of normative feedback and opportunites for social comparison increase as children progress through school.

For example, classrooms tend to become more formal and more structured in the upper grades, compared to early elementary school classrooms, which are more likely to be "open" (Arlin, 1976). The amount of whole-class instruction increases with grade, as do public response opportunities (Brophy & Evertson, 1981). Ability grouping is extended to mathematics in some upper grades (Parsons *et al.*, in press) and the use of letter grades increases (Gronlund, 1974). Brophy and Evertson (1981) found also that teachers are more likely to hold up students as good examples to the class in higher than in lower elementary grades. All of these shifts in classroom practices are associated with an increase in the availability and salience of normative performance feedback (Parsons *et al.*, in press). When children enter junior high and high school, normative information is particularly salient. Students are often ability grouped by whole classes, or by their entire curriculum (track), and most instruction is conducted with the entire class (Brophy & Evertson, 1978).

Given these shifts in the availability and salience of normative information, it is not surprising that children's attention to and concern with normative feedback increases as they advance through school. This is not to say that changes within the child, such as in the ability to process normative information, are not factors in their increased interest in social comparison. Indeed, preoperational children's lack of interest in normative feedback may be related to their inability to seriate (e.g., "I'm smarter than Dick but not as smart as Susan") and also to their lack of a concept of a stable ability. But the aforementioned environmental changes probably reinforce whatever changes occur in the child. Thus, children's interest in social comparative information might be accelerated or decelerated by creating certain kinds of educational environments that make salient social comparison, or that de-emphasize it.

SUMMARY

Changes in children's use of evaluative feedback have been proposed to explain findings that children's self-perceptions of competence and expectations for success decline over time in school and increasingly conform to objective (e.g., test scores) and symbolic (e.g., grades) indices of their relative academic performance. Children are believed to begin school attending primarily to social feedback. As they progress through the first few grades in school, objective performance feedback and symbolic representation of performance become more salient and meaningful. Children learn that high academic performance is valued and they give increased attention to social comparative information. By the third or fourth grade, most children attend to, process, and understand the significance of objective and symbolic performance feedback, both mastery based and normatively based.

During the first few years of elementary school, children also assume that effort and ability covary with performance outcomes. Thus, a successful outcome demonstrates both high ability and high effort. Since effort is under the child's own control, positive outcomes can be expected regardless of past performance. Not until about the sixth grade do children have a fully developed concept of ability as a stable factor which can limit the effects of effort on performance outcomes.

Development in children's cognitive processing abilities unquestionably affects their use of performance feedback, and consequently their achievement-related cognitions. Changes in the educational context, including the nature of evaluation and classroom structural variables, undoubtedly occur partly in response to these developmental differences in children's responsiveness and interpretation of performance feedback. However, the changes in the evaluative context may also serve to reinforce, extend, or delay the child's developmental changes.

The proposed relationships among achievement-related cognitions, processing of performance feedback and the educational environment are summarized in Figure 1. The box on the right-hand side lists developmental changes in children's achievement-related cognitions. In the

---

CHILD'S PROCESSING OF PERFORMANCE FEEDBACK

Attention to social feedback declines; attention to objective performance feedback and symbolic representation of performance increases.

Inclination to socially compare increases.

Consideration of normative information contained in grades increases.

Objective achievement-related judgments increasingly differentiated from desires.

Concept of effort and ability increasingly differentiated; concept of ability as a stable factor which limits the effectiveness of effort not fully developed until the age of about 11.

↑

CLASSROOM ENVIRONMENT

Structure and formality of classroom environment increases.

Amount of social reinforcement declines; social reinforcement increasingly contingent upon academic performance, decreasingly contingent upon good behavior.

Opportunities for social comparison increase:
-individualizational decreases;
-whole-class instruction increases;
-stable ability grouping and tracking increase;
-use of letter grades increases.

ACHIEVEMENT-RELATED COGNITIONS

Expectations for future success decline; strength of correlation between expectations and past performance outcomes increases.

Self-evaluation of competence declines; strength of correlation between self-evaluations and objective indices of performance or teachers' evaluations increases.

Causal attributions for performance outcomes increasingly differentiated—from effort (which is not distinguished from ability) to effort and ability as conceptually distinct causal factors; importance of ability, relative to effort, as a cause of performance outcomes increases.

Figure 1. Developmental change in achievement-related cognitions.

upper-left-hand box are changes in children's processing of performance feedback which are presumed to underlie changes in their achievement-related cognitions. Characteristics of the educational environment that are believed to reinforce these developmental changes in processing evaluative information are summarized in the lower-left-hand box.

DEVELOPMENTAL CHANGE IN VALUES, AFFECTS, AND GOALS

There is a sad paradox in the development of children's achievement related cognitions. Most children learn to value high performance based on a normative standard. But a normative standard, by definition, precludes all children reaching the relatively high level of performance to which they learn to aspire. Moreover, by sixth grade, children have developed a concept of stable ability which limits the effectiveness of effort. Thus, by the time children enter junior high school, high achievement relative to peers may be perceived by many as hopeless.

This paradox may be an important factor in the development of negative affects toward school and the precipitous decline in self-perceptions of competence associated with junior high school entry. Relatively poor achievers generally develop the most negative affect toward school (Berk, Rose, & Stewart, 1970). Their negative affects may be in part the result of socialization at home. But it is also likely to be caused by frustration stemming from a perceived inability to achieve what they have been socialized to value in school, if not at home.

Because some emotions involve cognitions (Weiner, 1979), changes in children's emotional lives in the classroom should also be associated with development of achievement-related cognitions (see Stipek, 1983, for further discussion). Unfortunately, less is known about the development of affective responses to achievement outcomes than is known about cognitions, such as those described in the previous sections. Yet, emotions are believed to be important determinants of achievement behavior (Weiner, 1980a, 1980b).

In the absence of developmental data on children's emotional experience in academic settings, we might speculate that an increase in negative achievement-related emotions—such as anxiety, fear, shame, feelings of incompetence, and embarrassment—would accompany the aforementioned development of achievement-related cognitions. As normative feedback becomes more important, pride in accomplishments and some other positive emotions related to performance outcomes (e.g., pride) may only result from achievements that compare favorably to classmates' achievements. Because many children will necessarily fail to achieve success by this standard, we might expect the emotional experiences of some children to be increasingly negative as they advance through school.

With regard to goals, one might speculate that performance feedback is related to the observed shift described earlier from an intrinsic, mastery motive to a concern with extrinsic reinforcement for achievement outcomes. As grades and other symbols of achievement are emphasized more in classrooms, and as these symbols of high achievement become increasingly meaningful and desirable to children, their attention is directed away from engaging in achievement tasks to experience feelings of competency, and toward engaging in tasks to obtain salient symbolic rewards. Attention to symbolic rewards has been shown to undermine intrinsic motivation in achievement situations (Maehr & Stallings, 1972). Parsons *et al.* (in press) suggest that classrooms also become more formal and more controlled as children advance in grade and that this also causes a decline in intrinsic motivation.

CONCLUSION

I once interviewed 96 children at the beginning of first grade; they all claimed to be among the smartest in their class (Stipek, 1977). But, the actual performance of many of these children fell significantly short of their expectations. Some of them, by any objective standard an adult would use, failed miserably. Many papers came back with more answers marked wrong than right. At the end of the year, these children were still working on letter recognition while most of their classmates were reading stories out of primary texts. Interviews of these relatively low-achieving children at the end of the school year revealed a remarkable ignorance of their poor academic performance. Feedback that for me unambiguously indicated low ability seemed not to be interpreted in this way by these first graders.

Other research reviewed in this chapter is generally consistent with my own observations. Until about the second or third grade, children's achievement-related cognitions—including their self-perceptions of competence, their expectations for success and their causal attributions for performance outcomes—remain generally positive. Thereafter, children's achievement cognitions, and probably their accompanying emotions, increasingly reflect their actual relative performance in the classroom. Attitudes toward school become more negative, on the average, and children tend to shift their attention to extrinsic rewards for academic outcomes.

Information-processing skills and other developments in the child no doubt contribute to these changes in achievement-motivational constructs. But we need to consider changes across grades in educational environments which might also contribute to children's achievement motivation, and consequently, their achievement behavior.

If the educational environment was all that was important, teachers throughout the elementary grades and beyond would be able to maintain a high level of motivation by maintaining the same educational environment that children typically experience in kindergarten and first grade. The task of educational researchers would be to carefully observe classrooms in the early grades and package their methods for teachers of later grades. To some degree, this may be a worthwile task. The focus on skill mastery rather than on normative performance, the less formal and more individualized instruction, and other characteristics presumed to be common in early elementary classrooms may indeed help maintain positive achievement-related cognitions, attitudes, and emotions beyond the first few grades in school. But these strategies would probably not be as successful with older children as they are with younger children. Achievement motivation develops as a function of a complex interaction between changes in the child and in the environment. Only through a better understanding of this reciprocal relationship can we build a model of achievement motivation that is developmentally sound and useful for designing educational programs that optimally motivate children at all ages.

ACKNOWLEDGMENTS

The author is grateful to Sandra Graham and Terrence Mason for helpful comments on previous drafts of this chapter.

REFERENCES

Anderson, L., Evertson, C., & Brophy, J. An experimental study of effective teaching in first-grade reading groups. *Elementary School Journal*, 1979, *79*, 193–223.

Anderson, R., & Faust, G. *Educational Psychology: The science of instruction and learning* (4th ed.). New York: Dodd, Mead, & Co., 1973.

Apple, M., & King, W. What do schools teach? In G. Willis (Ed.) *Qualitative evaluations: Concepts and cases in curriculum criticism.* Berkeley, CA: McCutchan, 1978.

Arlin, M. Open education and pupils' attitudes. *Elementary School Journal,* 1976, *76,* 219–228.

Atkinson, J. *An introduction to motivation.* Princeton, NJ: Van Nostrand, 1964.

Ausubel, D., Novak, J., & Hanesian, H. *Educational psychology: A cognitive view.* New York: Holt, Rinehart, & Winston, 1978.

Berk, L., Rose, M., & Stewart, D. Attitudes of English and American children toward their school experience. *Journal of Educational Psychology,* 1970, *61,* 33–40.

Biehler, R., & Snowman, J. *Psychology applied to teaching* (4th ed.). Boston: Houghton, 1982.

Blumenfeld, P. C. & Pintrich, P. R. *Children's perceptions of school and schoolwork: Age, sex, social class, individual and classroom differences.* Paper presented at the Annual American Educational Research Association Meeting, New York, 1982.

Blumenfeld, P., Pintrich, P., Meece, J., & Wessels, K. The formation and role of self perceptions of ability in elementary classrooms. *The Elementary School Journal,* 1982, *82,* 401–420.

Blumenfeld, P., Wessels, K., Pintrich, P., & Meece, J. *Age and sex differences in the impact of teacher communications on self-perceptions.* Paper presented at the Biennial Society for Research in Child Development Meeting, Boston, 1981.

Boggiano, A., & Ruble, D. Competence and the overjustification effect: A developmental study. *Journal of Personality and Social Psychology,* 1979, *37,* 1462–1468.

Brophy, J. Teacher praise: A functional analysis. *Review of Educational Research,* 1981, *51,* 5–32.

Brophy, J., & Evertson, C. Context variables in teaching. *Educational Psychologist,* 1978, *12,* 310–316.

Brophy, J., & Evertson, C. *Student characteristics and teaching.* New York: Longman, 1981.

Clifford, M. Validity of expectation: A developmental function. *Alberta Journal of Educational Research,* 1975, *21,* 11–17.

Clifford, M. The effects of quantitative feedback on children's expectation of success. *British Journal of Educational Psychology,* 1978, *48,* 220–226.

Clifford, M. *Practicing educational psychology.* Boston: Houghton, 1981.

Covington, M., & Beery, R. *Self-worth and school learning.* New York: Holt, Rinehart, & Winston, 1976.

Crandall, V. C. Achievement behavior in the young child. In W. Hartup (Ed.), *The young child: Reviews of research.* Washington, DC: National Association for the Education of Young Children, 1967.

deCharms, R. The origins of competence and achievement motivation in personal causation. In L. J. Fyans, Jr. (Ed.), *Achievement motivation: Recent trends in theory and research.* New York: Plenum, 1980.

Dweck, C. Theories of intelligence and achievement motivation. In S. Paris, G. Olson, & H. Stevenson (Eds.) *Learning and motivation in the classroom.* Hillsdale, NJ: Erlbaum, in press.

Entwisle, D., & Hayduk, L. *Too great expectations: The academic outlook of young children.* Baltimore, MD: Johns Hopkins University Press, 1978.

Eshel, Y., & Klein, Z. Development of academic self-concept of lower-class and middle-class primary school children. *Journal of Educational Psychology,* 1981, *73,* 287–293.

Flavell, J., Friedrichs, A., & Hoyt, J. Developmental changes in memorization processes. *Cognitive Psychology,* 1970, *1,* 324–340.

Freedman, J., Sears, D., & Carlsmith, J. *Social psychology.* (4th ed.). Englewood Cliffs, NJ: Prentice-Hall, 1981.

Goss, A. Estimated versus actual physical strength in three ethnic groups. *Child Development*, 1968, *39*, 283–290.

Gottfried, E. *Grade, sex, and race differences in academic intrinsic motivation.* Paper presented at the Annual American Educational Research Association Meeting, Los Angeles, April 1981.

Gronlund, N. *Improving marking and reporting in classroom instruction: A title in the current topics in classroom instruction series.* New York: Macmillan, 1974.

Haladyna, T., & Thomas, G. The attitudes of elementary school children toward school and subject matters. *Journal of Experimental Education*, 1979, *48*, 18–23.

Harari, O., & Covington, M. Reactions to achievement from a teacher and student perspective: A developmental analysis. *American Educational Research Journal*, 1981, *18*, 15–28.

Harter, S. Effectance motivation reconsidered: Toward a developmental model. *Human Development*, 1978, *21*, 34–64.

Harter, S. A new self-report scale of intrinsic versus extrinsic orientation in the classroom: Motivational and informational components. *Developmental Psychology*, 1981, *17*, 300–312. (a)

Harter, S. A model of mastery motivation in children: Individual differences and developmental change. In A. Pick (Ed.), *Minnesota Symposium on Child Psychology* (Vol. 14). Hillsdale, NJ: Erlbaum, 1981. (b)

Holt, J. *How children fail.* New York: Pitman, 1964.

Inhelder, B., & Piaget, J. *The early growth of logic in the child.* New York: Norton, 1964.

Jackson, P. *Life in classrooms.* New York: Holt, Rinehart, & Winston, 1968.

Karabenick, J., & Heller, K. A developmental study of effort and ability attributions. *Developmental Psychology*, 1976, *12*, 559–560.

Kohlberg, L. Stage and sequence: The cognitive-developmental approach to socialization. In D. Goslin (Ed.), *Handbook of socialization theory and research.* Chicago: McNally, 1969.

Kun, A. Development of the magnitude-covariation and compensations schemata in ability and effort attributions of performance. *Child Development*, 1977, *48*, 862–873.

Kun, A., Parsons, J., & Ruble, D. Development of integration processes using ability and effort information to predict outcome. *Developmental Psychology*, 1974, *10*, 721–732.

Lewis, M., Wall, M. & Aronfreed, J. Developmental change in the relative values of social and nonsocial reinforcement. *Journal of Experimental Psychology*, 1963, *66*, 133–137.

Maehr, M., & Stallings, W. Freedom from external evaluation. *Child Development*, 1972, *43*, 177–185.

Meid, E. *The effects of two types of success and failure on children's discrimination learning and evaluation of performance.* Unpublished manuscript, Yale University, 1971.

Meyer, W-U., Bachmann, M., Biermann, U., Hempelmann, M., Ploger, F., & Spiller, H. The informational value of evaluative behavior: Influences of praise and blame on perceptions of ability. *Journal of Educational Psychology*, 1979, *71*, 259–268.

Miller, A. *Self-recognitory schemes and achievement behavior: A developmental study.* Doctoral dissertation, Purdue University, 1982.

Mosatche, H., & Bragonier, P. An observational study of social comparison in preschoolers. *Child Development*, 1981, *52*, 376–378.

Neale, D., & Proshek, J. School-related attitudes of culturally disadvantaged elementary school children. *Journal of Educational Psychology*, 1967, *58*, 238–244.

Nicholls, J. The development of the concepts of effort and ability, perceptions of academic attainment and the understanding that difficult tasks require more ability. *Child Development*, 1978, *49*, 800–814.

Nicholls, J. The development of perception of own attainment and causal attributions for success and failure in reading. *Journal of Educational Psychology*, 1979, *71*, 94–99.

Nicholls, J., & Miller, A. Development and its discontents: The differentiation of the concept of ability. In J. Nicholls (Ed.), *The development of achievement motivation*. Greenwich, CT: JAI Press, in press.

Parsons, J. *The development of children's evaluative judgments*. Unpublished dissertation, UCLA, 1974.

Parsons, J., Adler, T., Futterman, R., Goff, S., Kaczala, C., Meece, J., & Midgley, C. Expectancies, values, and academic behaviors. In J. Spence (Ed.), *Perspectives on achievement and achievement motivation*. San Francisco: Freeman, in press.

Parsons, J., Midgley, C., & Adler, T. Age-related changes in the school environment: Effects on achievement motivation. In J. Nicholls (Ed.), *The development of achievement motivation*. Greenwich, CT: JAI Press, in press.

Parsons, J., Moses, L., & Yulish-Muszynski, S. *The development of attributions, expectancies and persistence*. Paper presented at the Annual Meeting of the American Psychological Association, San Francisco, 1977.

Parsons, J., & Ruble, D. Attributional processes related to the development of achievement-related affect and expectancy. *American Psychological Association Proceedings 80th Annual Convention*, 1972, 105–106.

Parsons, J. & Ruble, D. The development of achievement-related expectancies. *Child Development*, 1977, *48*, 1975–1979.

Phillips, B. Age changes in accuracy of self-perceptions. *Child Development*, 1963, *34*, 1041–1046.

Piaget, J. De quelques formes primitives de causalite chez l' enfant. *L'Annee Psychologie*, 1925, *26*, 31–71.

Piaget, J. *The child's conception of physical causality*. London: Routledge & Kegan Paul, 1930.

Rholes, W., Blackwell, J., Jordan, C., & Walters, C. A developmental study of learned helplessness. *Developmental Psychology*, 1980, *16*, 616–624.

Rosen, B., & D'Andrade, R. The psychological origins of achievement motivations. *Sociometry*, 1959, *22*, 185–218.

Rosenberg, M. *Conceiving the self*. New York: Basic Books, 1979.

Ruble, D. A developmental perspective on the theories of achievement motivation. In L. Fyans, Jr. (Ed.), *Achievement motivation: Recent trends in theory and research*. New York: Plenum, 1980.

Ruble, D., Boggiano, A., Feldman, N., & Loebl, J. Developmental analysis of the role of social comparison in self-evaluation. *Developmental Psychology*, 1980, *16*, 105–115.

Ruble, D., Feldman, N., & Boggiano, A. Social comparison between young children in achievement situations. *Developmental Psychology*, 1976, *12*, 192–197.

Ruble, D., Parsons, J., & Ross, J. Self-evaluative responses of children in an achievement setting. *Child Development*, 1976, *47*, 990–997.

Shaklee, H. Development in inferences of ability and task difficulty. *Child Development*, 1976, *47*, 1051–1057.

Shaklee, H., & Tucker, D. Cognitive bases of development in inferences of ability. *Child Development*, 1979, *50*, 904–907.

Simmons, R., Blyth, D., Van Cleave, E., & Bush, D. Entry into early adolescence: The impact of school structure, puberty, and early dating on self-esteem. *American Sociological Review*, 1979, *44*, 928–967.

Simmons, R., Rosenberg, F., & Rosenberg, M. Disturbance in the self-image of adolescence. *American Sociological Review*, 1973, *38*, 553–568.

Spear, P., & Armstrong, S. Effects of performance expectancies created by peer comparison as related to social reinforcement, task difficulty and age of child. *Journal of Experimental Child Psychology*, 1978, *25*, 254–266.

Stipek, D. *Changes during first grade in children's social-motivational development.* Doctoral dissertation, Yale University, 1977.

Stipek, D. Children's perceptions of their own and their classmates' ability. *Journal of Educational Psychology*, 1981, *73*, 404–410.

Stipek, D. Young children's performance expectations: Logical analysis or wishful thinking? In J. Nicholls (Ed.), *The development of achievement motivation.* Greenwich, CT: JAI Press, in press.

Stipek, D. A developmental analysis of pride and shame. *Human Development*, 1983, *26*, 42–54.

Stipek, D., & Hoffman, J. Development of children's performance-related judgments. *Child Development*, 1980, *51*, 912–914.

Stipek, D., Roberts, T., & Sanborn, M. Children's performance expectations for themselves and another child. Unpublished manuscript, Graduate School of Education, UCLA, 1983.

Stipek, D., & Tannatt, L. Children's judgments of their own and their peers' academic competence. *Journal of Educational Psychology*, in press.

Veroff, J. Social comparison and the development of achievement motivation. In C. Smith (Ed.), *Achievement-related motives in children.* New York: Russell Sage Foundation, 1969.

Weiner, B. A theory of motivation for some classroom experiences. *Journal of Educational Psychology*, 1979, *71*, 3–25.

Weiner, B. A cognitive (attribution)-emotion-action model of motivated behavior: An analysis of judgments of help-giving. *Journal of Personality and Social Psychology*, 1980, *39*, 186–200. (a)

Weiner, B. The role of affect in rationale (attributional) approaches to human motivation. *Educational Researcher*, 1980, *9*, 4–11. (b)

Weiner, B., Anderson, A., & Prawat, R. Affective experience in the classroom. Unpublished manuscript, UCLA, 1982.

Weisz, J. Perceived Control and learned helplessness among mentally retarded and nonretarded children: A developmental analysis. *Developmental Psychology*, 1979, *15*, 311–319.

Winterbottom, M. The relation of need for achievement to learning experiences in independence and mastery. In J. Atkinson (Ed.), *Motives in fantasy, action, and society.* Princeton: Van Nostrand, 1958.

Yamamoto, K., Thomas, E., & Karns, E. School-related attitudes in middle-school age students. *American Educational Research Journal*, 1969, *6*, 191–206.

Yussen, S., & Berman, L. Memory predictions for recall and recognition in first-, third-, and fifth-grade children. *Developmental Psychology*, 1981, *17*, 224–229.

Yussen, S., & Levy, V. Developmental changes in predicting one's own span of short-term memory. *Journal of Experimental Child Psychology*, 1975, *19*, 502–508.

PART III

The Student's Environment: Classroom and Situational Factors

6

Competitive, Cooperative, and
Individualistic Goal Structures:
A Cognitive-Motivational Analysis

Carole Ames

OVERVIEW OF COMPETITIVE VERSUS
NONCOMPETITIVE STRUCTURES

Since 1970, there has been considerable attention given to the relative
efficacy of competitive versus cooperative social structures in promoting
various social and achievement outcomes (for reviews, see Johnson &
Johnson, 1974; Johnson, Maruyama, Johnson, Nelson, & Skon, 1981;
Slavin, 1983). Although research on competitive versus alternative noncompetitive structures dates back to as early as 1920, the focus of this
literature has concerned achievement gains and social relationships
among students covering a wide range of ages and content areas. While
cooperative based structures have been highly touted for promoting
higher achievement and self-esteem in students (Johnson *et al.*, 1981;
Johnson, Johnson, & Scott, 1978), this research is not without refutation
(e.g., Cotton & Cook, 1982; Michaels, 1977; Slavin, 1977). Despite the
lingering controversies, one point remains clear and that is that substantially more attention has been directed toward predicting these outcomes than to understanding the motivational processes that mediate
these outcomes.

In Johnson *et al.*'s (1981) analysis of 121 research studies dealing with the effects of alternative goal structures on achievement and productivity within the educational realm, motivation was mentioned as a moderating variable in less than 10 of these studies. And, in these studies, motivation was treated as either an individual difference factor or was not directly measured but was merely presumed to covary with outcome. Only recently has the research on different types of goal–reward structures begun to examine cognitive and self-evaluative motivational factors as they are affected by the type of structure which, in turn, influences the direction of subsequent social and achievement behaviors. While motivation is a mediating construct in achievement, motivation may also be viewed as a goal in itself and this has not been addressed in most of the literature on goal–reward structures. Yet, understanding the psychology of motivation within different structures seems to be inextricably linked to certain educational outcomes such as continuing motivation (Maehr,1976), self-worth (Covington & Beery, 1976), reasons for learning (Kukla, 1978; Nicholls, 1979, 1982), intrinsic motivation (Deci, 1975), and achievement behaviors (Weiner, 1979). Thus, in addition to asking the question "Which type of structure leads to greater achievement or less achievement?" we should also be addressing questions such as "What is the psychological meaning of success and failure to the student within different goal–reward structures? How does the goal structure influence students' self-evaluations and cognitive–motivational thought processes?"

In this chapter, I examine these broad issues in an attempt to come to some understanding of the motivational processes implicit in cooperative, competitive, and individualistic structures. In the first sections of the chapter, I explore the self-evaluative and esteem-related consequences of different structures. From there, I move to proposing how these different types of structures may be tapping different motivational systems that have different origins and different meanings for students, particularly high and low achievers. Now let us turn to these motivational issues.

SALIENCE OF INFORMATIONAL CUES

How students evaluate their performances is foremost a function of whether they perceive themselves as successful or not. Whatever the reason or extenuating circumstance, students who perform poorly do not receive as positive evaluations nor do they feel as satisfied with their performance as students who perform well. Generally, we can say with some assurance that success enhances students' feelings of competence and failure diminishes their feelings of worth. Besides this outcome information (i.e., subjective perceptions of success or failure), there are other sources of information in achievement settings that influence children's self-evaluations and resulting motivation, for example, prior performance on similar tasks and relevant others' performance. This section attends to how the goal–reward structure of an achievement setting affects the salience of various information sources that children use in making self-evaluations.

That competitive reward structures are a pervasive phenomenon in American schools has been documented by many investigative observers of the classroom (Johnson & Johnson, 1975; Levine, 1983, Pepitone, 1980). A competitive structure describes a situation of negative interdependence among students, that is, students' gains or rewards are negatively related. The possibility or opportunity for one student to attain a goal or receive rewards is reduced when others are successful. In school, rewards are judiciously given, but in competitively structured classrooms; rewards are reserved for those getting right answers or the most right answers. John Holt (1964) illustrates the value of being right in the following anecdote: "'Well, I didn't get that answer,' said Jimmy, 'I got . . .' but before he could say any more, the teacher said 'Now Jimmy, I'm sure we don't want to hear any wrong answers.' And that was the last word out of Jimmy" (p. 142). The presence of competitive systems of evaluation solicits students' interest in comparing their own performance with that of others; but even in classrooms where students' goals and the rules governing the distribution of rewards are unclear or ambiguous, students learn to cope with this environmental uncertainty through comparison with their peers. Levine (1983) describes the classroom as a situation of forced social comparison where students are continually overwhelmed with information about their peers' performances. Thus, the use of social comparison information (how one compares with relevant others) is critical in competitive structures and is exacerbated by the extant ambiguity of many classroom reward systems.

Unlike competitive structures, within individualized (or success oriented, mastery-based) structures where rewards are based on self-improvement (e.g., Covington, present volume, Chapter 3; Covington & Beery, 1976; Slavin, 1983), the emphasis is not on comparing oneself with others, but instead on comparing one's present level of performance with one's prior achievements. In individualized settings, students' achievements are independent of each other and the opportunity for the attainment of rewards is equal across students. A student's task performance becomes a step in a process of learning or achieving mastery, and as such, the consistency or inconsistency of one's performance over time must remain highly salient for realistic goalsetting and expectancies. Thus, the salience of past performance information should be strong in individualized settings because this information is central to a "process" of achieving.

That individualistic and competitive structures differéntially affect the centrality of past performance information in children's self-evaluations is supported by the recent findings of Ames and Ames (1981). In this study, children either competed with one another or worked individually on a novel achievement-related task. The competing children were incited to try to win and the children working alone were given a challenge to try to do their best. Social comparison information was available in the competitive setting but not in the individual setting. An important feature of this study was what occurred prior to the competitive or individualized performance situation and that involved having each child complete several preliminary trials at similar tasks over which a performance history of predominantly success or failure was established. Thus, all children had information regarding their past performance, and then either performed successfully (won) or unsuccessfully (lost) on a similar task within a competitive or individualistic structure. While we might expect the final performance to color the children's self-evaluations, we were more interested in determining if the situational context also impacted the utility of past versus present performance information. Our findings showed that the past performance information was important to children's self-evaluations only in the individualized setting. In fact, in the individualized setting, past performance and final performance accounted for almost equal proportions of the variance in children's self-reward (ω^2 = .24 & .25) and feelings of satisfaction (ω^2 = .24 & .19). In contrast, in competitive settings, final performance accounted for 28% of the variance in self-reward and 33% of the variance in satisfaction and past performance accounted for 0% of the variance on both measures. Figure 1 illustrates the difference in self-reward as a function of the final outcome (success or failure) v the prior performance (success or failure). What we see is that in the individual setting a prior failure tempered the positive effects of success or winning and prior success lessened the negative impact of failure or losing. It is apparent that past performance as a source of information was little utilized in competitive settings. Thus, while consistency or inconsistency of one's performance over time or trials is a dominant cue for self-evaluation in individualized settings; social comparison information, alone, is the cue utilized in competitive settings. Inasmuch as some views of achievement motivation emphasize the development of a mastery or

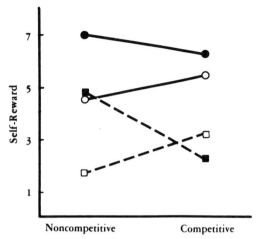

Figure 1.   Self-reward as a function of past and immediate performance (based on data from Ames & Ames, 1981); solid circles and solid line refers to success–success; open circles and solid line refers to failure–success; solid squares and broken line refers to success–failure; open squares and broken line refers to failure–failure.

process orientation (Block, 1977; Covington, present volume Chapter 3; Nicholls, 1979) that focuses children's attention on the continuities of their performance over time, the situational context appears to be an important facilitator or inhibitor of such an orientation.

Cooperative structures differ from competitive and individualistic structures in that they describe a situation of positive interdependence among a group of students, that is, group members share in the rewards or punishments as a function of their combined group performance. To the student, group outcome is new information pertaining to the outcome of the group. Just how important is this group outcome information to a student's self-evaluation? To what extent are esteem-related evaluations a function of personal productiveness versus group productiveness? A recent study (Ames, 1981) designed to compare the effects of competitive versus cooperative structures on children's self-perceptions showed that the outcome of a cooperative group was an important factor influencing children's self-evaluations, particularly their affective reactions. Fifth- and sixth-grade children were tested in pairs and prizes were promised to the winner in the competition or to both group members if they achieved a specific goal in the cooperative condition. The experimental manipulations were such that the relative performances within each pair of children were discrepant, that is, one child performed at a high level on the task and the other performed at a low level on the task. Further, within the cooperative structure, both successful and unsuccessful group outcomes were studied. This particular design allowed us to look at the salience of the individual performance or contribution to the group product relative to the performance of the group. The results showed that within the cooperative structure, the group outcome information was central to the process of self-evaluation. The group outcome affected children's perceptions of their own ability and their feelings of satisfaction as well as other esteem-based evaluations. The group outcome had the effect of moderating the positive or negative influence of the child's own high or low performance. That is, a group success tended to alleviate the otherwise negative self-perceptions that evolve from a poor individual performance; however, group failure tempered the positive self-perceptions of a high performer. Thus, the outcome of a cooperative group appears to be highly salient information for student self-evaluations; and, going a step further, we might suggest that cooperative structures can serve to modify intrapersonal perceptions of students either positively or negatively depending upon the outcome of the group.

Across competitive, cooperative, and individualistic structures, one source of information is constant and that is the individual's own level of achievement, and this information is important to students' esteem-related evaluations. But, beyond this, the consistency of one's performance over time in individualized settings and the group outcome in cooperative settings are also critical determinants of self-evaluation and affect how one's own individual performance is processed and interpreted. Quite clearly, the social comparison information (one's winning or losing) is preeminent to children's self-perceptions in competitive settings to the exclusion of other information when it is available. Motivating children for self-improvement may not be compatible with the demands of competitive situations in which the child's attention is singly focussed on the final outcome of winning or losing. Competitive or normative based evaluations offer little solace to the low achiever whose performance may only improve in small increments—small performance gains are of little or no importance when one is still losing. Thus, we can see how children who are similar in achievement patterns may hold discrepant self-views as a function of the type of goal–reward structure that defines the learning–working environment.

AFFECTIVE VALUE OF SUCCESS AND FAILURE

While success experiences lead to states of general satisfaction, there is considerable reason to believe that success is differentially valued as a function of the social context. Ames and Felker (1979) describe the value of success in competitive contexts as follows: "The critical factor for positive reward evaluation is outperforming another person, not merely achieving a high level of performance or receiving an external reinforcement." The basis for this statement was our finding that children judged a successful performance on an achievement task as most deserving of reward when it was defined as winning in a competitive situation. The fact that children in cooperative or individual situations were described as performing equally well was subordinate to the information that one performance (competitive) occasioned a win and the other did not. The conclusion that children place more value on winning than on performing a task well has been reached by several others (for example, Barnett & Andrews, 1977; Johnson & Johnson, 1974; Levine, 1983).

Winning incurs inflated levels of personal satisfaction and self-aggrandizement. Motives for self-aggrandizement are evident when we examine two sources of data, first by comparing self-reward by winners versus reward given to winners by losers. Supporting the relationship between self-interest motives and winning, self-reward by competitive winners has consistently been found to be greater than the reward given to a losing competitor (Ames, 1978, 1981; Ames, Ames, & Felker, 1977). A magnification of self-reward has not occurred in noncompetitive structures. Further, children have been found to give themselves more reward for winning than they give to others for winning—that is, children are more generous to themselves when they are winners than when they are rewarding another for winning (Ames, 1981; Barnett & Andrews, 1977).

For obvious reasons, we may be more concerned with the esteem-related consequences of academic failure than of success and we might ask if the negative consequences of failure might be attenuated or accentuated as a function of the social context. What we find is that just as winning bolsters the ego, losing in competition appears to deflate the ego. There is substantial evidence to suggest that failure in competitive settings has more negative consequences for one's self-esteem than failure in noncompetitive settings (Ames et al., 1977; Roberts, Kleiber, & Duda, 1981). Low-level attainments contribute to general dissatisfaction even in noncompetitive environments but the severity or level of affect depends on the structure of the achievement setting. That competitive contingencies accentuate the self-directed negativism that accompanies failure has been a consistent finding across our research (Ames, 1978, 1981; Ames et al., 1977; Ames & Felker, 1979). Children evaluate the poor performances of others as least satisfying when they involve a competitive loss; as well, children report significantly lower levels of satisfaction following a failure in competitive settings (see Figure 2).

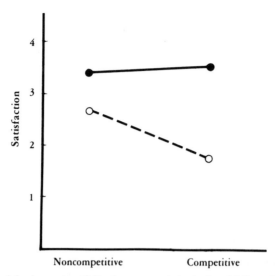

Figure 2.   Satisfaction ratings following success (winning) and failure (losing) (based on Ames *et al.*, 1977); solid line and circles refer to success; broken line and open circles refer to failure.

Competitive failure is also accompanied by increased levels of self-criticism. In fact, the findings from our research suggest that losing in competitive settings magnifies negative affect more than winning enhances positive affect (see Figure 2). While winning evokes self-aggrandizing motives, the findings are strong that failing in competitive structures elicits feelings of nondeservingness and dissatisfaction; and because competition engenders a situation of many losers and few winners, an esteem rating for this structure must necessarily be low.

As much as failure in competitive settings fosters conditions for negative esteem and personal dissatisfaction, the consequences of failure in cooperatively structured settings seems to be dependent upon the group outcome. Low-performing children seem to feel as satisfied with their level of performance as high performers are with their performance when they are part of a cooperative group that is successful in achieving its goal. In the Ames (1981) study that compared competitive to cooperative structures, children in competitive and unsuccessful cooperative group situations expressed the most dissatisfaction. Figure 3 illustrates how feelings of satisfaction vary as a function of the personal outcome in competitive structures and as a function of the group outcome in cooperative structures. Cooperative structures receive high esteem-ratings with a strong qualification. Because affective reactions to success and failure are largely a function of the group outcome, children in unsuccessful groups feel less satisfied, regardless of whether they personally performed well or poorly. For a low-achieving child, cooperative structures in which the group is successful in its goal accomplishment may provide an important mechanism for esteem-building by helping the child feel better about his or her performance.

We have also found that some students may be more sensitive to social context cues than others as a function of their own self-concept. Individual characteristics of students (achievement level, gender, self-concept) have long been suspected of influencing the perception and interpretation of relevant information (Weinstein, 1982; Weinstein & Middlestat, 1979). In our research, children who can be characterized as high versus low in self-concept have been found to differ in their responsiveness to social context cues. From a social learning perspective, high self-concept children tend to judge themselves more favorably than low self-concept children (Bandura, 1977). We have found that high self-concept children do, in fact, engage in more self-congratulatory behavior following successful experiences than do low-self-concept children (Ames, 1978). However, we have also found that expressions of personal dissatisfaction are not limited to those who hold a priori negative self-views. Even high self-concept children become self-punitive

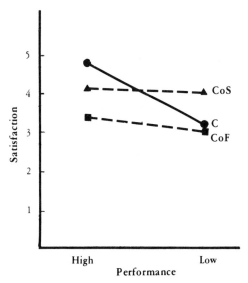

Figure 3. Satisfaction ratings following high and low performances in competitive (C), cooperatively successful (CoS) and cooperatively failing (CoF) groups (based on Ames, 1981).

when they experience failure in competitive settings. Specifically, we found that low-self-concept children were more self-punitive than high self-concept children in noncompetitively defined settings, but the high group became equally self-critical in competitive settings (Ames, 1978). Thus, while success evokes self-congratulations by high-self-concept children and failure evokes self-criticism by low-self-concept children, losing in competitive settings creates a condition for self-criticism even in the high-self-concept child. Making a similar point about the affective consequences of social comparison, Bandura (1977) writes "talented individuals who have high aspirations that are possible but difficult to realize are especially vulnerable to self-dissatisfaction despite their notable achievements." Over time, competition can conceivably threaten the positive self-evaluation held by a high self-concept student (see also Covington & Beery, 1976). Observed declines in self-concept over the school years may, in part, be due to the competitive nature of most classrooms.

Thus, the social context of an achievement setting does seem to be a potent contributor to children's affective responses. Inasmuch as feelings of encouragement are related to general states of satisfaction, cooperative structures that insure group success can be a real boon to low achievers.

PERCEPTIONS OF INDIVIDUAL DIFFERENCES

In situation X, students' perceptions of their own ability relative to other students' ability are not markedly different. While students are cognizant of different levels of performance, they do not infer ability differences from this information. In situation Y, however, students' self and interpersonal perceptions are not congruent, instead their own perceived ability is markedly higher or lower than the perceived ability of others. Two questions arise relevant to the occurrence of similar v discrepant interpersonal perceptions; first, what contributes to this phenomenon and secondly, what are the potential consequences of these perceptions for student motivation?

Our research has shown that the reward–goal structure of an achievement setting is an important factor contributing to congruities or incongruities in self–other perceptions. Consistent across our research (Ames, 1978, 1981; Ames et al., 1977; Ames & Felker, 1979) is the finding that competition creates a situation of strong differences in interpersonal perceptions. Winners perceive themselves as more capable and more deserving of reward than their losing counterparts; and losers perceive themselves as inferior on these same factors as compared to their perceptions of the winning others. Even when children are not actively involved in competition, they tend to employ similar rules when judging others who are competing (Ames & Felker, 1979). Inasmuch as perceptions of inequality arise in competitive settings, perceptions of equality prevail in cooperative (Ames, 1981; Ames & Felker, 1979) and noncompetitive (Ames, 1978; Ames et al., 1977) situations. In spite of real differences in levels of performance, children tend to perceive their own ability and deservingness as similar to others. Whereas the presence of normative criteria in competitive settings appears to accentuate a recognition of differences across individuals, the presence of a team relationship in cooperative structures or the absence of social comparison needs in noncompetitive situations appears to minimize these differences in perceptions and create a norm for equality.

Whether children who perform alongside each other hold similar or dissimilar interpersonal perceptions of ability and worthiness is likely to mediate certain achievement behaviors, for example, *dropping out* (perceiving oneself as less capable than others), *self-aggrandizement* (perceiving oneself as more capable than others). Nicholls (1979) suggests that inequalities in academic motivation evolve in competitive environments and these inequalities arise because of a perceived difference in abilities. Accordingly, the presence of perceived-low-ability students is a source of motivation for high ability students and the presence of high-ability students debilitates the motivation of low ability students (Nicholls, 1979). Within this conceptualization, disparate self–other perceptions in competitive settings serve to maximize differences in student motivation. In noncompetitive structures, however, the tendency for children to perceive each other similarly may provide the basis for interpersonal attraction and the prosocial behaviors that are often observed in these settings. Cooperative structures may focus children less on the real differences in their performance because their own performance is more tied to the group effort than to any one individual.

Findings comparable to the students' interpersonal perceptions have emerged in the study of teachers' evaluations of students. Ames and McKelvie (1982) provided experienced teachers with information about a student's ability, effort, and task performance within either a competitive or cooperative reward structure. Each teacher was asked to evaluate eight different students (representing all combinations of ability, effort and performance) who were all depicted as performing within a competitive or a cooperative classroom structure. In comparing teachers' reward to high versus low performers within each structural condition, it was found that teachers' evaluations of high and low performers were more discrepant in competitive than in the cooperative conditions. These evaluations included perceptions of the child's deservingness of reward as well as positive or negative affect that would be expressed to the child. Expectancy theory tells us that teachers' perceptions can be transmitted to students through verbal and nonverbal cues (Brophy & Good, 1974; Good, 1980). Further, students apparently perceive that teachers do give differential treatment to high and low achievers (Weinstein, Marshall, Brattesani, & Middlestat, 1982). If teachers' evaluations mediate the differential behaviors accorded to high and low achievers, the differential treatment of high and low achievers should be greater in competitive classrooms. As a result of her own research, Weinstein (1982) offers "public comparability" as the factor differentiating classrooms where there is more perceived differential treatment of high and low achievers. We might speculate then that the teacher-created "environment" should be more comparable across students in noncompetitive classrooms regardless of their performance. The implication here is that the structure of the classroom situation may be an important factor that serves to enhance, create, restrict, differentiate, or equalize motivational opportunities for students (see also Weinstein, 1982). To the extent that a classroom is competitively structured, we should expect to find strong differences in specific teacher behaviors toward high and low achieving students. What is apparent is that the structure of the classroom appears to create a climate for differentiation or similarity and these perceptions are shared by students and teachers.

GOAL STRUCTURES AS MOTIVATIONAL
SYSTEMS

Cooperation and competition are often viewed as behaviors that are directed to a task situation; however, in this chapter, they are being viewed as situational factors that impinge upon a child's motivation and achievement-related cognitions. The motivational effects of competitive, cooperative, and individualistic structures have typically been assessed by looking at achievement as the outcome variable. From indices of high achievement, the inference is made about the presence or absence or degree of motivation. Herewith, motivation is viewed as a quantitative variable, that is, achievement and motivation are positively related. However, there is reason to hypothesize that the motivational consequences of these three goal structures differ qualitatively, whether or not they differ quantitatively. In the preceding sections, alone, goal structure was shown to be a critical factor that differentially influences the salience of performance information cues, the affective value of success and failure, and the perception of individual differences. Going a step further, what is now proposed is that the motivational processes within the different goal structures can be meaningfully related to distinct motivational orientations—self-worth (Covington, present volume Chapter 3) or ego-involvement (Nicholls, 1979), moral responsibility, and achievement motivation (Weiner, 1979).

The flow model in Figure 4 serves as an organizer for the subsequent sections of the chapter. Briefly summarized, three motivational systems are posited as relating to competitive, cooperative and individualistic goal structures. The motivational processes within each structure can be analyzed in relation to the dispositional factors that provide the basis for self-evaluation and attribution. Self-evaluation and attribution derive from different sources of performance information and result in different affective consequences. A competitive structure promotes an egoistic or social comparative orientation, a cooperative structure elicits a moral orientation, and an individualistic structure evokes an achievement-mastery orientation. These motivational systems are now discussed.

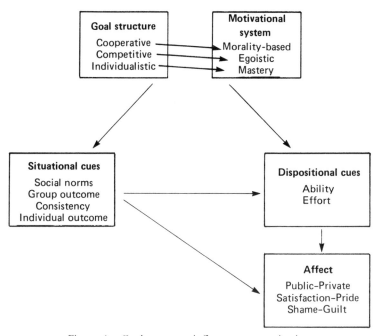

Figure 4.   Goal structure influences on motivation.

COMPETITIVE MOTIVATIONAL SYSTEM

In competition, winning is "everything" and there is substantial evidence to show that individuals will cheat, deny others of critical resources, and compete in subtle and not so subtle ways in their quest for success. Even in the context of organized sports where building character is often an intended objective, Kleiber and Roberts (1981) have found that children value winning over fairness. That competition pervades most American classrooms is no surprise to even a casual observer. Children are socialized into competitive thinking quite early in their school careers when they see, for example, that only the best work gets posted, the rows who are finished first get to line up first, smart students are accorded special privileges, students are grouped by ability, and so forth. Even young children "read" that differential treatment is given to high and low achievers (Weinstein, 1982) and believe that "winners" are smarter, happier and more deserving of reward in competitive than in noncompetitive situations (Ames & Felker, 1979). Normative comparisons in the classroom are explicit in grading practices and in teacher behavior as well as implicit in teachers' communications (e.g., "I like the way Allan is working."). Anecdotally, I have found on many occasions that teachers will indicate that they purposely try to de-emphasize competition in their classroom, but they readily acknowledge that they frequently wait to formulate their grading criteria until after they see the distribution of test scores. The point here is that competition has many faces and underscores the student's life in many, if not most, classrooms.

Nicholls (1979) suggests that competition is like an ego-involved situation such that students' attention is directed on their own ability to perform or win, rather than on "how" to do the task at hand. Covington and Beery (1976) characterize competition as a situation where only the most able are motivated and where less-able students' sense of self-worth is threatened. Common to these views is the emphasis on ability. Opportunities to win are directly related to one's ability. When an individual perceives that his or her ability is not competitive, self-worth is threatened and if alternative goals are not available, self-defeatism is the outcome. The basis of a competitive system of motivation is that the competitive structure focuses children on their ability and resulting self-ascriptions of ability are precariously linked to perceptions of winning or losing. That is, self-evaluations of ability covary with one's performance in relation to others' or to social norms and mediate subsequent affect and achievement behaviors (see Figure 4). A number of empirical investigations support this view.

In a typical experiment where we have compared competitive to contrasting noncompetitive structures, children's self-evaluations and affective reactions to their success or failure have been assessed (e.g., Ames, 1978; Ames & Ames, 1981; Ames *et al.*, 1977; Ames, 1983). In each of these studies, children's performances at a novel achievement-related task were experimentally manipulated so that one child in a pair performed at a high level (winning) and another child performed at a low level (losing). Across these studies, some involved promised rewards for performing well or winning while others only provided an instructional set of either trying to do well or trying to win. This latter factor, whether or not children actually received rewards for winning, did not appear to be critical; the mere announcement of winners appeared sufficient for instilling a competitive orientation. Consistent across these studies is the finding that competition increased the salience of ability as a factor mediating one's performance. Competitive winners self-aggrandize their ability, judging themselves as smarter than their competitors. Losers, on the other hand, deplore their situation and self-attribute incompetence. Even when children are asked to evaluate others, the ascription of high and low ability to winners and losers is more discrepant in competitive than in cooperatively defined settings (Ames & Felker, 1979).

Not only do competitive structures accentuate the salience of ability, but children's levels of satisfaction seem to be related to self-perceptions of ability. In the Ames *et al.* study (1977), self-perceptions of ability and affect were significantly related in competitive settings ($r = .65, p < .01$), but the relationship between ability and affect was not evident in noncompetitive settings. The centrality of self-ascriptions of ability to resulting affect is a consistent finding in related research that has involved competition-like situations. Nicholls (1975), for example, had children compare their own performance to a chart illustrating "how well kids your age do" and found an ability–affect linkage. Covington and Omelich (1979a) provided college age students with a mock normal distribution of scores on an exam and asked students to imagine that they had failed the test. Their findings showed that negative affect was maximized when students attributed failure to low ability. In a subsequent study using a similar paradigm (Covington & Omelich, 1979b), they found a similar relationship, although weaker, between ability attributions and positive affect following successful performances. When Halperin and Abrams (1978) asked college students to attribute their performance on a midterm exam, success and failure were attributed to ability, with the failure–lack-of-ability attribution being stronger for males than females. In these studies, social comparison was made explicit and ability emerged as the primary attribute mediating affect. Thus, there is reason to suggest that self-attributions of ability mediate affective reactions to success and failure within a competitive context.

That achievement related cognitions are related to affective reactions has been well documented, but those conditions that enhance an ability versus an effort–affect linkage have not yet been well articulated. What is suggested here is that competition is a condition that favors the use of ability as an attribute that distinguishes success and failure and that mediates subsequent affective responses.

Why do competitive situations make ability such a salient attribute for judging one's performance? From an information-processing point of view, social norms (consensus information) provide the most information about one's ability (Frieze & Weiner, 1971; Kelley, 1973). Succeeding when others fail or failing when others succeed implies that one has more ability or less (assuming that effort is constant) than others. Our research, however, suggests that it is not merely the social nature of an achievement setting that focuses children on ability cues; for when children have been rewarded for participation, trying, or cooperating, ability has not emerged as the primary factor that differentiates the self-evaluations of high and low performers. When the situation is competitively structured, however, self-ascriptions of ability covary with outcome. From an information processing point of view, then, when social norms for performance are highlighted, ability becomes a salient cue. Competitive situations may also involve ego-involving or self-worth motivational biases. Because competitive structures exaggerate the value of winning, self-perceptions of ability are easily aggrandized by the occurrence of success and self-worth is enhanced. Failure or losing leads to defensive strategies (e.g., attributions to luck) to protect self-worth (Covington & Beery, 1976); but when impossible, the ego-involvement of the situation produces low ability ascriptions and potential performance disabilities (Carver & Scheier, 1982). Nicholls (1979) suggests that it may be the increased self-awareness and the perceived importance of the terminal outcome (winning) that contributes to an ability focus.

Self-evaluations of ability may also have some perceived instrumental importance in competitive settings. Determining that one is able or not able to succeed has prima facie value if future similar situations are anticipated. An early evaluation of one's ability makes the future predictable and knowing what is likely to happen in the future is important in competitive settings where winning is positively valued and losing is negatively valued. Because ability is a stable trait, similar future performances are expected and anxiety over future competitive encounters may be partially alleviated. Even an attribution to luck could reduce anxiety because it implies "I am not responsible." Particularly in the case of failure, a private judgment of low ability, even if premature, allows one to defend against future failure, for example, by not trying or by dropping out (see Covington & Beery, 1976).

That individuals self-attribute high ability after winning is consistent with a self-worth perspective. Ability attributions for success trigger feelings of competence and confidence in addition to the more general feeling of satisfaction (Weiner, Russell, & Lerman, 1978, 1979). Pride in competition evolves from knowing one is smart and can win again. But how can the losers maintain and enhance self-worth? Ability attributions for failure are associated with "public shame" (Covington & Omelich, 1979a), which probably encompasses the affects of embarrassment and humiliation (Weiner et al., 1979). Clearly, students engage in many behaviors for avoiding the self-attribution of low ability and these have been extensively discussed by Covington and Beery (1976). However, it is not achievement situations per se that foster this "defensive maneuvering"—instead it is the competitiveness of the situation. Failure or losing connotes low ability and public shame results. Essentially students are "forced" into this potentially negative attribution–affect system when there is no reasonable alternative.

In sum, then, research that has involved competitive-based structures has implicated ability as the relevant attribution and has shown that ability attributions mediate the general affective state of satisfaction. While Brown and Weiner (in press) have suggested that anticipating future performances or that the importance of an achievement situation itself may elicit an ability–outcome covariation, competition certainly appears to be an ability-moderated motivational system that is consistent with a self-worth view of motivation. The cultural value placed on winning (being number one) may make all competitive situations "important ones." Whether unimportant competitive situations can be defined and whether they also lead to an ability focus is an empirical question. Based on recent formulations by Weiner and his colleagues (Weiner et al., 1979), we might speculate that the more specific affects associated with success in competition include public pride, competence, and confidence while public shame, embarassment and humiliation are the affects associated with losing. These attribution-dependent affects do not represent a positive achievement orientation following failure. The motivational dilemma of the low-ability, low-achieving student concerns engaging in behaviors that assure success or diminish the effects of failure or resign oneself to the self- and other-attributed level of low ability.

COOPERATIVE MOTIVATIONAL SYSTEM

A cooperative social situation is one in which the goals of separate individuals are shared (Deutsch, 1949; Johnson & Johnson, 1975). Cooperation involves working toward a common goal such that group members receive common rewards for attainment (or punishment for nonattainment) of goals; for example, there is a positive relationship between an individual's rewards and the achievements of the group. For a young child, cooperation is often equated with helping, sharing, taking turns. It is not infrequent that young children are admonished to "cooperate and share." Indeed, helping behaviors are often evident in cooperative situations and are implicit in many models of cooperative learning (Aronson, 1978; Slavin, 1978). According to Staub (1978), we encounter some conceptual problems when we try to differentiate cooperation from helping. Staub provides the following example: "In a marriage it is understood that the partners will do things for each other that are necessary to satisfy each other's needs, to attain shared goals external to the relationship, as well as to maintain a positive relationship" (p. 382). Here, helping is as much for purposes of mutual benefit or gain as it is to benefit the other. In the classroom, cooperative behaviors (helping) are critical to goal attainment in many cooperative learning structures (e.g., TGT, STAD, JIGSAW). Johnson and Johnson (1975) and Slavin (1983) attest that students' helping one another is a motivational component of cooperative structures and mediates achievement and learning. The dependence of each student's reward on the success of the group is thought to elicit helping behaviors (Hamblin, Hathaway, & Wodarski, 1971; Slavin, 1983). Helping is assisting others as well as doing one's share of the work on a cooperative task. As a consequence, the concepts of helping and cooperating are not always distinct; and when helping another benefits the group, helpfulness may be a type of cooperation (Staub, 1978). At the minimum, helping behavior appears to be a critical process variable that is activated by cooperative structures.

Inherent in cooperative structures, then, is a concept of shared effort, and the positive interdependence among students implies shared goals and shared rewards. To the extent that cooperation elicits norms for helping, cooperatively based structures involve some aspects of a moral situation. Even when students are afforded little opportunity to help each other directly, cooperative structures nevertheless create social interdependency among group members that is characteristic of moral situations. The implication of this argument is that if cooperative and moral situations emphasize the importance of similar behaviors, the motivational system that evolves in these situations may, in fact, be quite similar.

In moral situations, the focus for evaluation is intention or how willing one is to put forth effort. In an exemplary study by Weiner and Peter (1973), children of varying ages were asked to evaluate the moral (helping) behavior of a hypothetical child when provided with information about the child's ability, intent (whether he or she tried to help), and the outcome of the behavior. From the results of this study, they concluded that moral situations are primarily intent-oriented systems, that is, behavior is judged according to the intent of the actor. Within a moral domain then, perceived intention or willingness to put forth effort is important in the evaluation of behavior. If cooperative situations parallel the moral domain, we would also expect to find a valuing of effort within the achievement context of cooperation. While Weiner and Peter found that effort tended to be subordinate to outcome as an important determinant of evaluation in the achievement domain, their description of an achievement situation was individually (e.g., "_____ is working on a puzzle. He did not solve it.") not cooperatively structured. They suggested that the importance attributed to outcome or personal productiveness in achievement reflects a cultural bias favoring an individualistic–competitive orientation. Their argument parlays the role that situational and cultural factors have in achievement cognitions and judgments. We can speculate that if the situational context in the Weiner and Peter study had manded a cooperative orientation, effort may have been more uniformly valued in the achievement domain and the findings would have paralleled the moral context. In the absence of research that directly tests this assertion, we can first look to other cultures where social interdependence and group goals are stressed in the achievement domain (e.g., Japan), and we find that those behaviors that demonstrate group commitment (contributing to the group goal, effort) are positively valued and associated with success (Maehr & Nicholls, 1980; Torney-Purta & Schwille, 1982). The congruity between cooperative and moral situations centers on their common valuing of intent–effort directed toward some external goal. Inasmuch as cooperative structures evoke a moral orientation, effort should be of primary value. However, it is not the individualistic conception of effort (trying hard for one's own gain) that is reflected by the Protestant ethic; instead it is a conception of effort that serves group goals and demonstrates social responsibility. The distinction between groupdirected versus individually directed effort does not mean that one fits less within an achievement orientation than the other (see Maehr & Nicholls, 1980); it does, however, distinguish different goals. Within a cooperative structure, effort is demonstrated to fulfill group commitments to achieve group goals.

That primary importance is attached to behavior pursuant to the achievement of the group should have several implications. First, we might expect that the focus of attention would be centered on the group performance over and above any individual characteristics (within the realm of situational factors in Figure 4). In support of this, we have found that in the evaluation of achievement behavior, the productiveness of the group is as important as the productiveness of the individual. Specifically, children are perceived as similar in ability (and deserving of reward) when they are described as working in a cooperative group even when their performances are markedly discrepant (Ames & Felker, 1979; Ames & McKelvie, 1982). The presence of a team relationship appears to create a perception of equality; and equality, more than equity, governs the distribution of rewards. Cooperative structures appear to convey a norm of "perceived similarity" when children are involved in real performance settings as well as when they respond to hypothetical situations. A sense that "we are in this together" underscores an underlying belief structure that is closely aligned with cooperative settings. Thus, whereas competitive situations foster perceptions of differences, cooperative structures contribute to perceptions of similarity.

That the group goal or achievement is preeminent in importance is also found when we examine the effects of different group outcomes on self-evaluations. If group productiveness is valued, we should find differences in children's self-evaluations as a function of successful versus unsuccessful group outcomes even when individual performances might be alike. That is, low individual achievement should be differentially evaluated if the individual is in a successful group versus an unsuccessful group. This line of reasoning was tested in a recent study (Ames, 1981). In this study, children were paired to work at a novel achievement task in either cooperative or competitive settings. Within the cooperative structure, both successful and unsuccessful groups were studied—successful groups achieved a predesignated goal and unsuccessful groups did not. The performance of the individual child was also manipulated so that within each pair, one child achieved a high level performance and the other child a low level performance. Relevant to the preceding issue are the findings that showed that whether the cooperative group was successful or not influenced children's evaluations of their ability and their resulting affect (see Figure 5). A successful group outcome depressed the self-evaluations of a high performer. What is striking here is that a low achiever who might otherwise maintain self-perceptions of low ability is bolstered by the positive group outcome. Whereas winning enhances self-perceptions of ability in competitive situations, successful group outcomes have a similar effect in cooperative situations. Our findings suggest that many of the positive consequences (e.g., heightened self-esteem) attributed to cooperative structures may, in actuality, be more a function of the group outcome; than the cooperative structure itself. The potential impact of unsuccessful groups has been a much neglected factor in the research on cooperation. Within cooperative

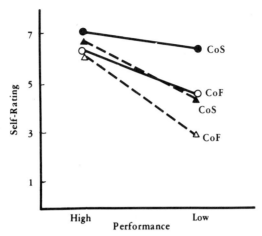

Figure 5. Self-evaluation following high and low performances in cooperatively successful (CoS) and Failing (CoF) groups (based on Ames, 1981); solid lines refer to ability; broken lines refer to deservedness of reward.

structures, then, group outcome or productiveness appears to be a critical factor for the study of motivation. We cannot predict self-evaluations solely by looking at individual achievements; children attend to group outcome information and the effects of negative outcomes deserve special attention in future research on cooperation.

When we look at the interpersonal evaluations within cooperative groups we find further support for the parallel between cooperative and moral situations. The evaluation system in the moral domain is based on blame, rather than reward. That is, individuals are less rewarded for upholding social norms than they are punished for behaviors that violate social norms and expectations. Moral situations involve the impartation of blame for negative behaviors. As we look within cooperative groups, the performance of the low performer may be viewed as unacceptable or deviant. This low performer may be viewed as a target for blame in that he or she "ought" to have made a better contribution to the group and has seemingly failed to fulfill a commitment to the group. However, we find that individual "failure" becomes most salient when the group fails. When group members are asked to distribute rewards, the low performer is given substantially less reward when the group has failed than when it has been successful (Ames, 1981). In the circumstance of group failure, the question of responsibility becomes important and the low contributor is judged negatively and apparently "punished" with reduced reward. Like a moral system, the negative outcome evokes blame for the individual who seemingly "caused" the failure. Cooperative structures, however are not situations of blame when the group succeeds, only when the group fails; that is, when expectations for both group and individual productivity are violated.

What has been argued here is that cooperative structures share certain features of moral situations. Cooperative situations are achievement settings; and while performance outcome is an important factor, unlike competitive situations, an individual's performance must be interpreted within the context of the group performance. Cooperative and moral situations are social in nature, involving interdependency. Characteristically, there is a strong element of helping behavior in cooperative settings, whether it involves directly assisting another or doing one's part of the task. Finally, implied in cooperative group situations is the norm of fulfilling one's commitment to the group.

Because cooperation reflects primarily a moral system, intent-based cues should be salient. We might speculate that the attribution of not trying mediated the assignment of low reward to the poor performer. The high-performing child's thought sequences may have been "I did well; I could do this task; therefore he should have been able to do it. He must not have tried." This seems especially plausible since children were paired within achievement levels. While we found that low performers self-attributed low ability, but generally not low effort, they might have been unwilling to self-attribute low effort because of an anticipation of blame. In this case, an attribution of low ability avoids public blame even though it might elicit personal shame. Clearly, the attribution–affect linkage in cooperative structures is in need of further research.

In sum, certain linkages and similarities have been noted to present the case that cooperative structures may involve a morally based motivational system. In each situation, sanctions are directed to fulfill an obligation to the group by putting forth effort to assure group success. Slavin (1983) has found that children in classes that use cooperative learning agree with statements such as "other children in my class want me to work hard." When cooperation is described as increasing students' motivation to learn (e.g., Slavin, 1983), it is not synonymous with Nicholls' description of a motivation to understand and gain ability; nor is it like Covington's self-worth motive; instead it implies a moral responsibility of being motivated to fulfill one's obligation to the group by putting forth effort. It is a task orientation only in the sense that cooperation implies an obligation to the group task. The effects of cooperative structures on learning are mediated by motivational factors that involve the concept of "ought"—that one ought to pull one's weight, to contribute, to satisfy peer norms and sanctions.

INDIVIDUALISTIC MOTIVATION SYSTEM

Alternative and somewhat contrasting conceptions of individualistic structures have evolved in the literature. Common to most views, individualism implies an independence of goals such that one individual's rewards are not dependent upon another's (Johnson & Johnson, 1974). Individualistic structures have also been described as producing self-competition in that performance evaluations are based on external criteria (Johnson & Johnson, 1979). In competitive settings the external criteria are social norms, and the criteria are defined in relation to some absolute standard in individualized settings. This perspective suggests that competitive and individualistic structures are similar in that they both focus on external standards for performance evaluation, and as such, they should elicit similar patterns of attribution and affect. Studies that have defined individualism within this framework have found that individual reward contingencies yield patters of attribution (e.g., Ames & Felker, 1979; Nicholls, 1975) and general affect (Garibaldi, 1979) similar to interpersonal competition and more extrinsically based motivation than cooperative structures (Johnson, Johnson, Johnson, & Anderson, 1976). Taken together, these studies suggest that the motivational consequences of individualized structures are potentially rather negative.

Alternative conceptions of individualized structures, however, focus less on external standards and instead emphasize self-generated cues for evaluating one's achievement. An implied "request" for self-improvement embodies what has been called success- and mastery-oriented structures (Covington, present volume, Chapter 3; Covington & Beery, 1976) and origin-like classrooms (deCharms, 1976). The common factor across these approaches is the focus on the instrumentality of one's behavior for achieving task mastery, that is, a valuing of effort. Individualistic structures, here, are sharply contrasted to competitive structures in that they have a stronger task focus and the self-awareness that is endogenous to competitive structures (Nicholls, 1979) is minimized. Perceptions of the task should also have different origins. In competitive structures, a determination of task difficulty involves a self-assessment of ability relative to the ability of others, but in individualized settings, task difficulty should require a determination of the amount of effort required relative to one's present status and the objective. It is presumed that a perception of "can" is necessary in an individualized structure ("I can do this if I try."); if this assumption is not self-evident, children are likely to engage in social comparison. Clearly, within our culture a non-competitive setting can be quickly translated into a competitive one when some level of uncertainty reigns (Alvarez & Pader, 1979; Levine, 1983). Thus, individualized structures that emphasize self-improvement and that get students involved in the task should make effort the criterion for self-evaluation.

In our research, our first attempt (Ames et al., 1977) to define a structure that would provide a contrast to competition was what was labeled a "noncompetitive" situation; and although it involved a social situation, in many respects it resembled an individualistic orientation. In this investigation, which contrasted competitive and noncompetitive structures, children in the noncompetitive setting were told that they would receive a prize for their participation. Essentially, there were no external performance criteria nor was there any performance evaluation; they were rewarded for participating which they may have interpreted as becoming involved in the task. Ratings were taken on several self-attribution (e.g., ability, effort) and affect (satisfaction) scales. Our findings showed a positive relationship between effort attributions and satisfaction ($r = .40$, $p < .05$) in the noncompetitive condition. Feelings of satisfaction were a function of self-attributions of effort. This relationship did not emerge in the competitive setting. A perceived effort attribution–affect linkage is the crux of Weiner's analysis of achievement behavior (Weiner, 1979; Weiner & Kukla, 1970). That is, pride and shame result from the attribution of success and failure to effort.

This early study gave us reason to suspect that a perceived effort–outcome covariation might prevail in settings that minimize needs for social comparison. In a subsequent study, however, we found that when externally defined goals were present, the situation appeared to be interpreted in a self-competitive manner, that is, attributions for success and failure paralleled those of a competitive condition (Ames & Felker, 1979). In this study, the individual situation had two components, a single performance outcome and absolute standards for evaluation, both of which may have made ability more salient than effort in differentiating success and failure. We suspected that a solicitation of task engagement might be necessary to instill an individualistic orientation. Further, we felt that a time dimension (i.e., performance over time trials) may be an implicit feature of individualistic structures. Our thinking led us to study children's causal attributions for success and failure within individualistic (defined as "try to solve as many puzzles as you can") and competitive ("who will be the winner") structures. In addition to these differing task orientations, children were involved with the task over several trials prior to the imposition of the competitive or individualistic goal orientation. Thus, the individual situation had both a task engagement component as well as a "performance over time" component. Confirming our expectations, the findings showed that effort attributions were associated more with individualistic than with competitive outcomes. Children believed that effort accounted for both high and low performances more in the individual than in the competitive situation. A more recent study (Ames, 1983) that will be described subsequently in more detail provides strong confirmation of the effort– outcome linkage in individualistic structures when trying is emphasized.

Recently, Heckhausen and Krug (1982) have described several curriculum-based modifications that embody an individual perspective (i.e., focus on continuity of performance over time, self-improvement). The cumulative findings of this research provides field-based evidence supporting the relationship between individualized programs and attributions to effort-related factors (e.g., motivation, interest). Covington (this volume, Chapter 3) in a field study using a mastery-based learning approach with college students has demonstrated how the opportunity for self-improvement (multiple test options) seems to be a critical factor for eliciting perceptions of personal control through effort.

Consistent across these field and lab investigations is the conception of individualized structures as involving the inculcation of "trying." The presence of absolute standards alone may make children goal-focused; and when children are goal focused, individualism becomes self-competition. Opportunities for self-improvement or for performance over time–trials in addition to noncompetitively prescribed standards may be critical for establishing an effort focus. In other words, a task or process focus may be necessary to convey a belief that effort mediates success and failure. There is some initial evidence that children are more process-oriented in individualized settings, in that children tend to use more self-instructional statements (e.g., "I need to concentrate") when they are performing in individualized than in competitive settings (Ames, 1983).

A belief that effort and achievement outcomes are causally linked is the basis for Weiner's model of achievement motivation (e.g., Weiner, 1979). This achievement motive appears to be aroused when there is a "self-challenge" and seems to evolve when students are encouraged to try but seems less likely to appear when there are solely external criteria or incentives for defining success (no self-improvement opportunity) and when situations are competitively defined. External incentives do not seem to be necessary for the maintenance of behavior over time (Alschuler, 1973) and may even undermine the occurrence of achievement behavior (Lepper & Greene, 1975). Thus, what is proposed is that an outcome → effort → personal pride/shame linkage is elicited within an individualistic structure where trying is made salient through self challenge, the solicitation of effort, or opportunities for self improvement (see Figure 4).

In addition to a self percept that performance and effort covary over time and events other achievement-related cognitions have recently become associated with positive and negative achievement orientations. Diener and Dweck (1978), for example, suggest that children who exhibit mastery versus helpless behaviors differ in their use of self-instructional and self-monitoring ("I need to concentrate, pay attention") cognitions and these cognitions purportedly reflect a mastery or positive achievement orientation. In their research, the mastery children became very solution-focused when they encountered failure; that is, they engaged in self-instructions in an attempt to improve their performance and attended to the amount of effort that might be necessary for effective task performance.

This research suggests that a variety of cognitive-motivational thought patterns (e.g., attributions to ability vs. effort, use of general cognitive strategies) may be associated with positive and negative achievement orientations. The following study (Ames, 1983) was designed to extend this work by examining these cognitions as a function of differing goal structures. While the research discussed thus far tends to support the relationship between ability attributions and competitive structures and between effort attributions and individualistic structures, could there also be differences in how children approach a task? We reasoned that if individualistic structures focus children on how to do a task and on how to improve their performance, correspondingly, they should also employ self-instructional strategies. That is, if an individualistic structure promotes a process or mastery orientation, children should actively search for ways to improve their performance through self-instructions.

In this study, (Ames, 1983) high, middle, and low achievement level fifth- and sixth-grade children were randomly assigned to competitive or individualistic goal structure conditions, controlling for achievement level, sex, and grade level. The children were tested individually or in pairs in the competitive condition such that all achievement levels were equally represented in each condition and children were paired within achievement level. The experimental situation involved two separate tasks of six line-drawn puzzles, which the children had to trace. The children performed at either a high (predominantly solvable puzzles) or a low (predominantly insolvable puzzles) level. In the competitive condition, each child was exhorted to try to be the winner. In the individualized condition, the children were told to try to solve as many puzzles as they could and to try to solve more puzzles the second time. Thus, the individual condition involved both criteria that were mentioned earlier, performance over time and opportunity for self-improvement. After the second task and while anticipating a third task, the children responded to a questionnaire which contained statements relating to attributions (ability vs. effort-related) a child might make about his or her performance, self-directed instructions a child might make about his or her next performance, and affective reactions to his or her performance. These statements were based on the categories Diener and Dweck (1978) derived from children's voluntary verbalizations during a task performance. The children read all the statements and were asked to circle those statements that told what the child was "thinking right now." The results showed that children selected more ability-related attributional statements in the competitive than in the individualized structure ($p < .01$). Conversely, children selected more effort-related ($p < .01$) and self-instructional ($p < .001$) statements in the individual than in the competitive setting. Further, in the individualistic structure, self-instructional statements (e.g., "I will work carefully . . . I will take my time . . . I will make a plan.") were used significantly more often than any other category of statement. Next most frequent were statements indicating attribution to effort-related factors. These findings indicate that individualistic structures create a mastery orientation that extends beyond the perceived effort–outcome covariation, evidenced by the predominant use of self-instructional statements. Further these findings suggest a linkage between the occurrence of attribution-related (effort) cognitions and coping strategies (self-instructions) in the individual condition.

Here, we have found support for the ability focus that evolves in competitive structures. Children exhibit a strong self-focus, believing that their ability is the factor that differentiates success and failure. Within the individualistic structure, however, we find further support for a strong achievement orientation. Not only do children attribute their performance to effort, they also think about how to do the task. Whereas many achievement change programs involve some form of attribution retraining or cognitive modification, these findings suggest that individualistic structures may produce the same motivational effects. Thus, an achievement (effort–outcome attribution) and task mastery (self-instructions) motivation appear to be generated in individualized settings where opportunities for improvement are provided.

CONCLUSION

The educational research literature that pits one type of goal–reward structure against another in relation to immediate achievement outcomes may miss or overlook other important psychological processes that are important to long-term motivation and learning. The psychological processes that have been discussed in this chapter include children's self-attributions and related cognitive self-evaluations as well as general affective reactions to success and failure. Three different motivational systems have been proposed, corresponding to competitive, cooperative, and individualistic goal structures. While these contrasting goal structures may contribute to similar or dissimilar levels of achievement, it has been argued that they do elicit different types of motivation. As a consequence, students may be socialized into a preferred motivational system, may develop different components of a self-evaluation system, and may rely on certain information sources as a function of the goal-reward structure they experience over time. Thus, based on certain value-related decisions, the structure of the learning environment may provide opportunities for students to realize certain goals and not others by influencing student motivational processes and achievement patterns.

REFERENCES

Alshuler, A. *Developing achievement motivation in adolescents.* Englewood Cliffs, NJ: Educational Technology, 1973.

Alvarez, C., & Pader, O. Cooperative and competitive behaviors of Cuban-American and Anglo-American children. *Journal of Psychology,* 1979, *101,* 265–271.

Ames, C. Children's achievement attributions and self-reinforcement: Effects of self-concept and competitive reward structure. *Journal of Educational Psychology,* 1978, *70,* 345–355.

Ames, C. Competitive versus cooperative reward structures: The influence of individual and group performance factors on achievement attributions and affect. *American Educational Research Journal,* 1981, *18,* 273–287.

Ames, C. *A study of cognitive-motivational thought processes in competitive and individualistic goal structures.* Manuscript submitted for publication, 1983.

Ames, C., & Ames, R. Competitive versus individualistic goal structures: The salience of past performance information for causal attributions and affect. *Journal of Educational Psychology,* 1981, *73,* 411–418.

Ames, C., Ames, R., & Felker, D. Effects of competitive reward structure and valence of outcome on children's achievement attributions. *Journal of Educational Psychology,* 1977, *69,* 1–8.

Ames, C., & Felker, D. An examination of children's attributions and achievement-related evaluations in competitive, cooperative, and individualistic reward structures. *Journal of Educational Psychology,* 1979, *71,* 413–420.

Ames, C., & McKelvie, S. *Evaluation of student achievement behavior within cooperative and competitive reward structures.* Paper presented at the Annual American Educational Research Association meeting, New York, 1982.

Aronson, E. *The jigsaw classroom.* Beverly Hills, CA: Sage, 1978.

Bandura, A. *Social learning theory*. Englewood Cliffs, NJ: Prentice-Hall, 1977.

Barnett, M., & Andrews, J. Sex differences in children's reward allocation under competitive and cooperative instructional sets. *Developmental Psychology*, 1977, *13*, 85–86.

Block, J. Motivation, evaluation and mastery learning. *UCLA Educator*, 1977, *12*, 31–37.

Brophy, J., & Good, T. *Teacher-student relationships: Causes and consequences*. New York: Holt, Rinehart, & Winston, 1974.

Brown, J., & Weiner, B. Affective consequences of ability versus effort ascriptions: Empirical controversies, resolutions and quandries. *Journal of Educational Psychology*, in press.

Carver, C., & Scheier, M. Outcome expectancy, locus of attribution for expectancy, and self-directed attention as determinants of evaluations and performance. *Journal of Experimental Social Psychology*, 1982, *18*, 184–200.

Cotton, J., & Cook, M. Meta-analyses and the effects of various reward systems: Some different conclusions from Johnson *et al. Psychological Bulletin*, 1982, *92*, 176–183.

Covington, M., & Beery, R. *Self-worth and school learning*. New York: Holt, Rinehart, & Winston, 1976.

Covington, M., & Omelich, C. Effort: The double-edged sword in school achievement. *Journal of Educational Psychology*, 1979, *71*, 169–182. (a)

Covington, M., & Omelich, C. It's best to be able and virtuous too: Student and teacher evaluative responses to successful effort. *Journal of Educational Psychology*, 1979, *71*, 688–700. (b)

deCharms, R. *Enhancing motivation: Change in the classroom*. New York: Irvington, 1976.

Deci, E. *Intrinsic motivation*. New York: Plenum, 1975.

Deutsch, M. A theory of cooperation and competition. *Human Relations*, 1949, *2*, 129–152.

Diener, C., & Dweck, C. An analysis of learned helplessness: Continuous changes in performance, strategy, and achievement cognitions following failure. *Journal of Personality and Social Psychology*, 1978, *36*, 451–462.

Frieze, I., & Weiner, B. Cue utilization and attributional judgments for success and failure. *Journal of Personality*, 1971, *39*, 591–605.

Garibaldi, A. Affective contributions of cooperative and group goal structures. *Journal of Educational Psychology*, 1979, *71*, 788–794.

Good, T. Classroom expectations: Teacher and pupil interactions. In J. McMillan (Ed.), *Social psychology of school learning*. New York: Academic Press, 1980.

Halperin, M., & Abrams, D. Sex differences in predicting final examination grades: The influence of past performance, attributions and achievement motivation. *Journal of Educational Psychology*, 1978, *70*, 763–771.

Hamblin, R., Hathaway, C., & Wodarski, J. Group contingencies, peer tutoring and accelerating academic achievement. In E. Ramp & W. Hopkins (Eds.), *A new direction in education: Behavior analysis*. Lawrence, KS: University of Kansas, 1971.

Heckhausen, H., & Krug, S. Motive modification. In A. Stewart (Ed.), *Motivation and society*. San Francisco: Jossey Bass, 1982.

Holt, J. *How children fail*. New York: Pittman, 1964.

Johnson, D., & Johnson, R. Instructional goal structure: Cooperative competitive or individualistic. *Review of Educational Research*, 1974, *44*, 213–240.

Johnson, D., & Johnson, R. *Learning together and alone: Cooperation, competition and individualization*. Englewood Cliffs, NJ: Prentice-Hall, 1975.

Johnson, D., & Johnson, R. Cooperation, competition, and individualization. In H. Walberg (Ed.), *Educational environments and effects*. Berkeley, CA: McCutchan, 1979.

Johnson, D., Johnson, R., Johnson, J., & Anderson, D. The effects of cooperative vs. individualized instruction on student prosocial behavior, attitudes toward learning and achievement. *Journal of Educational Psychology*, 1976, *68*, 446–452.

Johnson, D., Johnson, R., & Scott, L. The effects of cooperative and individualistic instruction on student attitudes and achievement. *Journal of Social Psychology*, 1978, *104*, 207–216.

Johnson, D., Maruyama, G., Johnson, R., Nelson, D., & Skon, L. Effects of cooperative, competitive, and individualistic goal structures on achievement: A meta-analysis. *Psychological Bulletin*, 1981, *89*, 47–62.

Kelley, H. The process of causal attribution. *American Psychologist*, 1973, *28*, 107–128.

Kleiber, D., & Roberts, G. The effects of sport experience in the development of social character: An exploratory investigation. *Journal of Sport Psychology*, 1981, *3*, 114–122.

Kukla, A. An attributional theory of choice. In L. Berkowitz (Ed.), *Advances in experimental social psychology* (Vol. 2). New York: Academic Press, 1978.

Lepper, M., & Greene, D. Turning play into work: Effects of adult surveillance and extrinsic rewards on children's intrinsic motivation. *Journal of Personality and Social Psychology*, 1975, *31*, 479–486.

Levine, J. Social comparison and education. In J. Levine & M. Wang (Eds.), *Teachers and student perceptions: Implications for learning*. New Jersey: Erlbaum, 1983.

Maehr, M. Continuing motivation: An analysis of a seldom considered educational outcome. *Review of Educational Research*, 1976, *46*, 443–462.

Maehr, M., & Nicholls, J. Culture and achievement motivation: A second look. In N. Warren (Ed.), *Studies in cross-cultural psychology*. New York: Academic Press, 1980.

Michaels, J. Classroom reward structures and academic performance.*Review of Educational Research*, 1977, *47*, 87–99.

Nicholls, J. Causal attributions and other achievement-related cognitions: Effects of task outcome, attainment value, and sex. *Journal of Personality and Social Psychology*, 1975, *31*, 379–389.

Nicholls, J. Quality and equality in intellectual development: The role of motivation in education. *American Psychologist*, 1979, *34*, 1071–1084.

Nicholls, J. Motivation theory and its applications to education. In S. Paris, G. Olson, & H. Stevenson (Eds.), *Learning and motivation in the classroom*. Hillsdale, NJ: Erlbaum, 1982.

Pepitone, E. *Children in cooperation and competition: Toward a developmental social psychology*. Lexington, MA: Heath, 1980.

Roberts, G., Kleiber, D., & Duda, J. An analysis of motivation in children's sport: The role of perceived competence in participation. *Journal of Sport Psychology*, 1981, *3*, 206–216.

Slavin, R. Classroom reward structure: Analytical and practical review. *Review of Educational Research*, 1977, *47*, 633–650.

Slavin, R. Student teams and achievement divisions. *Journal of Research and Development in Education*, 1978, *12*, 39–49.

Slavin, R. *Cooperative learning*. New York: Longman, 1983.

Staub, E. *Positive social behavior and morality*. New York: Academic Press, 1978.

Torney-Purta, J., & Schwille, J. The value learned in school: Policy and practice in industrialized countries. Washington, D.C.: National Commission on Excellence in Education, 1982.

Weiner, B. A theory of motivation for some classroom experiences. *Journal of Educational Psychology*, 1979, *71*, 3–25.

Weiner, B., & Kukla, A. An attributional analysis of achievement motivation. *Journal of Personality and Social Psychology*, 1970, *15*, 1–20.

Weiner, B., & Peter, N. A cognitive developmental analysis of achievement and moral judgments. *Developmental Psychology*, 1973, *9*, 290–309.

Weiner, B., Russell, D., & Lerman, D. Affective consequences of causal ascriptions. In J. H.

Harvey, W. Ickes, & R. Kidd (Eds.), *New directions in attribution research* (Vol. 2). Hillsdale, NJ: Erlbaum, 1978.

Weiner, B., Russell, D., & Lerman, D. The cognition–emotion process in achievement-related contexts. *Journal of Personality and Social Psychology*, 1979, *37*, 1211–1220.

Weinstein, R. *Expectations in the classroom*. Presented at the Annual American Educational Research Association meeting, New York, 1982.

Weinstein, R., Marshall, H., Brattesani, K., & Middlestat, S. Student perceptions of differential teacher treatment in open and traditional classrooms. *Journal of Educational Psychology*, 1982, *74*, 678–692.

Weinstein, R., & Middlestat, S. Student perceptions of teacher interactions with male high and low achievers. *Journal of Educational Psychology*, 1979, *71*, 421–431.

7

Socioeconomic Status and Ethnic Group Differences in Achievement Motivation*

Harris Cooper
David Y. H. Tom

OVERVIEW

This chapter begins with a brief discussion of the definition of achievement motivation and then reviews several theories of how achievement motivation is acquired. Particular attention is paid to how theorists explain the differences that exist between ethnic groups and socioeconomic statuses in the strength of their need to achieve.

The body of the chapter reviews 43 studies that compared different ethnic groups and socioeconomic statuses (SES), using need for achievement as the dependent measure. The review applies some quantitative techniques for combining the results of independent studies, as well as more traditional, narrative procedures. Finally, current problems in studying ethnic and SES differences in achievement motivation are discussed along with suggestions for future research.

*Thanks are extended to Martin Maehr for providing several bibliographies.

209

McClelland

McClelland defined achievement motivation in terms of "competition" and "standards of excellence" (McClelland, Atkinson, Clark, & Lowell, 1953). He argued that people who were high in achievement motivation tended to strive for high goals or levels of excellence that they set for themselves (McClelland, 1955a; 1955b; 1961; McClelland, Atkinson, Clark, & Lowell, 1953; McClelland, Clark, Roby, & Atkinson, 1958).

McClelland (1955a, 1961) maintained that independence training by parents played a crucial role in determining the future achievement motivation of the child. In particular, he suggested that achievement motivation was associated with the mother's stress on independence and self-reliance at an early age. McClelland and his associates found that mothers of sons with strong needs for achievement expected their offspring to be independent earlier in life than did mothers of sons low in need for achievement. In addition, mothers of boys with strong need for achievement tended to reduce the number of restrictions imposed on their sons' behavior as the child grew older, whereas mothers of boys with weak achievement strivings tended to increase the number of behavioral restrictions. Also, McClelland, Rindlibacher, and deCharms (1955) found that sons who felt their fathers had rejected them had higher need for achievement than sons who felt their fathers had loved and accepted them. In sum, various cultural and family factors were offered by McClelland as contributing to offsprings' attitudes toward independence, which in turn influenced the strength of their achievement motivation.

Rosen

Rosen (1959) stated that achievement motivation provided an impetus or drive for the person to excel, and that certain value orientations, as well as educational or occupational aspirations, seemed to help channel one's behavior toward these self-imposed standards or goals. For Rosen, achievement motivation was delineated by one's need to excel, which has origins early in a child's life.

Rosen reinforced much of McClelland's theory, including the notion that mothers of sons with strong needs for achievement were more dominant and had higher aspirations for their children (Rosen & D'Andrade, 1959). Rosen also suggested, however, that boys seemed to acquire more of their independence and autonomy from their fathers. Mothers, on the other hand, provided the driving impetus for success and tended to be more a catalyst for achievement aspirations than fathers. Rosen felt that achievement training and independence training were both elements of achievement motivation and that, in contrast to McClelland, achievement training was the more important of the two.

In achievement training, parents try to instill high standards of success in their child, urging the child to do as well as possible. In independence training, parents try to instill some sense of self-reliance and responsibility in the child. According to Rosen, these two elements together make up achievement motivation.

Mothers were thought by Rosen to contribute more to achievement training, and fathers to independence training. Because the influence of mothers on sons is much stronger than that of fathers, achievement training was deemed more important in fostering a high need for achievement (Rosen, 1959; Rosen & D'Andrade, 1959; Winterbottom, 1958).

Two other major factors discussed by Rosen are value orientations, which facilitate the implementation of achievement-motivated behavior, and educational or occupational aspirations. Both of these factors, together with achievement motivation, make up what Rosen called the Achievement Syndrome.

Atkinson

Atkinson and Raynor (1974, 1978) theorized that there were not one but two achievement-related motives acquired and demonstrated by people. One motive was to achieve and the other was to avoid failure. Atkinson and Raynor (1974) maintained that three variables contributed to an individual's tendency to achieve success. First, there was a personality variable or some intrinsic motive to approach success. Second, there was a strength of expectancy (or probability) that success will follow task performance. Third, there existed some index of attractiveness of the success of a particular activity, or its incentive value.

Similarly, Atkinson and Raynor (1974) identified a tendency to avoid the performance of achievement-related activities. The components of this tendency were (1) a motive to avoid failure or the humiliation and possible embarrassment experienced when failure is encountered; (2) an expectancy or probability that an act will result in failure; and (3) the incentive value of failure. For example, when a person fears failure at an easy task, the potential embarrassment encountered is to be avoided at all costs.

Maehr

Maehr's definition of achievement motivation contained three elements:

> achievement motivation refers first of all to behavior that occurs in reference to a *standard of excellence* and can thus be evaluated in terms of success and failure. A second defining condition is that the individual must in some sense *be responsible for the outcome.* Third, there is some level of *challenge* and, therewith, some sense of uncertainty involved [Maehr, 1974b, p. 888; italics in original].

Maehr's theory of achievement motivation was founded on the basis of what he termed "naturalistic" concepts of research and study (Maehr, 1974b). Incorporating the interactive nature of personality and situations, Maehr maintained that what is deemed achievement-oriented behavior in some cultures is not in others (Maehr, 1974a, 1974b; Maehr & Nicholls, 1980). Maehr defined three forms of achievement motivation.

1. *Ability-oriented motivation*, which he described as "striving to maintain a favorable perception of one's ability. That is, the goal of the behavior is to maximize the subjective probability of attributing high ability to oneself" (Maehr & Nicholls, 1980, pp. 236–237);
2. *Task-oriented motivation*, whereby the primary goal is to solve a problem or complete a task for its own intrinsic value, and not for the purposes of demonstrating one's skill on task performance; and
3. *Social-approval-oriented motivation*, which can be viewed as trying to maximize the chances of attributing a high amount of effort to the self, while minimizing the chances of attributing low effort to self (Maehr & Nicholls, 1980).

Maehr argued that what is important is defining which *settings* in various cultures call for achievement motivation to be present or absent. Additionally, it must be determined how each specific culture defines achievement motivation, and what culture-specific goals people strive for.

SOCIOECONOMIC STATUS, RACE, AND ACHIEVEMENT MOTIVATION

McClelland

McClelland's original theory of achievement motivation was an outgrowth of Max Weber's "Protestant work ethic" hypothesis (Weber, 1930). McClelland maintained that, in light of Weber's thesis, Protestant families stressed independence and self-reliance as a result of their religious training and background. This stress on self-reliance and productivity was in marked contrast to Catholic and Roman Catholic families, especially with regard to economic productivity.

McClelland proposed that Protestant families instilled strong need for achievement in their children as a result of the Protestants rebelling against the religious teachings of the time. However, McClelland also uncovered evidence of an interaction between ethnicity and religion. With religion held constant, Irish Catholics scored significantly higher than Italian Catholics in need for achievement (McClelland *et al.*, 1955). McClelland explained this finding in terms of the Irish fostering independence at an earlier age than the Italians. One factor not taken into account was the possible influences of Irish Protestants in facilitating earlier self-reliance on the part of their Catholic countrymen. Nevertheless, McClelland and his associates maintained that differences between ethnic and religious groups could be explained in terms of the attitude of parents toward early independence training, especially in the role of the mother toward the son.

With regard to SES, McClelland (1955a, 1955b) found that SES was closely tied to the nurturance, assistance, and training given by the parents. The higher the educational level of parents, the earlier the onset of independence training (McClelland, 1955a; 1955b).

In support of this conclusion, achievement motivation was found strongest in middle-SES boys whose mothers fostered early self-reliance and mastery (Winterbottom, 1958). It was also found that middle-SES parents placed a greater emphasis on independence training than lower-SES parents (McClelland *et al.*, 1955; Rosen, 1959).

Rosen

Rosen's (1959) basic premise was that racial and ethnic groups varied considerably in their orientation toward achievement, especially as determined by traditional measures of desire for status and upward social mobility. For example, Jews, Greeks, and Anglo-American (white) Protestants seemed to be more individualistic, active, and future-oriented in their outlook on raising a family and overall striving to succeed in life.

Rosen found that aspiration levels were usually expressed in terms of educational and occupational strivings. There were differences in how various cultures and religious groups expressed their orientation toward education; Protestants stressed education as a means of furthering a career and social status, while Jews stressed education for enhanced prestige, authority, and chances for a better marriage. Afro-Americans (blacks) did not find high educational aspirations to be realistic. Rosen suggested Afro-Americans were more passive and present-oriented. Afro-Americans' pessimism and cynicism concerning the realities of life in an Anglo-American dominated society may be due to their limited opportunity for education and economic well-being. As a result, Afro-Americans would not do well on need-for-achievement measures because of differences in their historical background and place in society.

Rosen found that SES accounted for more of the variance in achievement motivation than ethnicity. He concluded that SES is a better predictor of achievement motivation because of its focus on status improvement caused by the achievement values of certain SES levels.

Katz

As part of a broad examination of the academic motivation of ethnic-minority children, Katz (1967) questioned whether the achievement motive was general or independent for specific achievement domains. For example, a child might be motivated to achieve in athletics but not academics. Katz was especially concerned about the potential specificity of the motive because the projective techniques used to measure achievement striving made no attempt to distinguish need for achievement in different settings. Katz (1967) wrote, "the lower-class Negro pupil's disinterest in classroom learning may be less a matter of his lacking the achievement motive than of its being directed into nonintellectual pursuits" (p. 144). Like Rosen, Katz also speculated that SES differences in child-rearing practices probably contributed more to achievement motivation differences than did ethnic differences.

Maehr

In line with Katz' thinking, Maehr (1974b) maintained that the development of achievement motivation must be examined from the context of the individual and the cultural or ethnic group of which he or she is a member. Achievement-motivated behavior thus depends on and varies from culture to culture. Low need for achievement may be due to erroneous assumptions about motivational inferiority. Different cultures may hold differing orientations toward the concept of achievement, and may base success upon goals that differ significantly from one another. For example, achievement motivation among Afro-Americans must incorporate subjective concepts involving the social structure and meaning that is given to a situation by the individual. Similarly, there is evidence that competition in the classroom may elicit achievement behavior in middle-SES but not lower-SES children (Maehr & Shogren, 1971). Thus, various SES groups may respond differently depending on the mode of feedback employed, the cultural and social setting in which the person exists, and the goals perceived as being worthwhile by the individual. Maehr suggests, then, that the typical competition-oriented classroom may not be an appropriate place to measure differences in need for achievement. Also, lower-SES subjects do not exhibit strong need for achievement, but it is possible that the traditional tests of achievement motivation do not adequately measure need for achievement in other than middle- or upper-SES subjects.

THE PRESENT RESEARCH REVIEW

In 1967, Katz was able to find only two small-sample studies that compared white and black individuals. Given the strong emphasis theorists have placed on the role of culture in the development of achievement motivation, however, it is not surprising to find that in the intervening years numerous studies have compared different ethnic groups and socioeconomic statuses on need for achievement. In the pages that follow, a comprehensive review of these studies is presented. The review employs some of the recently developed statistical procedures for synthesizing research, including the combination of probability levels from studies testing the same hypothesis and the generation of effect-size estimates. Cooper (1982) has argued that more rigorous, scientific procedures must be employed in research reviews if social scientists hope to maintain their claim to objectivity. Cooper outlines procedures that establish the literature review as a unique type of research requiring the same attention to methodology that is demanded in primary research. The present review was conducted using these procedures as guidelines.

METHODS

STUDY RETRIEVAL PROCEDURES

Study retrieval began with an on-line computer search of the *Psychological Abstracts* and the *Educational Resources Information Center*. In order to uncover studies involving SES, the computer was instructed to retrieve studies whose abstracts or index terms included the words *achievement with motivation* crossed with the words *socioeconomic status, income level, social class, lower class, middle class, parent occupation, parent education,* or *parent background.* To uncover studies involving ethnicity, the phrase *achievement with motivation* was crossed with the words *ethnic, cultural, racial,* or *religion.*

The search uncovered 333 abstracts. Of these, a reading of the abstracts revealed 95 were potentially relevant. Sixty-six full reports were available in the university library and these were retrieved and read. These studies were then supplemented through references cited in previous theoretical works and relevant empirical studies. Ultimately, a total of 43 study reports were found that contained at least one relevant comparison.

CRITERIA FOR DETERMINING THE RELEVANCE OF
STUDIES

First, only studies that appeared in referreed journals were considered. This restriction creates a publication bias in the results of the review because of prejudice against the null hypothesis (see Greenwald, 1975). At the same time, however, unpublished research has two disadvantages. First, unpublished reports have not had the benefit of reviewer scrutiny to ensure that their methods are at least adequate. Second, because of the international nature of the present topic, a large percentage of unpublished reports appear in rather obscure sources not available in most libraries. Indeed, this international quality also affected the percentage of published reports that were unretrievable in a United States research university library (69%). Although it would be optimal to attempt to retrieve all studies by contacting the primary researchers, experience with past reviews (see Findley & Cooper, 1981) indicated that these inquiries are rarely successful. Instead, in order to test the possible effect of publication bias on the review outcome, certain statistical descriptors were generated that assess the cumulative results' resistance to undiscovered null findings (see discussion following).

Only studies that employed individuals as the unit of analysis were included in the review. Studies examining covariation in aggregate national statistics were not used. Thus, a study which correlated countries' gross national product with achievement motivation would not be considered relevant.

For purposes of this study, religion was considered an ethnic category, but few studies examining religion were uncovered. While this would not be a good general practice (many ethnic groups share the same religion), we felt readers would be interested in descriptions of these studies.

The primary criterion for inclusion of a study was that it contained a statistical comparison of at least two SES or ethnic groups on a measure of achievement motivation or a closely related component of achievement motivation (dependent variables are described here subsequently).

Characteristics of Individual Studies

The following design characteristics of relevant studies were obtained from the journal articles:

1. Type of comparison, whether SES or ethnic group. In the case of SES comparisons, the indexes used to measure SES were noted. For ethnic comparisons, the group names were taken.
2. Sample size
3. Type of need for achievement measure. Three types were distinguished. About half of the studies employed the Thematic Apperception Test (TAT; McClelland *et al.*, 1958). The TAT consists of card drawings about which subjects are asked to write stories or protocols. The stories are then judged for how much of their content relates to achievement strivings. Along with the TAT, researchers also employed other projective techniques, for example, the French Test of Insight (French, 1958) and line drawings (Mingione, 1965). Finally, some researchers used closed-ended item measures, like the Prestatic Motivation Scale (Hermans, 1970). The different closed-ended item indexes of need for achievement were rarely used in more than one study.
4. Geographic location of samples
5. Participant age or educational level
6. Participant gender (males only, females only, or both)
7. Sample characteristics. This category was used to indicate whether the primary researchers had employed a restricted economic level (in ethnicity studies) or ethnic mix (in SES studies) in choosing participants for the research.

In addition to the design characteristics, the results of each comparison in a study were classified according to (1) the direction of its finding, (2) its significance level and (3) its d-index effect size (see subsequent text).

Identification of Comparisons

Some studies reported the results of more than one relevant comparison. This could occur if (1) more than one measure of need for achievement was administered, or (2) samples were subdivided into subpopulations and separate results reported. This might be done for cross-validation purposes or to report statistics according to some theoretically relevant subpopulation characteristic (e.g., gender). In such cases, effect sizes and significance levels were weighted in any statistical analysis so that each study contributed equally to a given comparison. However, studies might also contribute more than one comparison by (1) containing more than two ethnic groups or (2) reporting results separately for different socioeconomic statuses of a single ethnic group. In these cases, comparisons were considered independent.

Categorization of Comparisons

Comparisons were grouped into six major categories:

1. Comparisons among SES groups using United States participants
2. Comparisons between Anglo-Americans and Afro-Americans
3. Comparisons between Anglo-Americans and other United States ethnic groups
4. Comparions among non-Anglo-Americans
5. Comparisons between persons from the United States and from other countries
6. Comparisons among persons from other countries

Only the SES and Anglo- versus Afro-American comparisons generated sufficient replications (13 for SES, 10 for Anglo–Afro-American) to justify the use of statistical combining procedures. Beyond these, the most frequently replicated comparison was between Mexican- and Anglo-Americans (four replications). Therefore, the results of studies in the last four categories are presented separately and without statistical synthesis.

A Note on Nomenclature

Needless to say, a variety of labels for ethnic groups were uncovered, some of which might today be considered pejorative due to their derivation. It is important that researchers strive to rid their work of such labels, especially in topic areas that can easily be misconstrued as perpetrating invidious comparisons. In this chapter, we describe ethnic groups by their country of origin and/or residence. However, for stylistic reasons, the term *Americans* is used to mean persons living in the United States, with no offense intended to persons north or south of the United States border. When this level of specificity failed us, we used the labels employed by the primary researchers.

QUANTIFYING OUTCOMES OF REVIEWS

Two primary methods for examining quantitative outcomes across studies were employed. The first method of aggregation involved combining probabilities from separate comparisons by adding their associated z scores (see Cooper, 1979). This procedure, referred to as the Stouffer Method (Mosteller & Bush, 1954), is straightforward and easy to compute when probability levels are reported. Z scores associated with the probability values are computed for each hypothesis test and the z scores are summed and divided by the square root of the number of tests. The result is itself a z score that can be interpreted as gauging the probability that the set of study results could have been generated by chance. In the present application, when a study reported a nonsignificant result and no p level was given, a p level of .50 and accompanying z score of 0.00 was assumed. Also, some studies contained more than one nonindependent comparison. These comparisons were weighted (by the reciprocal of the number of comparisons in the study) so that each study contributed equally to the combined result.

The method of combining probabilities has some interpretive problems, however. First, as previously noted, studies with significant p levels are more likely to be published than are studies with nonsignificant p levels. This leads to what Rosenthal (1979a) called "the file drawer problem." As a means for gauging the potential impact of relevant but unretrieved null studies, Rosenthal (1979a) and Cooper (1979) presented equivalent procedures for estimating the number of null-sum studies needed to increase a combined probability above a chosen level of significance. In this review, a fail-safe N (N_{fs}) was computed using procedures described by Cooper (1979). The fail-safe N indicates the number of additional studies with a summed null finding that would be needed to increase the cumulative probability above the $p = .05$ level. Cooper (1979) states,

> The fail-safe N is an important descriptive statistic in that it allows a reader to easily evaluate the "strength" exhibited in a review against the felt completeness of the review's sampling procedure. However, a limitation of the fail-safe N

should be pointed out. It is an appropriate guide for the reader only if the assumption of a summed null relation in undiscovered studies is acceptable. It is always possible that a smaller number of studies exist that have a summed Z-score of equal but negative value to the sum of those reviewed. The plausibility of this alternative also should be considered by the reader [p. 135].

An *effect size* measures "the degree to which the phenomenon is present in the population or the degree to which the null hypothesis is false" (Cohen, 1977, pp. 9–10). The best known measure of effect size is the correlation coefficient. The effect size used in this review was the d index (Cohen, 1977). The d index gauges the difference between two group means in terms of their common (average) standard deviation. The d index transforms the result from any two-group comparison into a common standardized metric. Findings from a number of studies can then be combined and analyzed simultaneously. If $d = .3$, it means that $\frac{3}{10}$ of a standard deviation separates the average persons in the two groups.

The d indexes can be calculated by the following formula:

$$d = \frac{\bar{X} \text{ Group A} - \bar{X} \text{ Group B}}{\text{average } SD \text{ of Groups A \& B}}$$

Groups A and B could be either different socioeconomic statuses or Anglo- and Afro-Americans, depending on the nature of the comparison. However, effect sizes were most often computed through transformation of t and F ratios (see Friedman, 1968). Some of the t and F values were estimated by the significance level and the sample size when (1) no group means were reported and only the value of multiple degree of freedom statistics was given, or (2) nonparametric statistics or percentages were used. Finally, if a study reported a nonsignificant result and not enough information was provided to determine the effect size, a d index of 0.00 was assumed.

Cohen (1977) also presents several measures of distribution overlap meant to enhance the interpretability of effect size indexes. The overlap measure employed in this review, called U_3, tells the percentage of the population with the smaller mean that is exceeded by the average person in the population with the larger mean. For instance, if $d = .3$, then $U_3 = 61.8$, signifying that the average person in the higher-meaned group exceeded 61.8% of the people in the lower-meaned group. A table for converting the d index to U_3 is presented by Cohen (1977, p. 22).

RESULTS

SOCIOECONOMIC STATUS IN THE UNITED STATES

Thirteen of the studies compared the achievement strivings of different SES groups in the United States. Table 1 lists many of the features of these studies. The mean year of appearance of the study reported was 1969. The earliest report appeared in 1958, the most recent study reported here appeared in 1980. A total of 5158 individuals participated in the studies, which ranged in size from 38 to 1588. Participants were drawn mainly from the eastern half of the United States. Four studies made no attempt to control the background of participants, whereas nine studies included some form of restriction on the ethnic or intellectual background of sampled individuals. Six studies examined males only, one study examined females only, five studies did not differentiate between the genders, and one study reported results separately for males and females. Finally, a broad spectrum of age and educational levels was sampled, ranging from 3-year-old children to college students.

Nearly all of the studies measured SES by indexing the education, occupation, or income of the participant's father. Scales for identifying SES included the Index of Status Characteristics, the Hollingshead Four Factor Index of Social Status, and the Duncan Scale, though many studies used less formal techniques. Need for achievement was most often measured using the TAT (seven studies). The remainder of the studies used closed-ended item questionnaires, except one (Hall, 1972), which used both types of measures.

The thirteen studies overwhelmingly supported the notion that a stronger need for achievement is associated with higher SES. Only four of the studies did not support this conclusion. Jacobs (1972) reported a nonsignificant difference between socioeconomic statuses on need for achievement coupled with nearly equal SES means. Fleming (1978) reported nonsignificant differences but did not report the direction of the finding. Lefkowitz and Fraser (1980) reported eight nonsignificant comparisons among subsamples, six of which were associated with stronger need for achievement among higher SES participants and two of which found the opposite relation. Notably, these studies were conducted on the smallest number of participants. Finally, Gruenfeld, Weissenberg, and Loh (1973) reported one nonsignificant difference that showed stronger achievement strivings among middle- than among lower-SES high school students and one comparison showing no appreciable difference. The remaining nine studies reported significantly stronger

TABLE 1

Comparisons among SES Groups in the United States

Author(s)	Year	Social class index[a]	Need for achievement measure	Location	Subpopulation	Gender	Education[b]	Direction	Average d-index
Lefkowitz & Fraser	1980	Education and income	Modified TAT	NYC	Anglo- & Afro-Americans	Male	College	3 Comp. + / 1 Comp. −	+.18
Fleming	1978	Education	TAT	MA	Afro-Americans	Female	College & non-college adults	Not given	0
Dielman, Barton, & Cattell	1973	Education	Item scale	IL	Uncontrolled	Both	JHS	Positive	+.50
Gruenfeld, Weissenberg, & Loh	1973	Education and occupation	Item scale	NY	Catholics and Protestants	Males	HS	1 Comp. + / 1 Comp. =	0
Adkins & Payne	1972	Ethnic groups	Item scale	Various	10 ethnic groups	Both	Preschool	Positive	+.12[c]
Hall	1972	Index of status characteristics	TAT and item scale	CA	Anglo- and Mexican-Americans	Both	College	Positive	+.22
Jacobs	1972	Occupation	TAT	Midwest	Mentally handicapped	Male	ES	Equal	0

Stein	1970	Duncan scale	Item scale	NY	Uncontrolled	Both	JHS	Positive	+.36
Turner	1970	Occupation	TAT	South	Uncontrolled	Male	JHS	Positive	+.98
McDonald	1964	Education and occupation	Item scale	MI	Anglo	Both	HS	Positive	+.51
Rosen	1961	Hollingshead	TAT	Northeast	6 ethnic groups	Males	ES	Positive	+.20[c]
Douvan	1956	Occupation	TAT	Midwest	Uncontrolled	Both	HS	1 Comp. + 1 Comp. =	+.43
Rosen	1956	Hollingshead	TAT	CN	Anglo	Male	HS	Positive	+.75[c]

[a] All SES indexes are based on father's status.
[b] ES = elementary school; JHS = junior high school; HS = high school.
[c] Estimated from incomplete data.

need for achievement in higher socioeconomic statuses across all measures and/or subsamples of participants.

The combined z-score across the 13 studies (weighted for number of comparisons per study) was 11.41. A run of studies showing this pattern of results would occur by chance less than once in 100,000 trials. The number of null-sum studies needed in order to reverse the conclusion, using the $p < .05$ level of significance, is 613. Rosenthal (1979b) presented a tolerance level to estimate the possible bias caused by unretrieved studies. He suggested that if the fail-safe N was 5 times greater than the number of known studies plus 10, then a conclusion could be considered "resistant." In the present case, Rosenthal's tolerance level would be 75 studies, well below the fail-safe N.

The average d-index across the 13 studies was $d = +.33$. This means that the average participant in the higher-SES groups had a stronger need for achievement than 63% of the participants in the lower-SES groups.

ANGLO- AND AFRO-AMERICANS

Ten of the studies compared Anglo- and Afro-Americans. Table 2 lists several important characteristics of each study. The mean year of publication of the studies was 1972, the earliest publication date was 1959, and the most recent reported here was 1980. A total of 1739 Anglo-Americans and 934 Afro-Americans participated. The smallest sample compared 32 Anglo- with 31 Afro-Americans. The largest sample compared 516 Anglo- with 202 Afro-Americans. Participants were drawn mostly from eastern locations in the United States, but a wide variety of age groups was represented. Seven studies were conducted on undifferentiated samples of males and females, two contained only males, and one reported separate results for male and female subsamples. Three of the studies reported results separately for two different samples of people and one study reported results for four separate samples. Two studies contained two different measures of achievement motivation. In the statistical analysis presented here, the significance levels and d indexes from studies with multiple comparisons were weighted so that all 10 studies contributed equally to the overall result.

Two studies used only the TAT to measure need for achievement. Four studies used other projective tests, whereas three studies used closed-ended item response measures. One study used both types of measures.

Five of the studies compared Anglo- and Afro-Americans drawn from

TABLE 2

Comparisons between Anglo- and Afro-Americans

Author(s)	Year	Need-for-achievement measure	Location	Subpopulation	Gender	Education[a]	Direction of finding	Average d-index
Lefkowitz & Fraser	1980	Modified TAT and item scale	NYC	Uncontrolled	Male	College	Equal on TAT Afro on item scale	−.22
DeBord	1977	TAT	TN	Lower income	Male	ES	Anglos	+.29
Ruhland & Feld	1977	Projective	MI	Low SES	Both	ES	Anglos	+.30
Ramirez & Price-Williams	1976	Projective	TX	Catholics	Both	ES	Anglos	+.65
Hall	1975	Projective	PA	Lower income	Both	College	Equal	0
Dielman, Barton, & Cattell	1973	Item scale	IL	Uncontrolled	Both	JHS	Equal	0
Adkins & Payne	1972	Item scale	Various	Various	Both	Preschool	One sample Afros One sample Anglos	+.07[b]
Mingione	1968	Projective	CN	Lower income	Both	ES	Three samples Anglos Fifth-grade females Afros	+.07
Mingione	1965	Projective	NC	Lower income	Both	ES	Anglo	+.34
Rosen	1959	TAT	Northeast	Five Anglo groups	Both	All	Anglo	+.19[b]

[a]ES = elementary school; JHS = junior high school.
[b]d-indexes were estimated from incomplete data.

lower-SES backgrounds. Five did not control for the SES of participants. Of these, two reported that income was confounded with race, that is, that the Anglo-American sample was of higher SES than the Afro-American sample.

Of those 10 studies, 5 reported Anglo-Americans had stronger achievement motivation, and 3 reported mixed results. Of the mixed results, 2 reported no differences between groups and 1 found higher need for achievement among Anglo-Americans on one measure and among Afro-Americans on another measure. Two studies found conflicting results for different subsamples. In Mingione's (1968) study, 3 subsamples showed a stronger need for achievement among Anglo-Americans and one among Afro-Americans. In Adkins and Payne (1972), a significant difference favoring Anglo-Americans was accompanied by a nonsignificant comparison favoring Afro-Americans.

Taking the significance levels of these comparisons into account (and weighting by the reciprocal of the number of comparisons within studies), the combined probability that this run of results could have occurred by chance was less than one in 100,000 (combine $Z = 5.97$). The hypothesis that Anglo-Americans have stronger need for achievement than Afro-Americans was firmly supported. The number of null-sum studies needed in order to reduce the cumulative result to $p > .05$ was 121. Rosenthal's (1979b) resistance value for estimating the likely number of unretrieved studies in this case would be 45, well within the fail-safe N.

The average d-index across the 10 studies was $d = +.17$, with Anglo-Americans the higher-meaned group. Thus, the average Anglo-American had a stronger need for achievement than 56% of the Afro-Americans in these studies.

Study comparisons that revealed either stronger achievement motivation among Afro-Americans or no differences were contrasted with results supporting the overall conclusion. Two interesting covariances were uncovered. First, both studies conducted on samples drawn from college student populations reported results counter to the overall finding. Hall (1975) gave the French's Test of Insight to male lower- and lower-middle-SES students in a northern urban-junior-college. She reported nonsignificant F-statistics of less than 2.00 on all motivation variables. Lefkowitz and Fraser (1980) gave two achievement motivation tests, a modified TAT and a closed-ended item scale, to students at the College of the City University of New York. They found nearly identical ($F = 0.1$) means on the TAT and a nonsignificantly stronger ($p < .1$) Afro-American mean on the closed-ended item scale. This result is especially surprising because Anglo-Americans also reported their parents had higher incomes than those reported by Afro-American students. No study demonstrated higher need for achievement among Anglo- than Afro-American college students.

The Lefkowitz and Fraser (1980) study had a second methodological characteristic apparently related to the study's outcome. All three studies that measured need for achievement through closed-ended item responses reported equivocal results. Lefkowitz and Fraser (1980) used Herman's Prestatic Motivation Test, containing Guttman-scaled measures of attitude and behavior. Dielman, Barton, and Cattell (1973) used the School Motivation Analysis Test, a 20-item objective scale measuring 15 factors of motivation and interest and found no differences on any items. Adkins and Payne (1972) used a device called Gumpgookies which asked children to respond by choosing between two forced-choice alternatives. It should be pointed out, however, that Adkins *et al.'s* finding of no difference between the groups compared Afro-Americans from Los Angeles with Anglo-Americans from rural Oregon, a sampling distinction that introduces many possible confounds to the result. In the other studies, location was controlled across ethnic groups.

The use of college student samples and/or closed-ended items could account for all results contrary to the overall conclusion except one. Mingione (1968) gave a sentence completion measure (projective technique) to lower income fifth and seventh graders from Hartford, Connecticut. Results were reported separately for each grade level and each student gender. Among seventh graders, Afro-American females showed a nonsignificantly higher achievement-motivation than their Anglo-American counterparts. All other comparisons favored Anglo-Americans.

ANGLO- AND NON-ANGLO-AMERICANS

Nine of the studies compared Anglo-Americans with other American ethnic groups. Four of these studies compared Anglo- and Mexican-Americans. Few of the studies specified the ethnic makeup of the American sample, but sample restrictions concerning location, age, and educational level were nearly always mentioned. Thus, we should assume that most of the American samples were predominantly Anglo-American.

Only one of the four comparisons involving Mexican-Americans found a significant difference. Hall (1972) compared community college students of both genders on a school-related-aspirations subscale from the Inventory of Self-Appraisal. She found that Mexican-Americans had lower aspirations than a sample of lower-SES Americans. Two other studies (Barberio, 1967; Evans & Anderson, 1973), one conducted in New Mexico and one in California, compared Anglo-Americans and Mexican-Americans of both genders within an age range of 12–15 years old. Neither study uncovered a significant difference but both reported more achievement striving among the Anglo-American sample. Finally, a study by Ramirez and Price-Williams (1976) compared fourth graders in a Houston Catholic school on a projective measure of need for achievement. They also distinguished between male and female subsamples. This study revealed nearly equal need for achievement scores among males but slightly stronger achievement scores for Anglo-American than for Mexican-American females. In sum, these comparisons demonstrate a fairly consistent pattern of higher need for achievement among Anglo- than among Mexican-Americans. The studies vary greatly with regard to age and location of participants, suggesting the uncovered difference may be fairly general but also that it requires further replication.

Two studies have compared Anglo-Americans with Native Americans of different tribes. Reboussin and Goldstein (1966) compared first-year college students on the French Test of Insight. One sample comprised Navahos who were enrolled at a junior college for Native Americans specializing in technical skills. The Anglo-American sample was drawn randomly from introductory psychology courses at the University of Kansas. The results revealed stronger need for achievement among the Navahos for both the male and female subpopulations. This result was contrary to predictions. The researchers speculated it may have been caused by the Navaho participants not being representative of the larger Navaho population. Query, Query, and Singh (1975) also used the French Test of Insight to compare the need for achievement of Sioux and Chippewa Native-Americans with Anglo-Americans. This study reported a nonsignificant trend for Anglo-Americans to have stronger need for achievement.

Mingione (1968) compared Anglo-Americans with Americans of Puerto Rican origin. Participants were drawn from the fifth and seventh grades of two schools serving lower-SES areas in Hartford, Connecticut. A sentence-completion task was scored for achievement content. Although all comparisons were statistically nonsignificant, Anglo-Americans had stronger need for achievement than Puerto Rican Americans for all groups except seventh-grade females. Among them, Puerto Rican Americans scored higher than their counterparts.

Hines (1973a) compared Greek-born and United States–born Greek-

Americans with Anglo-Americans, using the TAT. Participants resided in Syracuse, New York and in Columbus, Ohio. Participants were recruited through local universities and churches. Greek-born Americans had higher need for achievement than non-Greek-Americans. American-born Greeks also outscored non-Greek-Americans but not significantly so. The author attributes the result to the behavior of Greek mothers and to strong family ties.

Finally, a study by Husaini (1974) presented a classification problem. It involved a comparison of Americans with Hindus from Bombay, India who were college juniors or seniors in the United States. Thus, this study might be more suitable for discussion under the comparisons of Americans with other countries section. Regardless, a TAT administered to both groups revealed significantly stronger achievement strivings among Americans.

NON-ANGLO-AMERICANS

Seven researchers have compared different non-Anglo-American ethnic groups within the United States. Most of these occurred as part of larger studies that also included Anglo-Americans. Several of the studies cited have already been described here or can be found in Tables 1 and 2.

Three studies involved Americans of Hispanic origin. Ramirez and Price-Williams (1976; see preceding description) found that Mexican-American children had stronger need for achievement than Afro-Americans, whereas Mingione (1968) found only nonsignificant differences between Afro-Americans and American children from Puerto Rico (though, Afro-American children had generally stronger need for achievement). In a within-group study, Evans and Anderson (1973) compared English- and Spanish-speaking Mexican-Americans on a questionnaire designed to measure educational aspirations. No difference between the groups was found.

Hines's within-group study (1973a; see aforementioned description) found that Greek-Americans born in Greece had nonsignificantly higher need for achievement scores than Greek-Americans born in the United States. The explanation for this finding may be that a select group of highly motivated individuals choose to emigrate. As this group or their offspring face the realities of life in a culture dominated by another group, this motivation may be dissipated somewhat.

Sloggett, Gallimore, and Kubany (1970) compared the TAT scores of Filipino-Americans, Japanese-Americans, and high- and low-achieving Hawaiian-Americans. Participants were all male high-school-students from a low-income neighborhood, except the high-achieving Hawaiians, who attended a private school. Japanese-Americans had higher achievement needs than both the Hawaiian-American groups. The Filipino-Americans scored second highest but were not significantly different from any group. High- and low-achieving Hawaiian-Americans also did not differ from one another.

Two of the studies contained a number of ethnic breakdowns within American society. Rosen (1959) administered the TAT to six different ethnic groups residing in six different northeastern states. Through a purposive sample with the aid of religious, ethnic, and service organizations, 954 participants were recruited. A complex set of significance levels was produced by the following descending order of need for achievement scores: Greeks, Jews, Protestants, Italians, French-Canadians, and Afro-Americans. Greeks, Jews, and Protestants did not differ significantly. The largest difference was between the French-Canadians and Afro-Americans on the one hand and all of the other groups.

Finally, Adkins and Payne (1972) conducted a study involving 1588 American children from 10 ethnic groups. The 10 groups included middle-SES Mormons, Catholics, and Jews, and lower-SES Puerto Rican-Americans, urban Afro-Americans, white rural Anglo-Americans, Hawaiians, Asian-Americans, Mexican-Americans, and Native Americans. Samples were drawn from eight different communities, confounded with ethnic group. The children ranged from ages 3–6 years old. The need for achievement measure was a 75-item test called Gumpgookies. The middle-SES groups did not differ among themselves. Among the lower-SES groups, Afro-Americans, rural Anglo-Americans, and Puerto Ricans outscored the other four groups.

The results of comparisons among non-Anglo-Americans generally support the notion that those groups most assimilated to Anglo-American culture score highest on need for achievement measures. This finding is most dramatic when the non-Anglo-American group does not speak English. We must point out, however, that especially when a language barrier exists, it is not clear whether the measured difference is due to an actual motivation difference or problems created by cultural bias in testing. Also, there is some evidence that "newly arrived" ethnic groups demonstrate strong achievement motivation.

PEOPLE FROM THE UNITED STATES AND FROM OTHER
COUNTRIES

Eight of the studies compared persons from the United States with those from other countries. The major problem with six of these studies is that they sample people from specific geographic locations within the countries. This means the results of the comparison might not apply to citizens located elsewhere in the same country or to a random sample of all locations. These six studies are reviewed first.

Two studies compared Americans with Indians. Meade (1971) compared Hindu students attending college in northern India with American college students (college not identified) in terms of their responses on sentence-completion measures of achievement striving. All participants were male. He found a more pronounced future orientation in the responses of the American students, regardless of whether the topic of the sentence was educational, occupational, economic, or political. Ghei (1973) compared the need-for-achievement scores of female college students. The Americans were enrolled in a state university (probably in Wisconsin) and the Indians attended a major university in northern India. Participants were administered a 225-item personal preference schedule, of which 29 items produced significant differences in responses between the two cultures. Several of these appeared to tap achievement motivation, for example, "I like to stay up late working in order to get a job done," and "I like to do my very best in whatever I undertake." In all cases, the Indian women were more likely to endorse the statements, indicating stronger achievement motivation. It is not clear why the American versus Indian comparisons of males and females produced results in opposite directions. Differences in populations sampled and measuring instruments preclude any strong theoretical interpretation until a more controlled comparison is undertaken.

Two other studies compared young adults from rural New York state with foreign counterparts. Gruenfeld, Weissenberg, and Loh (1973) compared the need for achievement of high school students from rural New York with high school students from Lima, Peru using Likert scale measurements of self-reliance and future achievement motivation. The Americans scored nonsignificantly higher than the Peruvians on future-achievement orientation but significantly lower on self-reliance. The authors suggest this result may be due to American students believing that "the relation between ability and merit is in reality less than perfect in American society" (p. 47). Botha (1971) administered the TAT to both male and female college students in rural New York and in Lebanon. The Lebanon sample had a higher "hostile press" score than the Americans, meaning they expressed a greater fear of failure.

The Hines study (1973a; described previously) compared Americans with Greek residents of Athens and with New Zealanders residing in either Wellington or Auckland. Greeks scored highest on the TAT, followed by Americans and by New Zealanders, respectively.

Rosen (1962) compared the TAT scores of Brazilian and American adolescent boys. The Brazilian boys were drawn from two cities, whereas Americans represented six ethnic groups from four northeastern states. He found higher achievement motivation among the Americans.

The final two studies to be reviewed have the advantage of having used a random or purposively broad sampling of participants. Hines (1974) collected achievement motivation data on samples from Britain, Australia, New Zealand and the United States. Samples were drawn using random selections from business directories and university catalogs. Among a group of middle managers, Hines found the British scored higher on a nonprojective measure of achievement motivation than Americans, Australians scored about equal to Americans, and New Zealanders scored lower than Americans. Among educators, Americans scored slightly higher than the British but considerably higher than New Zealanders. Finally, Elizur (1979) compared the achievement motivation scores of middle managers in the United States and Israel. In both countries, samples were taken from diverse business organizations. Elizur used a complex index of the achievement motive and complex analysis techniques, but concluded in general that the need for achievement was higher among the Americans.

These studies present a mixed bag of results that defy generalization. As noted previously, each ethnic group comparison is confounded by the location and social status of the particular individuals in the sample. Perhaps the best that can be said is that Americans do not have a monopoly on achievement motivation. In about half of the comparisons, the non-American sample displayed stronger need for achievement than the Americans.

COMPARISONS NOT INVOLVING AMERICANS

Socioeconomic Status

Several studies have been conducted that examined SES and/or ethnicity differences in achievement motivation among subpopulations of countries other than the United States.

Two studies of SES and achievement striving have been conducted in South America. Gruenfeld et al. (1973) examined the relation of SES to need for achievement among Peruvian high school students (mentioned here previously). They found no differences among seven different schools serving various socioeconomic statuses in students' academic self-reliance or future achievement orientation. Rosen (1962) classified Brazilian boys according to the education and occupation level of their father. Curiously, he found that boys of the lowest SES outscored boys of the highest SES (but not boys in the second or third highest status groups). He suggested that children in the highest SES in Brazil are typically pampered and over-indulged, a child-rearing practice not associated with strong achievement strivings.

Tidrick (1971) examined the relation between SES (indexed by parent's education and occupation) and need for achievement among male, Jamaican college students. She found the expected positive relation. Interestingly, she also found that students who planned to emigrate from Jamaica had greater need for achievement than those who planned to stay. She attributes this finding to Jamaica's generally poor economic condition but also notes that the emigration of high-need-for-achievement people from poor economies creates a vicious cycle.

Inkson (1971) related SES (father's occupation) to the TAT scores of high-ability English teenagers. The product–moment correlation between the two variables was $r = +.27$ ($p < .02$). Need for achievement was also related to the boys' future occupational choices. Boys with strong need for achievement had a particular liking for business and engineering occupations.

Two studies of SES and need for achievement in India were uncovered. Gokulnathan (1970) examined the SES–need-for-achievement relation among Indian youths who belonged to a "higher intelligence" group. Using parents' education, occupation, and income as separate indexes, Gokulnathan found only father's occupation to be significantly positively associated with need for achievement ($r = +.35$, $p < .05$). In a more detailed study of Indian youths, Gokulnathan and Mehta (1972) report consistently positive, but nonsignificant, relations between SES indexes (father's education, occupation, and income) and TAT scores of a sample of boys and girls drawn from 14 secondary schools located in and around the city of Dibrogarh. The weak positive relation was found even when the sample was subdivided by gender, areas of residence (urban vs. rural), and tribal versus nontribal culture.

It seems, then, that the relation between social class and need for achievement is fairly robust across cultures. Regardless of country and subpopulation within country, a generally positive relation between social status and achievement striving can be expected.

Ethnicity

The opportunity to compare ethnic groups within and among countries other than the United States has not been missed by researchers.

The problem, of course, is making theoretical sense of these studies' outcomes, because the ethnic distinctions are often somewhat obscure to all but natives of the countries involved and are often severely confounded with SES or location. In addition, none of these ethnic comparisons has undergone replication. A brief review of these studies follows.

Kanungo and Bhatnagar (1978) compared the achievement motivation of English- and French-speaking Canadian high-school students in Montreal. They found the French-speaking youths set more difficult goals, preferred tasks with greater responsibility and relied more heavily on personal competence. No differences between the youths were found on need for feedback, emphasis on planning, or future orientation.

McClelland, Sturr, Knapp, and Wendt (1958) compared Protestant and Catholic boys from the city of Kaiserslauten, Germany. They found the Protestant boys were higher in need for achievement. McClelland *et al.* chose this sample because the two ethnic groups had lived side by side for many centuries, meaning migration patterns would not be confounded with ethnic differences.

Hines (1973b) examined achievement motivation in four groups of adult Pacific Islanders. Results indicated that Maoris and European New Zealanders had the highest need for achievement, followed by Cook Islanders and Western Samoans, in that order. Hines suggested that this result is predictable from the degree of exposure of each ethnic group to European schooling and child-rearing practices. Hines (1973a; see above) also reported Greek New Zealanders had higher need for achievement than non-Greek New Zealanders.

In a study of Australians from six ethnic groups, Marjoribanks (1979) administered a semistructured interview to the parents of 11-year-old children. He found that achievement orientation was strongest among Anglo-Australians of a middle-SES background. Lower-SES Anglo-Australians, Greeks, British, and Croations did not differ from one another in achievement striving, whereas southern Italian families scored lowest on achievement orientation.

Hines (1974) compared random samples of Britons, Australians, and New Zealanders from four occupational categories: entrepreneur, middle manager, educator, and student (described here previously). For all possible occupations the British scored highest and the New Zealanders scored lowest.

Morsbach (1969) compared Afrikaan-speaking and English-speaking South African high-school and university students. English-speaking students scored higher than Afrikaan-speaking students on a 12-item need for achievement scale. Morsbach attributes this to the English students' traditionally stronger entrepreneurial background.

Gokulnathan and Mehta (1972), in the aforementioned study, found that Mongolian Indians had higher need for achievement than did Hindus. They attribute the difference to well-documented child-rearing practices that are consistent with need-for-achievement theory.

Finally, Melikian, Ginsberg, Cuceloglu and Lynn (1971) gave a need for achievement questionnaire to male university-students from five countries. Afghanistan students scored highest, followed by Brazilians, Saudi Arabians, Turks, and English, in that order. Melikian *et al.* note that the low scoring of the English was consistent with results reported by McClelland. This result, however, appears to be at odds with those of the preceding Hines (1974) report.

As noted, it is exceedingly difficult to make theoretical statements based on the outcomes of these studies. What is needed is an ordering of cultures based on their emphasis on child-rearing practices believed to underlie achievement motivation (i.e., independence and achievement training).

DISCUSSION

Empirical research comparing SES and ethnic groups, with regard to need for achievement, has revealed some interesting relations. Confident statements of relations, however, appear to be limited only to American SES and to Anglo- versus Afro-American comparisons. These comparisons have undergone the necessary repeated testings and have demonstrated sufficient control of extraneous variables. The rest of the cross-cultural research is plagued by serious confounds involving the location, economic background, and education of restricted samples. A study by Reboussin and Goldstein (1966) is illustrative of the problem. They compared Native Americans from the Navaho tribe with introductory psychology students at the University of Kansas and found stronger need for achievement among Navahos. The Navahos, however, were sampled from a technical school. Thus, the question remains whether the difference they found was attributable to ethnic background or to the educational restrictions placed on the samples. The authors themselves opt for the latter explanation. Reboussin and Goldstein's (1966) study is not unique in this regard—nearly all of the cross-cultural research requires important qualifications based on threats to internal validity.

There are two solutions to the problems associated with making cross-cultural comparisons. First, large-scale studies involving broad, random, or purposive sampling need to be conducted. The problem with this approach, of course, is cost. Second, multiple replications with restricted but well-described samples need to accumulate. The problem with this solution is that most cross-cultural comparisons do not generate or sustain enough research interest to produce the needed replications.

Until one of these approaches to cross-cultural comparisons is undertaken, it is suggested that strong statements concerning ethnic differences in need for achievement be eschewed. The remainder of our remarks are limited to inferences stemming from SES comparisons in America and Anglo- versus Afro-American differences.

SOCIOECONOMIC STATUS IN AMERICA

The accumulated research clearly demonstrated that higher SES is associated with stronger need for achievement. This is not surprising because all theories predict this result. The only possible exception to this conclusion might concern the highest SES groups. First, the vast majority of studies examining SES compared participants from lower- and middle-SES backgrounds. Therefore, little is known about the highest income groups. More definitively, a study by Rosen (1962) showed considerably lower achievement strivings among the highest SES boys in Brazil than among the next two highest SES groups. A similar, but much less dramatic, finding appeared in Rosen's (1962) United States sample.

Future research in the SES area might profitably be directed toward sampling wealthy economic groups. If high-income groups were found to lack achievement motivation, this result might still be interpretable with present theories. This would be the case if it were also demonstrated that these groups begin independence training at a later age, as suggested by Rosen (1962).

ANGLO- AND AFRO-AMERICANS

It also appears that Anglo-Americans have stronger need for achievement than Afro-Americans. This finding, however, has several qualifications. First, researchers (e.g., Thompson, 1939) have long suspected that the Anglo-American appearance of the TAT figures might diminish their relevance or alter their interpretation by Afro-Americans. To test this notion, Lefkowitz and Fraser (1980) varied the race of TAT figures and TAT presenters for Anglo- and Afro-American college students. They found the highest TAT scores were obtained by the Afro-American students who were tested by an Anglo-American clinician using TAT cards modified to depict Afro-Americans. The lowest scores were obtained by Anglo-Americans viewing the standard TAT cards administered by Afro-American clinicians.

The literature review tended to support this notion that when racial identities are balanced or removed from stimulus materials the difference between Anglo- and Afro-Americans' need for achievement scores is lessened or disappears. The question of which measure of Afro-American need-for-achievement (with Afro-, Anglo-, or race-removed stimuli) is most valid, however, is extremely complex. It involves considering the potential uses of the measure the researcher has in mind. For example, until the racial bias is removed from the entire educational system, Afro-American responses to stimuli containing Anglo-Americans may be most predictive of these students' actual academic achievements.

From a theoretical viewpoint, it may also be that Afro-Americans are not motivated by the *situations* depicted in the TAT measure of achievement motivation. Maehr and Nicholls (1980) suggested that traditional measures of need for achievement fail to take account of the differential situational norms and social cues various cultures use to signify that achievement striving is acceptable.

The literature review also revealed no evidence that the achievement strivings of Anglo- and Afro-American collegians differ from one another. This finding is especially noteworthy because of the higher dropout rate among Afro-American collegians. Apparently, a lack of motivation is not the cause of this phenomenon.

In general, the interaction between need-for-achievement scores and participant, presenter, and race of the figure, as well as the lack of difference found among college populations substantiates Maehr's (1974a, 1974b) notion that definitions and scores on achievement-motivation tests will be culturally relative.

A COMPARISON OF THE TWO FACTORS

Two important questions relate to the intersection of the SES and Anglo- versus Afro-American findings. The first is Which is more important? and the second is Do social class differences between Anglo- and Afro-Americans explain the racial difference (along with stimulus biases)?

The d-index estimates generated from the uncovered literature indicated that the SES effect is clearly the larger of the two ($d = +.33$ for SES versus $d = +.17$ for race). This finding corroborates Rosen's (1959) earlier assertion. However, it is not clear that with SES held constant, the Anglo- versus Afro-American difference would disappear entirely. Several of the reviewed studies included controls that established similar SES backgrounds among participants but still produced the racial difference. Studies are needed that will systematically examine both SES and racial differences in the same design. Until such studies are conducted the present evidence can only be considered suggestive.

FUTURE RELATED-RESEARCH

Several potential directions for research have been suggested. Most of these have involved ways to make future examinations of ethnic and SES differences in achievement strivings more interpretable. It is also important that future research attempt to identify the mechanisms that mediate the relation. For instance, all of the theoretical formulations propose that differences in child-rearing practices (specifically, variation in the degree or onset of achievement and independence training) cause the ethnic and SES differences. In a sense, then, when populations are identified by ethnicity or by SES these variables serve as proxies for the true causal agents. Future researchers interested in these relations would maximize their contributions by simultaneously studying how ethnic and SES background affects child rearing and how, in turn, child rearing affects achievement motivation.

Finally, ethnic and SES differences in achievement motivation might be better understood if more was known about other associated cognitive differences among groups. For instance, the work of Weiner (1974, 1979) and his colleagues has attempted to "tease apart" achievement motivation by identifying the causal attributions that lead an individual to persist at achievement behavior. Ethnic and SES differences in causal ascriptions for achievement success and failure have rarely been the subject of study. These differences, however, reveal important insights for understanding differences in achievement striving among social groups.

REFERENCES

Adkins, D. C., & Payne, F. D. Motivation factor scores and response set for ten ethnic–cultural groups of preschool children. *American Educational Research Journal*, 1972, 9, 557–572.

Atkinson, H. W., & Raynor, J. O. (Eds.). *Motivation and achievement.* Washington, DC: Winston, 1974.

Atkinson, J. W., & Raynor, J. O. *Personality, motivation, and achievement.* Washington, DC: Hemisphere, 1978.

Barberio, R. The relationship between achievement motivation and ethnicity in Anglo-American and Mexican-American junior high school students. *Psychological Record,* 1967, *17,* 263–266.

Botha, E. The achievement motive in three cultures. *Journal of Social Psychology,* 1971, *85,* 163–170.

Cohen, J. *Statistical power analysis for the behavioral sciences* (2nd ed.). New York: Academic Press, 1977.

Cooper, H. Statistically combining independent studies: A meta-analysis of sex differences in conformity research. *Journal of Personality and Social Psychology,* 1979, *37,* 131–146.

Cooper, H. Scientific guidelines for conducting integrative research reviews. *Review of Educational Research,* 1982, *52,* 291–302.

DeBord, L. W. The achievement syndrome in lower-class boys. *Sociometry,* 1977, *40,* 190–196.

Dielman, T. E., Barton, K., & Cattell, R. B. Prediction of objective motivation test scores in adolescence from family demographic variables. *Psychological Reports,* 1973, *32,* 873–874.

Douvan, E. Social status and success strivings. *Journal of Abnormal and Social Psychology,* 1956, *52,* 219–223.

Elizur, D. Assessing achievement motive of American and Israeli managers: Design and application of a three-facet measure. *Applied Psychological Measurement,* 1979, *3,* 201–212.

Evans, F. B., & Anderson, J. G. The psychocultural origins of achievement motivation: The Mexican-American family. *Sociology of Education,* 1973, *46,* 396–416.

Findley, M., & Cooper, H. Introductory social psychology textbook citations: A comparison in five research areas. *Personality and Social Psychology Bulletin,* 1981, *7,* 173–176.

Fleming, J. Fear of success, achievement-related motives and behavior in black college women. *Journal of Personality,* 1978, *46,* 694–716.

French, E. G. Some characteristics of achievement motivation. In J. W. Atkinson (Ed.), *Motives in fantasy, action, and society.* Princeton, New Jersey: Van Nostrand, 1958.

Friedman, H. Magnitude of experimental effect and a table for its rapid estimation. *Psychological Bulletin,* 1968, *40,* 245–251.

Ghei, S. N. Female personality patterns in two cultures. *Psychological Reports,* 1973, *33,* 759–762.

Gokulnathan, P. P. Social class and educational achievement in relation to achievement motivation measured by an objective test. *Indian Journal of Psychology,* 1970, *45,* 67–74.

Gokulnathan, P. P., & Mehta, P. Achievement motive in tribal and nontribal Assamese secondary school adolescents. *Indian Educational Review,* 1972, *7,* 67–90.

Greenwald, A. Consequences of prejudice against the null hypothesis. *Psychological Bulletin,* 1975, *82,* 1–20.

Gruenfeld, L., Weissenberg, P., & Loh, W. Achievement values, cognitive values, and social class. *International Journal of Psychology,* 1973, *8,* 41–49.

Hall, E. R. Motivation and achievement in black and white junior college students. *Journal of Social Psychology,* 1975, *97,* 107–113.

Hall, L. H. Personality variables of achieving and non-achieving Mexican-American and other community college freshmen. *Journal of Educational Research,* 1972, *65,* 224–228.

Hermans, H. J. M. A questionnaire measure of achievement motivation. *Journal of Applied Psychology*, 1970, *54*, 353–363.

Hines, G. H. The persistence of Greek achievement motivation across time and culture. *International Journal of Psychology*, 1973, *8*, 285–288.(a)

Hines, G. H. Motivational correlates of Pacific Islanders in urban environments. *Journal of Psychology*, 1973, *83*, 247–249.(b)

Hines, G. H. Achievement motivation levels of immigrants in New Zealand. *Journal of Cross-Cultural Psychology*, 1974, *5*, 37–47.

Husaini, B. A. Achievement motivation and self-esteem: A cross-cultural study. *Indian Journal of Psychology*, 1974, *49*, 100–108.

Inkson, J. H. K. Achievement motivation and occupational choice. *Australian Journal of Psychology*, 1971, *23*, 225–234.

Jacobs, S. Acquisition of achievement motive among mentally retarded boys. *Sociology of Education*, 1972, *45*, 223–232.

Kanungo, R. N., & Bhatnagar, J. K. Achievement orientation and occupational values: A comparative study of young French and English Canadians. *Canadian Journal of Behavioral Science*, 1978, *10*, 202–213.

Katz, I. The socialization of academic motivation in minority group children. In D. Levine (Ed.), *Nebraska Symposium on Motivation*. Lincoln: University of Nebraska Press, 1967.

Lefkowitz, J., & Fraser, A. W. Assessment of achievement and power motivation of Blacks and Whites, using a Black and White TAT, with Black and White administrators. *Journal of Applied Psychology*, 1980, *65*, 685–696.

McClelland, D. C. (Ed.). *Studies in motivation*. New York: Appleton-Century-Crofts, 1955. (a)

McClelland, D. C. Measuring motivation in phantasy: The achievement motive. In D. C. McClelland (Ed.), *Studies in motivation*. New York: Appleton-Century-Crofts, 1955. (b)

McClelland, D. C. *The achieving society*. Princeton, NJ: Van Nostrand, 1961.

McClelland, D. C., Atkinson, J. W., Clark, R. A., & Lowel, E. J. *The achievement motive*. New York: Appleton-Century-Crofts, 1953.

McClelland, D. C., Clark, R. A., Roby, T. B., & Atkinson, J. W. The effect of the need for achievement on thematic apperception. In J. W. Atkinson (Ed.), *Motives in fantasy, action, and society*. Princeton, NJ: Van Nostrand, 1958.

McClelland, D. C., Rindlibacher, A., & deCharms, R. Religious and other sources of parental attitudes toward independence training. In D. C. McClelland (Ed.), *Studies in motivation*. New York: Appleton-Century-Crofts, 1955.

McClelland, D. C., Sturr, J. F., Knapp, R. H., & Wendt, H. W. Obligations to self and society in the United States and Germany. *Journal of Abnormal and Social Psychology*, 1958, *56*, 245–255.

McDonald, K. H. The relationship of socioeconomic status to an objective measure of motivation. *Personnel and Guidance Journal*, 1964, *42*, 997–1002.

Maehr, M. L. *Sociocultural origins of achievement*. Monterey, CA: Brooks/Cole, 1974. (a)

Maehr, M. L. Culture and achievement motivation. *American Psychologist*, 1974, *29*, 887–896. (b)

Maehr, M. L., & Nicholls, J. G. Culture and achievement motivation: A second look. In N. Warren (Ed.), *Studies in cross-cultural psychology* (Vol. 3). New York: Academic Press, 1980.

Maehr, M. L., & Shogren, D. D. Atkinson's theory of achievement motivation: First step toward a theory of academic motivation? *Review of Educational Research*, 1971, *41*, 143–161.

Marjoribanks, K. Ethclass, the achievement syndrome, and children's cognitive performance. *Journal of Educational Research*, 1979, *72*, 327–333.

Meade, R. D. Future time perspectives of college students in America and in India. *Journal of Social Psychology*, 1971, *83*, 175–182.

Melikian, L., Ginsberg, A., Cuceloglu, D., & Lynn, R. Achievement motivation in Afghanistan, Brazil, Saudi Arabia, and Turkey. *Journal of Social Psychology*, 1971, *83*, 183–184.

Mingione, A. D. Need for achievement in Negro and White children. *Journal of Consulting Psychology*, 1965, *29*, 108–111.

Mingione, A. D. Need for achievement in Negro, White, and Puerto Rican children. *Journal of Consulting and Clinical Psychology*, 1968, *32*, 94–95.

Morsbach, H. A cross-cultural study of achievement motivation and achievement values in two South African groups. *Journal of Social Psychology*, 1969, *79*, 267–268.

Mosteller, F. M., & Bush, R. R. Selected quantitative techniques. In G. Lindzey (Ed.), *Handbook of social psychology* (Vol. 1): *Theory and method*. Cambridge, MA: Addison-Wesley, 1954.

Query, J. M. N., Query, W. T., & Singh, D. Independence training, need achievement, and need affiliation: A comparison between White and Indian children. *International Journal of Psychology*, 1975, *10*, 255–268.

Ramirez, M., & Price-Williams, D. R. Achievement motivation in children of three ethnic groups in the United States. *Journal of Cross-Cultural Psychology*, 1976, *7*, 49–60.

Reboussin, R., & Goldstein, J. W. Achievement motivation in Navaho and white students. *American Anthropologist*, 1966, *68*, 740–745.

Rosen, B. C. The achievement syndrome: A psychocultural dimension of social stratification. *American Sociological Review*, 1956, *21*, 203–211.

Rosen, B. C. Race, ethnicity, and the achievement syndrome. *American Sociological Review*, 1959, *24*, 47–60.

Rosen, B. C. Family structure and achievement motivation. *American Sociological Review*, 1961, *26*, 574–584.

Rosen, B. C. Socialization and achievement motivation in Brazil. *American Sociological Review*, 1962, *27*, 612–624.

Rosen, B. C., & D'Andrade, R. The psychosocial origins of achievement motivation. *Sociometry*, 1959, *22*, 185–218.

Rosenthal, R. The "file drawer problem" and tolerance for null results. *Psychological Bulletin*, 1979, *86*, 638–641. (a)

Rosenthal, R. Replications and their relative utilities. *Replications in Social Psychology*, 1979, *1*, 15–23. (b)

Ruhland, D., & Feld, S. The development of achievement motivation in black and white children. *Child Development*, 1977, *48*, 1362–1368.

Sloggett, B. B., Gallimore, R., & Kubany, E. S. A comparative analysis of fantasy need achievement among high and low achieving male Hawaiian-Americans. *Journal of Cross-Cultural Psychology*, 1970, *1*, 53–61.

Stein, A. H. The effects of sex-role standards for achievement and sex-role preference on three determinants of achievement motivation. *Developmental Psychology*, 1970, *4*, 219–231.

Thompson, C. E. The Thompson modification of the Thematic Apperception Test. *Journal of Projective Techniques*, 1939, *13*, 469–478.

Tidrick, K. Need for achievement, social class, and intention to emigrate in Jamaican students. *Social and Economic Issues*, 1971, *20*, 52–60.

Turner, J. T. Entrepreneurial environments and the emergence of achievement motivation in adolescent males. *Sociometry*, 1970, *33*, 147–165.

Weber, M. *The Protestant work ethic and the spirit of capitalism (T. Parsons, trans.).* New York:
Scribner, 1930.

Weiner, B. *Achievement motivation and attribution theory.* New Jersey: General Learning Press,
1974.

Weiner, B. A theory of motivation for some classroom experiences. *Journal of Educational
Psychology*, 1979, *71*, 3–25.

Winterbottom, M. The relation of childhood training in independence to achievement
motivation. In J. W. Atkinson (Ed.), *Motives in fantasy, action, and society.* Princeton, NJ:
Van Nostrand, 1958.

PART IV

Designs to Optimize Student Motivation

8

Debilitating Motivation and Testing: A Major Educational Problem—Possible Solutions and Policy Applications*

Kennedy T. Hill

STUDENT MOTIVATION AND EDUCATIONAL TESTING

It has long been recognized that motivation plays an important role in students' educational achievement and performance, as is reflected throughout this volume. The present chapter deals with a relatively specific but important aspect of motivation and achievement: debilitating effects of anxiety on educational-test performance. A 20-year program of research is reviewed, which initially focused on the causes and consequences of negative test motivation and more recently has focused on solutions to the problem, and policy applications. In this first section,

*The research reported herein was supported in part by Research Grants NIE G-76-0086 and NIE G-80-0015 from the National Institute of Education to the author and by United States Public Health Service Training Grant HD-00244 from the National Institute of Child Health and Human Development to the Developmental Psychology Program, Department of Psychology, University of Illinois, Urbana-Champaign. The preparation of this chapter was also supported in part by Research Grant NIE G-80-0015.

the problem is defined, and research on its nature and scope is reviewed. Then, the second section comprises a review of research on the development and evaluation of teaching and testing solutions to the problem. Finally, recommendations for research, practice, and policy are discussed.

THE PROBLEM

The educational problem being addressed is that due to evaluation anxiety in educational-testing situations, many students fail to show what they have learned (Hill, 1980). Recent evidence suggests that up to 10 million students in this country, at both the elementary and secondary school levels, are affected significantly each year by the problem of debilitating test-motivation and deficiencies in test-taking skills.

Children and older students who report high test-anxiety or negative success–failure attributions with regard to test performance usually perform poorly on standardized achievement tests, aptitude tests, and many other educational tests (Hill, 1980). The interfering effects of negative motivation on performance can perhaps be seen most clearly in the formal testing situation. Highly test-anxious students perform quite well, however, under optimal testing conditions or when given special instruction about the tests. This suggests that such children do, in fact, know the material being tested but are unable to show their knowledge in many test situations. Many tests, then, provide a low, invalid estimate of these students' mastery of whatever is being tested. This makes the test results less useful in evaluating and making decisions about either the individual student or the educational program in which the student is taking part.

DEBILITATING TEST-MOTIVATION

Although there has been long-standing interest in the study of motivational determinants of children's learning and performance, only recently has there been research on the effects of coping and test-taking skills on children's test performance (Hill, 1980; Hill & Wigfield, in press).

Atkinson and his colleagues (Atkinson & Feather, 1966; Atkinson & Raynor, 1974) demonstrated in their pioneering work with college students the importance of achievement motivation in determining risk-taking and task persistence as well as performance level itself. Interfering effects of test anxiety were shown to be particularly strong in highly evaluative situations, such as educational testing (Atkinson, 1980).

At about this same time, the Sarason group (Sarason, Davidson, Lighthall, Waite, & Ruebush, 1960; Sarason, Hill, & Zimbardo, 1964; see Ruebush, 1963) was finding strong debilitating effects of test anxiety on elementary school children's test performance and school progress. They also found that the interfering effects of test anxiety obtained in highly evaluative testing conditions diminished and occasionally even reversed in relaxed, game-like conditions, at least on certain experimental tasks (see Hill, 1972).

The third and most recent major approach to the study of achievement-related motives in children is attribution theory, as developed by Weiner and his colleagues (Weiner, 1972, 1977). This work has emphasized the cognitive underpinnings of motivational effects, especially children's attributions for their successes and failures in school situations. Children who lack confidence in their ability credit their successes to luck or to the task being easy and their failures to lack of ability, and they show a pattern of low performance, low achievement-motivation, and high test-anxiety (see Hill, 1980).

There has been relatively little applied research extending theory and findings on achievement motivation, test anxiety, and success–failure attributions to teaching children specifically how to cope with the demands and pressures of actual educational testing (Hill & Wigfield, in press). In a relevant training study, Dweck (1975) found that children who show learned helplessness can be taught to persist at school-like problem-solving tasks by showing them that their failure is due to lack of effort, not to lack of ability (see also Dweck & Goetz, 1980).

There has also been relatively little research with children focusing on the training of test-taking strategies, test wiseness, and other aspects of test-taking instruction, which are often referred to as *coaching* (Hill, 1980; Hill & Wigfield, in press). Even in the growing literature on coaching high school and college students to take aptitude and related tests, there has been relatively little research on motivation effects, either in their own right or in interaction with coaching effects (see Pike, 1979, for a review of this literature, and Sarason, 1980, for a review of the adult literature on test anxiety).

An important question is how many and which kinds of students are affected by debilitating test motivation and test-taking skill deficits? At present, this can be estimated from the correlation of test anxiety with educational-test performance. In a major longitudinal study of lower- and middle-socioeconomic-status (SES) children, Hill and Sarason (1966) found that the correlation between test anxiety and achievement-test performance increased from near .00 in first grade to about −.25 in third grade to −.45 in sixth grade. The data suggests that the interfering effects of negative motivation on test performance, seen in the pattern of high test-anxiety and low performance scores, increases across the elementary school years. Effects were equally strong for boys and girls when both anxiety and defensiveness measures were considered.

More recently Willig, Harnisch, Hill, and Maehr (1983) have extended these findings in a study of low-income black, white, and Hispanic elementary and junior high school students. Test anxiety correlated negatively with test performance for boys and girls in all three ethnic groups, the correlations averaging −.27 for black, −.35 for white, and −.48 for Hispanic students (see Hill, 1980). Success–failure attributions also correlated predictably with test performance, most strongly for black students. For instance, black students who attributed their success to luck and failures to lack of ability obtained lower scores on mathematics tests than students showing positive attributions.

The most comprehensive demonstration of how motivation measures relate to test performance comes from a collaborative statewide testing project with the Illinois State Board of Education (see Fyans, 1979; Hill, 1979). Test anxiety and success–failure attribution measures were included in statewide sampling of some 5000 white, 650 black, and 850 other minority students from low- and middle-income backgrounds. Students were drawn at random from 300 schools throughout the state at grades 4, 8, and 11. Test anxiety and success–failure attributions correlated with performance on reading and mathematics achievement tests, as predicted for all ethnic groups, both genders, and all ages. Correlations increased across the three grade levels so that by eleventh grade, test anxiety correlated −.60 with achievement test performance (Fyans, 1979).

The correlation between test anxiety and test performance is one way to estimate the strength of the effects of motivation on test performance. Another way of estimating the strength of the effect for individual children comes from the Hill and Sarason (1966) longitudinal study reviewed earlier. These investigators compared the achievement-test performance of the 10% most test-anxious and 10% least test-anxious students in the fifth and sixth grades. They found that the highly anxious group was about a year behind the school-district average on standardized reading and mathematics achievement-tests, while the low anxious group was a year ahead. For instance, the two groups differed by 20–28 months in reading achievement for boys and girls from the two grade levels. There was virtually no overlap in test performance between the two groups, suggesting very strong effects of debilitating test-motivation on test performance. The 10% most test-anxious students would represent approximately three students in a typical elementary school classroom, and two or three million students nationwide in our elementary schools. In addition, another 10–15% of the students would have significant (although not as strong) problems with test motivation and test-taking skills. We estimate that up to five million elementary and five million junior high and high school students have the potential to benefit significantly from the teaching and testing programs under development.

The Hill and Sarason (1966) study also provides data bearing on the question of the generality of test-motivation effects (see also Sarason *et al.*, 1964). In this longitudinal study, test anxiety correlated with all areas of achievement tests and with intelligence-test performance as well. Test anxiety also related negatively to school report-card grades, and, in fact, predicted grades about as well as achievement-test scores. High test-anxiety students were also more than twice as likely to be held back and to repeat a grade than low-anxiety students. Test anxiety, then, had strong effects on all measures of school progress and performance. Other studies extending the research to a variety of tests, school learning tasks, and general problem-solving measures have found similar results (see Hill, 1972, 1980; Hill & Wigfield, in press).

In summary, test anxiety and success–failure attribution measures correlate increasingly with test performance across the elementary and secondary school years for boys and girls from all socioeconomic backgrounds. The problem of debilitating test-motivation and test-taking skill deficits, then, is a serious and widespread one.

It has been assumed in discussing the correlations between negative test-motivation and test performance that motivation is the causal factor—for instance, it is test anxiety that leads to low test-performance. It is possible, of course, that the causality runs in the opposite direction—that students who do not know the material and do poorly on tests become anxious in test situations. A series of studies have been carried out suggesting that motivation is, in fact, the causal factor in the motivation-performance correlations. One major study is reviewed here, to illustrate the issues and typical findings. Other studies supporting this conclusion are reviewed in the section on critical testing parameters.

Hill and Eaton (1977) carried out an initial, basic-research study bearing directly on the causality issue. They investigated the effects of time pressure on the performance of fifth- and sixth-grade students on basic arithmetic computation problems, presumably mastered several years earlier. Children were tested individually either in a *success–failure condition* in which they could complete only two-thirds of the problems they attempted, or in a *success-only condition* in which they were given as much time as they wanted to do problems. The success–failure condition, then, involved strong time-pressure, both actual and as perceived by the child.

The major results for the Hill and Eaton (1977) study are presented in Figure 1, which depicts the performance rate and accuracy for the low (LA), middle (MA), and high (HA) test-anxiety students tested in the two conditions. As can be seen, under the time pressure of mixed success–failure, high test-anxiety students take twice as long to do the problems and still make over three times as many errors as low-anxiety children. In contrast, in the success-only condition without time pressure, high-anxiety students almost catch up in performance, going about as fast and making just a few more errors than their low-anxiety counterparts. It is clear that the high-anxiety students had mastered basic mathematics computations, as they showed in the success-only condition; but they could not show their mastery under the pressure of time limits and failure in the mixed success–failure condition. The results suggest, then, that high-test-anxiety children's poor performance under highly evaluative testing-conditions is due to motivational and test-taking problems and not to poor mastery of the skills being tested.

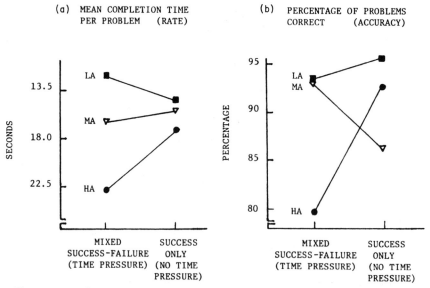

Figure 1. Performance as a function of test-anxiety- and time-pressure-induced success–failure experiences. (Based on Figure 1, Hill and Eaton, with the Y-axis inverted so that superior performance is at the top of the axis; reproduced by permission of the American Psychological Association, © 1977). Squares represent low anxiety (LA); triangles represent middle anxiety (MA); circles represent high anxiety (HA).

The strength of the debilitating effects of test anxiety in this study are noteworthy, with several-fold deficits in both rate and accuracy of the performance. As will be seen shortly, similar effects are obtained in research involving actual achievement-test situations.

Given the importance of testing and the competitive nature of our society, it is perhaps not surprising that pressure exists in many test situations, and that effects of debilitating test-motivation are so strong. Several recent changes in the nature and use of tests in our schools should, moreover, make the problem worse. Approximately three-quarters of the states have requirements for some form of minimal competency testing—for example, for promotion through the grades or for graduation from high school. Fear of failure and social disapproval underlie many of the debilitating effects of test motivation (Atkinson & Feather, 1966; Hill, 1976; Sarason et al., 1960). Because the consequences of failing minimal-competency tests are both negative and public, debilitating motivation-effects should become even stronger for competency tests than for current tests.

The recent public demand for greater accountability in public education has been responded to by decision and policy makers. This has led to increased use of achievement, competency, college admissions, and other standardized tests to evaluate teachers, educational programs, and school districts. This trend produces demands for higher test-scores, which are presumed to reflect greater learning. But these demands can also increase pressure in the testing situation. Paradoxically, this could result in greater negative test-motivation and lower test-performance. There is, in fact, evidence from cross-cultural research that debilitating effects of motivation are stronger when high test-performance becomes more important, whether at certain ages, such as the "11-plus" exams in England (see Sarason et al., 1960), or throughout a culture (see Maehr, 1978; Maehr & Nicholls, 1980).

It seems clear that tests play an important role in the educational progress and lives of students and will continue to do so in the forseeable future. Debilitating test-motivation should, if anything, become an even more serious and widespread problem in our society, as tests become even more important in the assessment of both individual students and the United States educational system itself.

CRITICAL TESTING CHARACTERISTICS

Most achievement tests, aptitude tests, and other formal, standardized educational tests have features that make them different from other

school experiences, including classroom tests. This is especially true for
elementary-school children. It is the uniqueness, and in this sense ar-
tificiality of standardized tests, in fact, that both allows debilitating test-
motivation to operate so strongly and makes it possible to study and
develop solutions to the problem. The research on testing parameters
reviewed in this section (and on classroom teaching programs discussed
later) moves from controlled laboratory-experiments to field-research,
developing and evaluating changes in school achievement-testing programs. This means educational solutions to the problem of debilitating
test-motivation can be empirically validated, and research-based policy
applications can be developed—something rare, given the nature of
most significant educational problems.

A series of studies in our program of research over the past 10 years,
as well as the work of others, has suggested three major features of
standardized testing contributing to motivational and test-taking skill
effects: (1) time limits and time pressure; (2) difficulty of test material;
and (3) test instructions, question and answer formats, and other testing
mechanics (see Hill, 1977, 1980; Hill & Wigfield, in press).

The preceding Hill and Eaton (1977) study represented a major demonstration of the debilitating effects of time pressure on performance of
high-anxiety children. Eaton (1979) followed up this research by showing that children who became anxious over a period of 2 school-years
showed interfering effects of test anxiety under time pressure, but performed well when time limits were removed, whereas children who decreased in anxiety over that time performed well under both conditions.
In other words, a change in test anxiety over two years related to performance under different testing-conditions in the same way that current
anxiety does.

Plass and Hill (1979) extended the Hill and Eaton findings to a more
natural test-like situation by using age-appropriate math word-prob-
lems, small-group testing, and group-imposed time limits. Plass and Hill
found that high-anxiety students showed low performance under time
pressure, but much higher performance, especially for boys, when time
limits were greatly relaxed. Importantly, they also found differences in
test-taking strategy between anxiety groups. Students' accuracy and
problem-solving rate (average time per test problem) were examined
jointly. Under time pressure, low-anxiety students showed an optimal
high-performing intermediate rate, middle-anxiety students showed a
less optimal, slow, cautious rate, and high anxiety students showed a fast,
inaccurate rate. When time pressure was removed, middle-anxiety students went faster and tried more problems, and high anxiety students
slowed down and were more accurate. Both groups completed more

problems correctly and had a higher test score. Teaching children an intermediate, optimal rate is, in fact, an important component of the teaching program under development.

Hill, Wigfield, and Plass (1980) have recently found similar optimizing effects in school–university research on actual achievement testing at the junior-high-school level. Staff of the collaborating school shared our concern about motivation and test-taking problems. It was decided to give the school's regular reading and mathematics achievement tests to seventh and eighth graders under one of four conditions: standard testing conditions, a relaxed time-limits condition (giving students twice the usual time for each test), a condition providing information about test difficulty, and a combined optimizing condition providing both extra time and test-difficulty information.

Hill *et al.* (1980) found that low-anxiety students did about twice as well as high anxiety students under the standard testing-conditions. But, when time limits were relaxed, either alone or in combination with information about test difficulty, middle and high test-anxiety students showed much higher, optimal test-performance, especially eighth graders. The data suggest, then, that in the actual achievement-testing situation, the low performance of high-anxiety students is due to debilitating motivational-effects (that can be reversed) and not to lack of mastery of the material being tested.

Several lines of research have suggested that the second critical testing characteristics, difficult test-materials and resulting failure on many test problems, contributes strongly to the motivational and other test-taking problems of anxious, failure-prone students. Zigler and his colleagues (Zigler, Abelson, & Seitz, 1973; Zigler & Butterfield, 1968; see Zigler & Harter, 1969) found increases in IQ-test performance of black and white low-income preschool and young elementary-school children under optimal test conditions. In these studies, each child in the optimizing condition was given an easier problem after several consecutive incorrect responses on the IQ test, to reduce the amount of failure, especially continuous failure. The tester also portrayed a supportive role in the optimizing condition. Children in the optimizing condition showed significant increases in IQ-test performance compared to a control group. This optimizing research again illustrates the importance of both success–failure experiences and evaluative reactions from the adult examiner, in determining motivational effects (see Fyans, 1980; Hill, 1976; 1980).

Williams (1976; see also Hill, 1980) found that the addition of information about test difficulty enhanced the performance of high-anxiety older elementary school students in small-group testing involving age-appropriate verbal problems. The difficulty information was designed to provide children with more realistic expectations for how well they would do on the test, to lessen the negative motivational effects of failure. The students were also reassured that the tester would be pleased if they tried hard and did their best. Optimizing instructions similar to these are included in the teaching program discussed in the section on classroom teaching activities.

The third major testing characteristic that contributes to the low performance of students with negative motivation and with test-taking skill deficits are aspects of testing mechanics, including the instructions, question and answer formats, and computerized answer sheets used in the upper elementary school and later grades. Awareness of the importance of these factors has grown over the past 5 years, as we have worked in close collaboration with classroom teachers in developing the teaching program under study. It became clear early that many students had difficulty understanding the sometimes long and complex test instructions. These instructions may change several times within a single subtest of an achievement test, for example in a language arts test. Many of the question and answer formats of tests are unfamiliar to children, especially first or second graders who may never have taken a standardized test—for instance, how to read a paragraph and answer both factual and inferential questions about it. Computerized answer sheets, introduced about the third or fourth grade in many achievement tests, present additional problems for many students. Research (leading to the 10-session teaching program reviewed in the next section on solutions) strongly suggests that many students perform below their capacity on standardized tests because they do not understand instructions or know how to answer the questions, as opposed to not understanding the material being tested.

Several additional ways in which achievement and other standardized tests differ from classroom tests may contribute to test-motivation effects, for example, test length and/or how often they are taken. Classroom tests are usually fairly short exercises, perhaps lasting 5–15 minutes for younger elementary school children and increasing in length to a class period (45–50 minutes) for junior high and high school students. This is in contrast to a standardized achievement test, which might require children to work for well over an hour (with short breaks between subtests) each day for several days, as early as the first or second grade. This is a very long time for such young children to work at peak efficiency while meeting all of the demands of testing; this is especially true for high test-anxiety children, who generally have trouble attending and staying on task (Nottelmann & Hill, 1977; Sarason, 1975; Wine, 1980).

With regard to frequency, teachers often give spelling, mathematics, and other classroom tests weekly, if not daily, at the elementary-school level. Classroom testing is also frequent at the secondary-school level. Achievement and other standardized tests are typically given just once a year—sometimes less often. This is why children and older students do not have the opportunity to become familiar with and to master many testing parameters. Given all of the demands and unique aspects of standardized testing, it is not surprising that many students develop debilitating test-motivation and are unable to show optimal test-performance. We turn now to new assessment, testing, and teaching programs that show promise of alleviating the problem.

DEVELOPING SOLUTIONS AND RECOMMENDATIONS

COLLABORATIVE SCHOOL–UNIVERSITY RESEARCH

The field research reviewed here—developing educational solutions to the problem of debilitating test motivation—involves what we have come to call the collaborative school–university research approach (Bodine & Hill, 1983; see Hill, 1980; Hill & Wigfield, in press). All of the research reviewed here has been carried out in full collaboration with teachers, school administrators, and state education agency staff. These educational practitioners and our project staff have often met weekly, working together on all phases of the research, from initial planning through implementing and evaluating the programs to disseminating findings. The research has required strong long-term commitment and involvement from both practitioners and researchers as the project has evolved over the years.

Our model for research development and educational change involves implementing and validating programs at increasingly broader levels. New measuring-instruments, testing procedures, and teaching activities are typically developed and initially tested in collaborating individual schools. The programs are then implemented and evaluated at the school-district level with in-service training of school staff and using a full intervention–control group or other appropriate research design. The next step in the model is to implement the assessment, testing, or teaching activities at a statewide level, again using a full research design. By this time, both the in-service training of school staff and the programs themselves have become increasingly refined and efficient. The final step is to research and apply the work at the national level, for instance, by holding workshops for educational practitioners working with national testing programs.

This model of increasingly broad application of programs has several advantages. The programs are validated across larger and more diverse populations of students and schools. Effective teaching and testing activities are replicated, improved, and made more efficient at each successive level. It is important that the model involves teaching and testing programs being validated at each level before being introduced and tested at the next level. This makes successful application of the programs at the broader level more likely. This, in turn, increases the interest of school staff, test developers, and others involved in educational testing in using the programs.

The three major components of our long-term program of research seeking to develop solutions to the problem of debilitating test-motivation are (1) cost-effective ways of assessing test motivation, (2) testing procedures and programs designed to optimize all students' test performance, and (3) classroom training programs teaching coping and test-taking skills. More recent, current collaborative school–university research efforts in each of three areas are reviewed, followed by discussion of an integrated assessment, testing, and teaching program, and policy applications.

ASSESSMENT OF STUDENT TEST-MOTIVATION

A critical first need in any program attempting to deal with the problem of debilitating test-motivation is the ability to assess such motivation in a straightforward and cost-efficient way. This allows for demonstration of the nature and strength of interfering motivational effects on test performance, identifies students for whom debilitating motivation is likely a problem, and helps assess the effectiveness of whatever teaching and testing programs are introduced to solve the problem. Perhaps the most important value of assessing the interfering effects of negative motivation on test performance is to make the seriousness of the problem known to practitioners, parents, policy makers, and the public. Without such awareness, there will be little interest in implementing teaching and testing programs designed to solve the problem.

The major measure of motivation used in research on test anxiety has been the Test Anxiety Scale for Children (TASC) and the accompanying Lie Scale for Children (LSC) developed by the Sarason group (Sarason *et al.*, 1960; see also Dusek, 1980; Hill, 1972). The 30-item TASC self-report questionnaire has been found to have excellent reliability and predictive power, especially when combined with the LSC scale, designed to correct for defensiveness tendencies (see Hill & Sarason, 1966).

Feld and Lewis (1969) made an important contribution to the measurement of test anxiety in developing a parallel, relaxed form of the TASC with items restated to ask children if they feel relaxed or comfortable, as opposed to worried, while taking tests or in other evaluative situations. In our collaborative research projects, we have found that school staff and parents prefer use of the relaxed form of the TASC because of its positive nature.

Our collaborative school–university research on assessment of test anxiety has focused on developing shorter, more cost-efficient versions of the relaxed 30-item form of the TASC for widespread application (Harnisch, Hill, & Fyans, 1980; see also Hill & Wigfield, in press). The scale has been shortened and validated as part of long-term collaborative projects with educational practitioners at the school-district and state level. The collaborating Illinois State Board of Education and local school-district staff have come to call the relaxed form of the TASC the Test Comfort Index (TCI). It has been possible to reduce the 30-item TCI to 7- and 14-item versions with good internal consistency and predictive validity. Most of the questions in the 7-item TCI ask students if they are relaxed in the test situation. The 7-item TCI has been validated in school district and statewide testing programs involving more than 6000 students in grades 4, 8, and 11 and has been found to have similar internal consistency and predictive power as the 30-item TASC and TCI (see Fyans, 1979; Harnisch et al., 1980; Hill, 1979). It takes about 5 minutes to administer. The 7-item form of the TCI is called the Test Comfort Index in this chapter and is recommended for both research and application.

The second major motivational measure used in the aforementioned district and statewide projects concerns students' attributions of their successes and failures in the test or in the general school situation (Fyans, 1979; Hill, 1979). A 10-question, one-page questionnaire has been developed measuring five key attributions with regard to both success and failure in the test situation. The first four are those Weiner focused on (1977) in his long-term program of research: ability, effort, luck, and task difficulty. The fifth attribution is a new one developed as part of the program of research reviewed here and asks students whether they think they succeed because they are good at taking tests or fail because they are not good at taking tests. This new measure is designed to assess whether students have confidence (success attribution) or lack confi-

dence (failure attribution) in their test-taking ability. This 10-item attribution scale also has been validated in school district and statewide
testing programs (in conjunction with the Comfort Index) and takes just
several minutes to administer at the elementary- and secondary-school
levels (Fyans, 1979; Hill, 1979). Development of the Comfort Index and
the attribution scales reflects well the collaborative school–university
research model. The research moved from the school building and the
school district to the statewide-testing level as the scales were refined and
validated.

DEVELOPING OPTIMAL TESTING PROCEDURES AND
PROGRAMS

The research on optimal testing conditions reviewed earlier suggests
three critical testing characteristics underlying debilitating motivational
effects on test performance: time limits and time pressure, difficulty of
test content, and instructions and test mechanics. The educational programs under development address each of these.

Time limits that create time pressure for a fair number of students
may be the most critical aspect of standardized testing that contributes to
debilitating motivation-effects. It also is the easiest characteristic to
change of those most relevant to motivation. All of the research reviewed earlier found that longer time-limits significantly facilitated the
test performance of high test-anxiety, failure-prone students. It should
be emphasized that it is the time pressure perceived or experienced by
the student that determines motivational effects, not the time limit itself.
If 90% of the students finish a given subtest of an achievement test, far
more than 10% will experience time pressure. In addition to the 10% of
the students who do not finish, 10–25% more may have to hurry to
finish or may be distracted by the time limits. Further, any student not
finishing or having trouble finishing any subtest of an achievement test
may experience time pressure on subsequent subtests. In the optimizing
studies reviewed earlier, the high test anxiety groups showing strong
gains when time limits were relaxed included 20–30% of the subjects
tested. It appears quite possible that one-fourth to one-third or more of
elementary school children, particularly those with high test anxiety,
experience at least some time pressure on a typical standardized achievement test. These students could benefit considerably from a relaxing of
time limits.

The research reviewed earlier suggests that an additional 50–100%

more time compared to that given on many current achievement tests would greatly reduce time pressure and facilitate the performance of students now experiencing debilitating test motivation. Increasing the typical time limits used in standardized achievement tests would, of course, result in new but still completely standardized norms for the tests. Relaxed time-limits would seem to be particularly important for competency testing programs used to assess basic academic skills that should be mastered for promotion or graduation. The primary interest here presumably is whether the student has mastered the skills and can demonstrate them in a reasonable amount of time, not necessarily under time pressure.

Test difficulty is the second testing characteristic that contributes to debilitating motivational effects. The research by Zigler's group (see Zigler & Harter, 1969) and the Williams (1976) and Hill, Wigfield, and Plass (1980) studies reviewed earlier all suggest variations in item difficulty and test instructions that can ameliorate the interfering effects of test anxiety. The Zigler work shows the detrimental effect of a continuous high level of failure, and our work shows the facilitating effect of providing information and reassurance about test difficulty and realistic performance expectancies.

The impact of test failure should be particularly strong for the high-test-anxiety, low-performing student of primary interest in the program of research under review. Such a student, if performing well-below age norm, will miss many if not most problems on many standardized tests. If the problems come in increasing order of difficulty, as they do on many tests, such students will tend to give up and not try later problems they could have completed (see Dweck & Goetz, 1980; Hutt, 1947). The situation becomes worse if children of several grade levels take the same form of a test—for example, first and second graders; fifth and sixth graders; seventh, eighth, and ninth graders, and so on. Children at the youngest age-level taking a given form of an achievement test obviously face a more difficult test than children at the oldest age-level taking the same form of the test.

Ideally all students would take achievement, aptitude, and other tests whose difficulty level is bracketed around their current ability level. It is not feasible, however, to administer alternate forms of a test at many levels of difficulty to different children at a given grade level for a norm-reference test. Some achievement-test instruction manuals, however, encourage giving the next-lower-level test to students known to be performing well-below age norm. This practice would be encouraged, perhaps expanded to include tests several levels below grade level for high anxiety, very low-performing students. Many of these students give up quickly and do not even try on achievement tests designed for their grade level (see Dweck, 1975).

Developing tests with appropriate difficulty level for each elementary school and junior high school grade level (instead of giving the same form to multiple grade-levels) would also be commended (Hill, 1980). This would lessen the problem of excessive difficulty level for many students while maintaining a completely standardized norm-reference test for each grade level.

The third major testing characteristic that can contribute strongly to debilitating motivational effects are testing mechanics such as instructions, question and answer formats, and computerized answer sheets (Hill & Wigfield, in press). Few would argue with the recommendation that test instructions and mechanics be clear and easy to understand and follow. However, many elementary-school students have difficulty with various aspects of test mechanics, typical of many current achievement and other educational tests. This is particularly so for younger elementary-school students and students with motivational and test-taking problems. Recommendations will be made for how to change standardized test instructions and mechanics in order to obtain optimal estimates of achievement for all students, after considering collaborative school–university research that develops new classroom programs to teach test-taking skills.

It will take time, of course, for new testing procedures that minimize debilitating test-motivation and optimize performance to be fully developed, validated, and incorporated into standardized-testing programs. In the meantime, a dual testing program could be implemented at the individual school, or at the district, state, or national level to determine different students' learning and achievement. In such a program, students could be tested twice, once under current, standard testing conditions, and a second time under optimal testing-conditions. In the latter condition, students might be given more time, an easier form of the test, and some basic instruction on test mechanics and test-taking skills. Initially, at least, some students would have to be tested twice under standard testing conditions to serve as a test–retest control group.

It would be expected that students experiencing debilitating test-motivation (such as test anxiety) and lacking effective test-taking skills would show stronger gains between the standard and the optimizing testing condition than students with positive motivation and good test-taking skills (or anxious students retested in the standard testing condition). Such results would confirm that the learning and achievement of high test-anxiety, failure-prone students is underestimated by the current testing procedures. At the same time, such results would identify students with motivational and test-taking problems who would be most likely to benefit from the new teaching programs described in the next section.

Such a dual testing program could be quite cost-effective. Not all students would need to be tested twice and not all portions of an achievement or other standardized test need be readministered. The dual testing program would be most important for students identified as having debilitating test-motivation, from the school-wide assessment procedures described earlier, from recommendations by teachers or parents, and from low test-performances. Students might be retested in only certain areas—for example, reading paragraphs and math computation. Finally, a school district might implement such a dual testing program in only some of its schools and only at certain grade levels, depending on student needs and school staff interest in the problem. The program could then be expanded to other grade levels and other schools in the district if gains under the optimizing testing conditions warrant it. Following the next section on new teaching activities, we turn to recommendations for how to integrate such a dual testing program with the motivational assessment and teaching programs under development.

DEVELOPING CLASSROOM TEACHING ACTIVITIES

The assessment and optimal testing-condition research just discussed, as well as the theory and basic research reviewed earlier, all point to the need to teach students the motivational coping and test-taking skills needed for optimal test-performance. Teachers and school administrators have emphasized throughout our collaboration the difficulty many elementary-school students have in meeting the many demands of standardized testing, especially students experiencing debilitating test-motivation or lacking test-taking skills. It seems unlikely the demands of testing will decrease in the near future—if anything, they are likely to increase. Developing classroom-teaching activities that show children how to cope with the demands of testing became a high priority for school staff and for our project staff.

One of our first efforts in this area was development of an individualized classroom tutorial program designed to help students develop the test-taking skills needed to perform optimally on timed classroom-arithmetic-tests (see Hill & Wigfield, in press). The program has been developed at the second- through fourth-grade level in full collaboration with classroom teachers in the participating elementary school.

The tutorial program has been fully implemented and is being evaluated in four third- and fourth-grade classrooms involving over 100 students. Throughout the school year, all students in the participating classrooms take a mathematics test twice a week under rather strict time limits to help students learn to perform quickly and accurately in a formal testing-situation as well as to confirm they have mastered their math facts. Children in the four collaborating classrooms take a 3-minute, 60-item test with problems from several levels of the child's current math activities. Here students must show 100% accuracy on recently learned as well as currently learning materials. For example, a student learning his "7's" in multiplication would have to complete, with perfect accuracy, in 3 minutes, 20 problems with 7's, 20 problems with 6's (the previous multiplication set learned), and 20 problems with lower multiplication numbers (learned earlier in the school year).

Students are chosen for the tutorial program based on low performance on the classroom tests and on teacher ratings of their test-taking skills, their general motivation in school, and their level of mastery of math facts. Most children taking part in the tutorial program have problems in all three areas, including many high test-anxiety, low-performing children.

The tutorial program is designed to individually diagnose and remediate students' debilitating-motivation and test-taking skill deficits as well as to provide some supplemental instruction. Tutorial activities are designed to facilitate positive test motivation, on-task behavior, effective problem-solving strategies, and mastery of math facts. Tutoring was carried out by trained undergraduates and project staff and typically continued for several months for most children taking part in the program. Children's performance on the twice-weekly classroom math tests was charted across the semester for each student.

Ongoing analyses (Bodine & Hill, 1983) are indicating that about one-third of the tutored students show excellent progress in response to tutoring, one-third good progress, and one-third little or no progress. Considering the test-taking, motivational, and learning problems exhibited by the group being tutored, the classroom teachers and our project staff find these results most encouraging. Teacher reports and ratings, as well as tutor observations, also indicate positive gains in test motivation for most children taking part in the program, including some of those not yet showing classroom test performance gains.

In summary, the case study data suggest that the tutorial program is proving to be quite successful in helping students with severe test-taking and learning problems to develop positive motivation and effective coping and test-taking skills. In doing so, the tutorial project has helped clarify the dynamics of debilitating test-motivation and test-taking skill deficits. A drawback of the tutorial program, in terms of widespread application, is that it is expensive to implement. The tutoring requires trained personnel and frequent individual sessions with each student, as well as fairly extensive record-keeping. It may not be practical for such a tutorial program to be incorporated into many schools' ongoing programs. Instead, cost-efficient, classroom group-teaching programs, that have been developed in part out of the tutorial program, may be the most feasible vehicle for addressing the problem of debilitating test-motivation nationally.

Our major effort in the development of such group teaching programs helps students develop all of the coping and test-taking skills needed to perform optimally on tests (Ambuel, Hartman, Nandakumar, & Hill, 1983; see Hill & Wigfield, in press). It comprises 8–10 30-minute-sessions in the classroom. This is our most advanced intervention research to date, both in terms of the scope of the (teaching) program and the degree of collaboration with school staff.

The classroom teaching programs being developed integrate and build on all of our earlier work reviewed here, as well as the research literature (see Hill 1980; Hill & Wigfield, in press). In particular the teaching program includes activities suggested by the earlier experimental research, the optimal testing-procedure studies, the ongoing tutorial project just reviewed, and the informal projects with collaborating teachers. These last projects include developing classroom learning-exercises in test-like format, a brief classroom-discussion of the general purposes and major elements of testing, and a practice testing session providing students some familiarity with test instructions and format.

The classroom teaching program was initially developed and implemented at the second-grade level for several reasons. First, this is the grade level at which students in the collaborating school district first take a standardized achievement test. Teachers have indicated that many students have considerable difficulty taking their first such test. Second, many of the tutorial and informal teaching activities had been piloted at this age level and collaborating teachers had a strong interest in further developing the program. And third, the nature and demands of testing are simpler and more straightforward at this grade level than at later ones, making it somewhat more feasible to initially develop a comprehensive, effective teaching program.

The motivational coping skills and other test-taking skills taught in the initial eight-$\frac{1}{2}$-hour-session teaching program for the second-grade level are summarized in Table 1 (Ambuel et al., 1983). As can be seen in Table 1, both general and specific coping and test-taking skills are taught

TABLE 1

Summary of Test-Taking Skills and Motivational Dispositions

1. General Test Skills and Knowledge
   a. Be comfortable and sit where you can write easily.
   b. Sit where you can easily hear the teacher.
   c. Pay attention to the teacher when she or he talks.
   d. The teacher can help you understand how to work on the test, but can not tell you the answer to a problem on the test.
   e. The purpose of the test is to find out what children know and what each child knows. This helps the teacher teach.
   f. Taking tests is something we learn to do in school.

2. Positive Motivation: Doing Your Best
   a. Do your best. Your teacher will be really pleased if you try to do your best.
   b. If you finish a section before time is up, go back and check your answers. Do not disturb others; instead, work quietly at your desk.
   c. Before the test begins, remember to carefully listen to your teacher, take a deep breath, and feel relaxed.

3. Positive Motivation—Expectancy Reassurance
   a. Some tests have some very hard problems. Do not worry if you cannot do some problems.
   b. Some tests have problems that you will not understand. Do not worry. The teacher has not taught you everything on these tests. Just skip a problem if you do not understand it at all.
   c. If you work hard but do not finish a test, do not worry about it! The most important thing to me is that you try hard and do as well as you can. Everybody can do their best if they keep at it. I know you will do a good job if you try!

4. Test Strategy and Problem-Solving Skills
   a. There is only *one* best answer.
   b. If you do not know the right answer but have some idea, choose the answer that you *think* is best.
   c. Do what you know first. If you cannot answer a problem or it is taking a lot of time, move on to the next one. You can come back later if you have time.
   d. Do not rush. If you work *too fast* you can make careless errors. You have to work carefully.
   e. Do not work too slowly. Do the problems at a moderate rate.
   f. Keep track of where you are working on the page by keeping one hand on this spot.

5. Test Mechanics and Instructions
   a. Various skills are taught, many relating to specific areas of tests.
   b. The specific skills taught are listed in the script for each session of the classroom teaching program.

across the eight sessions. The motivational focus is on coping with the major factors identified in the basic and applied research reviewed earlier, including time limits, difficulty level, and the need for concentration and persistent, on-task behavior. The test-taking skill focus is on how to deal with test instructions, question and answer formats, and other testing mechanics, again both general to testing and specific to particular content areas.

The first session involved a general discussion of the purpose and general nature of achievement testing, an overview of the teaching program, and an introduction to some of the major coping and test-taking skills. The subsequent seven sessions each focused on a specific area within language arts, reading, or mathematics sampled by most major achievement tests. For instance, achievement tests typically have two subtests in mathematics, one dealing with computation and one with problem solving. In each session the teacher made some general and specific points about time limits, task difficulty, and testing mechanics as they relate to motivation and test-taking skills. Children learned these points as they were exposed to and learned to deal with test instructions and prototypic question and answer formats. The scripts for the eight sessions and the content of the practice-test problems were developed specifically for the teaching program by the collaborating teachers. None of the materials come from any test. The purpose of the program, of course, is to teach students how to take tests, not the content of tests themselves.

The collaborating school staff and our project group developed an experimental–control group design with pre- and postprogram measures. Premeasures of academic skills were deemed necessary to control for possible baseline differences among individual students or among classrooms. Premeasures in reading and language arts were developed specifically for the project, and a mathematics premeasure was available for most students from a school competency test. All premeasures were given under normal classroom-work conditions (without time limits, formal test instructions, etc.) in order to have as accurate a baseline measure of achievement as possible in each major area. The postmeasure was performance on the actual achievement test administered by the collaborating school district each year, in this case the Comprehensive Tests of Basic Skills (CTBS).

The teaching program was implemented in two multi-age classrooms with 34 second-grade students total, while three similar classrooms with 31 students total served as a control group. Analyses of baseline measures revealed differences in favor of the teaching group in mathematics competency and in one of the six language arts and reading subtest areas (language mechanics), but with minimal differences in the other five areas. There were minimal differences in all of the baseline premeasures between the two rooms in the teaching program and among the three rooms serving as a control group. There also were minimal differences between the two rooms in the teaching program and among the three rooms in the control group on the CTBS results discussed next. These findings indicate that findings are not tied to specific classrooms.

The major results for this study come from analyses of covariance (ANCOVA) of the number of problems correct on each portion of the CTBS achievement test with the appropriate baseline premeasure covaried out (the mathematics competency score, for example, in analyses of the CTBS mathematics scores).

The teaching group showed consistently higher performance on the CTBS achievement test than the control group, with baseline differences removed. Results for the teaching-program effect from the ANCOVA are summarized in Table 2. As can be seen in Table 2, results were strong and often significant in the language arts and reading areas, but weaker in the mathematics domain. In language arts, there was a very

TABLE 2

Summary of Significant Differences between Teaching and Control Classrooms on CTBS Achievement Test Scores

| | | | | | Mean percentile[a] | |
| | | | | | Teaching classrooms | Control classrooms |
General area	Specific score	F	df	p		
Language arts						
	Language mechanics	16.75	1/62	<.001	75	57
	Spelling	<1	1/62	n.s.	46	49
	Language expression	8.69	1/62	<.01	72	59
	Total language arts	25.49	1/62	<.001	65	58
Reading						
	Vocabulary	8.58	1/62	<.01	75	61
	Sentences	2.23	1/62	.14	56	52
	Passages (paragraphs)	2.77	1/62	<.10	55	49
	Total reading	7.86	1/62	<.01	67	55
Mathematics						
	Computation	1.49	1/52	n.s.	69	61
	Concepts and application	<1	1/52	n.s.	67	65
	Total mathematics	<1	1/52	n.s.	70	64
Total CTBS achievement test score		4.52	1/48	<.05	71	61

[a]Percentiles calculated from adjusted group-means (with baseline partialled out) using the CTBS examiner's manual.

significant teaching-program effect for language mechanics and language expression and, therefore, for the total language arts score. Adjusted for baseline, the teaching group scored 18 percentile points higher than the control group on the language mechanics subtest. Turning to the reading area, there was a very significant teaching-program effect (14 percentile points) for the vocabulary achievement subtest and borderline or near borderline effects for sentences and reading passages (paragraphs). The result of these effects is a very significant teaching-program effect for the total reading score. Students in the teaching program tended to score higher than the control group on both mathematics subtests but, as can be seen in Table 2, this effect failed to approach significance for these two subtests or for the total mathematics score. Perhaps the higher initial math scores for the teaching group, the smaller sample-size in these analyses (some of the students did not have the district competency-test premeasure), and the relatively straightforward format of the tests in this area combined to produce weaker effects for the teaching program in the math area.

Finally, and most importantly, students in the teaching program obtained significantly higher overall CTBS achievement test scores than students in the control group. Again, corrected for baseline, students in the teaching program scored 71 percentile points for the overall test while students in the control group scored 61 percentile points (see the bottom of Table 2).

To summarize the major results, then, the eight-session classroom teaching-program at the second-grade level resulted in significant gains on three of the achievement-test subtests, with borderline gains on two more. The teaching group had significantly higher scores on two of the three major area scores, in language arts and reading, as well as on the total achievement-test score. The gain from the teaching program was 10 percentile points on the overall achievement test and ranged as high as 18 percentile points on subtests. The achievement test, of course, was given under normal testing conditions.

Additional analyses of variance were carried out entering either the students' baseline performance level, TCI score, or teacher ratings of their test-taking problems as blocked, independent variables to see if effects of the teaching program interacted with students' baseline ability or motivational dispositions. Although test motivation-effects generally have not developed by this age (Hill, 1980), it was expected that, if anything, program effects would be stronger for low-performing children beginning to show test-motivation problems. The blocking analyses revealed that the teaching program effects were general and did not interact at this age with either baseline academic ability level or test-taking problems. We would expect both of these interactions to be signif-icant in the middle and late elementary-school years, when test anxiety and other debilitating motivation-effects become significant and strong, pressure to perform well on tests increases, and achievement and other educational tests themselves become more demanding in terms of time pressure, difficulty level, and complexity of test instructions and me-chanics (see Hill, 1980; Hill & Wigfield, in press).

Encouraged by these initial results, teachers from the collaborating school and our project staff are currently implementing and evaluating an enhanced and refined 10-$\frac{1}{2}$-hour-session teaching program for stu-dents in grades two through six. Based on teacher and project-staff evaluation of the second-grade project and analysis of test-taking-skill needs in later elementary-school grades, the program was expanded to 10 sessions. It now includes two initial-sessions reviewing the nature and purpose of testing, the coping and test-taking skills to be taught, the kinds of test mechanics to be learned, and the use of computerized answer sheets. There are also two sessions devoted to how to take read-ing tests involving paragraphs with both factual and inferential multiple-choice questions. Collaborating teachers feel this is one of the most diffi-cult test-formats to deal with, especially for high-anxiety students tested under time pressure.

Collaborating teachers developed the script for the 10-session pro-gram, with versions for grades two, three, four, and five–six. Teachers have also developed the more-than-500 original items needed for the premeasures, the teaching sessions, and the extra work sheets for the seven areas of achievement for the different age-levels. School staff have worked closely with our research-project staff in developing the design to evaluate the program's effectiveness. This involvement and contribu-tion from teachers illustrates the collaborative nature of the program of research.

All 10 teachers working with students in grades three through six in the collaborating school are taking part in the implementation and val-idation of the 10-session teaching program. An experimental–control-group design with pre- and postmeasures is again being used. Six teach-ers are giving the program, and four are serving as control groups. Premeasures in reading, language arts, and mathematics have been de-veloped specifically for the project. The postmeasure again is the CTBS achievement-test given each year by the collaborating school district un-der standard conditions. Debilitating test-motivation is being measured by the TCI and the success–failure attributions specific to the test situa-tion reviewed earlier. Participating teachers are also making pre- and postratings of debilitating motivation, test-taking problems, and academic-skill mastery. It is expected that the teaching program will facilitate optimal test-performance at all age levels, especially for older students experiencing debilitating test-motivation and test-taking skill deficits.

If the teaching program proves to be effective in the collaborating elementary school, the next step will be to introduce and validate the program in other schools in the collaborating school district. This would demonstrate the feasibility of implementing the program through regular in-service training of teachers who had not collaborated in the development of the program. A district-wide project would also make it possible to assess the effectiveness of the program with a large number and wide variety of students at different grade levels. Successful implementation of the program at the broader school-district level would suggest it is ready for widespread implementation.

Another focus of future research will be to develop a shorter version of the teaching program for use in school district, state, and national testing programs. For instance, the first two $\frac{1}{2}$-hour sessions reviewing the nature and purposes of testing and explaining the major coping and test-taking skills taught in the program might be combined into a single teaching session given the day before achievement or other educational testing. The teaching-program sessions dealing with specific areas of testing (reading paragraphs, math computation, etc.) might be shortened to 10–20-minute sessions introducing each area of testing. Presumably such a shortened program would not be as effective as the full 10-session teaching activity. On the other hand, a shorter program might be sufficiently effective with enough students with motivational and other test-taking problems to warrant its use in educational testing programs. It would be desirable initially to validate such a shortened form of the teaching program in a large-scale testing project in order to test for the strength and nature of its effects across different students, grade levels, and schools.

GENERAL RECOMMENDATIONS AND CLOSING COMMENTS

Specific applications of the new motivational assessment, testing, and teaching programs under development were discussed when reviewing each program. Concluding comments focus on some of the general implications of the work for educational research, practice, and policy.

The research literature cited earlier, as well as the program of research reviewed here, suggests the importance of motivation and test-taking skills as determinants of elementary (and older) school students' performance on achievement and other educational tests. As seen earlier, correlational survey-research suggests that the achievement-test performance of as many as five million elementary-school (and as many secondary-school) students may be significantly affected by debilitating test-motivation. Further, while achievement testing has been focused on in much of the relevant research, similar results have been obtained for intelligence, aptitude, classroom, and other educational tests when they have been studied (Hill & Wigfield, in press).

The program of research reviewed here demonstrates the value of long-term collaborative research with school and state agency staff (see also, for example, deCharms, 1976, and deCharms Chapter 9, present volume). The collaborating teachers, school administrators, and state educational agency staff have made major contributions in all phases of the present program of research, including clarifying the nature of the specific problem, developing the new testing and teaching programs, and planning, carrying out, and disseminating the research. The education solutions being developed would not be possible without the strong involvement and commitment both of practitioners and of our research staff. The paradox of such collaborative school–university research is that it enhances our understanding of the basic phenomenon, while solutions are developed to the educational problem at hand: in this case, debilitating test-motivation. The dozens of practitioners taking part in the long-term program of research have contributed enormous insight into the nature and consequences of test motivation and test-taking skills, in the process of developing and evaluating intervention programs.

The present research suggests the need and value of an integrative approach to the problem of debilitating test-motivation and test-taking skill deficits. The assessment research suggests the usefulness of the 7-item Test Comfort Index and accompanying test success–failure attribution questionnaire as cost-effective measures of test motivation. The optimal test-condition research indicates the need to relax time pressure, adjust difficulty level of a test around low-performing student's current academic ability level, and to simplify test instructions and mechanics. The dual testing program described earlier can both demonstrate the presence of debilitating test motivation and suggest benefits from intervention efforts.

School districts could combine the assessment procedures, the dual testing program, and the 10-session classroom teaching-activities into an integrated program. The assessment and dual-testing components would identify the strength and scope of the problem and suggest which students should benefit most from optimal testing-procedures and the classroom teaching-program. The programs would become even more cost-efficient over time as the students with the greatest needs and the tests most susceptible to the problem were better pinpointed. Some students with test-taking problems will need the full 10-session teaching program, while others may need just the shortened version, now under development. Students may also need and benefit more from the teaching program at some grade levels than at others. One instance would be the first time a student takes an achievement test, typically in the early elementary school years. Another instance would be the first time the student encounters computerized answer sheets, fairly complex test instructions, and test items appropriate to students 1 or 2 years older, typically in the middle elementary school years.

Assessment of motivation, optimal testing procedures, and greater test-taking instruction could also become part of local, state, and national tests and testing programs. Statewide testing in Illinois has already shown the feasibility and value of incorporating motivation measures into large-scale testing programs. The suggested modifications in time limits, difficulty level of material for the students being tested, and instructions and test mechanics can all be incorporated into testing programs; again, many already have been in the statewide testing in Illinois. It may also be possible to incorporate into standardized testing programs the major components of the 10-session teaching program, in a shortened form, as discussed earlier. But, this last possibility awaits future research development and validation.

The program of research reviewed here suggests the value of carrying out research developing solutions to educational problems in full collaboration with staff from participating schools. The work can then be extended outward to increasingly broad school district, state, and national levels. Different components of the educational programs reviewed here presently have been developed and tested at the school building, school district, or statewide level. When fully developed and validated, the programs will have the potential for enhancing the positive test-motivation, as well as for facilitating the test performance of millions of students in this country. This would be of significant benefit to the students and would enhance our ability to evaluate our educational system, as well.

ACKNOWLEDGMENT

The author wishes to thank Carole and Russell Ames, Andrew Hartman, and Allan Wigfield for their helpful comments on an earlier draft of this chapter.

REFERENCES

Ambuel, B., Hartman, A., Nandakumar, R., & Hill, K. T. *Teaching children how to take tests: Overcoming negative motivation and test-taking skills deficits.* Paper presented at the annual meeting of the American Educational Research Association, Montreal, April 1983.

Atkinson, J. W. Motivational effects in so-called tests of ability and educational achievement. In L. J. Fyans (Ed.), *Achievement motivation: Recent trends in theory and research.* New York, Plenum, 1980.

Atkinson, J. W., & Feather, N. T. *A theory of achievement motivation.* New York: Wiley, 1966.

Atkinson, J. W., & Raynor, J. O. *Motivation and achievement.* Washington, DC: Winston, 1974.

Bodine, R., & Hill, K. T. *Field and experimental research on student motivation: Practitioners and researchers working together to advance knowledge and implement effective education programs.* Symposium presented at the annual meeting of the American Educational Research Association, Montreal, April 1983.

deCharms, R. *Enhancing motivation: Change in the classroom.* New York: Irvington, 1976.

Dusek, J. B. The development of test anxiety in children. In I. G. Sarason (Ed.), *Test anxiety: Theory, research and applications.* Hillsdale, NJ: Erlbaum, 1980.

Dweck, C. S. The role of expectations and attributions in the alleviation of learned helplessness. *Journal of Personality and Social Psychology,* 1975, *11,* 674–685.

Dweck, C. S., & Goetz, T. E. Attributions and learned helplessness. In J. H. Harvey, W. Ickes, & R. F. Kidd (Eds.), *New directions in attribution research* (Vol. 2). Hillsdale, NJ: Erlbaum, 1980.

Eaton, W. O. Profile approach to longitudinal data: Test anxiety and success–failure experiences. *Developmental Psychology,* 1979, *15,* 344–345.

Feld, S. C., & Lewis, J. The assessment of achievement anxieties in children. In C. P. Smith (Ed.), *Achievement-related motives in children.* New York: Sage, 1969.

Fyans, L. J. *Test anxiety, test comfort, and student achievement test performance.* Paper presented at the Educational Testing Service, Princeton, New Jersey, July 1979.

Fyans, L. J., Jr. (Ed.). *Achievement-motivation: Recent trends in theory and research.* New York: Plenum, 1980.

Harnisch, D. L., Hill, K. T., & Fyans, L. J. *Development of a shorter, more reliable and more valid measure of test motivation.* Paper presented at the annual meeting of the National Council on Measurement in Education, Boston, April 1980.

Hill, K. T. Anxiety in the evaluative context. In W. W. Hartup (Ed.), *The young child* (Vol. 2). Washington, DC: National Association for the Education of Young Children, 1972.

Hill, K. T. Individual differences in children's response to adult presence and evaluative reactions. *Merrill-Palmer Quarterly,* 1976, *22,* 99–104, 118–123.

Hill, K. T. The relation of evaluative practices to test anxiety and achievement motivation. *UCLA Educator,* 1977, *19,* 15–21.

Hill, K. T. *Eliminating motivational testing error by developing optimal testing procedures and teaching test-taking skills.* Paper presented at the Educational Testing Service, Princeton, New Jersey, 1979.

Hill, K. T. Motivation, evaluation and educational testing policy. In L. J. Fyans (Ed.), *Achievement motivation: Recent trends in theory and research.* New York: Plenum, 1980.

Hill, K. T., & Eaton, W. O. The interaction of test anxiety and success–failure experiences in determining children's arithmetic performance. *Developmental Psychology,* 1977, *13,* 205–211.

Hill, K. T., & Sarason, S. B. The relation of test anxiety and defensiveness to test and school performance over the elementary school years. *Monographs of the Society for Research in Child Development*, 1966, *31* (2, Serial No. 104).

Hill, K. T., & Wigfield, A. Test anxiety: A major educational problem and what can be done about it. *Elementary School Journal*, in press.

Hill, K. T., Wigfield, A., & Plass, J. A. *Effects of different kinds of optimizing instructions on seventh- and eighth-grade children's achievement test performance.* Paper presented at the annual meeting of the American Educational Research Association, Boston, 1980.

Hutt, M. L. "Consecutive" and "adaptive" testing with the revised Stanford-Binet. *Journal of Consulting Psychology*, 1947, *11*, 93–104.

Maehr, M. L. Sociocultural origins of achievement motivation. In D. Bar-Tal & L. Saxe (Eds.), *Social psychology of education: Theory and research.* New York: Hemisphere, 1978.

Maehr, M. L., & Nicholls, J. A second look at culture and achievement motivation. In N. Warren (Ed.), *Studies in cross-cultural psychology* (Vol. 3). New York: Academic Press, 1980.

Nottelmann, E. D., & Hill, K. T. Test anxiety and off-task behavior in evaluative situations. *Child Development*, 1977, *48*, 225–231.

Pike, L. W. Short-term instruction, testwiseness, and the scholastic aptitude test. New York: College Entrance Examination Board Research and Development Report, 1979.

Plass, J. A., & Hill, K. T. *Optimizing children's achievement test performance: The role of time pressure, evaluation anxiety, and sex.* Paper presented at the Biennial meeting of the Society for Research in Child Development, San Francisco, March 1979.

Ruebush, B. K. Anxiety. In H. W. Stevenson, J. Kagan, & C. Spiker (Eds.), *Sixty-second yearbook of the national society for the study of education* (Part 1): *Child psychology.* Chicago: University of Chicago Press, 1963.

Sarason, I. G. Test anxiety, attention and the general problem of anxiety. In C. D. Spielberger and I. G. Sarason (Eds.), *Stress and anxiety* (Vol. 1). Washington, DC: Hemisphere Press, 1975.

Sarason, I. G. (Ed.), *Test anxiety: Theory, research and applications.* Hillsdale, NJ: Erlbaum, 1980.

Sarason, S. B., Davidson, K. S., Lighthall, F. F., Waite, R. R., & Ruebush, B. K. *Anxiety in elementary school children.* New York: Wiley, 1960.

Sarason, S. B., Hill, K. T., & Zimbardo, P. G. A longitudinal study of the relation of test anxiety to performance on intelligence and achievement tests. *Monographs of the Society for Research in Child Development*, 1964, *29* (7, Serial No. 98).

Weiner, B. *Theories of motivation: From mechanism to cognition.* Chicago: Markham, 1972.

Weiner, B. An attributional approach for educational psychology. In L. S. Shulman (Ed.), *Review of research in education* (Vol. 4). Istasca, IL: Peacock, 1977. (A publication of the American Educational Research Association.)

Williams, J. P. *Individual differences in achievement test presentation and evaluation anxiety.* Unpublished doctoral dissertation, University of Illinois at Urbana-Champaign, 1976.

Willig, A. C., Harnisch, D. L., Hill, K. T., & Maehr, M. L. Sociocultural and educational correlates of success–failure attributions and evaluation anxiety in the school setting for Black, Hispanic, and Anglo children. *American Educational Research Journal*, 1983, *20*, 385–410.

Wine, J. D. Cognitive-attentional theory of test anxiety. In I. G. Sarason (Ed.), *Test anxiety: Theory, research and applications.* Hillsdale, NJ: Erlbaum, 1980.

Zigler, E., Abelson, W. D., & Seitz, V. Motivational factors in the performance of economically disadvantaged children on the Peabody Picture Vocabulary Test. *Child Development*, 1973, *44*, 294–303.

Zigler, E., & Butterfield, E. C. Motivational aspects of change in IQ test performance of culturally deprived nursery school children. *Child Development*, 1968, *39*, 1–14.

Zigler, E., & Harter, S. The socialization of the mentally retarded. In D. A. Goslin (Ed.), *Handbook of socialization theory and research*. Chicago: McNally, 1969.

9

Motivation Enhancement in Educational Settings*

Richard deCharms

OVERVIEW

There are several common, yet apparently different, ways of thinking about learning and teaching. One is that the learner is developing habits; the teacher demonstrates the correct responses, the learner imitates those responses, and the teacher strengthens (reinforces) them into good habits. Another is that the learner is a passive receptacle and the teacher fills the receptacle with knowledge, as one fills a cup from a pitcher. A third is that the learner is an active agent engaged in interaction with the environment; the teacher helps to initiate the interaction, as one sets a stage for a drama but cannot completely control the action.

Working teachers probably use vestiges of each kind of thinking in everyday teaching. They can learn much about habit-formation and knowledge acquisition, storage, and retrieval, from the psychology of learning and thinking. As to the learner as agent, the teacher is given a warm feeling of rightness and little else to go on. We can train habits, we can impart knowledge, but how do we enhance agency?

*Research reported was partially supported by Grants from the Carnegie Corporation, the National Institute of Mental Health, and the Spencer Foundation.

275

Teacher training courses often extoll the concept of active learning, yet when it comes right down to what to do in the classroom, the teacher is trained to use specific responses (methods). If teachers of teachers are to facilitate discrimination between training for good habits, imparting knowledge, and enhancing agency, they must practice their own preaching.

We have chosen to use the word *enhancing* in contrast to training (of habits) or teaching (of knowledge) because motivation cannot be trained or taught. Specific methods do not work. Yet, teachers *can* enhance agency in a pupil, and what is more they can also enhance habit formation by going a step beyond training. They can even enhance knowledge acquisition by going a step beyond teaching facts. Agency involves doing something. Doing something involves thinking, as well as responding. And thinking and doing involve the person in causing some event in the world. The concept of *personal causation* is central to the combination of doing, thinking, and learning, whether a result of habit, cognition reception, or agency.

THE GUIDING CONCEPTUALIZATION

THE CONCEPT OF PERSONAL CAUSATION

Personal causation means doing something intentionally to produce a change. A habit is learned so that it can be used in action. Knowledge is learned so that it can be used to guide action. *Agency* is the reasonable use of knowledge and habits (learned responses) to produce desirable changes. So agency, knowledgeable doing, combines habit and knowledge. The payoff is the desired change.

When habits and knowledge, combined with motivation, are adequate, agency is successful; when they are inadequate, agency is unsuccessful. When attempted agency is successful, the agent has caused the desired change and feels that he or she has originated it. When agency is unsuccessful, the person has not caused the change—some other agent or object has interfered with personal causation and the person feels that he or she is a pawn.

The outcome or effect of doing something may be thought of as a reward or a reinforcer. As currently used, however, the concept of reinforcer does not apply to all the known meanings of the concept of successful and, especially, unsuccessful agency. Rigorously defined, a *reinforcer* (as in reinforced concrete) is an observable event that increases the probability of the observable response that preceded it. Yet, failure often increases attempts to succeed and success reduces the necessity to attempt further. By refining the concept of reinforcement, these objections can be met. However, the vivid image of the objectivity of an observable strengthener of behavior begins to pale when we are forced further from the original concept toward unobservable reinforcement of undefined cognitive events and toward the even more subjective concept of self-reinforcement. No one can deny the value of the reinforcement concept used in radical behaviorism. Nor is it deniable that we can use the argot of radical behaviorism to describe an agency event; but we are using an *argot*—a specialized jargon that often conceals the true import of agency.

We go beyond the limitations of the rigorous definitions of reinforcement to use the concept of personal causation. We assume a priori that being the cause of desired changes is the aim of actions of agency. There is no substitute for personal causation because that is the way we understand our own actions and those of others. If causing desired changes (being effective) is primary in action, it becomes a superordinate, although in some sense secondary, aim in itself. Not only do we desire the specific effect, we desire to produce it ourselves. It is not enough that we can reproduce another person's mathematical proof, we are prone to desire production of our own. Sometimes, simple assurance that we can do something, without actually doing it in fact, something like turning off a distracting noise, is enough to affect our actions.

The centrality of personal causation in human agency is an assumption or a guiding conceptualization. It is not a fact and it *cannot* be demonstrated empirically. It is, therefore, much like the proposition that all learning is a function of reinforcement. What *can* be done is to try consistently to analyze learning and human agency from the point of view of the assumption of the centrality of personal causation. Using such a guiding conceptualization, the teacher, the educator, or the psychologist can design experiences to enhance (or diminish) personal causation in self and others to see what difference it makes. Using such a guiding conceptualization is consistent within itself because teachers, educators, or psychologists are themselves trying to make a change, and they are only asking others to do what they are trying to do.

PERCEPTION VERSUS EXPERIENCE

The concept of personal causation has its roots in Fritz Heider's discussion of the perceived locus of causality for behavior (Heider, 1944,

1958). The perception of the locus of causality as internal or external to the action is the cornerstone of attribution theory (Jones, Kanous, Kelley, Nisbett, Valins, & Weiner, 1971) in social psychology. At first, I thought of personal causation as the *perception* of internal locus of causality (deCharms, 1968). Applied to others, that is what it is, but more and more I became interested in going beyond third-person attribution (deCharms & Shea, 1976) to the first-person experience of personal causation. As a result more and more I dropped the phrase "perception of internal locus of causality" in favor of "experience of . . . ."

ORIGIN AND PAWN

Along with (in fact temporally preceding) the shift from "perception" to "experience," we sought to shorten the phrase "perception–experience of internal locus of causality" and its pair "the experience of external locus." For the sake of brevity, we (those of us involved in the Carnegie Project), dubbed the negative experience of external locus of causality for our behavior, the *pawn* experience—the feeling of being externally pushed around. The more positive experience of internal locus of causality for behavior we dubbed the *origin* experience because of the strong sense of originating our own actions.

The origin–pawn terminology had the advantage that it apparently captured a common human experience and was quickly grasped by teachers and students. At the same time it had the disadvantage of oversimplifying a complex phenomenon. The advantage led to easy communication at a superficial level and at the same time led to misconceptions even among ourselves when attempting more sophisticated analysis.

MISCONCEPTIONS FOSTERED BY THE ORIGIN CONCEPT

There are two misconceptions that we must address. First, origin–pawn terminology led us to talk as if (and others to conclude that) there are two kinds of people, origins and pawns. *This kind of gross characterization is manifestly false.* Would that it were so simple. Both people and situations can be characterized as more or less origin (people) or origin-enhancing (situations). In short, we are all origins some of the time and pawns some of the time. Some situations can turn almost anyone into a pawn, but even in a Nazi concentration camp, a man like Bruno Bettelheim can maintain vestiges of originship by studying his own reactions. And his conclusion was that it was this ability that saved his sanity, if not his very life (see Bettelheim, 1943).

The second misconception was that to treat persons as origins, you let them do as they please. This misconception has devastating effects in the educational setting. It was captured in the 1960s by the anecdote of the child who asked the teacher, "Do we *have* to do what we want to do?" As pointed out by Plimpton (in deCharms, 1976, pp. 162–175) the origin-enhancing teacher is not a *laissez-faire* teacher (literally a teacher who lets students do whatever they want). The origin classroom is not even a democratic classroom because students cannot be expected to vote on all issues. Ruminations on this misconception led us to consider the amount of structure imposed on a class by a teacher and to propose the "curvilinear hypothesis."

CHOICE, FREEDOM, RESPONSIBILITY, AND OWNERSHIP OF BEHAVIOR

The complexity of the origin concept forced us to consider all of the related concepts—choice, freedom, responsibility, and ownership of behavior. The guiding conceptualization was broadened to include them. In a nutshell, originating one's own actions implies choice; choice is experienced as freedom; choice imposes responsibility for choice-related actions and enhances the feeling that the action is "mine" (ownership of action). Put in the negative, having actions imposed from without (pawn behaviors) abrogates choice; lack of choice is experienced as bondage, releases one from responsibility, and allows, even encourages, the feeling that the action is "not mine." Some evidence for the validity of the connections in this chain of reasoning are presented here subsequently.

THE HIDDEN COSTS OF REWARDS

In 1968 (deCharms, 1968, pp. 329–332), using the guiding conceptualization of personal causation, I predicted a paradoxical effect of an extrinsic reinforcer on an intrinsically motivated action. The logic was that if an action is freely initiated through choice and then it is discovered that someone else desires the actor to do the action so much that the other will reward him or her for doing it, then the actor may lose the feeling of freedom, ownership, and choice. If the personal causation analysis is valid, the actor should continue the action only as long as the extrinsic reinforcer is offered. Subsequently, with no reinforcer, the action should disappear or diminish. Lepper, Greene, and Nisbett (1973) have given dramatic support to this hypothesis. They selected preschool children who originally chose from several other possible activities to draw with felt pens although no external incentive was offered. Some of these children were subsequently offered a prize for drawing while others were not. Later, back in the situation where choice between several activities was available, but no prize was offered, the children who had received the prize were significantly less prone to choose to draw with felt pens than were the children who had not received the prize. Since the original study, a considerable literature has appeared confirming the phenomena. The interest generated by this hypothesis stems from the apparent contradiction of strict reinforcement theory, which should predict that the prize (reinforcer) would increase rather than decrease the probability of the felt-pen-drawing response.

Several explanations of the phenomenon, dubbed "the hidden costs of rewards," have been offered. These include some that extend reinforcement theory to self-perception theory (Lepper & Greene, 1978) and one by Deci (1975, 1980), in terms of competency and self-determination, which has close ties to the personal causation thesis. This vast literature shows both the importance of choice (the condition for being in Lepper's study was choice of activity) and the danger of uncritical use of reinforcers (for more on the careful use of rewards in the classroom see de-Charms, 1983).

THE CURVILINEAR HYPOTHESIS

As I learned more about personal causation, pondered the misconceptions sometimes fostered by the origin concept, and wondered about the effects of reinforcement on motivation, I gradually came to think of the relationship between classroom structure and pupil motivation as curvilinear. A rigidly structured classroom should inhibit pupil motivation, just as an unstructured classroom should inhibit motivation.

A classroom with the right amount of structure should *enhance* motivation. But what is the right amount of structure and, for that matter, what is structure? Number of choices permitted pupils and amount of teacher dominance in the classroom seemed to be two concepts that had three advantages: both seemed intuitively to be related to structure, both were more easily operationalized than structure itself, and both were related to motivation (Lewin, Lippitt, & White, 1939; Perlmuter & Monty, 1979). Further, teacher dominance in the classroom would most naturally be negatively related to pupil choice—the more the teacher dominated the fewer choices the pupils would have. Often two negatively related variables produce a curvilinear relationship with a third variable.

For example, Eckert Hess (1959, pp. 44–77) explained the phenomenon of "imprinting" in wild fowl as a curvilinear function where a particular set of responses wax and then wane as a function of time since the chick hatched. He showed that ability to perform the responses was a positive linear function of time (maturation) and an interfering response (fear) that was also a linear function of time. The combination of the two produced the typical peak period in which "imprinting" is maximum and before or after which it is less effective or nonexistent. Similarly, Atkinson (1958) has shown that risk-taking behavior is a curvilinear function of risk and has analyzed risk into the two negatively related variables of incentive value and probability of success. By direct analogy to the preceding, we hypothesized a curvilinear relationship growing out of the three variables: teacher dominance, number of choices available to pupils, and pupil motivation.

RAWL'S ARISTOTELEAN HYPOTHESIS—A JUST
CLASSROOM

The conceptualization just sketched has in part guided and in part been guided by our empirical research since the 1970s. Early on, we devised a longitudinal study to investigate the possibility of helping teachers to treat children as origins. Our intent was to test the hypothesis that children who are treated as origins would feel personal causation, would learn origin behavior, and would gain more academically. The Carnegie Project and the follow-up research subsequent to it (which is described here subsequently) investigated the relationships among helping teachers to enhance motivation, the teachers' classroom behavior, and the pupils' motivation and academic achievement. The Carnegie Project was successful in increasing originship in children and that result led to a questioning of the ethics of such a project. Had we, in helping children to be origins, trained them to treat others as pawns? Was the classroom with enhanced originship in the children a just classroom?

To gain some insight into this question we use the analogy between a just classroom and what the moral philosopher, John Rawls, calls *The Just Society*. The analogy was strengthened by the apparent similarity of our central concept of personal causation and Rawl's central concept that he calls the Aristotelean principle.

The Aristotelean Principle is stated by Rawls (1971, p. 426) as follows: "other things equal, human beings enjoy the exercise of their realized capacities (their innate or trained abilities), and this enjoyment increases the more the capacity is realized, or the greater its complexity." Put another way, Rawls is saying that a basic principle of human psychology contained within Aristotle's Nicomachean Ethics (if not explicitly stated) is that for humans, *doing what they can do well is a basic "human good."* He goes on to say, "The Aristotelean Principle is a principle of motivation" (p. 427). With regard to enjoyment and rewards Rawls says

> The Aristotelean Principle characterizes human beings as importantly moved . . . by the desire to do things enjoyed simply for their own sakes, . . . The marks of such enjoyed activities are many, varying from the manner and way in which they are done to the persistence with which they are returned to at a later time. Indeed, we do them without the incentive of evident reward, and allowing us to engage in them can itself act often as a reward for doing other things [p. 431–432].

The psychological evidence for such behavior is contained in White's (1959) famous article on competence motivation which, incidentally, is cited by Rawls.

Connecting Rawl's Aristotelean Principle with personal causation produced the hypothesis that origin-trained children might differ from untrained children in their conception of their relation to others. Trained origins might learn to treat others as pawns, a result that we would not like to see. Or they might have what we considered a more mature origin orientation, tempered by a sense of responsibility, and treat others as equal origins.

What follows is the description of attempts to use the broad-ranging guiding conceptualization of personal causation to produce desired changes in educational settings—usually inner-city elementary schools.

THE EVIDENCE

THE CARNEGIE PROJECT

In the spring of 1967 we designed a project to help teachers enhance personal causation in low-income black elementary schoolchildren. The project was a longitudinal study. Measures of motivation and academic achievement were obtained on the pupils at the end of each school year for 4 years, from fifth to eighth grades. The experimental treatment involved training teachers who taught the children in sixth and seventh grade and used motivation-enhancing exercises in their classrooms. The students who constituted the experimental subjects received training in their classrooms plus the regular curriculum throughout the year from motivation-trained teachers. Control subjects experienced only the regular curriculum from nonmotivation-trained teachers.

Personal Causation Training

The experimental manipulation was accomplished through a two-step process. First, the teachers attended a motivation training session. Second, the teachers and the university staff designed exercises that the teachers used throughout the year in their classrooms.

The experimental teachers were paid to attend a week-long residential personal-causation training-course prior to meeting their class in the fall. The major sections of the course were designed (1) to encourage self-study and evaluation of personal motives; (2) to acquaint the participants with thoughts and behavior characteristics of people with different motives, such as affiliation, achievement, and power; (3) to show the value of careful planning and realistic goal-setting in relation to any motive; and (4) to promote origin rather than pawn behavior (for details see deCharms, 1976, Chapter 4). During the year following their training, when they were teaching the experimental children, the teachers met regularly with the research staff and helped to design classroom exercises that they then implemented. The exercises were designed to emphasize four major concepts, namely, (1) the self-concept, (2) achievement motivation, (3) realistic goal setting, and (4) the origin–pawn concept.

It would consume too much space to describe here in any detail all of these classroom exercises (for details see deCharms, 1976, Chapter 4). Each unit lasted for about 10 weeks and occupied about $\frac{1}{2}$ hour of class time at least 3–4 days of each week. "The Real Me" unit asked the children to compose a notebook of personal statements about themselves and their relations to others. The "Person Perception" unit stressed interpersonal sensitivity and cognitive complexity, designed to enhance ego-development (Loevinger & Wessler, 1970). "Stories of Achievement" asked the children each week to write an imaginative story from a supplied skeleton plot composed of achievement-motivation categories (e.g., write about a hero who is trying to do something better than he or she did it before). The "Spelling Game" involved realistic goal-setting in a spelling bee in which the child could choose easy, moderate, or difficult words that were scaled to personal ability. Extensive "Origin Manuals" were introduced last to bring together concepts used in previous units under the origin–pawn rubric. They stressed internal realistic goal-setting, planning, personal responsibility, feelings of personal ·causation and self-confidence, and the negative feelings of being pushed around.

Results: Origin–Pawn Variable

Did the children show more origin behavior as a result of personal causation training? The origin–pawn variable was measured through content analysis of thought samples. The rationale for this derived from Bridgman's (1959) concept of operational analysis of "introspectional words in the private mode" (p. 38) and Polanyi's (1958) concept of personal knowledge. As a result of several theoretical seminars and an intensive observation study of children in an experimental classroom, Plimpton (see deCharms, 1976, Appendix A) developed a scoring manual that was applicable to the thought samples that we had collected each year using a form of data collection procedure developed by McClelland, Atkinson, Clark, and Lowell (1953).

The children's stories were coded for presence or absence of six origin–pawn categories, namely: (1) internal goal setting, (2) internal determination of instrumental activity, (3) reality perception, (4) personal responsibility, (5) self-confidence, and (6) internal control. Each story received 1 point for each category and, because the children wrote six stories, the origin–pawn score could range from 0 to 36. Considerable effort was expended (deCharms, 1971) on such things as coder reliability, test–retest reliability, internal consistency, and predictive validity of the new measure.

The origin–pawn coding system was applied to stories written by the children at the end of their fifth, sixth, and seventh grades. The fifth-grade data constitute the pretraining measure, sixth- and seventh-grade data are postmeasures for both experimentals and controls for both years. Because some children received training in both sixth and seventh grades, some only in sixth, some only in seventh, and some no training at all; these data were analyzed as a 2×2 factorial design. The data are longitudinal in that we had origin measures for each year on all subjects in the analysis.

The simplest predictions would have been that the origin score would have increased as a function of training and would have not increased when training did not intervene. Figure 1 shows that this is clearly the case.

The mean origin scores increased from about 5 to 12 as a function of

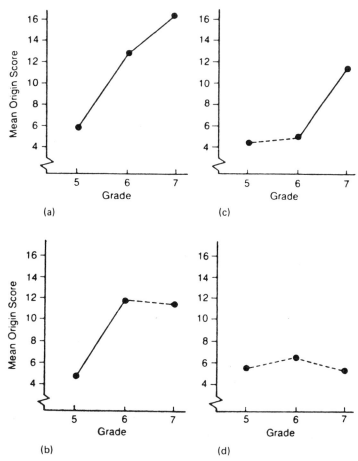

Figure 1.   Mean origin score with (solid lines) and without (broken lines) motivational training: (a) sixth- and seventh-grade training (N = 57); (b) sixth-grade training only (N = 27); (c) seventh-grade training only (N = 41); (d) no-training controls (N = 50).

training. It did not decline significantly in a follow-up year. In every case where there was training, the mean origin score increased significantly (p < .001). In no case where training did not occur did the mean differences even approach significance.

There is clear evidence that the personal-causation training affected the way children write imaginative stories. After training, the characters in the stories more often set their own goals, determine their own instrumental activity, are more realistic, take more personal responsibility for their action, and are more self-confident: all subcategories of the origin–pawn score increase.

Results: Academic Achievement

In the school district where this research was performed, the Iowa Test of Basic Skills (Lindquist & Hieronymous, 1955) was administered at the end of each year and the teachers and administrators were most concerned about the grade placement scores of the children. Success and failure of both teachers and children are often seen in terms of the results of the Iowa Test of Basic Skills.

By fifth grade the children in the district were typically more than $\frac{1}{2}$ year behind national norms in grade placement. As the years pass and the children go on to higher grades they fall farther behind. This trend of gaining less than the normal full year in grade placement over a year of school was significantly alleviated by the personal-causation training. Figure 2 shows the decrement from grade placement of experimental and control children in fifth, sixth, and seventh grades. The experimentals received personal-causation training in both sixth and seventh grades, the controls received no training. This most global analysis showed significant effects of the training on academic achievement during both years.

More detailed analyses indicated that the training significantly affected both genders, but had more effect on the boys than on the girls. Language skills were most strongly affected overall, although arithmetic skills were also enhanced during the first year. Reading skills seemed to be least affected by the training. Other types of school behavior on which

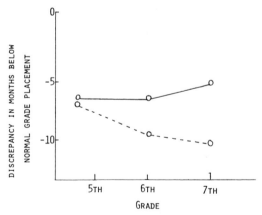

Figure 2.   Mean discrepancy in months from normal grade placement on the composite Iowa Test of Basic Skills. Experimentals ($N = 112$) are indicated by a solid line; controls ($N = 64$) are indicated by a broken line. Discrepancy from fifth to sixth grade, $p < .05$; discrepancy from sixth to seventh grade, $p < .1$.

we had reliable data were attendance records and tardies. Both absences and tardies were significantly reduced in the trained classes in the sixth-grade compared with fifth-grade records and the reverse was true—more absences and tardies—for the control children. Clearly, personal causation training did significantly affect the academic achievement and other school behavior of the children.

Other types of origin behavior were also affected by the training. In the sixth-grade spelling game the children became progressively more moderate in their risk taking, a finding that, when coupled with the reality perception category in content analysis of the stories, may be called increased realistic goal setting. Shea (1969) found this same effect with the experimental children, using a risk-taking measure involving arithmetic problems, although here the effect interacted with Rotter's measure of internal versus external control of reinforcement (Battle, 1962; Rotter, 1966). The significant difference in realistic goal-setting for arithmetic problems held only for the "externals." The externals were the most extreme risk takers in the control classes and were much less extreme after training in the experimental group. All of the data give evidence that personal-causation training does increase origin-related behavior in children. We may now ask, "What are the characteristics of an origin classroom?"

CHARACTERISTICS OF AN ORIGIN CLASSROOM

The Right Stuff: Not a Laissez-faire Classroom

Tom Wolfe says you have to have "the right stuff" to be in the top echelons of military flyers. At a more mundane and yet more subtle level a teacher has to have the right stuff to be highly successful in enhancing motivation. The right stuff, among other things, is the right amount of structure: too much is too bad—too little is chaos.

We learned this dramatically the second year of the Carnegie Project. A teacher left the summer workshop determined to treat his new seventh graders as origins. When he first met his class, he asked them to arrange the moveable desks into a circle. The class then proceeded to discuss what they would do that year. His plan was to have them decide everything by majority vote. When he returned to the first meeting with the staff after school had started he reported that treating students as origins was a failure and impossible to maintain as it resulted in chaos. Apparently, he had moved from too much structure to too little.

We first thought of structure along the traditional (and ambiguous) dimensions of autocratic–democratic–laissez-faire (White & Lippitt, 1960). Clearly the origin classroom is not a laissez-faire classroom but it is not even a democratic classroom as we discovered later (see the following), because a critical aspect in an origin classroom is individual choice. The democratic process (majority rules) denies the minority their choice and hence treats them as pawns.

Classroom observations had turned our interest to teacher behavior but in the Carnegie Project we had few quantifiable data on what untrained teachers did to develop origin classrooms, although we knew that some teachers (in the control group) succeeded quite well without training. This became the focus of later projects. Possibly more important than what trained teachers do is the students' perception of what the teachers do. To measure the students' *experience* of the origin classroom, Koenigs and Hess (see deCharms, 1976, Appendix B) developed the Origin Climate Questionnaire. The measure was derived from the six major categories that we had found to distinguish origin behavior from pawn behavior. Twenty-four questions were developed that asked the students whether the teacher (1) encouraged goal setting, (2) allowed students to determine their own activities in pursuing goals, (3) stressed realistic goal setting, (4) encouraged students to take personal responsibility for their actions, and (5) instilled self-confidence in them.

Students of experimental and control teachers filled out the questionnaire at the end of the year. A random selection of six boys and six girls was chosen from each classroom to give a mean origin score for each class. The students of the trained teachers experienced them as more encouraging of origin behavior (compared to students of the control teachers) in two replications of 20 and 26 classrooms ($p < .01$ and $p < .06$, respectively). An analysis of a subgroup showed that the effects on the teachers' classroom behavior lasted for at least 1 year after they had been formally associated with the project and almost 2 years after they received their initial personal causation training. The students did see and report significant differences between the classroom behavior of the trained teachers and that of untrained teachers. The trained teachers treated the children more as origins.

The origin climate questionnaire has lead to another misunderstanding of our research. The questionnaire *is not a measure of the individual child's level of motivation* and cannot be substituted for the preceding thought-sample measure. In fact, it is not significantly correlated with the origin measure derived from thought samples (in two samples of inner-city children the correlations were $r = +.10$, $N = 109$, $p > .25$; $r = +.13$, $N = 132$, $p > .10$). The Origin Climate Questionnaire is a measure of the average experience of the class members of that class with that teacher. The score used in analyses is an average for each classroom. Clear evidence that the measure varies as a function of the teacher, not of the students, was found. In one study, 17 teachers taught two different classes and both scores for each teacher (same teacher, different children) were correlated. The result was a correlation of +.72, demonstrating that the mean for the teacher related primarily to the way her classroom procedures were perceived rather than to the particular students that filled out the questionnaire. Later (under "agents of origin influence"), further evidence using the origin climate questionnaire is reviewed but for now let us return to characteristics of the origin-trained classrooms.

A Responsible and Just Classroom

Extensive observations in one origin classroom led Plimpton to conclude that

> Once the rules were established in the beginning of the year . . . the teacher intentionally gave the students all the freedom possible within the limits of a classroom setting. But with the freedom the students also had to assume *personal* and *collective responsibility*. . . . once this system of working together has developed, the teacher does very little to control the children. Indeed, the children are controlling themselves. *But* a classroom society built on controls from within, warmth, acceptance and mutual respect is not created overnight. Nor is it developed by a laissez-faire teacher. She must be firm and consistant in her behavior, consistently seeking the good of the children in ways that they can understand [deCharms, 1976, pp. 167–168; emphasis in original].

Responsibility to others is central to Rawl's concept of the just society. In general terms we may ask of our procedures, Can origin training be done in a way that is commensurate with the maxim that "the activities favored by the Aristotelean Principle are good for other persons as well"? (Rawls, 1971, p. 429). A person acting as an origin is not acting in a vacuum. The importance of the significant other parties to the interaction in the acquisition of personal causation cannot be ignored. Is the free, independent, autonomous origin, in fact, a monster who attempts to run rough-shod over all who chance to get in the way? Did our training turn out monster origins or responsible origins?

Rawls assumes that the exercise of one's realized abilities, under the Aristotelean Principle, involves activities that "fellow associates are likely to support . . . as promoting the common interest and also take pleasure in as displays of human excellence" (p. 429). Assuming that training and education are applied to cognitive capacities or skills, there seems to be no conflict with "the principles of right," but what about training and education (origin training) in capacities for interaction with, and perhaps manipulation of other persons? What about the person who delights in the exercise of this capacity as a "con artist"?

This kind of question was raised poignantly during the first year of the Carnegie Project. In the spring of 1968 some 400 inner-city sixthgrade children were nearing the end of a year of motivation training. I happened to be briefly out of the country on the day (April fourth) that Martin Luther King was murdered. In the days that followed that incident, the overseas news of riots in Washington, and so on, was alarming. A colleague with whom I was traveling said to me, "Now that you have trained all those kids in the ghetto to be origins, what do you think they will do?" The importance of the aspect of personal responsibility in our motivation training had never loomed so large.

When I arrived back in the United States, I asked the teachers if there had been any incidents in the schools involving motivation-trained children. In one school there was one white teacher and the windows in her automobile had been broken. Neither she nor her students were receiving motivation training. The trained teacher who reported the incident, however, also revealed that members of her own class who were receiving origin training had come to her asking, in essence, what was the responsible thing for them to do. They knew who had broken the windows (the children in the white teacher's classroom) and they wanted neither to be blamed for it nor to reveal their knowledge to anyone but to their own teacher. The teacher was proud of the responsible way her trained children responded.

More than anecdotal data are available, however. Following the Carnegie Project, Muir (1977) designed a study to attempt deliberately to increase responsibility and ownership of action in sixth graders through the device of offering choices in the classroom. Results demonstrated an increased understanding of responsibility as a function of choice but the data fell short of showing relationships with responsible classroom behavior.

Origin Training and Power Motivation

In light of Rawl's theory the question of the effects of personal causation training on responsibility seems crucial. An unfortunate consequence of our adoption of the terms *origin* and *pawn* seems to be the assumption that for one person to be an origin others have to be pawns. An "I win, you lose," zero-sum view of the world would lead to this assumption. Our own conception of a more mature outlook, however, is that origins try to treat others as origins and this is what we tried to model for the teachers, and to get them in turn to transmit to the pupils.

We have tried to get some direct evidence concerning this issue. To do this we resorted to McClelland's concept of the power motive (McClelland, 1976). McClelland has suggested that although "people are suspicious of a man who wants power . . . surely this negative face of power is only part of the story. Power must have a positive face too" (p. 304). Consequenctly, he set out to devise measures of these "two faces of power" that he called "personalized power" (the negative face that we usually think of as raw power), and "socialized power" (the more positive face). Starting with the basic definition of the need for power (Uleman, 1966; Veroff, 1957; Winter, 1967) as a "concern for having a strong impact on others" (p. 305), McClelland continues, "there are two faces of power. One is turned toward seeking to win out over active adversaries. Life tends to be seen as a zero-sum game . . . the imagery is that of the 'law of the jungle.' . . . The other face of the power motive is more socialized . . . At the fantasy level it expresses itself in thoughts of exercising power for the benefit of others" (p. 306).

Fortunately for our purposes, McClelland has related personalized and socialized power directly to the origin–pawn concept in his definitions, especially in stressing the positive face. He says, for instance, that the role of the leader with socialized power motivation "is to strengthen and uplift, to make people feel like Origins, not Pawns of the sociopolitical system" (p. 307). Later he says, "the major goal of all of our educational exercises was to make the participants feel strong, like Origins rather than Pawns" (p. 309). And further, "The positive or socialized face of power is characterized by a concern for group goals, . . . in fantasy it leads to a concern with exercising influence *for* others . . . It functions in a way that makes members of a group feel like Origins rather than Pawns" (pp. 310–311).

With these definitions and descriptions of the two faces of power in mind, Wittcoff (1980) formulated the hypotheses that if origin training led to more responsible origin behavior, then personalized power scores should decrease and socialized power scores increase as a function of training. If, on the other hand, origin training led to the origin as monster phenomenon, then personalized power scores should increase and socialized power scores should decrease as a function of training.

In our files we had stories written by students in the original motivation training groups. Wittcoff selected protocols from a small group of students half of whom had received training in sixth grade and half of whom had not. For both groups protocols were available before training (end of fifth grade) and after the period when training occurred (end of sixth grade). Consequently, she could test the longitudinal change hypotheses directly.

The results of content analyses of the data demonstrated a moderate increase in socialized power scores for the trained students, whereas the untrained students remained essentially unchanged. For personalized power scores the origin-trained students showed a sizable decline, whereas the untrained students increased in personalized power. Combining socialized and personalized power scores into a composite score resulted in statistical significance.

These data are encouraging. What they tell us tentatively is that personalized power is on the increase in inner-city children when they are in middle elementary school and that origin training can reverse the trend and reduce the self-centered personalized power and even tend to augment the more culturally desirable socialized power. Origin training, with emphasis on responsible behavior, does not produce monster origins.

LONG-TERM EFFECTS OF ORIGIN ENHANCEMENT

Eleventh-Grade Follow-up

Two follow-up studies that have been completed since the original Carnegie study give evidence of long-term effects of training. H. Jackson (1976) designed a study to test the hypothesis that the students given origin training in late elementary school would still have higher origin scores than untrained students several years later. He also hypothesized that trained students would, by eleventh grade, be thinking ahead and planning for their future more than untrained students. He readministered the origin thought-sample measure and devised a semistructured interview to measure personal life goals and responsibility orientation. Even 4 years after training (11th grade), the previously trained students still had significantly higher origin scores. Jackson developed the Origin Behavior Index to content analyze the taped interviews of 79 students. The scores on this index were significantly higher for the randomly selected previously origin-trained students than for the untrained students. This result indicated that training affected career planning and responsible-type behaviors.

Effects of Training on High School Graduation

The second follow-up study occurred after the students, half of whom were trained in late elementary school, should have graduated from high school 5 years after training. Of course, many had not graduated. It was possible to show that for the boys the probability of graduating from high school was increased by origin training, that is, a significantly higher percentage of trained than untrained boys graduated. This finding was further substantiated by demonstrating that even among trained boys there was a higher probability of graduating for those who showed greater motivation change during the training. These data show the long-term effects (after 4 years) of personal causation training.

AGENTS OF ORIGIN INFLUENCE

Parents

Teachers often complain that they have very little influence on children and are especially powerless in combating negative influences from the home. Those who work with teachers often discount these complaints assuming that the teachers are just excusing their own inadequate teaching. In shaping basic predispositions of children, like their long-term motive dispositions, the teacher has either a formidable opponent or an ally in the child's parents, for no other reason than that any one teacher is a small part of a child's life compared to a parent. In shaping origin–pawn dispositions in a child, teachers and parents can reinforce or counteract each other's efforts. We have seen evidence that teachers can enhance originship, and in one study we went into the home to study mother–child interactions.

K. Jackson (1973) used a block-stacking game (Rosen & D'Andrade, 1959) that placed seventh-graders in a standardized interaction with their mothers. The blindfolded child was confronted with a large assortment of blocks and told to see how many blocks he or she could stack, one on top of another, with the nonpreferred hand in a 5-minute period. The mother was told that she might help the child but could not touch either the child or the blocks. K. Jackson trained three black male teachers to present this problem to 80 mother–child pairs from the inner-city in their homes. He developed a coding system to analyze the helping behavior of the mother. Directive statements by the mother were defined as those that completely controlled the movements of the child ("Move your hand to the right two inches and pick up that block").

The data from this study gave the best evidence yet of a curvilinear relationship between structure (number of Mother's directive statements) and a motivational predisposition (origin score of child). The relationship was clearly curvilinear for both boys and girls. The children with the highest-mean origin scores were those whose mothers neither controlled them completely (with a high number of directive statments), nor neglected them (with few directive statements). Children with the highest origin scores have mothers who give a moderate amount of help with their directing statements.

The mother who directs every act even before the child asks for help is over-nurturing and allowing the child little chance to develop personal causation. On the other hand, the mother who gives no help is neglecting the child and fostering a feeling of helplessness (Seligman, 1975) as a pawn. The child who experiences the mother as helping but not taking over, experiences a mutuality between self and mother in accomplishing the task. Such a child experiences personal causation.

Teachers

Following the K. Jackson study, we became interested in the possible effects of a teacher's behavior in the classroom and especially of teacher–pupil interaction. Spring (1974) used terminology from Thibaut and Riecken (1955) that describes *interpersonal influence* in terms of the billiard-ball conception of causality. If Person A tries to influence Person B, the influence attempt is called a "hit." If B's behavior is changed by the "hit" then B is said to be "steered." Spring developed an observation schedule in which the number of hits and steers made by a teacher or her or his pupils can be accurately recorded. She hypothesized that in a classroom where the teacher dominates, that is, where the ratio of teacher hits to pupil hits was very high, the pupils would feel little personal causation; whereas in a classroom where pupil hits and teacher hits were more equally distributed the feeling of personal causation in the children would be higher. Where the pupils dominate and "push the teacher around" the individual pupils may feel personal causation momentarily but ultimately nothing gets done. The hypothesis was a curvilinear relationship (similar to that found by K. Jackson in mother–child interaction) between pupils' hit ratio and their performance in the classroom. In a sample of 50 suburban and inner-city classrooms, Spring found virtually none where the pupil hit ratio was over 50%, but below this moderate level a significant linear relationship obtained. The more pupils can influence classroom activities, the more they feel personal causation and the more they learn.

Subsequent to this study, Koenigs, Fiedler, and deCharms (1977) fit Spring's[1] data into a chain of reasoning and data, from characteristics of the teacher, through teacher–pupil interaction and pupil reactions to the climate of the classroom, to academic achievement of the pupils. The measures used for these variables were Teacher Belief Systems (Harvey,

[1] Spring and Fiedler are the same person.

Prather, White, & Hoffmeister, 1968), pupil:hit ratio (Spring, 1974), origin climate of the classroom (deCharms, 1976, Appendix B), and the Iowa Test of Basic Skills (Lindquist & Hieronymous, 1955).

Harvey's Teacher Belief Systems scale measures four distinct, internally consistent predispositions. These "psychological filters" render the individual selective in personal perceptions of, feelings toward, and responses to ego-involving stimuli and events. Belief systems reflect a continuum ranging from the concrete to the abstract and signify personal predispositions regarding alternatives. Briefly, System I teachers rely on their authority role in the classroom to maintain order and to transmit information. They are absolutistic. System II individuals reject and react negatively to established norms and are equally absolutistic, but teachers are rarely System II. System III teachers value interpersonal harmony and seek to nurture a comfortable learning environment. System IV teachers desire and encouarge a flexible approach to learning in which relativity is emphasized in problem-solving.

The Spring pupil:hit ratio measures teacher–pupil verbal interaction and teacher–pupil relative ability to affect the classroom environment by influencing classroom activities. A high pupil:hit ratio indicates that the teacher is encouraging the students to initiate and to originate during classroom activities, that is, fostering origin behavior.

The origin climate questionnaire used by Koenigs *et al.* is a Likert-type questionnaire where the pupils rate the teacher and classroom on the six origin dimensions.

The data indicate that all the links in the chain from teacher belief systems to pupils' academic achievement are significantly related except the last between origin climate and academic achievement ($r = +.245$). This correlation is based on a reduced number of classrooms (25) on which the academic achievement measure was available. In our previous research (deCharms, 1976) the relationship between origin climate and academic achievement *was* significant.

The major finding of this study for our purposes is the importance of the teacher–pupil interaction in developing feelings of originship in the pupils. The correlation between pupil:hit ratio and origin climate of the classroom is $+.539$. This constitutes a further demonstration of the importance of the "other person," in this case the teacher, in the acquisition of personal causation.

Origin Teachers and Internal Locus of Control Teachers

Rotter (1966) and his associates have developed the concept of *internal* versus *external* locus of control of reinforcements that is often assumed to be the same as the origin–pawn concept. The confusion comes from the original derivation of personal causation (deCharms, 1968) from Heider's (1958) concept of perceived locus of causality for behavior. The theoretical bases of locus of control of reinforcements (social-learning theory) and of locus of causality for behavior (attribution theory) are quite different. And the questionnaire measure of locus of control of reinforcements is not correlated with the thought-sample origin measure (for 85 teachers, $r = +.11$, $p = .30$). What is interesting, however, is that both measures used with teachers predict average academic achievement of their pupils.

For the preceding Koenigs et $al.$ (1977) sample of 85 teachers, we had the questionnaire measures of locus of control of reinforcements and the thought-sample origin-measure. For their pupils we knew the classroom average on the Iowa Test of Basic Skills. Because there was no correlation between the two teacher measures, we could divide the teachers into four approximately equal groups by splitting the origin measure and the locus of control of reinforcements measure at the median. This resulted in high origin–internal teachers ($N = 16$), high origin–external teachers ($N = 23$), low origin–internal teachers ($N = 24$), and low origin–external teachers ($N = 22$). Obtaining mean Iowa Test of Basic Skill scores for the teachers' classes in each group allowed us to compute a 2×2 factorial analysis of variance with academic achievement of classes as the dependent variable. Internal locus of control of reinforcements teachers had higher academic achievement in their classrooms than did external locus of control teachers ($p < .04$). Similarly, high-origin teachers had higher means than did low-origin teachers ($p < .02$). There was no significant interaction. Clearly, although the two orientations of the teachers are uncorrelated, they each contribute independently to academic achievement of pupils.

WHEN ORIGIN ENHANCEMENT FAILED

If the exception improves the rule, then it is advantageous to have some failures to help improve origin-enhancement efforts. No one should conclude that our work with the teachers uniformly helped them or that their work with the pupils had positive effects with every child. In order to gain hypotheses about how to strengthen our procedures we examined the data very carefully for apparent failures.[2]

---

[2]So far every finding we have reported has been statistically highly significant with the most conservative analysis and most often replicated at least once. Some of our evidence for apparent failures is less firm and that almost by definition because we did not predict failure. Still we have looked for data rather than mere speculation.

Lack of Teacher Ownership

Our first failure was obvious. When the children that we had been following since the fifth grade entered eighth grade, we selected and trained a set of teachers to compare with untrained teachers and children. We were fortunate in that the school assigned both previously trained and previously untrained children to trained teachers. The same was true for untrained teachers. Consequently, we could observe differential effects on the pupils of previous training experiences and the new experience in eighth grade. Briefly, there was *no* difference between the origin scores or the academic achievement scores (Iowa Test of Basic Skills) for the pupils whose teachers attended our eighth-grade workshop compared to the pupils of control teachers, although previously (sixth and/or seventh grade) trained students were still significantly different on both measures from previously untrained students. We concluded that the eighth grade teacher workshops had failed and we wanted to know why.

There was an apparently obvious reason—the teachers did not develop or use special motivation-enhancing units in their classrooms as the teachers had in the years before. But then, we asked ourselves, why did they not use them? Our speculative answer, based only on impressions, was that they did not feel ownership of the units. After our successes with the sixth and seventh grade teachers we became complacent. We had the answers and we allowed the teachers to talk us into giving them the classroom units developed by the previous teachers rather than insisting that they develop their own. This, of course, was the easy way out for both staff and teachers. Although we provided materials for implementation of the units, the teachers only made a half-hearted effort to use the self-concept unit and later in the year they found ways to avoid using any of the other units. No teacher actually used the origin unit that had been provided them.

If our impressions of this failure are correct, they emphasize the difference between predeveloped units supplied to the teachers and units developed by and, hence, owned by the teachers. We would conclude that full implementation of origin enhancement by teachers can only be achieved by the hard work of developing new units with the teachers. This is completely commensurate with the theory of personal causation—that the teachers feel that *they* made the difference in their pupils rather than some packaged materials. *Packaged units will not do it.* For this reason we have become very suspicious of "teacher-proof" packages at least where motivation enhancement is concerned. The intensive work between staff and a limited number of teachers that is required to develop new units each year severely restricts the widespread implementation of these results. This was dramatically pointed out to us by Lee Cronbach in a comment that he made after I had presented some of our early results at an international congress. He said something like, "If we have some hundreds of thousands of teachers who need your techniques but you can only work with 20 per year, how can the techniques be implemented in a way to be more than a drop in the ocean?" This has troubled us, and led us to try concentrating on more specific teacher behaviors that encourage motivation (more on this here later).

Lack of Teacher Know-how

In 1974 we had another dramatic failure based on more concrete data. Koenigs *et al.* (1977) had found that teachers with origin classrooms encouraged pupils to interact with and to influence them. Such teachers were more often the flexible, complex poeple described by Harvey (Harvey *et al.*, 1968) with their measure of belief systems (Systems III or IV, not Systems I or II). Further, Murphy and Brown (1970) had shown some of the concrete behaviors used by System III and System IV teachers. We tried to put all of this together to give teachers concrete examples of what to do in their classrooms to encourage pupil participation that leads to feelings of originship in their pupils.

After intensive discussions in teacher workshops, we modeled inflexible, simplistic, pupil-influence-inhibiting behaviors as compared to flexible, complex, pupil-influence-inviting behaviors. Statistically significant data collected at the workshops from the teachers clearly demonstrated that they understood and could discriminate between the two types of behavior clusters that we called pawn enhancing versus origin enhancing. But when we went to their classrooms to observe, *we found no difference between their classrooms and nonworkshop participants* (See Cohen, Emrich & deCharms, 1976/1977 for the data). We interpreted these results using two concepts developed by the philosopher Gilbert Ryle (1949). We had taught the teachers to "know that" certain types of behavior enhance motivation but we had not taught them to "know *how*" to use those behaviors in their classrooms.

The following year we repeated the process with a new group of teachers and spent many hours with the teachers in the classroom developing ways to encourage pupil participation. Cohen (1979) modified the teacher–pupil influence measure (originally used in the Koenigs, *et al.*, 1977 study) to include two types of teacher influence attempts and two types of pupil influence attempts. Teacher influence was divided into *inviting influence from* the pupils and *imposing influence on* the pupils. The

modified observation instrument was used reliably in 17 trained teachers' classrooms and 14 control classrooms. Trained teachers, by the end
of the year, tended to use more inviting than imposing influence attempts compared to controls but the results were not statistically significant.

Change in pupil influence attempts were significant, however. Cohen
called disruptive influence attempts "noise" (a pupil, for instance, asks to
sharpen a pencil for the third time in 5 minutes). Noise should not
contribute constructively either to pupils' feelings of responsible originship or to classroom progress. Cohen's data showed a significant decrease in pupil "noise" influence attempts in the trained teachers' classrooms. Constructive influence attempts by pupils were dubbed "expressive" attempts by Cohen and there was a tendency for them to be used
more by pupils of trained teachers than by pupils of control teachers. A
composite score combining *enhancing* teacher influence (inviting minus
imposing) and *enhanced* pupil influence (expressive minus noise) by standardized scores showed a significant ($p < .05$) difference between
trained and untrained classroom scores.

Failure with Individual Children

Another way to highlight failures of motivation enhancement is to
look for groups of children who apparently were not helped even in
classes where training was successful overall. In the original Carnegie
study we identified a small group whose origin score did not increase as
a function of a year of training. They apparently resisted the training, so
we called them "resistors." The major characteristics of the resistors was
that they were unique in the trained classrooms in not improving on
academic achievement whereas all the others did.

To pursue the resistors further, we speculated that perhaps *pawns*
(arbitrarily defined as pupils with below median origin scores) preferred
a *pawn classroom environment* (defined as classrooms with below the median origin climate means). To eliminate the effects of training we concentrated on control classrooms only. In a 2×2 analysis of variance we
divided both scores at the median and used academic achievement as the
dependent measure. This analysis disconfirmed the hypothesis. Even
children below the median on origin score have higher achievement
scores in classrooms with high origin climate scores than in classrooms
with low origin climate scores. Apparently, even so-called pawns achieve
more in an origin climate. Incidentally, this analysis also demonstrated
that children above the median on origin score (compared to those be-

low the median) had significantly higher achievement scores even in the absence of any training. This demonstrates essentially a positive correlation between origin score and academic achievement in the average classroom without special training.[3]

Porter (1979) carried this line of thinking one step further hypothesizing that origin children would achieve more with origin teachers and that children with high affiliation motivation would achieve more with affiliative teachers. Affiliation motivation was scored reliably using the techniques reported in Atkinson (1958). Porter's hypotheses were both confirmed if IQ was not considered, but dropped below significance when IQ was covaried. The evidence suggests that similarity of dominant motive patterns between teacher and pupil may facilitate achievement. It also raises the question of whether some of the correlation between motive measures and IQ is spurious because it takes some motivation to do well on an intelligence test and some intelligence to do well on a motivation exercise. Although it is beyond this chapter's scope, Busch (1982) has recently followed this lead and succeeded in devising a purer measure of origin motivation to correlate with achievement scores.

The Right Amount of Structure: When Strong Teacher Control Is Needed

Recent evidence in music education indicates that it may be a mistake to prejudge the right amount of structure in teaching from an unsophisticated origin–pawn notion. Milak (1980) set out to compare two methods of teaching instrumental music to fourth- and fifth-grade students attempting their first experience with a brass instrument. Milak designed two teaching strategies that he called the "imposed learning method" and the "subject matter method." The *imposed learning method* was based on the premise that the student's state of inexperience dictates the instructional approach. The *subject matter method* is based on the premise that the demands of the instrument and traditional musical notation dictate the instructional approach.

In essence, the imposed method broke down behavioral components of instrumental playing and music reading into teacher-controlled movements and allowed the student to use the instrument only under the watchful eye of the instructor. (The students were not allowed to

---

[3]It should be noted that there is usually a positive correlation between origin score and IQ. As a result all data reported using achievement scores were controlled for IQ differences between groups by covariance analysis.

take the instrument home.) The subject matter method started with the full-blown musical notation and encouraged experimentation with the instrument in practice sessions at home. On the face of it the imposed method had all the elements of the pawn condition—no choice, strict supervision, no opportunity to explore. This could be seen as high structure. The subject matter method certainly was not low structure and came closer to moderate structure, but certainly allowed free, unsupervised experimentation at home.

Forty-eight fourth- and fifth-grade beginners (randomly assigned) experienced one of the two conditions (all under Milak's own tutelege) for 16 weeks in a private-school setting. In the imposed method, children had access to the instrument for three 30-minute sessions per week under supervision. Subject-matter children had the instrument at all times, experienced one 45-minute lesson per week and their parents reported approximately 100 minutes per week of practice at home. It is probable, then, that the subject-matter children had more time on the instrument than the imposed-method children did.

Milak used both standardized achievement tests and tape-recorded test sessions rated by impartial judges for quality of tone. Thus, he had evidence on achievement and on actual performance. On all seven subtests of the standardized test and on all four performance ratings there was a significant difference—the imposed learning method was superior.

Obviously, for beginning brass instrument players, the greater structure of supervised practice and step-by-step rhythm and pitch notation lead to greater achievement and performance increments after a semester of instruction. Yet, one might ask whether Milak's imposed-learning pupils were performing well and at the same time learning to hate it because it was *his* goal not theirs. Self-report measures of the children's attitudes toward the lessons, or a follow-up study of how long they retained interest in playing the instrument could test this hypothesis. Unfortunately, Milak's data contained neither attitude toward the instrument nor follow-up evidence.

Still the data can be interpreted motivationally as follows. For the children to feel personal causation, to feel that they originated their own behavior, their behavior must be effective. If the children tried to blow the horn and the result was an "ill wind that nobody blows good" they would feel that the instrument precluded their originating any successful behavior. With the close supervision of the teacher, however, they could attain greater success sooner and their behavior would lead to feelings of personal causation.

If the curvilinear hypothesis is correct, the right amount of supervision increased success while not reducing a feeling of ownership of the behavior too much. If supervision is so strict that children felt that their behavior was only done for the teacher, then personal causation would drop off despite the fact that performance remained high.

In the most recent project (deCharms & Natriello, 1981) in the series studying personal causation in the schools we attempted to move up one level. That is, instead of studying teacher–pupil relationships, we concentrated on teacher–administrator relationships with major emphasis on the school principal. The project was designed to investigate the relationship between evaluation procedures and teacher motivation. A curvilinear relationship was hypothesized between closeness of evaluation and teacher motivation and effort in teaching.

Six inner-city middle-school principals invited us to their schools, each of which housed approximately 180 teachers. A fieldworker was assigned to each school and given freedom to become engaged in some helpful project that they found in the school. They spent at least 1 day a week in the school for 8 months and wrote weekly reports. Later in the year, when the fieldworkers were familiar with the schools, more systematic data were collected. A teacher survey (completed by 97% of the teachers) included (1) the school origin-climate questionnaire (30 items), (2) task conceptions items (24), (3) evaluation and supervision items (60), (4) teacher-influence items (32), and (5) effort and effectiveness items (28).

The Habermas Hypothesis

According to Jurgen Habermas (1973), a sociocultural system that does not satisfy the basic motives of the workforce is faced with a motivational legitimation crisis. Translated into the subculture of an inner-city school system, this thesis suggests that demands on teachers (workforce) from the school district (organization) that tend to disrupt teacher motivation and ability to teach should lead to (1) teacher dissatisfaction (they feel like pawns), and (2) a crisis, in the form of inadequate teaching.

In an attempt to pursue this thesis, an index of organizational disruption of the teachers was constructed that discriminated significantly among schools and among teacher groups known (from observations) to be differentially organized.

TABLE 1

Mean School Origin Climate Scores
by Three Levels of Teacher Disruption

Level of teacher disruption	Mean school origin climate[a]
High	63.86 ($N = 34$)
Medium	69.77 ($N = 76$)
Low	90.12 ($N = 70$)
Total	76.57 ($N = 180$)

[a]$F = 3.5; p = .036.$

The disruption index was a simple summation of whether the teacher was arbitrarily assigned this year to (1) a new grade, (2) a new subject matter, (3) a new school, and (4) a new principal or other supervisor. A teacher who was in the same situation this year as last year was assigned a score of 0 on the index (as were 4 first-year teachers in the sample). A teacher for whom all the preceding variables had changed this year was assigned the highest score (4) on the disruption index. The rationale for this index followed naturally from the complaints of many teachers, some of whom had been shifted from teaching kindergarten to seventh grade, some of whom were reading specialists and were forced to teach math.

Considerable disruption can be seen from the percentage of teachers who had been arbitrarily assigned. Of all of the teachers, 61% had experienced some disruption, and 19% had experienced 3 or 4 disruptions. Organizationally, almost ⅔ of these teachers had been treated as pawns in this respect. That an origin climate prevailed in the least-disrupted groups and a pawn climate in the highly disrupted groups is clear from Table 1.

Teacher Evaluation and the Curvilinear Hypothesis

We hypothesized a curvilinear relationship between closeness of evaluation and self-reported teacher effectiveness. That is, we expected both loose and strict evaluation to reduce effectiveness as compared to a middle ground. Observations in the schools led to the strong impression that the norm of the principals was to avoid evaluation beyond that required by the district so the actual amount probably varied from loose to moderate with no principal showing overly close evaluation.

Commensurate with these observations, the teacher-survey data (where they reported both their experience of level of evaluation and their feelings of effectiveness) resulted not in a curvilinear relationship but in a linear one. The more evaluation effort by the principal (teacher report) the more the teachers felt effective. Perhaps, at least in these schools, more evaluation is needed to enhance teacher motivation.

PROBLEMS OF DISSEMINATION

The McBell Experience

As reported earlier, dissemination of the full-blown project for enhancing motivation is difficult because of the intense effort and time required of both staff and teachers. Our first attempt at dissemination at a distance forced us to shorten the contact time between staff and teachers. In 1979, the superintendents of two large suburban school districts (called here McBell) requested our help and we attempted a shortened version of the enhancing motivation project (Winingham, Wittcoff, & deCharms, 1980). A 3-day workshop was conducted each of 2 years with approximately 14 teachers. Staff visited teacher classrooms on roughly a monthly basis for approximately an hour. We concentrated on two things. First, we tried to train an energetic local staff administrator to carry on with a small group of teachers after our staff had left. Second, following our evidence on teacher ownership, we did not offer the teachers predesigned classroom units but insisted that they develop their own.

Data from both years indicated that trained teachers had higher origin climate scores than comparable controls but there was no data collected concerning motivation or achievement of pupils. As to further dissemination, the local group succeeded in using the techniques in a third district and this resulted in much enthusiasm. At present, hard data to evaluate this attempt are not available.

Classroom Settings and Origin Enhancement

As a result of the McBell experience, Winingham (1982) tried to devise an even shorter training workshop for teachers. She hypothesized that a major factor in enhancing motivation in classrooms was the atmosphere or "setting" established by the teacher. Perhaps teachers could learn quickly some classroom control techniques and enhance origin feelings without the more intensive training. Winingham, an accomplished inner-city teacher as well as a 10-year member of the enhancing motivation project described above, distinguished between three settings that she commonly saw when visiting classrooms.[4]

---

[4]The reader familiar with Bossert's (1979) task dimensions in classrooms will note similarities.

Setting 1 (Total Group Activity) is a classroom structure where the whole class is directed by the teacher. The teacher is the only source of information. The pupils are the passive recipients of instruction. There are few opportunities for pupils to take responsibility for their own learning or to accept responsibility with peers in interdependent relationships. Instructional activities include testing, pupil recitation, lecturing in all content areas. Organizational activities include preparation for ancillary classes, giving directions prior to independent seat work or distributing supplies.

Setting 2 (Independent Activity) involves structural conditions designed to promote engagement of pupils in activities on their own, individually, or in small groups. The teacher responds to pupils when assistance is requested or monitors pupil progress. This structure provided opportunities for pupils to accept personal responsibility and become actively involved in their own learning. It requires the pupils to work together, to help each other in interdependent relationships and to utilize one another as resources. Instructional activities include programmed learning, peer tutoring, chalkboard and experimental study units in all content areas. Organizational activities include class monitors for books, instructional supplies, audiovisual equipment, office messages, bulletin board teams, and daily attendance teams.

Setting 3 (Independent Activity and Small Group) involves structural conditions that foster the engagement of the majority of pupils in independent activities while the teacher is working simultaneously with a small group (e.g., a reading group). The teacher's influence is limited to one small group. Pupil access to the teacher is either passive, or ignored. Compared to Setting 1 this structure provides more opportunities for pupils to take responsibility for their own learning. The teacher is still the major human resource.

In the McBell study (Winingham et al., 1980), Winingham noted that the most prevalent classroom setting used by teachers was Setting 1 but that Setting 2 (the least prevalent) showed the highest pupil participation and influence as measured by the pupil influence ratio (Koenigs et al., 1977). She concluded that training teachers to use Setting 2 more often, in the context of a brief personal causation rationale, might result in enhanced pupil motivation and might also shorten and simplify training procedures. Teachers seemed to understand the settings very quickly when they were described and to have little difficulty in knowing how to implement Setting 2.

A short teacher-workshop was devised that could be implemented in two 3-hour afternoon sessions. This was combined with several visits to the teachers' classrooms for help and observation and, after 2 weeks, another 3-hour follow-up workshop. The total project, including data collection, took 6 weeks. Fourteen randomly selected sixth-grade inner-city teachers were trained and 16 comparable wait–control teachers formed a comparison group who waited to receive training until after data collection.

Winingham hypothesized that trained teachers compared to control(s) would have (1) a higher percentage of time spent in Setting 2, (2) higher mean pupil-influence ratio in Setting 2, (3) higher mean origin climate scores.

The data indicated that (1) the trained teachers spent a higher percentage of time in Setting 2 (54%) than the untrained teachers (32%; $F = 7.85$, $df = \frac{1}{28}$, $p < .01$) (2) trained teachers encouraged more influence attempts from pupils (mean pupil influence ratio = .50) than untrained teachers (mean pupil influence ratio = .37; $F = 13.5$, $df = \frac{1}{28}$, $p < .001$); (3) the trained teachers' pupils did not feel that they had more origin influence than the untrained teachers' pupils.

Two of her three hypotheses were confirmed. The lack of a relationship between training and the origin climate of the classroom was possibly the result of the brevity of the observation period and the fact that the project occurred near the end of the school year. In previous studies teachers received training before meeting a new class in the fall and the origin climate was measured 6 months later. In the Winingham study the pupils had been with the teacher for 6 months before the training and had probably resisted change of their well-established views of the classroom climate.

MAXIMIZING MOTIVATION
IN EDUCATIONAL SETTINGS

WHAT CAN TEACHERS DO?

The first and most important thing that teachers must do is to believe that all pupils can be origins, and that teachers *can* influence pupils in that direction. Put another way, teachers must believe that they themselves can be origins and can have desired effects on students. This attitude (that can be enhanced by training) must be applied even to the most recalcitrant of students (those who want to prove to the teacher that they cannot be trusted so that they will not have to take responsibility).

The second thing that teachers can do is to pursue the optimum amount of structure to fit the class's and, when possible, the individual's needs. We have documented two concrete ways that this can be done, namely (1) by giving carefully conceived choices and (2) by creating an atmosphere that encourages responsible pupil-influence attempts and independent activity (Setting 2).

A choice is between at least two alternatives: the alternatives must be understood. Initial choice experiences must be simple and short-ranged in order to produce a concentrated ownership experience. Slowly and gradually the time frame can be extended and the external structure lessened. The choice must, when possible, be personal. Majority rule negates the choices of the minority. The alternatives must be within the ability of the chooser, preferably of moderate difficulty. The teacher must be able to live with the choices. Offering a choice is promising that all the alternatives are acceptable. Setting 2 cannot be used all of the time, of course, but Winingham found that most teachers can find ways to use it more often in structuring both instructional and organizational activities in the classroom.

The most important thing to remember is that either extreme—riding herd or dropping the reins completely, too few or too many choices—depresses motivation and achievement. A vicious cycle can develop between the two extremes when the teacher tries to reduce restraints too suddenly. The resulting chaos causes the teacher, through anxiety, to clamp down even more than before. Such a cycle will be experienced by the pupils as capricious behavior.

WHAT CAN ADMINISTRATORS DO?

Preliminary evidence indicates that the principles for principals (and other administrators) working with teachers are the same as for teachers working with students. Our data showed that administrators simultaneously gave no choice and no guidance, too much and too little structure. Teachers were arbitrarily assigned unfamiliar subjects, grades, schools, and supervisors, leading to disruption, lowered motivation, and bad teaching. At the same time principals adopted a "hands off" policy toward teacher behavior in the classroom. This was apparently a result of anxiety over too much evaluation. Contrary to our expectations it appeared that principals *under*supervised, resulting in the desire by teachers for more rather than less evaluation.

Concretely, teachers and administrators could develop an evaluation procedure modeled after that suggested by Dornbusch and Scott (1975), using each of their six steps (task assignment, criteria setting, sampling behavior, assessment, communicating results, and planning improvement). This cooperative venture could stress responsible teacher influence, choices, and independent activity at each of the six steps.

REFERENCES

Atkinson, J. W. (Ed.) *Motives in fantasy, action and society*. Princeton, NJ: Van Nostrand, 1958.

Battle, E. *The relationship of social class and ethnic group to the attitude of internal versus external control of reinforcement in children*. Unpublished master's thesis, Ohio State University, 1962.

Bettelheim, B. Individual and mass behavior in extreme situations. *Journal of Abnormal and Social Psychology*, 1943, *38*, 417–452.

Bossert, S. *Tasks and social relationships in classrooms*. New York: Cambridge University Press. 1979.

Bridgman, P. W. *The way things are*. Cambridge, MA: Harvard University Press, 1959.

Busch, S. G. *A methodological study of the relationship between the concepts of motivation and intelligence and their contribution to academic achievement*. Unpublished doctoral dissertation, Washington University, St. Louis, MO, 1982.

Cohen, M. W. *Student influence in the classroom*. Unpublished doctoral dissertation, Washington University, St. Louis, MO, 1979.

Cohen, M. W., Emrich, A., & deCharms, R. Training teachers to enhance personal causation in students. *Interchange*, 1976–1977, *7*, 34–49.

deCharms, R. *Personal causation*. New York: Academic Press, 1968.

deCharms, R. Motivation measure for elementary school children. Final Report, U.S. Office of Education, 1971.

deCharms, R. *Enhancing motivation: Change in the classroom*. New York: Irvington, 1976.

deCharms, R. Intrinsic motivation, peer tutoring and cooperative learning. In J. M. Levine & M. C. Wang (Eds.), *Teacher and student perception: Implications for learning*. Hillsdale, NJ: Erlbaum, 1983.

deCharms, R. & Natriello, G. Evaluation and Teacher Motivation. Final report, Spencer Foundation, Washington University, St. Louis, MO, 1981.

deCharms, R., & Shea, D. J. Beyond attribution theory: The human conception of motivation and causality. In L. H. Strickland, F. E. Aboud, & K. J. Gergen (Eds.), *Social psychology in transition*. New York: Plenum, 1976.

Deci, E. L. *Intrinsic motivation*. New York: Plenum, 1975.

Deci, E. L. *The psychology of self-determination*. Lexington, MA: Heath, 1980.

Dornbusch, S. M., & Scott, W. R. *Evaluation and exercise of authority*. San Francisco: Jossey-Bass, 1975.

Habermas, J. *Theory and practice*. Boston: Beacon, 1973.

Harvey, O. J., Prather, M., White, B. J., & Hoffmeister, J. K. Teacher beliefs, classroom atmosphere and student performance. *American Educational Research Journal*, 1968, *5*, 151–166.

Heider, F. Social perception and phenomenal causality. *Psychology Review*, 1944, *51*, 358–374.

Heider, F. *The psychology of interpersonal relations*. New York: Wiley, 1958.

Hess, E. The relationship between imprinting and motivation. In M. R. Jones (Ed.), *Nebraska Symposium on Motivation*, Lincoln: Univ. of Nebraska Press, 1959.

Jackson, H. *An assessment of long-term effects of personal causation training*. Unpublished doctoral dissertation, Washington University, St. Louis, MO, 1976.

Jackson, K. W. *Maternal behavior correlates of child motivation in low income, black eighth grade children*. Unpublished doctoral dissertation, Washington University, St. Louis, MO, 1973.

Jones, E. E., Kanous, D. E., Kelley, H. H., Nisbett, R. E., Valins, S., Weiner, B. (Eds.). *Attribution: Perceiving the causes of behavior.* Morristown, NJ: General Learning Press, 1971.

Koenigs, S., Fiedler, M., & deCharms, R. Teacher beliefs, classroom interaction and personal causation. *Journal of Applied Social Psychology,* 1977, *7,* 95–114.

Lepper, M. R., Greene, D. *The hidden costs of reward.* Hillsdale, NJ: Erlbaum, 1978.

Lepper, M. R., Greene, D., & Nisbett, R. E. Undermining children's intrinsic interest with extrinsic rewards: A test of the "over-justification" hypothesis. *Journal of Personality and Social Psychology,* 1973, *28,* 129–137.

Lewin, K., Lippitt, R., & White, R. Patterns of agressive behavior in experimentally created social climates. *Journal of Sociology,* 1939, *10,* 271–299.

Lindquist, E. F., & Hieronymous, A. N. *Iowa Test of Basic Skills.* Boston: Houghton, 1955.

Loevinger, J., & Wessler, R. *Measuring ego development (Vol. 1): Construction and use of a sentence completion test.* San Francisco: Jossey-Bass, 1970.

McClelland, D. C. *Power: The inner experience.* New York: Irvington, 1976.

McClelland, D. C., Atkinson, J. W., Clark, R. A., & Lowell, E. L. *The achievement motive.* New York: Appleton-Century-Crofts, 1953.

Milak, J. J. *A comparison of two approaches of teaching brass instruments to elementary school children.* Unpublished doctoral dissertation, Washington University, St. Louis, MO, 1980.

Muir, M. S. *Personal responsibility training for elementary school children.* Unpublished doctoral dissertation, Washington University, St. Louis, MO, 1977.

Murphy, D. D., & Brown, M. M. Conceptual systems and teaching style. *American Educational Research Journal,* 1970, *7,* 529–540.

Perlmuter, L. C., & Monty, R. A. *Choice and perceived control.* Hillsdale, NJ: Erlbaum, 1979.

Polanyi, M. *Personal knowledge.* Chicago: University of Chicago Press, 1958.

Porter, J. *Person–environment interaction within the classroom setting.* Unpublished doctoral dissertation, Washington University, St. Louis, MO, 1979.

Rawls, J. *A theory of justice.* Cambridge, MA: Harvard University Press, 1971.

Rosen, B. C., & D'Andrade, R. G. The psychological origins of achievement motivation. *Sociometry,* 1959, *22,* 185–218.

Rotter, J. B. Generalized expectancies for internal versus external control of reinforcement. *Psychological Monographs,* 1966, *80,* (1, Whole No. 609).

Ryle, G. *The concept of mind.* New York: Barnes & Noble, 1949.

Seligman, M. E. P. *Helplessness.* San Francisco: Freeman, 1975.

Shea, D. J. *The effects of achievement motivation training on motivational and behavioral variables.* Unpublished doctoral dissertation, Washington University, St. Louis, MO, 1969.

Spring, M. F. *The development and validation of an observation measure of classroom influence.* Unpublished doctoral dissertation, Washington University, St. Louis, MO, 1974.

Thibaut, J. W., & Riecken, H. W. Some determinants and consequences of the perception of social causality. *Journal of Personality,* 1955, *24,* 113–133.

Uleman, J. A. *A new TAT measure of the need for power.* Unpublished doctoral dissertation, Harvard University, 1966.

Veroff, J. Development and validation of a projective measure of power motivation. *Journal of Abnormal and Social Psychology,* 1957, *54,* 1–8.

White, R. W. Motivation reconsidered: The concept of competence. *Psychological Review,* 1959, *66,* 297–333.

White, R., & Lippitt, R. Leader behavior and member reaction in three "social climates." In D. Cartwright & A. Zander (Eds.), *Group dynamics: Research and theory* (2nd ed.). Evanston, IL: Row, Peterson, & Co., 1960.

Winingham, B. R. *Helping teachers to encourage pupil influence: Classroom settings that enhance motivation.* Unpublished doctoral dissertation, Washington University, St. Louis, MO., 1982.

Winingham, B. R., Wittcoff, C., & deCharms, R. *Classroom settings and pupil influence.* Unpublished manuscript, Washington University, St. Louis, MO, 1980.

Winter, D. G. *Power motivation in thought and action.* Unpublished doctoral dissertation, Harvard University, 1967.

Wittcoff, C. *Power motivation in the schools.* Unpublished manuscript, Washington University, St. Louis, MO, 1980.

PART V

Discussant

10

Student Motivation: Some Reflections and Projections

Samuel Ball

OVERVIEW OF MOTIVATION

In the world of educational psychology, topics fashionable in one era become outmoded in the next only to return again still later, perhaps in some slightly altered form. Motivation, like narrow ties and padded shoulders, is a topic that has seen its popularity wax and wane. It is a topic whose centrality to educational psychology can hardly be challenged; so it is with a feeling of approval that we can note that it presently is waxing rather than waning.

I undertook a content analysis of articles published in the *Journal of Educational Psychology* in order to substantiate this assertion that student motivation has in recent years ceased being a neglected topic. The data base was all the articles published during a series of biennial periods and the results are presented in the following table.

It can be seen that motivation was ranked in the top half of the categories of articles published in 1919–1920, 1939–1940, 1959–1960, and 1979–1980—every second decade in regular rhythm. However, only in 1959–1960 and most recently (1979–1980) did motivation comprise more than 10% of the published material. The earlier articles on moti-

	On topic of motivation	
Biennial period	% of published articles	Ranking out of[1] 13 topic categories
1910–1911	<5%	10
1919–1920	5%	6
1929–1930	<5%	7
1939–1940	6%	4
1949–1950	<5%	9
1959–1960	11%	3
1969–1970	5%	8
1979–1980	13%	2

vation research in the *Journal of Educational Psychology* had been concerned with a potpourri of motivational subtopics including curiosity, reinforcement theory and research, interests, locus of control, values, and level of aspiration. In 1959–1960 the emphasis was on self-concept, mental health, and emotional factors underlying student achievement. In 1979–1980 there was not only a quantitative change but also a qualitative one, with the emphasis in the motivation articles reflecting the new theoretical formulations and understandings of the 1970s. This decade's articles were primarily concerned with attribution theory and research and with drawing together the diverse elements of motivation that had characterized earlier research.

The chapters of this volume on student motivation faithfully reflect these new emphases. Indeed Weiner, in his chapter, forcefully argues for the newer approach. He explicitly denigrates the major early historical theories of motivation (hedonistic- and homeostatic-based theories) arguing cogently (once again) for the need for a cognitively based theory. He adds two more points worth repeating: an educationally relevant theory of motivation has to come to terms with emotional states; and no single motivational concept can adequately explain motivation in the classroom.

Nicholls also addresses these important theoretical themes. While acknowledging the usefulness of a phenomenological approach to student motivation, he is too astute to fall into the trap of circularity that bedevilled, for example, much of the earlier theoretical work on curiosity. As Fowler (1965, p. 21) pointed out in the earlier theory on curiosity, a

[1]Examples of other categories are measurement–evaluation, psycholinguistics, cognition. A longer report of this study appears in the December, 1984 issue of the *Journal of Educational Psychology*.

child was considered curious because he or she displayed exploratory behavior. However, it was also argued that the reason for exploratory behavior was the possession of a curiosity drive or motive. It does not take a giant analogous leap to see the possibility of similar unwitting, circular descriptions and explanations marring attribution theory and research. Fortunately, current leaders in the attribution area, such as Weiner and Nicholls, are too sophisticated to be so seduced. Nicholls, while arguing for the "intentional" approach to understanding behavior, is aware of the need to obtain evidence of intentionality independent of outcome behavior.

The efforts made by Weiner and by Nicholls to integrate other motivation theories with attribution theory is also noteworthy. For example, Weiner's view is that there are a number of dimensions of causality, one of which is the locus of control dimension (internality–externality); and he relates that dimension to deCharmes's origin–pawn, Deci's intrinsic–extrinsic, and Brehm's freedom–constraint constructs. Similarly Nicholls integrates, at least to a degree, White's competency notions, ego involvement, level of aspiration, achievement motivation, test anxiety, and self-concept.

The fact that attribution theory can be used in an attempt to integrate some of the vast array of motivational constructs (Ball, 1977, p. 189) is itself a positive attribute of attribution theory. This attempt to provide a more elegant, less cluttered, motivational theory has clearly provided an impetus to research.

The chapters by Covington and by Maehr illustrate well the new vigor of research in motivation brought about in part by new theory. However, it must also be realized that the process is iterative and that empirical research findings help to clarify and "fine tune" theoretical formulations. Thus, Covington takes the construct of self-worth and from the research literature allows it to encompass otherwise such bewildering phenomena as self-deprecation, cheating, and unrealistically high goals. The early literature on the self (Wylie, 1979) tended to concentrate on positive and global aspects. The research cited by Covington looks at the realities of student underachievement, lack of involvement, and inactivity; and it relates these realities to the excessive use of failure-avoiding strategies. Covington's point, based on research, is that low effort in success is generally seen to be indicative of brilliance and low effort in failure deflects criticism of one's ability. This analysis is a clarification of the reasoning underlying most students' exam-time rhetoric, though it may not apply, as Nicholls and Stipek point out, to younger children.

Covington's fine tuning of motivational theory relates self-worth to learned helplessness and self-consistency (which he points out may be more valued than self-validation). From his interpretation of the research the contradiction between the consistency and self-worth literatures is resolved. The crucial factor, as Covington points out, is where on the continuum between effective coping and dysfunctioning an individual lies.

Similarly, Maehr develops new integrated theory from his incisive interpretations of the research literature. His Theory of Personal Investment might be called "Beyond Achievement Motivation" because it attempts to link achievement motivation with other theoretical positions, including theories that emphasize the sociocultural context of motivation. Of course for educators, any motivational theory that ignores the sociocultural context is a theory that denies the importance and influence of the teacher.

The first four chapters of this first volume on student motivation show clearly the great strides in theory and accompanying research that have taken place in the last decade. They provide a useful illustration of the interdependence of research and theory; they indicate how much progress is being attained in the integration and fine tuning of the theory; and they provide evidence of the heuristic value of the new theory as manifested in the increase in research articles published in, for example, the *Journal of Educational Psychology*.

DEVELOPMENTAL CONSIDERATIONS

The importance of an understanding of developmental aspects of student motivation became clear to me quite early in my teaching career when I discovered the amazing differences in response by first graders and by sixth graders to my assertion that I liked children who sit up straight. The first graders' backs would stiffen and arch as they literally bent over backwards to please me. The sixth graders would mostly smile pleasantly, if not quizzically, sensing another eccentricity of their young teacher.

Stipek, in her chapter, provides a much more scholarly and precise presentation of developmental considerations affecting student motivation. Interestingly, she validates the value of my early experience, noting that social reinforcement from the teacher may be highly motivating for young children (because they can immediately see it as bearing on their self-worth).

I did not begin this section of the chapter with a personal anecdote in order to trivialize the importance of developmental considerations. Indeed, as Stipek and the earlier chapter by Nicholls reveal, an understanding of developmental effects is crucial to an understanding of student motivation. We often blame schools for inhibiting children's curiosity and for lowering their levels of self-esteem. However, the reality appears to be that the trend over the school-age years seems to be in these directions as a matter of course and not necessarily as a result of the school's influence. Virtually all of the 96 children interviewed by Stipek at the start of their first-grade experience claimed to be the smartest in their group. Such distortions of reality are cute in young children but alarming in adolescents. Social comparisons eventually come into play to be used as evidence by individuals to evaluate their performance. As Stipek observes, it is rather natural for very young children, who learn such prodigious amounts on a day-to-day basis anyway, to think that they can achieve most things through natural talent. Increasing cognitive development enables them to realize limitations, through peer comparisons that were previously not part of their repertoire of self-evaluation evidence.

Developmental considerations seem equally important to an understanding of the application of attribution theory. Young children do not seem to differentiate between effort and ability in considering outcomes. Therefore, young children are not able to manipulate effort attributions in order to avoid the personal (internal) failure label and to maximize the personal ability label, whereas older children and adolescents are able to do so. Whether by conscious choice or by intuitive judgement, teachers of young children seem to appreciate this finding. Teachers of young children tend not to differentiate effort and ability in their feedback to their students. Nonetheless, it is important for us to understand *why* this occurs even if some of the practical applications have already been worked out on an experiential, folklore basis.

Perhaps the aspect that gives the greatest concern in the Stipek chapter is her admonition that there is an absence of comparative observation data concerning achievement-related behavior. This gap in the literature needs to be filled. Most young children seem so eager to learn and so confident in their ability to do so. Many, if not most, adolescents seem so lacking in confidence and so hesitant to try new learning experiences. We have argued that this is not just a matter of schooling; but it may not be just a matter of developmental changes either. The *interaction* of the school experience on developmental changes is an important but neglected area. Now that we are beginning to understand better the basic processes of adult motivation it is time to look at the etiology of underachievement and academic apathy. This requires initially the sort of exploratory research that Stipek herself carries out (Stipek, 1981) and it also requires a focus on interactions between sociocultural factors and motivational factors.

THE STUDENT'S ENVIRONMENT

Two chapters of this book, one by Carole Ames and the other by Cooper and Tom, though quite different in research style, both take up the challenge of trying to understand some of the relationships between social and cultural factors and motivation.

Carole Ames' chapter is an insightful analysis of one of the most value-laden areas in educational psychology—the area of competitive, cooperative, and individualistic approaches to learning. Educational program evaluation demonstrates that motivation can be a dependent variable, as well as an independent or moderator variable (Anderson, Ball, & Murphy, 1975). However, as Ames points out, educational researchers rarely view motivation as a goal (dependent variable) in itself—and she approaches the competition–cooperation literature as one area where student motivation can be seen as a research design dependent variable (or goal of the program). She makes a good case for seeing the motivational outcome as dependent upon the social system.

Because this is a value-laden area, personal and political as well as academic reactions inevitably arise when considering this literature. From the early research of Lewin, Lippitt, and White (1939) there has been a generally glowing report on the efficacy of cooperative social groupings over competitive or individualistic systems. Yet we know at the macro level, as in Poland and China, that communal cooperatives seem less efficient and productive than individual plots. As well, one wonders at the objectivity of some of the research designs, which have (included in my editorial experience) one treatment group being asked to discuss a topic cooperatively while members of the individualistic treatment group are told to read the written materials on the topic and to talk to no one. One of the results subsequently claimed was that cooperation leads to greater social interaction than individualistic instruction. We knew where that researcher's values lay.

Carole Ames is well aware of the difficulties inherent in the cooperation–competition literature and she indicates several complexities of interpreting the effects of social structures. For example, she points out that cooperative structures may be particularly beneficial for low-achieving children and that sensitivity to social context cues may be a function of self-concept.

Nonetheless, we are left with results that inevitably will be interpreted differently by people with different values. Is a lowering of self-esteem after early childhood deplorable or is it a proper realistic orientation? Is self-criticism to be avoided? If it is to be considered a negative outcome, what about other cultures where it is a social tool used extensively to obtain social cohesiveness? Is very high self-esteem, which appears a more likely result of cooperative systems, a special prize to be treasured or does it eventually lead to negative personality and achievement outcomes? Ames, fortunately and properly, concentrates on research findings and leaves a full-scale debate on the values issues to others. Her treatment leads to several important refinements in interpretation such as those summarized in the final paragraphs of her chapter, where she shows linkages between various types of attributions and various social structures.

The scope of the task set by Ames in her chapter is too wide to allow her the labor of following up in detail all of the research issues that she has raised. Here are two examples that lend themselves to further investigation. To what extent are teachers also affected by competitive and cooperative systems? Is it losing that causes shame, embarrassment, and humiliation under competitive conditions or is it, rather, doing worse than publicly expected? (We note in the New Hampshire primaries leading up to the presidential elections that it is not winning or losing that counts but doing better or worse than expected. Note, for example, the events leading to President Johnson's decision not to seek a new term. He won the primary but his win was by a disappointingly small margin.)

Three other questions that arise from my reading of the Ames chapter follow.

1. Granted that most studies show that the motivational consequences of competitive structures are rather negative for most students, is this finding also true for the very talented? If the very talented benefit from competitive structures, then from a societal viewpoint such structures might still, overall, be beneficial even if at the expense of the less talented. The point is that questions of justice, equality, equity, and long-term productivity intrude so that decisions based on the research in this area cannot be allowed to rest solely on the research.

2. Why do so many of the competitive treatment conditions involve individual competitive situations? While individual competition (like singles matches in tennis) does occur, many teachers also use "team" competitive approaches (as do such organized sports as baseball, basketball, football, etc.). In many classrooms, the Bees and the Birds vie with each other to see who finishes a task first or who gets least errors. (In Aus-

tralia, the teams are more likely to be called Kangaroos, Koalas, and Wallabies). Does team competition garner the worst or the best of cooperative and competitive conditions? Working for team success seems to allow group pressures to increase productivity and team success to spread across the less-talented team members.

3. Would the more dramatic results seen in the research literature actually occur in typical classrooms? Teachers do not use pure cooperation, or pure competition, or pure individualization. Most teachers, even in the course of a few hours, use all three approaches to social structuring. Normative, competition-arousing evaluations are often followed by cooperative groupings only to be followed next by a lesson involving individualized bookwork. Without denying that different teachers emphasize different structures, we still need to know from simple observations what the real mixes happen to be in typical classrooms. Stipek pointed out in terms of developmental research the need for observational descriptive studies; and the need also seems apparent with respect to social structuring of the classroom.

The other chapter regarding environmental impact on student motivation is by Cooper and Tom and deals with socioeconomic status (SES) and ethnic group differences. They synthesize a variety of research studies using recently developed statistical procedures. From 333 abstracts consulted, 43 study reports were eventually used. These met stringent criteria relating to relevance, variables, design, and availability of results. They date back some time,because the mean date of the research report was 1969.

The importance of this metaanalysis lies both in the political as well as the theoretical–academic spheres. Any synthesis of scattered research has theoretical academic interest, helps to advance our understandings, and perhaps provides stronger support for current theory. However, when the synthesis concerns ethnicity, SES, and, so-called, race, its political importance is also paramount. One would need to have been in solitary confinement for a very long time not to have heard lay opinion confidently asserted to the detriment and denigration of various SES, ethnic, and racial groupings. Usually, the speaker stresses the poor motivation of the particular disadvantaged group under discussion at that time.

Cooper and Tom's synthesis of the research shows that members of the dominant culture have higher levels of achievement motivation than members of less-dominant subcultures; but perhaps the most important finding is that SES is positively related to achievement motivation in virtually all countries and cultures in which data were available and that the SES effect is larger in the United States than, say, the Anglo- versus Afro-American differences.

The fact that so many studies used a projective test with dubious reliability levels is a pity. Whether the obtained scores could be said to possess construct validity given the low reliability and given that the trait being measured is supposed to be relatively stable is a matter for considerable concern (Vidler, 1977, p. 75).

In any case Cooper and Tom have synthesized a long-running research area and have illustrated some very useful statistical tools. It will be only a matter of time before those tools have been applied to other bodies of research in the student motivation literature with aspects of self-esteem, anxiety, and curiosity being good candidates.

OPTIMIZING STUDENT LEARNING: PRACTICAL APPLICATIONS

The last chapters in this book present two quite different designs or applications for optimizing student learning. The first by Hill considers specific teaching and testing programs aimed at reducing the problem of debilitating student-motivation. It reviews and promotes in a most constructive way a variety of programs for all age–grade levels showing that debilitating motivation is not necessarily a terminal disease of students and can be either reversed or even innoculated against.

One variable considered is the troublesome one of anxiety. The negative overtones associated with anxiety have been accumulating since the time Freud studied it and they have been emphasized by such popular movie art as *High Anxiety*. The mental health movement seems convinced that anxiety is a negative factor with occasional severely debilitating manifestations. The question worth asking is whether this is a valid position to take when considering student motivation. I have argued elsewhere (Ball, 1983) that at least as far as important student-performance areas are concerned, lowering anxiety levels does not improve student performance and is more likely to reduce the overall level of student performance. One reason why many researchers find this argument disagreeable is the confusion generated by the frequent finding of a negative correlation between anxiety and performance. However, as we all know, such correlational findings do not necessarily imply causation in the direction of anxiety to performance, nor do they necessarily imply that reducing anxiety, on the average, improves student performance. Anxiety-reduction programs would seem to benefit only those students with particularly high anxiety.

Hill also draws attention to the recurring problem of dissemination. Excellent programs locked up in academic enclaves are, by definition, not going to help students. Ironically, the better the dissemination the more likely the program may be found to be wanting. This is because the quality of a program is, in part, dependent on the enthusiasm of the staff who implement the program, and the further they are removed from the program's originators, the less likely they are to retain the originators' enthusiasms. The further the dissmenination, the less enthused the program's staff.

The second of the chapters involving practical applications is written by deCharms—justifiably one of the most famous workers in the field of student motivation. DeCharms' origin–pawn presentations have acquired an enviable reputation and a growing, developing literature of research and evaluation. With a frankness that is refreshing, deCharms relates not only his present position but the mistakes and misconceptions that lie along the path he has traveled. It would be pretentious of me to summarize the clearly presented origin–pawn chapter. However, in the sections dealing with attempts to disseminate deCharms' motivational enhancement strategies, one factor bears repetition if only for the sake of emphasis. In training teachers it is well to put them through a similar process to that wanted for their students. The process may be more important than the message when it comes to motivation. The drawback is that dissemination becomes a matter of "intense effort and time" as deCharms admits in his section on dissemination. Under these conditions, how cost effective is the dissemination effort? That is the kind of question too infrequently asked.

Both Hill and deCharms present practical applications for enhancing student motivation; yet they do so with an appropriate underpinning of research and theory. While this may seem to be a perfectly obvious way of proceeding when considering practical applications, it is certainly not universal.

When I entered a teacher education course more than 30 years ago, it soon became apparent that my lecturers were stronger on exhortation than they were on practical suggestions. The consistent cry was that we young teachers must strive to motivate the student; but, apart from some dubious pieces of folklore, the practical suggestions were based more on the lecturers' personal experiences than on substantial theory or systematic research and evaluation.

Recently, I had the task of translating and summarizing the technical literature on motivation for practicing educators (Ball, 1982). The final section dealt with practical applications and my effort there left me less than satisfied with what we can tell practicing educators. Compared with 30 years ago, we are clearly in a better position concerning our theoretical understanding and research evidence. Despite that, we must remain hesitant in suggesting practical recipes for enhancing student motivation. In a fit of literary flamboyance, if not copping out from the task, I argued that theory and research provided the oils and the canvas but that it was still up to the teacher to paint the specific classroom picture— a picture that is appropriate in style and effect for the situation.

The chapters in the Ames and Ames volume on student motivation all present ideas and implications that have practical merit. Two of the chapters, as we have seen, emphasize a practical message to the reader. Nonetheless, despite a myriad of practical ideas, a problem remains because the more we understand, the more we realize our limitations. Throughout this book there are instances to show that with greater sophistication we must resort less to general recipes and palliatives and more to careful restrictive statements concerning our advice. "It depends" is an opening phrase that increasingly seems to dominate our advisory statements. If the student has a very positive self-concept, if the student has high anxiety, if the student has realistic goals, if the student had been making a strong effort—the qualifying "if's" abound. On the one hand, we congratulate ourselves with our increasing theoretical sophistication, but on the other hand, this reduces the generality of our practical advice. The answer to this apparent conundrum seems to be increasingly to professionalize the education of our educators from the mechanical training they used to receive. Attribution theory, for example, has many possibilities in terms of classroom applications but these applications have scarcely begun to be thought through; and obviously the validity of the applications would then need to be evaluated. As technology takes up some of the burden of the crasser aspects of teaching, teachers might be able to spend more time on the more professionally rewarding aspects including the delicate, difficult, enigmatic task of motivating students.

MEASURING MOTIVATION

David McClelland (1965) pointed out how theory and research seem to blossom only when appropriate measuring instruments have been developed. Once a measure becomes available then there is a sudden deluge of theory and research—at least so it seemed to him as he considered the need for achievement. Measurement is central to empirical research and to theory; all the chapters of this book provide testimony to this assertion.

Nicholls, in his chapter, explicitly draws our attention to this area of concern with his warning that it is foolish to assume uncritically that a test measures what its name asserts that it measures. *Nominal determinism* (the name determines the behavior) may work out in real life from time to time (for example, why else would people called Ames become so interested in studying other people's goals; and why is deCharms interested in influencing others?). Even so, Nicholls is right. Nominal determinism must be considered an unreliable approach to the study of measurement. The problem of construct validity is exacerbated when we are attempting to measure how others perceive and interpret events and situations in a phenomenological framework.

Two recent articles provide unhappy verification of the point that there may be problems in the area of attribution measurement. Maruyama (1982), using data from Elig and Frieze (1979), found that while two structured-methods of attribution measurement gave results similar to each other, this criterion-related validity was not shown by an unstructured, open-ended method. If different results are obtained using measures that allegedly are measuring the same constructs, then one or more of the measures is invalid.

A group at the University of Sydney (Marsh, Cairns, Relich, Barnes, & Debus, 1984) present much more disturbing evidence about measurement problems. They concluded that

1. Self-attributions for success differ systematically from self-attributions for failure so that outcome cannot be ignored in considering attributions.
2. Data obtained from self-attributions may bear little relationship to those obtained about fictional others in hypothetical situations. (See, too, Sohn, 1977).
3. Factor analysis studies fail to substantiate that part of Weiner's general motivational model that relates to bipolar factors.
4. Most measurement development has been to assess experimental manipulations rather than to assess individual differences and this has led, in turn, to insufficient consideration of basic, psychometric concerns. No satisfactory well-tried measure of individual differences in self-attributions exists.

It is not unknown in science for faulty theory and misleading research to have been built on the basis of imprecise measurement. Improved measurement has sometimes meant the sweeping away of the faulty theory. We need to do more work on the measurement of attributions in order to ensure that attribution theory and research is indeed properly based on reliable and valid measurement.

THE FUTURE OF STUDENT MOTIVATION

One would need to be a greater prophet than Samuel to predict with confidence the future trends in theory, research, and application related to student motivation. Not only has interest in the topic waxed and waned over the decades of this century, but the focus of interest has also been less than steady. The focus has moved from interests, to emotions, to level of aspiration, to self-concept, to curiosity, to anxiety, to achievement motivation and locus of control, and on to attribution theory with various interregnum periods dotted in between.

If the best predictor of the future can be seen in *present* performance, then attribution theory and research will continue to hold major attention with respect to student motivation. Much depends, of course, on the further unfolding of this area. As we have just discussed, one aspect of great importance will be the result of further psychometric examination and development of the measuring instruments. Will the measurement problems that choked off the popularity of research in areas like curiosity and creativity also crowd in on attribution research?

Stipek and Weisz (1981) point to other problems that have to be faced. Will the results obtained to date mainly from laboratory simulations hold up in real-life classrooms? (If they do not hold up, then the chances are that attribution theory in psychology may go the way of phlogiston theory in chemistry.) Stipek and Weisz also ask whether attributions are consistent across situations? If attributions lack consistency across related academic situations, then the usefulness of the theory in terms of teaching and student motivation is somewhat limited.

The amount of research activity in the attribution area is so great that the likelihood at this point is nonetheless for its healthy continuation in the immediate future. As well as the healthy future of attribution research, the future of attribution theory also can be predicted to be promising. One of the strongest features of attribution theory is its ability to incorporate or provide new meaning to other theories of motivation—theories such as achievement motivation, anxiety, locus of control, self-concept, and even the once-virile reinforcement theory. The absurdity of dozens of competing motivational concepts has finally become apparent and, like the corporate world, we will probably see more and more take-over bids, rationalizations, and amalgamations of the old disparate motivational constructs. The stronger constructs will survive and they will do so partly to the extent that they can be interrelated with other motivational constructs to form meaningful new apperception masses. Examples of this abound in this book, from social environments and self-concepts influencing attributions to locus of control and anxiety concepts being incorporated into a broader theoretical structure. There is no doubt that attribution theory will continue to have, at least in the short run, heuristic value.

Finally a word about the future of practical applications of attribution theory and research. The etiology of student attributions certainly needs more analytic research. Why do some students prefer stable, internal attributions across situations while others prefer, for example, external attributions which differ depending on the specific situation? From answers to these kinds of questions comes knowledge that will provide teachers with a better opportunity to influence student motivation.

The future is likely to bring greater complexities and less certain nostrums. Student motivation not only *seems* to be a complex topic—it *is* a complex topic and will remain so despite the less fractionated and less factional theory and research that is now emerging.

REFERENCES

Anderson, S. B., Ball, S., & Murphy, R. *Encyclopedia of Educational Evaluation*. San Francisco: Jossey-Bass, 1975.

Ball, S. *Motivation in Education*. New York: Academic Press, 1977.

Ball, S. Motivation. In H. Mitzel (Ed.), *Encyclopedia of Educational Research* (5th ed., Vol. 3). New York: Free Press, 1982.

Ball, S. What is the impact of anxiety on student performance in important examinations? In C. Spielberger (Ed.), *Test Anxiety Revisited*. New York: Hemisphere/McGraw Hill, 1984.

Elig, T. W., & Frieze, I. H. Measuring causal attributions for success and failure. *Journal of Personality and Social Psychology*, 1979, *37*, 621–634.

Fowler, H. *Curiosity and Exploratory Behavior*. New York: Macmillan, 1965.

Lewin, K., Lippitt, R., & White, R. K. Patterns of aggressive behavior in experimentally created social climates. *Journal of Social Psychology*, 1939, *10*, 217–299.

McClelland, D. Toward a theory of motive acquisition. *American Psychologist*, 1965, *20*, 321–333.

Marsh, H. W., Cairns, L., Relich, J., Barnes, J., & Debus, R. L. The relationship between dimensions of self-attribution and dimensions of self-concept. *Journal of Educational Psychology*, 1984, *76*, 1ff.

Maruyama, G. How should attributions be measured? A reanalysis of data from Elig and Frieze. *American Educational Research Journal*, 1982, *19*, 552–558.

Sohn, D. Affect-generating powers of effort and ability self attributions of success and failure. *Journal of Educational Psychology*, 1977, *69*, 500–505.

Stipek, J. D. Children's perceptions of their own and their classmates' ability. *Journal of Educational Psychology*, 1981, *73*, 404–410. (a)

Stipek, J. D., & Weisz, J. R. Perceived personal control and academic achievement. *Review of Educational Research*, 1981, *51*, 101–137. (b)

Vidler, D. Achievement Motivation. In S. Ball (Ed.), *Motivation in Education*. New York: Academic Press, 1977.

Wylie, R. C. *The Self-concept*. (Vol. 2). Lincoln: University of Nebraska Press, 1979.

Author Index

The numerals in italics indicate pages on which the complete references appear.

A

Abelson, W. D., 253, *273*
Abrams, D., 191, *205*
Abrams, L., 45, *69*
Abramson, L. Y., 21, *36*, 56, 57, *68*, 94, *108*
Adkins, D. C., 222, 225, 226, 227, 230, *238*
Adler, T., 66, *69*, 151, 152, *172*
Allport, G. W., 127, *142*
Alschuler, A., 201, *204*
Alshuler, A. S., 82, *108*
Alvarez, C., 200, *204*
Ambuel, B., 263, *272*
Ames, C., 45, 63, *68*, 82, 84, 93, 98, *108*, 180, 181, 183, 184, 185, 186, 187, 190, 191, 196, 197, 199, 200, 201, 202, *204*
Ames, C., 82, *108*
Ames, R., 45, 63, *68*, 123, *142*, 180, 183, 186, 187, 191, 200, *204*
Anderson, C. A., 22, 27, *36*
Anderson, D., 199, *205*
Anderson, J. G., 103, *108*, 228, *239*
Anderson, L., *170*
Anderson, R., 146, *170*
Anderson, S. B., 318, *326*
Andres, G. R., 27, *36*
Andrews, J., 183, *205*
Ankeny, N. C., *68*
Appelman, A. J., 80, 96, *108*
Apple, M., 160, *170*
Arkin, R. M., 48, *68*, 80, 96, *108*
Arlin, M., 165, *170*
Armstrong, S., 154, *173*
Aronfreed, J., 154, *172*
Aronson, E., 96, *108*, 194, *204*
Atkinson, H. W., 211, *239*
Atkinson, J. W., 2, *11*, 21, *36*, 40, *68*, 84, *108*, 116, 129, 131, 132, 135, *142*,

143, 151, *170*, 210, 217, *240*, 246, 247, 251, *272*, 281, 284, 300, *309*
Ausubel, D., 146, *170*

B

Bachmann, M., 156, *172*
Backman, C. W., 96, *112*
Ball, S., 314, 318, 321, 322, *326*
Bandura, A., 57, *68*
Barberio, R., 228, *239*
Barkow, J. W., 139, *142*
Barnes, J., 324, *326*
Barnett, M., 183, *205*
Barton, K., 222, 225, 227, *239*
Battle, E., *308*
Baumeister, R. F., 80, *108*
Beery, R., 57, 67, *69*, 82, 83, 84, 85, 88, 92, 97, *108*, *109*, 148, *171*
Berglas, S., 96, *108*
Berk, L., 168, *170*
Berman, L., 150, *174*
Betley, G., 45, *69*
Bettelheim, B., 279, *308*
Bhatnagar, J. K., 234, *240*
Biehler, R., 146, *170*
Biermann, U., 156, *172*
Birney, R. C., 82, *108*
Blackwell, J., 61, *72*, 149, *173*
Block, J. H., 97, *108*, 181, *205*
Bloom, B. S., 64, *68*, 124, *142*
Blumenfeld, P. C., 89, 90, *108*, 153, 156, 160, *171*
Bodine, R., 255, 262, *272*
Boggiano, A. K., 91, *111*, 164, 165, *171*, *173*
Bohrnstedt, G. W., 60, *69*
Boring, E. G., 115, *142*
Bossert, S., 89, *108*, *308*
Botha, E., 231, *239*
Bowles, S., 67, *68*

329

Subject Index